The Cruising Guide to the

Northwest Caribbean

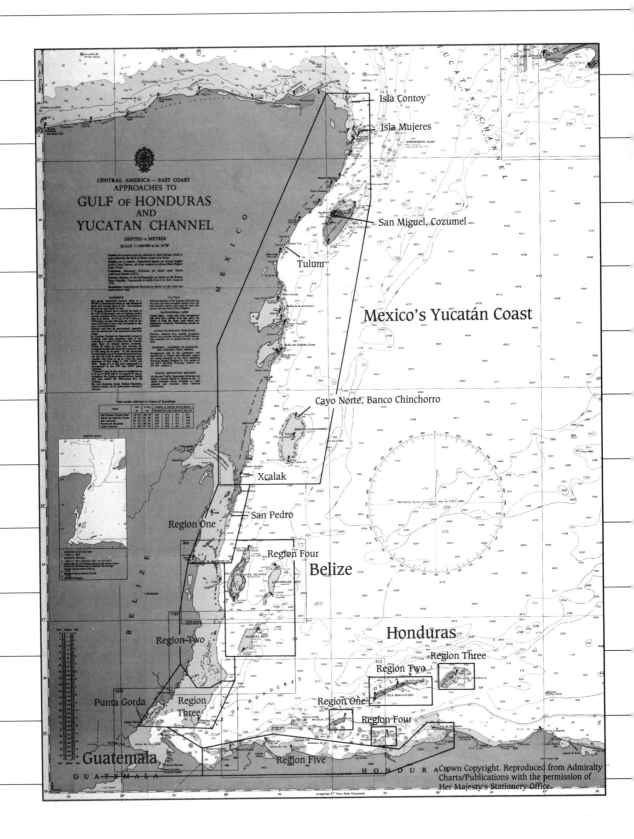

CENTRAL AMERICA — EAST COAST

APPROACHES TO

GULF OF HONDURAS
AND
YUCATAN CHANNEL

DEPTHS IN METRES

SCALE 1:1,000,000 at lat 16°30'

Isla Contoy

Isla Mujeres

San Miguel, Cozumel

Tulum

MEXICO

Mexico's Yucatán Coast

Cayo Norte, Banco Chinchorro

Xcalak

San Pedro

Region One

Region Four

Belize

Honduras

Region Three

Region Two

Region Two

Region One

Region Four

Region Three

Punta Gorda

Region Five

Guatemala

The Cruising Guide
to the
Northwest Caribbean

The Yucatán Coast of Mexico,

Belize, Guatemala, Honduras, and the

Bay Islands of Honduras

Nigel Calder

with Peter Hancock

International Marine
Camden, Maine

Published by International Marine®

10 9 8 7 6 5 4 3

*Dedicated to my parents, who
never attempted to rein in my sense of
adventure, even when I blew craters in the
lawn with homemade bombs!
May I have the wisdom to give my
children the same room to grow.*

Library of Congress Cataloging-in-Publication Data

Calder, Nigel.
    The cruising guide to the northwest Caribbean: the Yucatán Coast of Mexico, Belize, Guatemala, Honduras, and the Bay Islands of Honduras / Nigel Calder with Peter Hancock.
        p. cm.
    Includes index.
    ISBN 0-87742-303-2
    1. Yachts and Yachting—Caribbean Area—Guide-books. 2. Caribbean Area—Description and travel—1981—Guide-books. I. Hancock, Peter. II. Title.
GV817.C37C35 1991
917.29'0452—dc20   91-15982
                                                                  CIP

Design and Page Production by Watermark Design, Camden, ME
Edited by Pamela Salomon, Heidi Brugger
Illustrated by Terrie Frisbie
Photos by the Author
Imageset by High Resolution, Camden, ME
Printed by Arcata Graphics, Fairfield, PA

Questions regarding the content of this book should be addressed to:
International Marine
P.O. Box 220
Camden, ME 04843

Contents

Preface

We have had a lot of fun preparing this guide. As usual there are many people to thank. Top of the list is Peter Hancock. He sailed into the berth next to ours in Mandeville, Louisiana, in October of 1989 after singlehanding his 26-foot Contessa sloop, *Kylie*, across the Atlantic so that he could attend his daughter's wedding in Baton Rouge. We struck up an immediate friendship and sailed and traveled together for the next 12 months. Peter helped with every stage of this guide and was able, with his boat's shallower draft, to explore areas inaccessible to our 39-foot ketch, *Nada*.

Peter, a retired English literature teacher, kept the children—Pippin, age four, and Paul, age three—entertained during the day, then when they were asleep, he spent many a night reading Shakespeare to my wife, Terrie, and me. I believe he eventually read the entire collected works, but after a hard day's surveying I generally fell asleep after the children, so I have to take his and Terrie's word on this!

Numerous cruising sailors whom we met in our travels told us of their favorite anchorages, even though many disapproved of this guide since it will encourage more boats to visit "their" area. My thanks to all of them.

The governments of Mexico, Belize, Guatemala, and Honduras all supplied information of different sorts. Orlando Ochoa Palma guided us into the anchorage at Nicolas Cay, Belize. Dan Thompson and CEDAM International provided satellite mapping of Lighthouse Reef. Raymond Lemons, the librarian at the National Research Council Library in Washington, D.C., dug out some further information on Lighthouse, Glover's, and Turneffe reefs from an ancient Atoll Research Bulletin. Beth la Croix, formerly of Belize City and currently on the Rio Dulce, off the top of her head gave me numerous valuable pieces of navigational information on Belize's outlying reefs and cays, all of which proved to be remarkably accurate.

Jim Gorman, an excellent photographer and a wizard in the darkroom, did an outstanding job of converting my color slides to black-and-white photos. Terrie provided all the beautiful sketches with the exception of two done by her sister Renée.

Then there is, as always, the production team at International Marine—Jon Eaton, Pamela Salomon, Heidi Brugger, Molly Mulhern, and the rest of the crew.

Last but certainly not least, I must thank Terrie, once again, and the children. They rarely threatened to mutiny in spite of the fact that I repeatedly made us pull up anchors and head out of perfectly pristine anchorages only a few hours after arriving. We ran aground so many times, due to my insistence on sailing over every reef and shoal in sight to check depths, that now Terrie and I can launch the dinghy, lay out a kedge anchor, and pull ourselves off without saying a word—and the children know to stay in the cockpit, keep out of Daddy's way, and keep quiet.

Naturally, in spite of all this help, there are still mistakes in this guide. These are mine. If you find any, I would be grateful if you let me know about them.

Nigel Calder
Bridger, Montana
January 1991

Introduction

Between Peter Hancock and the Calder family, we have sailed to the fjords of Norway and the clouds of the Hebrides. We've ghosted past the dreaming spires of England, pushed east through the Mediterranean to the Black and Red seas, and cruised the Caribbean from one end of the West Indies to the other. In our travels we have found no region that can match the attractions of the 500-mile crescent of land and sea between the Yucatán Strait and the Gulf of Honduras.

Sandy, coconut-fringed beaches glowing orange in a tropical sunset; the jeweled colors and flashing shapes of fish darting around crags of pristine coral; the thrill of racing along at hull speed in the lee of Belize's great barrier reef, driven forward by a 20-knot tradewind over waves little higher than ripples; pushing slowly through fields of water hyacinths on Guatemala's jungle rivers, with parrots and monkeys in the orchid-draped trees; the magnificent Mayan ruins of Tikál; dazzling colors of medieval Christian pageantry intermingling with the pagan masques of the Mayan Indians; an almost perfect climate . . . the Northwest Caribbean has all this and more.

From the faded frescoes of the temple at Tulum, squatting on its Yucatecan seacliffs in the north, down through Belize and Guatemala to the Monkey God Palace of Copán in Honduras, the Maya are still a presence. Numbered today at more than two million; shy but friendly, they weave their unforgettable presence into the journeys of all who travel inland to marvel at the wonders of the region.

Few areas of similar size have such an amazing geographical diversity. The snowcapped, symmetrical, and still active volcanic peaks mirrored in Lake Atitlan are only 80 miles from the semidesert of the Rio Motagua. The lush jungle-clad gorge of the Rio Dulce stands in stark contrast to the dry limestone plateau of the Yucatán.

Isla Contoy and the island of Cochino Grande stand at the north and south gateways to the region. The former is a barely uplifted bed of limestone with underscored cliffs, sparse vegetation, and a parched countenance. The latter is a high island clothed in luxuriant tropical rain forest, with rocky headlands enclosing lovely white beaches. Between them stretches a 300-mile necklace of cays and reefs that has no equal for variety and beauty in the western hemisphere.

The entire area is a nature lover's delight, home to numerous exotic birds and endangered species, both ashore and in the ocean. Restricted in our movements as we were by two small children, we still saw frigate birds and boobies, parrots and toucans, howler and spider monkeys, manta rays, dolphins, manatees, flying fish, and turtles, and innumerable varieties of gorgeous tropical fish and reef corals.

Despite the region's compactness, in the course of our survey we covered 2,500 sea miles, not including passages made between Isla Mujeres and our home base of New Orleans. Even so, we left much unexplored—you could spend years gunkholing the area and still not know it well. Since we have been back in the United States, we have talked frequently of returning to take up where we left off, and probably will do so as early as next year. Before setting sail, you should be warned that the area is addictive. A number of longtime cruisers have kept returning, finally to remain permanently! If you still decide to go, I hope this guide helps you enjoy the Northwest Caribbean as much as we have.

Cautionary Notes

MAGNETIC VARIATIONS

All bearings and courses in this guide have been corrected to true north.

When this guide was written (1990), magnetic variation in the region ranged from approximately 1°E at Isla Mujeres to 3°E in Belizean waters, and back to 2°E in the Bay Islands of Honduras. In all areas the variation is decreasing by approximately 7 minutes annually.

In correcting bearings taken with a hand-bearing compass:

1° has been added to those taken between Isla Mujeres and the southern tip of Cozumel;

2° to those taken between the southern tip of Cozumel and northern Belize;

3° to those taken in Belizean and Guatemalan waters;

2° to those taken in the Bay Islands of Honduras and along the Honduran mainland.

To convert a bearing back to a magnetic heading, check your charts for the current variation in the relevant area, then make whatever adjustment is necessary.

To go from a *true* heading to a *magnetic* heading, you *deduct* easterly variation.

ACCURACY DISCLAIMERS

Most cruising guides warn the reader that the guide and its sketch charts are not to replace existing government charts and publications, then follow this with a disclaimer concerning the accuracy of the information in the guide.

In much of the region covered by this guide, however, either the available charts have insuffi-

cient detail for coastal piloting and gunkholing, or the charts contain so many inaccuracies that they are unreliable aids to navigation. I recognize that the normal disclaimer is a rather pointless and academic exercise; inevitably, this guide at times will substitute for government publications, or will fill a void in those publications. Indeed, the inadequacy of existing official publications is the primary rationale for this cruising guide.

It is therefore more important than ever that you, the reader, recognize the limitations of this guide.

This guide has been prepared by experienced small-boat sailors, not professional ocean surveyors. We have used the existing charts, with all their inadequacies; the depthsounders on our boats, with all their inaccuracies; and our hand-bearing compasses, with all the uncertainties of sights taken, sometimes in rough conditions.

I have spent hour upon hour perched on our spreaders to obtain a better view of the surrounding water. In calm conditions and good light, I have been able to see a considerable area and check for hazards with a fair degree of conviction. In rougher conditions and poor light, sometimes I saw little more than the water immediately surrounding our boat. This guide shows many anchorages that we, and others, have entered safely, but on occasion we may have slipped past dangerous, unseen coral heads just half a boat length away.

We also have made every effort to ensure the accuracy of the information in this guide, going so far as to sail back out of many of the trickier entries, and then come back in rigidly following our own instructions, sometimes repeating this maneuver two or three times as we refined and simplified the information. Nevertheless, we are bound to have made some mistakes. What is more, piloting information changes: Reefs grow and die; hurricanes blast new channels or extend existing cays; buoys and stakes are moved, lost, or changed; and so on.

Given the number of hazards—primarily coral

reefs—and the sheer complexity of covering the region, it becomes crucial that you, the reader, do not place a blind trust in the information in this guide.

In the Northwest Caribbean, more than any other region that we have sailed, it is important that you use a cruising guide simply as an adjunct to prudent navigation and piloting, and never as a substitute. Regardless of how seemingly precise the information in this guide is—and we have tried to make it precise—you should never try any of the reef entries unless conditions give you full control of your boat at all times and the light provides an adequate view of the bottom.

Neither the publisher nor the author can hold themselves responsible for any errors or omissions in the text or the sketch charts in this book. You must navigate with this in mind. Should you find any mistakes, ambiguities, omissions, or have other comments to make, we would very much like to hear from you. Please write to: Nigel Calder, c/o International Marine Publishing, P.O. Box 220, Camden, ME 04843. Your help will be gratefully received.

Part I

Preparations for Cruising the Northwest Caribbean

Background Information

HISTORY

Chichén Itzá, Uxmal, Palenque, Tikál, Copán . . . magnificent ruins that evoke the glory of the Mayan empire and inspire wonder in all who see them. The Northwest Caribbean is still Maya country; in fact, this guide's regional boundaries dovetail neatly into the boundaries of the Mayan Empire of old, and match the present-day spread of the surviving Indians.

From the northern coasts of the Yucatán to Honduras, you will still find purebred Mayans living very much as they did when Columbus first sighted these shores, and very much as they have done for the better part of 3,000 years. The *palapas* (palm-thatched houses), the slash-and-burn agriculture, the techniques of planting maize in the ashes with a pointed stick, the volcanic terraces in Guatemala, the time-honored traditions surrounding planting, harvesting, and life have all been handed down through the millenia, affected by each new wave of conquest but in many ways unchanged. Although the Mayans are nominally Catholics, they infused even the Catholic religion with their own religious beliefs to such an extent that, in some areas, it is difficult to determine who converted whom!

THE MAYAN EMPIRE

In the days when Europe was deep in the "Dark Ages," the Maya had developed a complex script, accumulated tremendously precise astronomical knowledge, invented an incredibly accurate calendar, and were building enormous temples, which had elaborately carved panels and histories in stone. Cities of tens of thousands supported what must have been an extensive, cultured aristocracy and priesthood. Mayan civilization soared to its greatest heights in the Central Area—the region from the southern Yucatán to western Honduras.

Early explorers and investigators painted a romantic picture of an essentially benign theocratic empire, but the picture that has emerged from recent research is far less sanguine. The Mayan empire was never a unified whole. It comprised a number of rival city states in a loose confederacy, each ruled by an aristocracy, not the priesthood, with alternating periods of warfare and uneasy peace. The bedrock upon which the achievements of the Mayans was erected was a highly productive agriculture. This cultivation included widespread terracing of the rich volcanic soils in Guatemala (which continues to this day) and large irrigation projects in other drier, less fertile areas. The agricultural surpluses fed the artisans and intellectuals, the aristocrats and priests who were responsible for the impressive artifacts and ruins that we see today.

Dozens of gods governed every aspect of life in a highly ritualized society. The Mayans had an obsession with blood sacrifice. Carvings and paintings show prisoners tortured and torn apart to glorify some ruler or sanctify some event. Where previ-

Stone carving of a Mayan lord from Palenque, circa A.D. 730.

ously certain images were thought to represent men pouring water over their penises, it is now recognized that these recorded the self-mutilation of this member. Other pictures show women lacerating their tongues by chewing on thorn-embedded ropes. Slaves, prisoners, and especially young children were slaughtered to solemnify events. Most of the tombs of lords in the pyramids contain remains of two or three other people sacrificed at the funeral.

The tremendous flowering of Mayan culture suddenly ceased around A.D. 900. Throughout the Central Area, the cities were abandoned, while a less dramatic depopulation occurred in the more northern regions. In the following centuries, waves of Mexican invaders at one time or another dominated much of the Mayan lands. In one or two regions a renaissance of sorts occurred, particularly at Chichén Itzá where there was much new construction. In general, however, nothing rivaled the magnificence of earlier centuries.

What happened? Epigraphists are slowly unravelling the mysteries of Mayan hieroglyphs. Together with archaeologists, botanists, art historians, ethnohistorians, and linguists, they are bringing us closer than ever before to an understanding of the history of the Mayan people. Still, no clear picture has emerged regarding what brought about the relatively sudden collapse of the great Mayan city states. Perhaps agricultural production could no longer support the burgeoning aristocracy and non-productive classes; maybe an epidemic swept the region; or possibly the peasants rose up and killed their oppressors, who took with them to their graves the remaining secrets of the Maya.

THE SPANISH CONQUEST

By the 1500s when the Spanish conquistadors arrived, almost all of the old cities and ceremonial

Stone carving of a Mayan warrior at Tikál.

centers had been long-since abandoned for good. The Maya had broken up into warring feudal states governed from walled cities. This lack of centralization forced the Spaniards to conquer the Mayan lands piecemeal; unlike the Aztec in Mexico, the Maya possessed no central authority that could be defeated. The Spaniards frequently employed one group of Mayas to make war on another.

The campaign was long and bloody, with immense cruelty on both sides, including the ritual sacrifice of captured Spaniards. The last major Mayan stronghold, on an island in Lake Peten Itza,

Guatemala, was not taken until 1697. Subsequently, the Spaniards and their successors had to deal with repeated revolts. As late as 1860, the Yucatán Maya rebelled and formed an independent kingdom, which was not fully absorbed into present-day Mexico until the 1930s.

POST CONQUEST

The conquistadors were more interested in loot than settlement. All of Central America was raided for treasure. One Spanish treasure fleet assembled regularly on Lago Izabal, Guatemala, shipping plundered goods that had been hauled overland by Indian slaves. From Lago Izabal the fleet made its way down the Rio Dulce to the Caribbean to run the gauntlet of pirates, privateers (pirates "licensed" by various European governments, primarily the French, British, and Dutch), and hurricanes on its journey back to Spain. A fort—the Castilio San Felipe—was built to defend the fleet at the point where the Rio Dulce exits Lago Izabal. This fort has been fully restored by the Guatemalan government and is well worth a visit.

Although Columbus landed on Guanaja, in the Bay Islands, the Spaniards' attempt to establish a settlement failed. In subsequent years, pirates, privateers, and buccaneers used the fabulous natural harbors on Roatan as temporary bases from time to time. There is a persistent local rumor that the infamous Henry Morgan was based in Port Royal harbor and from there organized his raids, including the sacking of Panama in 1670. Many of today's white, English-speaking population in the Bay Islands claim descent from these pirates.

The stories are colorful but not true. Morgan and other English pirates sailed out of Port Royal harbor, *Jamaica*, not Port Royal, Roatan. Pirates did make occasional layovers in the Bay Islands to seek shelter, careen ships, and hunt feral pigs and cattle (escaped domestic animals gone wild), but the first permanent white settlers were people involved in the export of logwood (highly valued in Europe for blue dye) from the Mosquito Coast of Nicaragua and from mainland Honduras. The first settlement (1638) was driven out by the Spaniards in 1642. English colonists returned intermittently until British troops were sent to organize a permanent colony in 1744. This colony grew steadily. In 1797, 5,000 rebellious "Black Caribs" were deported from St. Vincent to Roatan; then in 1838, a substantial number of former slaves from the Cayman Islands were also settled there.

Meanwhile the Indian population on the mainland was steadily decimated through slaughter, enslavement, and imported European diseases. At the same time, the Spaniards, faced with a shortage of European women, freely intermarried, which created today's majority mestizo population. The Indians were dispossessed of the more fertile lands. Great Spanish haciendas were established with subjugated Indian labor—a situation that remains fundamentally unchanged in spite of further centuries of upheaval.

Treasure and cash crops such as cacao, indigo, sugar, and tobacco exported back to Spain brought wealth to the colonial aristocracy. Cities were built, with churches, palaces, and universities. It was inevitable that sooner or later, resentment of the heavy bureaucratic hand of Spain and the hemorrhage of wealth back to the mother country would build and flare into revolt.

INDEPENDENCE

The American revolutionary war set in motion a tidal wave from the New World that was to engulf the old. In 1789 the French revolution overthrew the ancien régime. In its wake Napoleon conquered much of Europe, including Spain. For a time the Spanish colonies were left on their own while new, liberal political ideas were infusing the body politic. The defeat of Napoleon was followed by the restoration of the old, conservative regime in Spain, intent on undoing any moves toward liberalization or independence in the colonies.

The Mexicans were the first to rebel, followed almost immediately by the Captaincy General of Guatemala—Spain's Central American colonies—and the colonies in South America. Much of Central America celebrates its day of independence as September 15, 1821—exceptions in the region covered by this guide are Belize (September 21) and Mexico (September 16). A new and independent Mexican

Empire was established, embracing all of Central America, under the leadership of Iturbide.

Within two years Iturbide was assassinated and the Central American federation broke away from the empire. The next 15 years saw a continuous succession of civil wars within Central America as liberals and conservatives, church and state, and the various regions all jockeyed for power. In 1838 the federation broke up for good, more or less into today's countries of Nicaragua, El Salvador, Honduras, and Guatemala.

Belize, an almost uninhabited, bug-infested tropical jungle, was largely ignored, allowing small coastal settlements of British and their black slaves to maintain a toehold on the mainland in their pursuit of first logwood trees, then mahogany (after synthetic dyes killed the logwood industry). Similar settlements grew along the inhospitable Mosquito Coast of Nicaragua and in the Bay Islands. In the 1850s Britain, under pressure from the United States government, ceded its claims in Nicaragua and the Bay Islands to the Nicaraguan and Honduran governments, while Belize was elevated to the status of a full colony.

POST INDEPENDENCE

With the exception of Belize, the Central American states have been dominated by an intensely conservative, landed oligarchy. Brief interludes of liberal reform and constitutional democracy have been sandwiched between long stretches of often despotic dictatorship. The inequalities of land distribution and wealth have led to frequent revolts of the Indians and peasants, who generally have been brutally suppressed.

Since World War II, the population of the region has more than doubled. The Indians, in particular, crammed into tiny landholdings with no possibility for increasing food production, have been driven ever closer to starvation. All attempts at land reform have been met with staunch hostility by the landed oligarchies, which have used their national armies to wage war on their own people.

The ideologies adopted by those in rebellion have changed, with various socialist currents dominating the existing revolutionary groups. The fundamental causes of rebellion, however, are the same—inequitable distribution of land, which leaves millions in abject poverty while an elite minority accumulates and often squanders the national wealth. The result has been lengthy and bitter civil wars in Guatemala, El Salvador (not part of this cruising guide's ground), and to a lesser degree Honduras—and the level of destruction escalates as the various forces acquire increasingly modern weaponry.

The recent election of a "civilian" government in Guatemala (and also El Salvador) has been held up as proof of a steady process of U.S.-sponsored democratization. But it has not stopped the death-squad activities, nor widespread abuses of human rights. Unless the U.S. promotes human rights by tying all military aid to an observance of the rule of law, any new governments in this region are unlikely to break free of the shadows of their military establishments, and the "democracies" will, as so often before, be stillborn.

It is my hope that the current atmosphere of superpower detente and the global thawing of the cold war will lead to a thorough reappraisal of U.S. policies in the region. It cannot come too soon for the majority of those living in Central America.

BIBLIOGRAPHY

Many books cover the history of this region. I have selected three that give a feel for the past, the present, and the major issues of today. These, in turn, will suggest plenty of other reading to those who wish to pursue the subject in greater detail.

The Maya, by Michael D. Coe, published by Thames and Hudson, is a concise look at all aspects of the Mayan empire. It is, perhaps, a little academic for the lay reader, but a quick reading, without getting too bogged down in all the details, will give a good picture of the current understanding of the Maya.

Guatemala: A Nation in Turmoil, by Peter Calvert, published by Westview Press, is an equally concise, very readable account of the history of Guatemala to the present day.

War Against the Poor, by Jack Nelson-Pallmeyer,

published by Orbis Books, is a well-researched and documented, passionate attack on current United States government policy in Central America by a devout Christian and longtime resident in Central America.

POLITICS AND SECURITY

The political situation in Central America in the recent past has deterred many sailors from visiting this region. This is hardly surprising, but even at the height of the various insurgencies and counter-insurgencies, to all intents and purposes the visiting cruiser has never been in danger and has rarely seen any overt signs of the region's problems.

Take Guatemala, for example. The country has experienced low-level insurgency for more than 20 years while various military dictatorships have had one of the worst human rights records in Central America. Reputable human rights organizations estimate that the military has slaughtered tens of thousands of Guatemalans, often razing whole villages. Yet none of this has been visible to visiting yachts. Throughout this period, sailors entering the Rio Dulce have felt more welcomed by the local people and more secure than in many a city at home.

 I am not suggesting that the cruising community should ignore the political realities of the region; what I am saying is that in spite of the undercurrents of violence, you still can feel safe in this region. At the local level, the people are some of the friendliest in the Caribbean. We traveled extensively in Guatemala, in the Central Highlands, and up to Tikál, and were just overwhelmed by the beauty of the region, the spectacularly colorful native clothes, and the open and friendly nature of the Mayan Indian population. These are areas still subject to sporadic guerrilla activity—the mountains south of Antigua were bombed just before we arrived, and the day before we left the bus from Tikál was stopped and burned by guerillas—but both sides seem careful to keep tourists out of the crossfire. As a result, most visitors are completely unaware of any of these activities.

Crime against tourists, especially violent crime, is rare, excluding Belize City (which has a major problem with thieves). There is no need for anything more than ordinary security precautions (such as locking your outboard motor to your dinghy during the day and taking it off at night). In many areas you really don't need any security measures at all. This is a wonderful endorsement of the people, especially when you consider the enormous disparities in wealth between us and most of them.

The average cruiser is safer almost anywhere in this region than in many of the popular cruising grounds in the Virgin Islands and West Indies, not to mention most cities "back home" (wherever that happens to be).

DRUGS AND PIRACY

The second major concern of many people is the probability of running into trouble with drug-runners and drug-related violence. There would seem to be little doubt that a substantial part of the flow of drugs into the southern United States comes through this region. And yet, in three cruises in the area, the last one seven months in duration, we have neither encountered any drug traffic or traffickers nor heard any reports or rumors of such activity. The closest we have come was a warning from an inebriated Englishman in Tulum (on the Mexican coast) to watch out for *bandidos* in the Bahia de la Ascension. The only people we saw were local fishermen. My conclusion is that just as the political violence does not impinge on visitors, so too the drug trade hereabouts avoids us.

While on the subject of drugs, let me warn people who themselves indulge: We have been searched when clearing into all the countries in this guide, stopped and searched by the U.S. Coast Guard in international waters, and searched by local patrols in Belize. Unless you want to run the risk of losing your boat, throw your contraband drugs overboard.

FIREARMS

The political situation and the drug trade seem to lead naturally to a discussion of firearms. This is a very personal and emotional subject for many Americans. I intend to say little except that every country in this region is likely to take your firearms on entry and to hold them until you leave. If you attempt to enter without declaring weapons, especially handguns, rifles, semi-automatics, and automatics, and they are found on board during a subsequent search, you may find yourself in deep trouble.

Given the lack of threats to cruising sailors in this region, and the likelihood that any weapons will be locked up in someone else's custody for much of the time you are there, you must consider whether it really is worth bringing in weapons. Associate editor Peter Hancock got tired of the bureaucratic hassles occasioned by his rusty old shotgun. He tried to give it away to a port captain in Mexico, but without success. He finally succeeded in selling it to a port captain in Guatemala and has not missed it.

My own feelings are that a flare gun fired at close quarters would make a reasonably effective weapon. The odds of running into a situation where a heavier armament would end rather than add to your problems are minuscule.

If you do decide to keep firearms on board, install a sturdily built, custom-made gun cabinet with a hefty lock. This will sometimes persuade authorities to let you keep the arms on board. In this case when you enter the country, be sure to have customs put a note on your *zarpe* (see "Paperwork" on page 8) to the effect that the guns have been declared; otherwise the next official down the line will assume you have smuggled them in, which will cause all kinds of problems.

LANGUAGES

Mexico, Guatemala, and Honduras are all Spanish-speaking countries and little English is spoken, except by the white and black people in the Bay Islands (some of whom are insulted if you address them in Spanish!). All officials speak Spanish; very few understand any English.

Belize is English speaking, although you might not think so listening to the everyday speech. In the north and south, however, there are quite a few Spanish-speaking people who do not understand English.

Inland in all these countries are Mayan Indians who speak any number of different Mayan dialects.

It will make your trip a lot more enjoyable if you can acquire at least a little Spanish before you arrive, but this is by no means essential to getting around.

MONEY

The currencies are as follows:

- Mexico: the peso, which continues to slide steadily against the dollar;
- Belize: the Belizean dollar, which is pegged at 2:1 against the U.S. dollar;
- Guatemala: the quetzal, which after years of relative stability is now on a steady slide against the dollar;
- Honduras: the lempira, which for years was officially 2:1 against the U.S. dollar while it slowly slid on the black market to 4:1. In 1990 the banks briefly came into line with the black market, but the currency continues to slide.

Since the peso, quetzal, and lempira continue to drift downhill, it is not worth buying any of these currencies until you need them, and then only as much as you need. You should spend any surplus before leaving the relevant country; getting rid of it elsewhere will prove almost impossible!

VISA, MASTERCARD, AND AMERICAN EXPRESS. Do not plan to obtain cash advances with a Visa or MasterCard. This is only possible in Cancún and Cozumel, Mexico; at Barclay's Bank in Belize City; and at the American Bank in Guatemala City. The latter bank's telex machine was out of action every time we went there, and we could never get an advance; the bank would advance us a monthly limit of $100, in local currency only. CredoMatic in Guatemala City has links with various banks and also will give a cash advance against a Visa or MasterCard, but at a poor exchange rate and with a 5 percent commission, which adds up to a whopping 10 percent overhead.

There are no Visa or MasterCard facilities in the Bay Islands. Even when it is possible to use a credit card (such as when buying an airline ticket), you are strongly advised not to since you will be given the official exchange rate, which lags far behind the street rate even subsequent to the banks' raising their rate.

Where cash advances can be obtained with a Visa or MasterCard, few banks are willing to sell anything other than local currency. In Belize the banks are not allowed to sell you U.S. dollars or U.S. dollar-based traveler's checks, without proof that you are leaving the country—either a return airline ticket to a foreign country or a letter of authorization from the Central Bank of Belize. The American Bank in Guatemala City will sell U.S. dollar-based traveler's checks (when their telex is working) at a modest 2 percent commission. And that's it!

American Express cardholders can obtain cash or traveler's checks at AMEX offices. See their current listing.

CHANGING MONEY. U.S. dollars are acceptable throughout the region and dollar-based traveler's checks are easy to change except in more isolated places in Mexico and Guatemala.

In Mexico and Belize the banks give as good a rate as on the street (the black market). In Guatemala and Honduras the official exchange rate always lags behind the street rate. You will not have problems changing money on the street and will not have to wait in line for an hour in a bank. Consult other tourists for the current rate.

In Guatemala City the money changers hang out by the post office in Zone 1 (see page 183); all you have to do is walk down the street and you will be approached by several money changers. Don't take the first offer you receive; they can always be squeezed up a little!

There are no money-changing facilities in Relleno/Fronteras, the town on the Rio Dulce closest to the marinas and the Catamaran Hotel. It is best to acquire some quetzals in Livingston when checking into Guatemala. The Chinese grocery store on the right at the top of the street leading up from the town dock will cash both notes and traveler's checks. The rate lags behind Guatemala City but not too much. You will need about 100 quetzals to clear in, plus whatever else you expect to spend while on the Rio Dulce. If coming from Punta Gorda in Belize, you can buy quetzals at a similar rate from the supermarket in the center of town.

Such is the demand for U.S. dollars in the Bay Islands that many stores and restaurants will cash personal checks. Check around in Coxen's Hole and French Harbor. Please, don't bounce any checks; it spoils the trusting relationship for the rest of us.

SUMMARY. To avoid cash-flow problems, you should enter this region with a substantial float of dollars and traveler's checks. Do not place yourself in a position of dependence on a cash advance from a credit card or from overseas. If you should need to use a credit card to obtain cash, the most useful one is American Express.

PAPERWORK

PASSPORTS AND VISAS. Every crewmember needs an up-to-date passport to travel in this region. At various times, we have gone to the trouble and expense of obtaining visas for Guatemala and Honduras from the relevant consulates before leaving the U.S. It always has proved to be a waste of time and money. The entering officials have never recognized the visas and always insisted on issuing new ones—and charging for them.

Whenever traveling inland, be sure to carry your passport plus any visa or tourist card issued when you entered the country.

BOAT PAPERS. You will need a certificate of registration for your boat—a state registration slip (e.g., State of Louisiana) is adequate, but a U.S. Coast Guard certification looks more official. Occasionally you will be asked to produce a bill of sale to prove your ownership. In addition, as you enter and leave each country, you will need a crew list. In Belize, Guatemala, and Honduras, the relevant officials will type up the necessary paperwork for you, generally at no charge. Not so in Mexico where officials can be unbelievably difficult if you are not fully prepared with *seven* copies of everything, in impeccable Spanish. On page 70 you'll find a sample crew list that should get you by in Mexico. If possible, you should carry a portable typewriter and carbon paper on board (unless you have a word processor and printer) in case further documentation is required. When entering Belize you may be required to produce three copies of a list of all the groceries—dried, canned, fresh, and frozen—on board.

You must "clear in" and "clear out" of each country. If you arrive at your next destination without proper clearance from your last port-of-call, you will have major difficulties. The key document is universally known as a *zarpe*. It gives your boat name, some particulars, lists the crewmembers, and states that you have been cleared from such-and-such port to such-and-such port.

A zarpe is dated for its day of issue. If more than a few days elapse before your arrival at the stated destination, the officials there may give you a hard time. It is, of course, permissible to change your plans and sail somewhere else. The important thing is not to allow too long a period of time to elapse before arrival. If necessary you may have to claim engine problems or adverse winds.

Both Mexico and Honduras issue zarpes from port to port—you must clear in and out of each principal port—whereas once cleared into Belize and Guatemala, you are free to sail anywhere within these countries for the permitted time—generally 30 days in Belize; 90 days in Guatemala. After clearing in to Mexico or Honduras, you will need a zarpe to move on to the next port. At this time it is sometimes possible to talk the officials into listing *puntos intermedios* (intermediate points) on your new zarpe, in which case you should try to list every place you are likely to visit, up to and including the port you will clear out of when you leave the country. Officials in some ports may still come out to your boat and refuse to recognize this zarpe, requiring you to obtain a fresh one from them, but most times you will get by with it.

Belizean officials, especially those from Belize City who are used to dealing with big ships, do not like to see vessels in their waters for more than 24 hours without clearing in, or more than 24 hours after clearing out. They maintain regular patrols of the outlying cays and will check your paperwork (and search your boat), so play the game right and keep your papers straight. It is rarely more than a minor inconvenience and most officials are helpful, courteous (with the notable exception of San Miguel, Cozumel), and reasonably honest (with the notable exceptions of Coxen's Hole on Roatan and San Miguel).

Specific procedures for clearing in and out of in-dividual ports are covered in the relevant sections in the guide. As a result of communications I have had with various ministries in Mexico, I learned that they are reviewing the entry procedures for boats in order to simplify them. Perhaps we shall see improvements in procedures in the near future.

FISHING LICENSES. A license is required to fish anywhere in Mexican waters. If your boat is boarded and inspected at any time, discovery of a fishing pole or other tackle on board can be construed as proof that you have been fishing, so it is best to get a license. You can get a fishing license from Secretaria de Pesca, Alvaro Obregon #269, Mexico City, Mexico, from Mexican consulates in the U.S., or from the Department of Fisheries in Cancún and San Miguel, Cozumel.

CHANGES IN CREW. If at any time friends or crewmembers fly out to join you, they may be required to carry return tickets—even if they intend to sail back with you. Be sure to check with your airline or travel agent, since some airlines will not let you board without a return ticket, and some countries will not let you enter without one. Unused portions of a ticket can often be refunded at a later date.

Finally, parents of young children, be forewarned. If one of you is planning to sail a boat somewhere while the other partner flies out with the children to join the boat overseas, note that some airlines in the U.S. will not allow one parent with children to board an overseas flight without a notarized statement from the other parent granting permission to take the children out of the United States.

If you plan to fly out and leave your boat in a marina, you may need some paperwork showing that the boat is in responsible hands. Check with the marina (see "Leaving Your Boat" in Chapter 3).

FLAGS AND
FLAG ETIQUETTE

You will need a courtesy flag for each country you visit. These should be 12 inches by 15 inches or larger. If you make your own, be reasonably accurate. The Hondurans, in particular, can be real sticklers: Our flag was rejected because the stripes were too blue-green, as opposed to bright blue (in reality, this was just a gambit to try and extract *mordida*—a bribe). The courtesy flag is flown from the starboard spreader.

When first entering a country you fly a yellow flag—the Q (for quarantine) flag—which is taken down as soon as you are cleared in. Strictly speaking this should be flown from a separate hoist but on small boats it too is generally flown from the starboard spreader, below the courtesy flag.

Your national flag should be flown from a flagstaff at the stern, or from the rearmost topping lift on the boat (i.e., the main topping lift on a sloop or cutter; the mizzen on a ketch, yawl, or schooner). If you fly your flag on the same hoist as the courtesy flag, make sure it is *below* the courtesy flag!

PUBLIC HOLIDAYS

It is no good trying to clear in and out of a country on a public holiday. You will probably not be able to find the relevant officials, but if you do you may be charged overtime. Below are the chief holidays:

MEXICO:

January 1	New Year's Day
February 5	Constitution Day
March 21	Birthday of Benito Juarez
Varies	Good Friday
May 1	Labor Day
May 5	Anniversary of the Battle of Puebla
September 15,16	Independence Day (officially the 16th but celebration begins the night before)
October 12	Columbus Day
November 2	All Souls Day
November 20	Anniversary of the Mexican revolution
December 25	Christmas Day

BELIZE:

January 1	New Year's Day
March 9	Baron Bliss Day
Varies	Good Friday, Easter Saturday, and Easter Monday
May 1	Labor Day
May 24	Commonwealth Day
September 10	Commemoration of the Battle of St. George's Cay
September 21	Independence Day
October 12	Columbus Day
November 19	Garifuna Settlement Day
December 25	Christmas Day
December 26	Boxing Day

GUATEMALA:

January 1	New Year's Day
January 6	Epiphany
Varies	Wednesday to Sunday of Easter week
May 1	Labor Day
June 30	Anniversary of the revolution
August 15	Anniversary of the revolution (in Guatemala City only)
September 15	Independence Day
October 20	Revolution Day
November 1	All Saints Day
December 24	Christmas Eve Day
December 25	Christmas Day

HONDURAS:

January 1	New Year's Day
April 14	Day of the Americas
Varies	Easter Thursday to Sunday
May 1	Labor Day
September 15	Independence Day
October 3	Francisco Morazan Day
October 12	Discovery Day
October 21	Army Day
December 25	Christmas Day

DRESS CODE

Dress throughout the region covered by this guide tends to be uniformly informal, if not downright scruffy. Nevertheless, many of the people are deeply conservative and dress modestly. As a matter of basic respect to local custom, avoid wearing brief shorts and swimsuits except on beaches and in resorts that are accustomed to such attire.

The Boat

Onboard Systems for the Tropics

A cruising guide is not the proper place for me to air my prejudices on boat design and rig, spade rudders, and the like. With that in mind I have limited the following comments to the more important systems that make life aboard comfortable in the tropics, and how they are likely to be affected in this region. The points are in no particular order of importance

VENTILATION
AND SHADE

These two factors determine whether your boat will become a sauna or a cool and comfortable home. A full-length awning that shades most of the boat will have a major impact on interior temperatures. If you can't accommodate an awning this size, go for the largest you can handle. A number of books detail sturdy awning designs.

Once the boat is shaded, you must maintain an airflow through it. From this perspective you cannot have too many hatches, opening ports, and ventilators, but note that one good-size hatch is worth a dozen ports and ventilators. Equip the hatches with individual wind socks (such as those made by WindScoop) to funnel any breezes into your boat. If you design the awning so that it keeps rain off the wind socks, then you can leave hatches open during rain showers.

On those occasions when the wind dies, you will need a number of strategically placed DC fans: in the galley, the saloon, and over each berth.

INSECT SCREENS

Much of this region comes alive for an hour or two at dusk, when mosquitoes, sand flies, and no-see-ums take off in search of flesh. An anchorage open to the trade winds will have no problem, but if the wind dies, you will need screens for every opening in the boat—hatches, ventilators, and ports. Screens should be standard equipment on a cruising boat since this problem is not confined to the Northwest Caribbean. If you don't have screens, make some before setting out on your cruise.

REFRIGERATION

Keeping food cool is as important as keeping yourself cool. Food spoils rapidly in the tropics, where supplies of fresh produce are infrequent (see "Provisioning"). Without refrigeration you will soon be reduced to a diet of canned and dried food. A freezer is a particularly nice luxury since fresh meat is even scarcer than fresh produce. Furthermore, from time to time truly excellent cuts of meat can be bought very cheaply (e.g., on the Rio Dulce where we froze enough to carry us through Belize and the Bay Islands). In spite of the infrequency of supplies, our refrigeration system permits us to eat at least as well on board, and perhaps better, than we do when ashore in the States!

A refrigeration system is, unfortunately, a tremendous power hog. Boats coming down to the tropics from cooler regions up north frequently find

that their refrigeration units kill batteries and require extended engine running time at anchor for recharging, sometimes still not working effectively. If you have not tested your refrigeration system in a tropical environment, be sure to check its operating characteristics before leaving port, and make any alterations required. Keep the following points in mind:

ICEBOXES. Refrigerators need 3 to 4 inches of closed-cell foam on the sides and bottom, 2 inches on the lids. Freezers need 4 to 6 inches of foam with 3 inches on the lids. All lids should be double-sealed, and drains require a U-trap or plug to stop cold air from leaking out of the bottom of the icebox.

TWELVE-VOLT UNITS. Twelve-volt constant-cycling refrigeration units have an air-cooled or a water-cooled condenser, or both. Air-cooled units suffer an 8 percent or more loss in performance with every 10° Fahrenheit rise in the ambient air temperature. In the tropics cabin and engine room temperatures on a tightly closed boat frequently will rise to well over 100°F. As the unit's performance is declining, the heat loss from the icebox is increasing: All the variables are moving in the wrong direction. The unit may be only half as efficient in the tropics as in northern latitudes. If it is already running 20 minutes or more an hour in a cooler climate, it may run almost continuously in the tropics. Even then it may not cool effectively. Apart from killing your batteries, sooner or later the unit will burn out.

A water-cooled condenser is as much as 15 times more efficient than an air-cooled condenser. Even in the tropics water temperatures rarely exceed 85°F; I have never logged higher than 94°F. This is below normal cabin temperatures. *Any boat venturing into the tropics with refrigeration should have a water-cooled condenser,* both to conserve energy and to protect the refrigeration unit from excessively long running periods and high operating temperatures.

ENERGY SYSTEMS

Twelve-volt refrigeration systems are likely to consume 70 amp-hours or more a day in the tropics. Fan and light usage can easily add another 50 amp-hours, and then there are the boat's electronics and other miscellaneous systems. On the average boat, this adds up to a hefty load of 100 amp-hours or more a day.

Between charges the ship's batteries must carry this load. They will be regularly discharged and recharged ("cycled"). No automotive battery can hold up under this kind of usage—most will fail after just a few months. Before you head south, I strongly recommend you buy a set of good-quality deep-cycle batteries. These are custom-made to handle the kind of cycling service found on most cruising boats. Although expensive, they more than pay for themselves over their lifespan. You should have two separate banks of batteries, each with a minimum capacity of 2¹/₂ times the anticipated daily demand, and preferably four times the anticipated daily demand.

While energy consumption on a cruising boat is high, shoreside power is almost nonexistent in the region covered by this guide. Your ability to recharge your batteries will be almost totally dependent on your own generating capability.

Once you leave your slip, your alternator probably will become your primary charging device. To avoid long hours of engine-running at anchor, which is expensive both in fuel and maintenance and in wear and tear on the engine, I strongly advise you to buy a marine high-output alternator (130 to 160 amps) and a marine deep-cycle regulator. These will pay for themselves quite rapidly. Keep the old alternator and regulator as a spare, or better yet, buy a second high-output alternator and marine regulator. A good-size wind generator and as many *marine-grade* solar panels as you can handle would be another excellent investment. For a detailed discussion of all these topics, see *The Boatowner's Mechanical and Electrical Manual* (listed in the bibliography).

Many larger boats with generators are heavily loaded with AC equipment: air conditioners, a microwave, an electric stove, a blender, a coffee percolator, and so on. In normal circumstances, air conditioning is the only major power consumer that demands a continuous source of AC power. Almost all other AC devices are used only intermittently. These can be subdivided into major-load items (microwaves, stoves, water heaters) and minor-load items (almost everything else).

If your boat has adequate ventilation, air conditioning is often not needed. Then, with a little planning, you can concentrate use of the major-load items into just an hour or so of generator run time. Minor-load items operated intermittently throughout the rest of the day can be handled by a DC/AC inverter without running the generator.

With such a system, you can realize major savings in fuel consumption and generator wear and tear—more than enough to pay for the inverter, not to mention the reduction in noise, exhaust fumes, and heat. However, if you plan to use a DC/AC inverter this way—i.e., on anything more than the most minor and intermittent loads—a heavy strain will be placed on the DC system. It is absolutely essential to have a large bank of deep-cycle batteries and adequate charging capabilities. There is no benefit to transferring the generator load to the DC system if you must then run the main engine long hours to recharge the batteries!

Note that in many circumstances, since the generator will be run an hour or two every day for the major-load items, it makes more sense to fit a high-output alternator and marine regulator to this engine rather than to the main engine. In such circumstances it is also frequently more sensible to drive engine-driven refrigeration off the generator engine rather than off the main engine.

FUEL TANKAGE AND
OTHER CONSIDERATIONS

Getting to and from the Northwest Caribbean is likely to require at least one moderately long—500 or more miles—open-water passage. Once you are in the region, basic engine supplies—fuel, oil, and filters—are sometimes hard to come by (for sources of resupply see the next chapter). The average auxiliary-powered sailboat should carry 50 or more gallons of diesel, using jerry cans if necessary to supplement existing tankage; a powerboat should have at least a 1,000-mile range. You need to carry enough oil for at least two oil changes, plus the necessary filters. Similar considerations apply to generators.

Mexican fuel, in particular, has a lousy reputation and has been blamed for many an engine problem. I have to say, however, that we have filled up a number of times in Mexico and have never received contaminated fuel, whereas we received filthy fuel in the Bay Islands. In any event, it is advisable to buy a funnel with a multistage filter and to use this whenever taking on fuel (including in the United States). Your engine also needs a substantial primary filter with a see-through bowl in addition to the secondary (engine-mounted) filter. The see-through bowl permits you to spot any water or dirt in the fuel; it can then be bled off before affecting the engine. Powerboats need double primary filters with a valved manifold that allows either filter to be isolated and bled off without having to shut down the engine. If you are unlucky enough to take on dirty fuel, you may have to change the filters repeatedly before problems clear up, so carry a good stock of filters (at least half a dozen).

If your engine raw-water pump uses a rubber impeller (most do), you need to keep a couple of spare impellers on board. You also should have at least one spare belt for each belt on the engine. It would be as well to replace the alternator belt before setting out. Finally, if you plan on an extended cruise you need to carry two or three spares for each zinc "pencil" anode on the engine—there may be one on the block; there should be one on the heat exchanger, maybe others in the cooling side of the exhaust manifold, and perhaps in any water-cooled refrigeration condenser. Be sure to check these zincs every two or three months and replace them when *partially corroded*, not when eaten away completely. Beyond this your spares inventory is a matter of cruising style: Some people like to carry extensive spares; others very few.

STOVE FUELS

Almost all boats these days have propane stoves. Assuming you are so equipped, you should carry enough propane for at least a month's use, preferably two or three (depending on your cruising pace). Accessible sources of resupply are not common in this region (see the next chapter). In Guatemala, propane has been periodically unavailable since the government, which runs the fuel business, has been slow to pay its bills, and its supplies have been cut off from time to time.

If you have a kerosene or alcohol stove, I advise installing sufficient tankage for several months. Stove alcohol is a rare commodity indeed. Kerosene is not only rare but, when found, may be of poor quality, resulting in plugged up burners and endless problems. Kerosene stove users should carry enough fuel to see them through this region. They need to keep on board a couple of complete spare burners, needle valves, and the special tool needed to remove the nipples from the burners.

WATER TANKAGE AND

COLLECTION

Sources of clean drinking water are infrequent (see the next chapter). The minimum capacity should be adequate tankage for at least a month's use. Even if you have a watermaker, I still suggest a month's backup in case of watermaker failure. Be sure to bring plenty of spare filters for the watermaker.

Some form of rainwater collection system is an excellent idea. The simplest way to do this is to design low spots and drains into the main awning such that any rainwater can be funneled into buckets or the water tanks. Since strong gusty winds often accompany rain squalls, you must think about how to fasten down the awning so that the water runs off as desired. On boats with continuous bulwarks, if the decks are scrubbed during one rainshower, the deck drains can be plugged during the next and the entire boat used for rainwater collection. We have our tank fills set in the side decks. Once our boat is clean, we simply plug our deck drains, unscrew the fill fittings, and run the water straight into our tanks. In a good squall we can gather 200 gallons quite rapidly. However, you should not place any reliance on being able to collect rainwater during the dry season—from November through May—because precipitation in much of the region is very infrequent.

RATLINES OR MAST STEPS

One of the Northwest Caribbean's great attractions is the abundance of living coral. This, however, can become a navigator's nightmare. The only effective way to navigate through coral is to station a crewmember up the mast in good light. This vantage point provides an excellent picture of the surrounding water. This tactic demands ratlines or mast steps. On a boat with fore-and-aft shrouds, my preference is overwhelmingly in favor of wooden (not rope) ratlines in the shrouds. These provide a far more comfortable perch than mast steps. This is another item that will need installing before setting out.

RIGGING

Almost all boats today have swaged-on rigging fittings—the type of end fitting that is slipped onto the wire rope and then run through a press that compresses the metal of the fitting around the wire. The tropics can be hard on such fittings, particularly the lower terminals on rigging because minute quantities of salt water wick down the wire rope into the fitting and become trapped. The warm, humid tropical environment promotes galvanic corrosion, which destroys the fitting from the inside. This has been known to happen in as little as two years.

If your rigging fittings are more than two years old, you should inspect them closely before commencing any extended cruise. Look for any telltale rust streaks or minute cracks. Your spares kit could well include a length of wire rope as long as the longest stay on the boat, and appropriate end fittings such that it could be used to replace any stay or shroud that showed signs of failing. Sta-Lok and Norseman end fittings are without question the best for this purpose since they can be made up in the field with simple hand tools.

Roller reefers also can develop problems. Before departure check the bearings in the drum and upper swivel to see that they are free-turning without any roughness and with no undue amount of play. If in any doubt, have them replaced. Check the nylon inserts inside the upper swivel to see that these are not worn.

TRASH DISPOSAL

Trash is a problem. At sea, in deep water, bottles and cans can be sunk. Be sure to fill them with water first, smash them, or punch a hole in both ends of cans, so that nothing floats. Much other waste is biodegradable and can be disposed of over the side. Plastics, of course, must all be retained.

When in shallower waters and around reefs, you should retain all but animal and vegetable wastes, and dispose of your trash properly ashore. Since many of the smaller communities have no waste disposal facilities, it is important to not just hand the trash to some helpful boy on the dock, who might turn around and throw it in the sea when you leave. If you cannot find a proper bin in which to dispose of your trash, you should take it back on board.

Thankfully, public awareness of the irresponsibility of littering our oceans is on the rise and lawmakers are responding. At the beginning of 1989, the new International Marine Pollution Treaty—MARPOL V—came into effect. This bans the dumping of any plastics ("biodegradable" or not) at sea, and bans the dumping of other kinds of trash in inshore areas. The U.S. Coast Guard is responsible for enforcing the treaty in U.S. waters and will in future, when checking for drugs and compliance with safety regulations, also be looking to see that boats have a reasonable amount of garbage on board. Boats that have been at sea for some time yet have no trash on board will be issued a citation. Fines of up to $25,000 can be imposed on those found guilty of illegal dumping.

One of the things that impressed us most about the Northwest Caribbean—and stood out in stark contrast to many of the islands in the West Indies—was the lack of trash. Many of the smaller communities on outlying cays and islands are raked and swept daily. Let's play our part in keeping it this way. *Stow It—Don't Throw It!*

For more information write to the Center for Marine Conservation, 1725 DeSales Street NW, Washington, DC 20036, U.S.A. Tel: (202) 429-5609. They will send you a free copy of "A Citizen's Guide to Plastics in the Ocean."

Ground Tackle, Anchoring, and

Kedging Off

The Northwest Caribbean is guaranteed to put your ground tackle and anchoring skills to the test. There is every kind of bottom from heavy sand, in which any kind of an anchor will set fast and hard, to almost smooth rock, on which just about nothing will bite. Anchorages vary in depth from 7 to 70 feet, and from fully protected lagoons to open roadsteads with a heavy swell—the latter imposing severe snubbing loads on ground tackle and windlasses. Winds may come steadily from one direction or box every point of the compass, sometimes with considerable force.

GROUND TACKLE

Your ground tackle must be adequate to the challenge. You will not be able to upgrade it anywhere in this region. You will need two distinct kinds of anchor: a plow (CQR), or Bruce, both of which are excellent on sand and mud, and a Danforth (or equivalent), which generally will set much better in grassy bottoms and in thin-sand-over-rock bottoms—coral sand (common in Belize). A useful backup on rock is a heavy fisherman-type anchor—most convenient are the ones that can be dismantled and stowed in a locker. The table on page 18 gives suitable anchor sizes for a given boat.

All anchors should have a minimum of 10 to 15 feet of chain shackled to the anchor. Thereafter many people prefer a nylon rode, since it is lighter and easier to handle than chain, but I strongly recommend giving the primary anchor an all-chain rode (or at least 100 feet of chain). If you anchor on nylon around coral, any wind shift may cause the rode to wrap around a coral head and chafe through. We lost one of our secondary anchors in Belize in this fashion.

How much rode to carry? This is a function of depth and not boat size. When anchoring with an all-chain rode, you should use a scope of at least four times the water depth; with a nylon rode a scope of at least six times the water depth. Since some anchorages may be as much as 60 feet deep, an all-chain rode should be 240 feet (which is an awful lot of chain!) and a nylon rode 360 feet. There should be *at least* two rodes of this length on board. We carry 120 feet of chain on our primary anchor, 500 feet of ⅝-inch nylon on our secondary anchor, and 600 feet of ½-inch nylon as a backup. On rare occasions we have used the whole lot!

Except on the smallest boats an anchor windlass is a near-essential piece of equipment, especially where an all-chain rode is used. When anchoring in deeper water, the weight of maybe 60 feet of chain added to even a relatively lightweight anchor can become too heavy to handle. Before setting out to do the legwork for this guide, we installed an electric windlass, and it proved to be almost worth its weight in gold. With an electric windlass, if you are not satisfied with the way the anchor is lying, you think nothing of weighing it and resetting it. We now also regularly set two anchors (previously we might have set only one) since retrieving the second anchor is effortless. But perhaps the greatest boon of the electric windlass has been its ability to kedge us off painlessly after running aground. I will have more to say on this in a moment.

ANCHORING WITH

ONE ANCHOR

The normal procedure when setting just one anchor is to come head to wind, to wait until all forward

SUGGESTED ANCHOR SIZES

Anchor Type	Boat Length in Feet																
	28	30	32	34	36	38	40	42	44	46	48	50	52	54	56	58	60
Danforth Standard	S–1300		S–1600		S–2000		S–3000				S–3500						
Danforth Standard Deep	D–1150	D–1650			D–2000		D–2500		D–3750								
Danforth High-Tensile	H–1500				H–1800		H–2100		H–3600						H–4000		
Danforth High-Tensile Deepset	T–1800				T–2500				T–3000			T–4000					
Fortress	FX–16		FX–23				FX–37					FX–55			FX–85		
CQR		25		35		45		60				75					
Delta		22			35			55									
Bruce		22			33			44				66				110	

Note: This table is loosely based on manufacturers' claims of holding power. However, there is more to anchoring than this! In general the heavier your ground tackle the better. For example, in a hard or weed-covered bottom, extra weight may be necessary for the flukes to penetrate.

motion is lost, to drop the anchor, and then to pay out the required scope as the wind pushes the boat backwards. It is important to pay the line or chain out gradually so that it does not pile up on top of the anchor and snag a fluke, especially when using a Danforth-type anchor.

Most boats have more windage forward than aft. The head will blow off as the boat falls back. This is no problem. As you come toward the end of the desired scope, you must place a little tension on the line and *gradually* snub up the rode. This has the effect of easing the points of the anchor flukes into the bottom and is particularly important on grassy bottoms where the anchor must cut through the grass. If you snub up with a jerk, the anchor sometimes will skip across the bottom and is unlikely to set, especially on grassy or sand-over-rock bottoms.

When you snub the anchor, keep a foot on the rode. If the anchor is dragging, you will feel it quite clearly. Other symptoms will be the boat's failure to come head to wind and its continuing to move in relation to fixed objects ashore. If the anchor is dragging, sometimes paying out more scope will get it to set. Otherwise it will have to be retrieved and reset. Don't feel bad; we have made up to seven attempts before getting an adequate bite. This is where the electric windlass really shines!

Once the boat has snubbed up and the anchor has bitten firmly, we always back down in full reverse to really dig the anchor in. We start with a little throttle and gradually build to full throttle. If the anchor will not hold under this kind of a load, it is not going to hold in a strong blow. It is better to know now rather than later. If it just cannot be made to hold, you will need a second, and possibly a third, anchor—see below.

Once the anchor is set, if you are using all-chain rode, you must put on a snubbing line. This is a short (10- to 15-foot) length of nylon, which is secured to the chain and then cleated off to the samson post or main cleat. More chain is fed out until the snubber is taking all the load. Nylon has a considerable degree of stretch—up to 50 percent before breaking—and acts like a rubber band absorbing sudden loads from any wave action that builds up. Without such a snubber, the shocks from the pitching motion imparted to a boat by even quite small waves can break windlass shafts (we have sheared ours twice) and loosen windlass mountings.

Suggested snubbing line sizes vary for different weights of boat: For boats of up to 25,000 pounds, $^3/_8$-inch line should be used; up to 40,000 pounds, $^1/_2$-inch line; boats of more than 40,000 pounds should use $^5/_8$-inch line.

Many people use chain hooks to attach the snubbing line to the rode, but I find a rolling hitch perfectly adequate and easy to undo, even after it has been subjected to severe loads.

If your boat has a bowsprit, the anchor rode must be kept clear of the bobstay. If not, a nylon rode is likely to chafe through while chain will bang and grate noisily. When using a nylon rode, we simply run it through a snatch block on the end of the bowsprit. When using chain, we run the snubbing line through a hawse hole set a few feet back from the bow. The pull on the rode is now slightly off center, causing the boat to lie just off the wind and keeping the chain and snubber away from the bobstay.

The final task in most anchorages is to snorkel down and check the set of the anchor. If you are having trouble digging in the flukes, it is often possible—especially on grassy bottoms—to force them physically into the bottom enough to get the process started.

ANCHORING WITH
TWO ANCHORS

Two anchors are set to increase holding power, to hold a boat in a particular alignment, or to limit swinging room in crowded or restricted anchorages.

INCREASING HOLDING POWER. The closer two anchors are to being in line, the more effective they will be at increasing holding power. In any event, if swinging room is not a problem, they should be set no more than 30 to 40 degrees apart. The procedure is to set one anchor as above, power forward a little to one side of it, come past it so as to give the second some dragging room while setting, and then to drop the second anchor and set it. The rode on the first anchor should be left slack until the second anchor is properly dug in. Both rodes then can be adjusted to share the load.

MAINTAINING ALIGNMENT. Sometimes the effect of wind and current is to hold your boat broadside to the swell. Even a small swell can cause most boats to roll uncomfortably. In these circumstances a stern anchor sometimes will hold the boat into the seas and reduce a wild roll to a moderate pitch.

There are two approaches to setting a stern anchor:

- Set the bow anchor as before, back down with the waves (not the wind), paying out double the scope needed, and drop the stern anchor. Then pull forward to a point midway between the two anchors, setting the stern anchor in the process.
- Alternatively, throw out a stern anchor as you enter an anchorage, paying out rode as you head into the waves (not the wind) until the bow anchor is dropped, at which point you fall back, setting the bow anchor and taking in the slack on the stern anchor.

Either way you will need to keep both rodes taut to hold the boat out of alignment with the wind or current. If you have a long-keeled boat with moderate windage, you will find the maneuver frequently does not work satisfactorily—I have given up setting stern anchors!

LIMITING SWINGING ROOM. This procedure, sometimes known as a "Bahamian" or "running" moor, is used to limit swinging room. In the Bahamas this procedure is needed in crowded anchorages. In the Northwest Caribbean, the proximity of other boats is unlikely to be a problem, but the running moor is sometimes needed as insurance against wind shifts that might set your boat onto a reef. The same two approaches are used as in setting a stern anchor, except that both anchors are set off the bow rather than one being set off the stern.

The rodes are tightened and effectively hold the boat within a very small turning circle.

Sometimes boats that have fin keels and spade rudders and use nylon rodes experience problems with the rearward setting rode snagging the keel or rudder as the boat swings. Generally, leaving a little slack in this rode will solve the problem. Otherwise a weight will need to be slid down the rode to hold it down; a short length of chain shackled into a loop and lowered on a 10- to 15-foot pendant works well.

ANCHORING ON CORAL

Don't do it! The anchor will not bite but, at best, will snag a coral head. Any wind shift may pop it loose. Chain will wrap around coral heads and sometimes prove very hard to disentangle, and nylon rodes will chafe through. Worst of all is the damage you will be doing. A carelessly placed anchor dragging through coral can destroy *in minutes* something that took *hundreds of years* to grow. A few irresponsible cruising boats can rapidly wreck a pristine reef. This has happened repeatedly in other areas of the world (e.g., the Virgin Islands) as they became popular. Now, with greater public awareness of the fragility of our environment, there is no excuse for such marine vandalism.

There are almost always patches of sand and grassy areas adjacent to, or mixed in with, the coral reefs in the Northwest Caribbean. Both prudent seamanship and ecologically responsible behavior dictate that you seek out such patches whenever you are in reef areas. If necessary anchor well off a reef you wish to visit, then dinghy over to it. *Never, never throw an anchor down in coral!*

GOING AGROUND AND

KEDGING OFF

In the course of researching this guide, we ran aground more than 30 times, sometimes quite hard! This book is designed to save you from the same experience, but sooner or later we all run aground,

or get caught out by a wind shift while at anchor and get blown aground. Fortunately most of this area's various reefs, islands, and other features limit wave action so that running aground is an inconvenience rather than a boat-threatening situation. On sand and mud, in particular, no damage is done. Even on coral and rock, although the most nerve-wracking grating sounds may echo through the hull, damage to a well-constructed hull is generally minimal when there is no wave action. With wave action, of course, it is likely to be quite another story.

If you feel the boat touch the bottom, it is important to lose all motion as fast as possible. Cast off the sheets and, if under power, throw the boat in reverse (first shorten the dinghy painter if you are towing it, or you will wrap the painter around the propeller!). If the boat is not stuck too hard, the reverse propeller thrust will drive water under the hull and may wash it off the bottom. Swinging the wheel or tiller from side to side, combined with the crew moving rhythmically from side to side to set the boat rolling, will help to break the grip of mud.

If the engine fails to bring you off, throttle back before it overheats, so that the mud you have stirred up does not plug the water filter. If the boat can be brought broadside to the wind, and the sails are sheeted in hard, the boat will heel over. This may reduce your draft sufficiently to power off. Otherwise you will have to kedge off.

To kedge off, you row an anchor out and use the windlass to drag your boat off. Generally a boat must come off in the reverse of the direction it went on. However, if you take a chain rode and set the anchor behind your boat, the chain is likely to scrape against your topsides and scratch the paintwork as you take up the load on the windlass. What is more, on many boats, unless the rode is led more or less straight ahead, it drags around various plates, the forestay, the bow pulpit, or other obstructions rather than making a fair lead onto the bow roller. Much of your energy will be wasted in unwanted friction, and you may damage your boat.

Think about these things before setting the anchor. If the lead onto the bow roller is not going to be a fair one, use a nylon rode and rig up snatch blocks to make it a fair lead. Think about how the angles will change as you drag the head around.

Once the anchor is set, take up the slack on the

rode and crank away. In stubborn situations rock the boat as before, lay it over with the sails, and use the motor. It is a rare situation in which these techniques fail to bring a boat off.

If your boat remains stuck, you are going to need to reduce its draft. There is no need to start pumping out the tanks and throwing gear overboard! Set a second anchor well off to one side and toward your stern, attach your mainsail halyard to the anchor rode, and start winching away on the halyard winch. You should be able to pull the masthead down until the rail goes under. Now go back to the windlass and crank away on the kedge anchor once again.

Note that in some cases when you pull a boat down by the masthead, the sideways pull may damage the mainsail halyard sheave. A snatch block rigged just below the sheave will solve this problem. The loads generated also can cause some lightweight masts or rigs to collapse, but boats with lightweight masts have no business going offshore in the first place, since the stresses are no greater than those experienced in a knockdown.

BIBLIOGRAPHY

Boatowner's Mechanical and Electrical Manual, *Marine Diesel Engines*, and *Refrigeration for Pleasure Boats*, all by Nigel Calder and published by International Marine, explore in some detail 12-volt DC systems, diesel engines, refrigeration, rigging, and other topics touched on in this chapter.

Cruising Rigs and Rigging, by Ross Norgrove, also published by International Marine, has much useful information on rigging and awnings.

Anchoring, by Brian Fagan, (another International Marine book), is a useful handbook on this subject.

Supplies and Services

PROVISIONING AND WATER

There is nothing even resembling a well-stocked American supermarket anywhere in the Northwest Caribbean. In fact, in many areas, particularly Mexico and the cays of Belize, supplies are quite limited. Similarly, in many areas safe drinking water is hard to come by. The following are the principal places for resupply.

MEXICO. Isla Mujeres has a reasonably well-stocked supermarket, a good market for fresh produce, and drinking water on the fuel dock with depths of 8 feet alongside its outer end. Nothing between here and Belize City is as good or as convenient.

There are a couple of small supermarkets close to the marina at Puerto Aventuras, but their prices are high. Water is available, though brackish tasting, in all the slips.

Playa del Carmen has a reasonable stock of groceries and produce but no fresh water. San Miguel, Cozumel likewise has a reasonable stock of groceries and fresh produce, and water is available at the marina. From here south, grocery stores in Mexico are small, the choice is meager, and fresh produce is unreliable. Water is virtually unobtainable.

BELIZE. San Pedro on Ambergris Cay has a reasonable stock of groceries and fresh produce, and water is available from an outside faucet at the police station, but must be hauled in jerry cans.

Belize City has three well-stocked supermarkets, a fresh-produce market, and good water on the dock at the Fort George Hotel (six feet six inches on its outer end). However, there is frequently an uncomfortable swell running here, and tying up to the dock can be tricky.

South of Belize City there is no readily available water until the marinas on the Rio Dulce. Dangriga (Stann Creek) and Punta Gorda both have a reasonable selection of groceries and fresh produce, but as with Belize City the anchorages can be decidedly uncomfortable.

GUATEMALA. Livingston, at the mouth of the Rio Dulce, has adequate groceries and fresh produce, though more expensive than elsewhere in Guatemala. At Relleno/Fronteras—close to the three marinas on the Rio Dulce—there are several small grocery stores and excellent fresh produce. A refrigerated truck comes once a week from Guatemala City (Wednesdays, but check with the marinas) with first-class meat. Normally food orders must be placed a week ahead of time to be picked up the following week. Free drinking water is available at all the marinas.

Puerto Barrios has several stores, but you will have to walk the half mile or so to town. Drinking water is available at the Marina Lidimar (see the relevant section in the text).

HONDURAS. In the Bay Islands all settlements have some groceries with quite good shopping in Coxen's Hole (particularly at Warren's Supermarket), French Harbor, and Guanaja settlement. Drinking water is available at the old CSY dock in Brick Bay, at the French Harbor Yacht Club, and in Guanaja (although here it probably will have to be hauled in jerry cans since the dock is frequently occupied). All the principal mainland ports in Honduras have supplies but no facilities for taking on water.

FUEL

The following is a list of fuel docks that can accommodate a minimum six-foot draft (most will handle more): Isla Mujeres; Cay Chapel Marina, Belize; Fort

George Hotel, Belize City; the Shell dock opposite the Catamaran Hotel/Mañana Marina on the Rio Dulce; Warren's dock at Coxen's Hole, Roatan; the fuel dock in French Harbor; the Texaco dock in Guanaja Settlement (you may find the dock occupied, so do not count on filling up here).

Fuel is available in many other places (its availability is noted under the various anchorages in the cruising section of the text) but will have to be hauled in jerry cans.

HARDWARE

Basic household-type hardware (plumbing supplies, etc.) can be found in all the major towns (Isla Mujeres, San Miguel, Belize City, Puerto Barrios, French Harbor), but yacht hardware is virtually unobtainable with the exception of a limited number of items in French Harbor at Mariscos Agua Azul, a large hardware store alongside the fuel dock.

Importation of hardware is difficult, often takes weeks, and the parts sometimes never show up. In all these countries, any imported articles must be cleared through customs. To do this you have to find out where the objects are being held—the customs officials may not notify you of their arrival. Then you may be required to hire a recognized agent to clear the objects.

By international agreement anything sent to a "yacht in transit" should be free of duty, so be sure to have this placed on labeling, customs declarations, and paperwork. Even with such labeling officials may try to levy duties of up to 100 percent of the declared value. If possible, have the supplier also label the objects as "Replacement Under Warranty"; this will help you avoid duties.

You stand a much better chance of receiving the goods if they can be shipped via a courier service such as Federal Express or UPS Red Label. While such service is expensive, it may prove to be the cheapest option in the long run. What is clear is that one small, but critical, breakdown can mess up your cruising plans for weeks and lead to nearly endless frustration. For this reason your onboard spares inventory should be as comprehensive as you can accommodate.

BOATYARD FACILITIES AND PROFESSIONAL HELP

There are few haul-out or professional boatyard facilities in the entire Northwest Caribbean. In Belize City, Arthur Hoare has a marine railway up a haul-over creek that is capable of hauling quite large boats. He is a skilled boatbuilder. The controlling depth at the mouth of the creek used to be five feet, but it reportedly has been dredged to nine. To come in, you will need a local guide, and you will have to make arrangements to have the swing bridge opened. The yard is a little above the bridge.

"Haul-Out" Charley (Charley Carlson) has a very primitive yard in New Haven Bight, Belize. He can haul boats up to 40 feet long and with a seven-foot draft, but mostly just to do bottom jobs. Bring your own paint and other supplies since he has nothing. You also need plenty of bug spray here. There are no roads to his yard, no power, and he has no neighbors, so during your stay you have to camp out in your boat. He and his mate are skilled shipwrights and are capable of quite sophisticated repairs, but remember you have to supply all the materials.

At its Santo Tomas base—near Puerto Barrios—the Guatemalan Navy has an excellent facility, which can haul any yacht imaginable. It can be used by cruisers. The cost to lift and lower is comparable to, or higher than, the same services in the

States. Once your boat is out of the water, they have skilled painters, welders, and other professionals at very cheap labor rates ($2–$3 an hour in 1990). You can also work on your own boat. The base's security, as you might expect, is excellent! I have had mixed reports on this yard, with one boat receiving excellent service and another running into bureaucratic problems with the military.

The Honduran Navy has a similar facility at Puerto Cortes, and similar remarks apply.

The marine railway at the old CSY dock in Brick Bay, Roatan, is still operational. It was built to handle their fleet of CSY 44s, a heavy displacement, six-foot draft boat. In 1990 Romeo Silvestri was running the resort that has taken the place of CSY and was quite happy to let visiting yachts use the railway. You need to bring all your own supplies and do all your own work. Controlling depth entering is six feet.

The principal haul-out facilities in the whole region are two substantial marine railways in French Harbor. These service the shrimp-boat fleet. One is the A & D Dry Dock (run by Seth Arch, who monitors channel 16); the other is the Fisherman's Dry Dock (channel 22). Both have had previous experience with yachts, and can handle bottom jobs as well as most kinds of repairs, including work on fiberglass, steel, and wood hulls. Sandblasting and gelcoat blister repairs can be done. Bottom paint is available in the islands (Devoe), but it is best to bring your own. Similarily, for an Imron, Awlgrip, or Interthane Plus topsides paint job, you need to supply the paint and thinners.

I have had mixed reports on the quality of the workmanship. At the time of writing, A & D Dry Dock will not let you work on your own boat but is planning a new, smaller railway for pleasureboats. When the new railway is completed, owners will be permitted to work on their boats. If you are planning on a haul-out, try to write ahead and notify them (both addresses are: French Harbor, Roatan, Honduras, C.A.). Try to avoid hauling out in the months of June and July since these precede the opening of shrimp season and the yards are busy.

Refrigeration and electronic repairs can also be carried out in French Harbor. Searle Bodden at Transcoastal Marine Refrigeration (TMR) monitors channel 16; Dale Werden at Dale's Electronics monitors channel 68.

There is another operational marine railway in Savannah Bight, Guanaja, but I have no information on it.

MAIL DROPS

Getting your mail can be as difficult in the Northwest Caribbean as in any other place in the Caribbean. My editor tried for weeks to get a manuscript to me in Guatemala. Finallly he sent it by courier service to Belize City, and we sailed there to pick it up!

In any case, allow at least three weeks for first-class mail to make it from the United States or Europe, and considerably longer for packages (whether airmail or not). Packages and parcels present a special problem since they generally must clear customs. They may get held by the customs people who may, or may not, notify you of their arrival. Never have money sent through the mail. Particularly in Guatemala, the postal workers have a bad reputation for opening overseas mail in search of money.

Holders of American Express credit cards can use any American Express office as a mail drop. The following places also will hold mail for you, but you should as a rule notify them in advance when you will be coming through to pick it up. Have the envelopes marked: "Please hold for collection."

MEXICO. Marina Paraiso (Isla Mujeres), Isla Mujeres, Quintana Roo, Mexico. Telephone: 2-02-52.

Puerto Aventuras Marina, Carretera Chetumal, Cancún Km 269, AP No. 181, Quintana Roo, Mexico. Telephone: (987) 2-32-22.

BELIZE. The various post offices (San Pedro, Belize City, Dangriga, and Punta Gorda) will hold any mail addressed to: Yacht "...........", c/o General Delivery, The Post Office, Belize City (San Pedro, Dangriga, or Punta Gorda), Belize, C.A.

The Cay Chapel Marina will also hold mail (P.O. Box 192, Cay Chapel, Belize, Central America).

GUATEMALA. As already mentioned, Guatemala is something of a lost cause. However, mail does eventually filter through. On one occasion Clyde

Crocker, the owner of the Mañana Marina, received a call from the customs in Puerto Barrios to tell him he had an urgent package to pick up. He made the lengthy trip, only to be given a package of jelly beans (opened, of course) sent to our children for Easter. Needless to say, he wasn't very pleased!

The three marinas on the Rio Dulce will all hold mail. They are the Mañana Marina (the oldest and best known), Susanna's Laguna, and Mario's. Addresses for all are: Frontera Rio Dulce, Morales, Izabal, Guatemala, Central America.

THE BAY ISLANDS. The French Harbor Yacht Club will hold mail. For boats coming around from Panama, this is very often the first reliable maildrop in some time. The address is: French Harbor Yacht Club, French Harbor, Roatan, Bay Islands (Islas de la Bahia), Honduras, Central America.

PHOTOGRAPHIC

SUPPLIES

Kodachrome 64, Kodachrome mailers, and Kodachrome processing are not available anywhere in the Northwest Caribbean. Ektachrome and Fujichrome can be bought and processed in the larger cities, but are not always easy to find and are expensive. Print film and processing are more readily available in the cities, but not in Mexico south of Cozumel, in most of Belize, nor on the Rio Dulce. You are therefore advised to bring good stocks of film since you will want to take lots of pictures.

LEAVING YOUR BOAT

This whole region has such outstanding attractions inland that you should plan on making at least a couple of extended trips away from your boat. Many people also like to lay up their boats and fly home to visit friends and families, sometimes for a period of months. There are numerous protected anchorages throughout the Northwest Caribbean, but few with adequate access to shoreside transportation and airports, even fewer with good security, and almost none with full hurricane protection, should you want to leave your boat during hurricane season. The following are the best anchorages.

MEXICO. The Marina Paraiso on Isla Mujeres is an excellent base from which to explore the Yucatán. Security is good and the rates quite reasonable. Until the island took a direct hit from Hurricane Gilbert in 1988, the lagoon was considered an excellent hurricane hole. While a number of boats at the marina suffered damage to a greater or lesser degree during this hurricane, it must be remembered that Gilbert was a Class VI hurricane—the strongest category—and it went right over the island.

Access to Cancún on the mainland is cheap and easy (regular ferries). Cancún airport has by far the cheapest flights to and from the U.S. of any airport in the entire Northwest Caribbean. This is an excellent point at which to drop off, or pick up, squeamish crewmembers who wish to avoid crossing the Gulf of Mexico. The airport, however, is some distance out of town (20-plus kilometers, 12-plus miles) and there is no bus service. Taxis can be expensive—you should agree to a fare with your driver before taking off. Don't be shy about haggling—this is Mexico! If you are flying into Cancún, don't pick up a taxi outside the airport terminal building, but walk a couple of hundred yards across the parking lot to where the road exits the airport. After bargaining, fares from here are often one-third those at the terminal building.

Cancún has good bus connections to all the main tourist attractions in the Yucatán (Tulum, Chichén Itzá, Uxmal, Palenque, and the lovely old colonial city of Mérida) and several car rental agencies.

Puerto Aventuras Marina is also close to Cancún. This is a first-class marina with excellent security and protection (even in hurricanes)—and prices to match!

There is no other place in Mexico I would feel happy leaving our boat for even a day or two.

BELIZE. The only two places I would feel happy leaving our boat in Belize are the Cay Chapel Marina and the marina at Moho Cay just to the north of Belize City. The Cay Chapel Marina has been scooped out of the leeward side of the island. Beside the entrance channel is a large spoil heap. The resort, which owns the island, has a bulldozer. In the event of a hurricane passing this way, the marina manager ("Smitty") will bulldoze this spoil heap into the channel to close off the marina from all wave action. There would still be the wind, of course—Smitty hasn't figured out a way (yet!) to stop it. The marina is very secure. The resort runs regular flights to Belize City and a speedboat stops by every day.

The Moho Cay marina has also been scooped out of an island. It is closer to Belize City with a shuttle boat running to and from the mainland.

There are regular international flights in and out of Belize City, which is, after Cancún, the cheapest Caribbean destination for Americans. Interior flights connect Belize City with San Pedro, Dangriga, Placencia, and Punta Gorda. The last two are close to the best cruising grounds in Belize and are excellent spots from which to pick up and drop off guests coming for a short visit. Punta Gorda is also the best spot to pick up and drop off crewmembers who wish to make the trip up the Rio Dulce. From Belize City you can take a bus or rent a car to explore the resort area of San Ignacio and perhaps even travel as far as Tikál in Guatemala. This is one of the three possible ways of getting to this somewhat inaccessible site—a "must" for every visitor to this region (for more suggestions see page 184).

GUATEMALA. The Rio Dulce offers the ultimate in boat security. Fabulous protection from storms and hurricanes and a local population with virtually no crime. The three marinas (Mañana, Susanna's, and Mario's) are cheap by U.S. standards and provide better service—they will open your boat every day to air it out, pump the bilges, wash the decks, and run your machinery once a week if you so desire. The Catamaran Hotel also has a number of excellent slips.

Guatemala City ("Guate") is six hours and two bus rides away. The bus service is excellent, but the same cannot be said of the roads. However, they are constantly being improved. No car rentals are available outside Guatemala City. Guate has an international airport with good connections to the States, but the flights are much more expensive than those from Cancún or Belize City.

There is so much to see in Guatemala, and at such cheap prices, that even the most budget- and time-conscious cruiser should plan on spending an absolute minimum of two weeks inland, preferably a month. Many cruisers come intending to stay a week or two (like ourselves), end up staying months (like ourselves), and after leaving find themselves drawn back again (like ourselves).

THE BAY ISLANDS. The French Harbor Yacht Club has a very secure marina on Roatan. There is an armed guard; the docks are well built; and Old French Harbor, in which the marina is located, is an almost land-locked lagoon, providing good protection from just about anything short of a direct hit by a hurricane. Dock space is limited so, if you plan on leaving your boat, you should book ahead (French Harbor Marina, French Harbor, Roatan, Bay Islands, Honduras, Central America).

There is a taxi service to the airport at Coxen's Hole, which now has direct flights to Miami, Houston, and New Orleans. Tickets *bought in Honduras in lempiras* (the local currency) offer some of the cheapest flights in and out of the region, but this may change.

AN IMPORTANT NOTE. If you leave your boat to fly out of any of these countries, you may run into trouble with the officials at the airport when you attempt to leave. This is especially likely in Mexico and Guatemala. Ask a knowledgeable person at the marina where you plan to leave your boat about current regulations. You may need a cover letter or some other paperwork to show that the boat is in responsible hands.

Health and Medicines

The information given here is garnered from the best sources I could find and has been distilled through several years' personal experience of sailing in the tropics with my wife and small children (from birth). Since individuals vary greatly in their reactions to courses of treatment and medicines, what has worked for us may prove less effective, or even dangerous, for people with different constitutions or medical histories. Therefore, when reading this chapter, please remember that I am not a doctor! If you or your crew become worryingly ill, you must seek the aid of a qualified medical practitioner.

I would like to thank Dr. David Werner of the Hesperian Foundation and M.J. Colbourne of the London School of Hygiene and Tropical Medicine for reviewing this chapter, and for their helpful comments.

SEASICKNESS

Both Terrie and I, and our two children, suffer from seasickness, so I understand the misery it can cause. The children got sick even as babies (which the books say they are not supposed to do). We found there is nothing that can spoil a long passage faster than having to hang onto two seasick babies while helming the boat and feeling queasy yourself!

Over the years we have tried all kinds of remedies. Some worked; others failed us completely (in the latter category are "Sea-Bands" utilizing "acupressure," but other people swear by them). The most effective remedies all have side effects we would rather do without, so we tend to do without medication unless we feel really queasy. Staying up in the cockpit in the fresh air, focusing on the horizon, and perhaps taking on a responsibility such as helming the boat, help to a considerable extent. If you are below, it is best to lie down and close your eyes. When you become nauseated, it is often best to throw up and get it over with.

Of the medicines, scopalomine is extremely effective, especially the patches that you stick behind your ear. These generally confer immunity from sickness for three days, by which time most people have their sea legs. The side effects, however, can be quite pronounced and include a dry throat, restlessness, and difficulty in focusing on books and charts (the words and images tend to dance around). Antihistamines (the most common being Dramamine) are less effective and induce drowsiness, but if a crewmember is not needed it might be preferable to have him or her doze below rather than use scopalomine.

Our choice is a mixture of promethazine and ephedrine (25 mg. promethazine with 50 mg. ephedrine). This is something the Naval Aerospace Medical Research Laboratory at Pensacola, Florida, came up with after extensive testing. They found other drugs to be more effective (e.g., straight amphetamines—"speed") but with unacceptable side effects.

The promethazine/ephedrine is at least as effective as scopalomine, much more so than Dramamine, and has few noticeable side effects. Promethazine is an antihistamine which, if taken alone, will make you extremely drowsy, but ephedrine is a stimulant and the two seem to just about cancel out. The advantage of this mixture is that you only need to take it when you feel sick (as opposed to the scopalomine patches, which are put on before the start of a voyage and stay on), and if sick people can keep the pills down for half an hour, it will bring them out of the sickness.

Promethazine can be obtained only with a doctor's prescription. A pharmacist can make up the pills, or you can buy the promethazine and ephedrine tablets separately and just take the necessary dosage. You should need to take only one dose, with perhaps another 8 to 12 hours later, if the

sickness is not under control. You should discuss this, and all other medications suggested in this chapter, with your doctor for possible side effects, bearing in mind the individual histories of yourself and your crew.

GOOD HEALTH IN

TROPICAL CLIMATES

The rest of this chapter does not in any way constitute a first-aid manual—you should already have one on board. It is an attempt to describe some of the more common medical problems that can arise during visits to Central America with which you may not be familiar, and outlines ways to avoid them or deal with them.

There is no question that traveling to the tropics increases the risk of sickness. There are a number of reasons for this:

- The higher heat and humidity create a greater tendency to sweat. This, combined with the warm atmosphere, provides an excellent environment for fungi and bacteria to grow on the skin. As a result, various itches and rashes are quite common, and even tiny bites and pinpricks have a tendency to become infected. The sun also can cause serious sunburn.
- Many water supplies are contaminated, particularly with amoebas, bacteria, and viruses from human and animal fecal matter that cause diarrhea and other intestinal disorders.
- Sanitation is often poor at best. Flush toilets are rare, and even where they exist the plumbing often is not adequate to handle toilet paper. Used paper is frequently thrown into a bin, or the corner of the latrine. Various parasites and bacteria find their way via unwashed hands and flies from fecal matter onto food.

- Most food processing is not subject to the same rigorous public health standards as in the developed world.
- There are numerous amoebas, bacteria, and viruses to which the local population has developed a tolerance, but which cause sickness in newly infected visitors.
- Finally, diseases that have been all but eradicated in the developed countries are still widespread in parts of the undeveloped world. Of these, malaria is probably the greatest hazard in the Northwest Caribbean, although its incidence is generally limited to a few isolated outbreaks.

PREVENTION

Having read that list, do not become paranoid about visiting the Northwest Caribbean! It is by recognizing the problems that we can deduce a few simple measures which greatly reduce the risk of becoming sick. These measures should interfere very little, if at all, with your enjoyment of this region.

INNOCULATION. First and foremost of these measures, innoculation is especially important for children, who have weaker immune systems than adults. Most adults have already received a number of innoculations, many of which confer immunity for life; the beneficial effects of other immunizations tend to fade with time. Before leaving home, adults need to review their history of innoculations carefully and obtain boosters where necessary. Additional innoculations that are not part of the developed nations' routine immunizations are recommended for those visiting Central America.

The Ross Institute of Tropical Hygiene, an institution long associated with the field of tropical medicine, recommends the two schedules of innoculation in the accompanying table, "Innocula-

INNOCULATION SCHEDULES FOR VISITORS TO THE TROPICS

Schedule A	Week	Vaccine
	1	Yellow fever
	4	Typhoid and tetanus (1)
	7	Poliomyelitis (oral) (1)
	10	Typhoid and tetanus (2)
	13	Poliomyelitis (oral) (2)
	19	Poliomyelitis (oral) (3)
	36	Typhoid and tetanus (3)

Schedule B	Day	Vaccine
	1	Typhoid and tetanus (1) and poliomyelitis (oral) (1)
	5	Yellow fever
	28	Typhoid and tetanus (2) and poliomyelitis (oral) (2)

A third dose of tetanus vaccine and of poliomyelitis vaccine (oral) will be required later to complete the primary courses of immunization.

(ADAPTED FROM A TABLE, COURTESY OF THE ROSS INSTITUTE OF TROPICAL HYGIENE.)

Notes:
1. The Ross Institute recommends cholera immunization in Schedule B. I have omitted this innoculation because cholera is not common in Central America and travelers in particular are at very little risk; the vaccine is only 50 percent effective; and booster doses are required every six months.
2. Yellow fever is not a problem in Central America; it is a problem in Venezuela and Trinidad, so you need protection only if visiting these areas. Children under age one, and persons allergic to eggs, should not receive this vaccine.
3. Innoculations should not be given during pregnancy except in cases of medical emergency.
4. An innoculation with immune serum globulin just prior to departure should be considered for protection against hepatitis A, which is endemic to Central America. Since this only gives protection for a limited period of time and booster shots are required every four to six months, this innoculation must be considered in the light of your cruising plans.

tion Schedules for Visitors to the Tropics." Schedule A, the first and more effective, begins 36 weeks before the departure date so it is for those with plenty of time to complete the course; Schedule B begins one month before departure.

Most children from the developed world already have received a fair number of innoculations. The Ross Institute recommendations for juvenile visitors to the tropics are given in the accompanying table. You need to discuss these recommendations with your doctor in the light of the innoculations you and your children already have received, and to work out an appropriate schedule to complete the innoculations.

MALARIA. Malaria occurs from time to time in one or two areas covered by this guide. In 1990, outbreaks were reported around Tikál in Guatemala and in the Cayos Cochinos. In the latter instance, these were the first cases in more than 15 years, almost certainly imported from mainland Honduras.

INNOCULATION PROGRAM FOR CHILDREN VISITING THE TROPICS

Child's Age	Vaccine
3 months	DPT (1)—diphtheria, whooping cough, and tetanus
	OPV (1)—oral poliomyelitis
	BCG (1)—tuberculosis
4–8 weeks later	DPT (2)
	OPV (2)
4–8 weeks later	DPT (3)
	OPV (3)
10–12 months	Measles
18–24 months	DPT (4)
	OPV (4)
5 years	DT (1)—diphtheria and tetanus
	OPV (5)
12–14 years	DT (2)
	OPV (6)
	Rubella vaccine for girls (German measles)
	BCG (2)

(COURTESY OF THE ROSS INSTITUTE OF TROPICAL HYGIENE.)

The parasites that cause malaria are carried in the saliva of the anopheles mosquito. The disease is transmitted when a mosquito sucks blood from an infected person. After about one week, this mosquito can pass the disease on to anyone it bites. The anopheles mosquito only bites in the evening and after dark—the use of suitable bug repellants, wearing clothing with long pantlegs and sleeves when ashore in the evenings, and using mosquito screens on the boat at night, minimize the chances of being bitten. Various medicines will kill the malaria parasites should you get bitten. Of these, the most common is chloroquine (Aralen, Avloclor, Nivaquine, Resochin).

If you are visiting an area with a known outbreak of malaria, you should take chloroquine for two weeks before you arrive (to get it into your bloodstream), and continue taking it for six weeks after you leave (the parasites can lie dormant in the blood for some time before becoming active). Chloroquine can be bought over the counter at drugstores and supermarkets all over Central America. The prevention dose is 300 mg. *of base* to be taken once a week; this is generally two tablets—you must distinguish between the weight of each tablet and the amount of base it contains. Children from birth to 5 weeks old should receive a weekly dose of 37 mg. of base (one-eighth the adult dose); those 6 weeks to 11 months old, 75 mg. (one-fourth adult dose); 1 to 5 years old, 150 mg. of base; 6 to 12 years old, 225 mg. Children more than 12 years old should take the full adult dose of 300 mg. weekly.

Unfortunately, chloroquine-resistant strains of malaria are becoming widespread (e.g., in Panama and Venezuela). To date chloroquine has proved effective in the Northwest Caribbean, but you will need to check on the current situation. Where resistance has developed, one tablet a week of Maloprim (pyrimethamine-dapsone) is generally added to the dose of chloroquine given above.

Malaria needs to be taken seriously. If there is any question about its occurrence, the prophylactic dose should be taken—swallowing one or two tablets a week is a small price to pay for freedom from the disease. *This dose must be maintained for six weeks after leaving the infected region.* Many people have become seriously ill because they neglected to follow the entire program.

PROTECTION FROM THE SUN. Apart from the risk of sunburn, excessive long-term exposure to our sun is known to cause skin cancer. Sensible use of sunscreen or suntan lotion, hats, and clothing will guard against this.

Sunscreen and suntan lotion are hard to find throughout Central America. They can also be expensive. We had a tub of Desitin (for diaper rash) left over from the days when the children were in diapers and took to smearing this over their faces and shoulders. It is an extremely effective sunblock, does not wash off in water, and is inexpensive. It is white, however, which made them look like ghosts, but so what!

Sunglasses are needed to protect the eyes, particularly from reflected glare off the surface of the water.

PERSONAL HYGIENE. Most Americans are super-clean so hygiene is no problem. Where possible, a freshwater shower night and morning, with a regular change of clothes, will go a long way toward eliminating skin irritations caused by bacterial and fungal infections.

HYGIENE OF OTHERS. Here we have a major problem. Since we have no control over the hygiene of the local population, all fresh food—fruit, vegetables, and meat—bought in the tropics should be considered suspect, as should most salads or fresh fruits consumed in restaurants.

When eating out you should look for clean restaurants and eat only well-cooked foods. Avoid salads at all times. Fruit must be well washed in uncontaminated water or, better still, peeled. Peeled fruit is only as safe as the hygiene of the individual peeling it, so you should peel the fruit that you will eat.

Flies are a frequent carrier of parasites from fecal or decaying matter. Avoid eating any food left around fly-infested areas. This includes your own boat—keep food covered!

Do not drink local water or use ice in your drinks unless you know it is made from purified water. Don't eat ice cream or any other water- or milk-based product (e.g., yogurt, cheese) unless you know it is made from purifed water and/or pasteurized milk. If drinking bottled water, have it opened in front of you (it is not unknown for restauranteurs to fill the bottles from a faucet out back!). Soft-drink bottling plants almost always have their own water purification systems making these safe, as are drinks made from boiled water—tea, coffee, etc.

COOKING ABOARD. Preparing your own food is the safest way to avoid intestinal problems. Thoroughly wash all uncooked vegetables and fruits. Avoid lettuce and similar leafy greens altogether: they are too hard to clean properly and in any case have little nutritional value. All meats should be well cooked (sorry, rare-meat lovers).

Warm milk, yogurt, and soft cheese make a very fine environment in which to grow various harmful bacteria. Not only can diseases be transmitted from the cow itself, but also from the dirty hands of the person milking the cow. Use only pasteurized milk, yogurt, and cheese. To pasteurize milk yourself, boil or heat it to 144°F (62°C), keep it at this temperature for 30 minutes, then cool it rapidly. Powdered milk (made with purified water) is always safe. Once mixed, store it in a cool place as you would regular milk or it will rapidly sour.

If your water quality is at all questionable, boil water for drinking or food preparation for at least five minutes. At the first opportunity flush your tanks, pump, lines, and any filters with a chlorine solution (use chlorine bleach diluted with water) and then refill the tanks with safe water.

ASTHMA AND BRONCHITIS. Travelers who suffer from these chronic respiratory problems need to take an adequate supply of their regular medicines and inhalers. As a child I suffered from asthma, but had not had problems in 20 years until we ventured into the Central Highlands of Guatemala. There I suffered an allergic reaction to something in the atmosphere. Since it was the dry season and very dusty, I thought this might be the problem, but we returned in the rainy season with the same result. Subsequently I discovered that a number of other travelers experience similar problems in this area. There must be a mold or pollen in the atmosphere that sometimes triggers an asthmatic reaction.

SHOES. Always wear shoes in inhabited areas with poor sanitation. Such areas are rife with hook-worms, which can be picked up through the soles of the feet.

DENTAL CARE. Dentists are found only in the large cities of this region. You should have a thorough checkup before setting sail so that you can arrange to complete any overdue dental treatment. Regular brushing of teeth, with or without toothpaste, and the regular use of dental floss are essential to good oral hygiene.

EYEGLASSES. Opticians are, likewise, hard to come by. You should carry spare eyeglasses and leave a prescription with a friend or relative at home so that, if you should need another pair, they can be made up and mailed to you.

CURES

There is a limit to how thoroughly you can protect yourself from all risk of sickness in the tropics without cutting yourself off from the people. Sooner or later almost everybody who travels extensively in Central America gets sick, the most common complaint being some form of diarrhea. Luckily, this is usually little more than a temporary discomfort and inconvenience.

DIARRHEA. Diarrhea is caused by a number of infectious organisms. In almost all cases, the sufferer has watery stool with mild to severe stomach cramps. Most bouts last for one to three days, although we did once get a bout that took 10 days to clear. Occasionally, more serious strains of bacillary or amoebic dysentery are contracted, in which case there is likely to be blood and mucus in the stool, and/or recurrent bouts of diarrhea. When dysentery is suspected, consult a doctor.

Antibiotics are useless in treating most cases of diarrhea and often do more harm than good. The same is true of many supposed diarrhea remedies including neomycin, streptomycin, lodochlor-hydroxyquin (Entero-Vioform), paregoric, codeine, diphenoxylate with atropine (Lomotil), loperamide (Imodium), and kaolin and pectate (Kaopectate). The use of such medicines for children is strongly discouraged. Some will help harden up the stool but in doing so may interfere with the body's ability to rid itself of the infection, making it last longer or recur. The only time a binding medication (e.g., Lomotil, Kaopectate) is justified is in emergencies, such as when taking a long bus ride or when toilets are few and far between.

Unless blood is in the stool, or the diarrhea is persistent or recurrent, the best treatment is to take it easy and to drink lots of liquid (but not milk) to replace the fluids lost. Young children, in particular, can rapidly be put at great risk through dehydration. Recent research has shown that a cereal-based rehydration drink is the most effective way to combat dehydration. The best preparation is made with powdered or mashed rice to form a thin gruel, which is boiled and cooled. The exact quantity of rice is not critical. You should add about $1/2$ teaspoon salt per quart or liter of solution. You can purchase various powders (Oralyte, Dioralyte, Pediolyte) to mix with water for replacing body salts, but these sugar-based solutions are expensive for what they contain and are probably not as effective as the rice-based drink. Gatorade would likely work as well and be a lot cheaper.

The rehydration drink should be sipped every five minutes, day and night in serious cases of lost body fluids, or until normal urination is established. A large person needs 3 quarts a day; a small child at least 1 quart, or an 8-ounce glassful for every watery stool.

A person with diarrhea should start to eat if the diarrhea lasts for more than a day since the body still needs nourishment. Avoid fatty or greasy foods, raw fruit, highly seasoned food, milk products, and alcohol.

WORMS AND LICE. These parasites are commonly picked up by small children—ours have done it twice now (although, to be fair, I should note that the worms were contracted in Venezuela and Louisiana, U.S.A., not Central America!). Hookworms, threadworms, whipworms, and roundworms inhabit the intestinal tract. Eggs are deposited in feces or around the anus. They are transferred to the mouth through poor hygiene, through playing in the dirt, or, in the case of hookworms, through the skin of the feet when walking barefoot on infected ground or beaches.

Worm medicines containing piperazine (Antepar) clear up threadworms and roundworms. When one child is infected, all should get treatment. Thiabendazole or mebendazole are used against whipworms and hookworms, but thiabendazole has some nasty side effects and should not be used, while mebendazole (Vermox) must not be given to pregnant women and children under two years old.

Tapeworms and trichinosis can be acquired by eating infected meat that has been insufficiently cooked (any meat, not just pork, though pork is the more likely to be infected, which is easily understood after you have seen a few pigs rooting around in open sewers).

All forms of lice (head lice, body lice, and pubic lice, better known as crabs) are treated with a lotion containing gamma benzene hexachloride (Lindane, Kwell, Gammazane). This is relatively toxic, so avoid repeated use and do not use on babies. A safer product, available in the U.S., is Rid, or other similar formulations that use pyrethrine. Clothing and bedding should be boiled at the same time if at all possible. Benzyl benzoate cream is used on scabies.

FUNGAL INFECTIONS. Infections caused by fungi may occur on any part of the body, but most commonly affected are the areas between the toes (athlete's foot) and around the genitals (jock itch). Most infections grow in the form of a ring (ringworm). All should be regularly washed with soap and water, dried, and, if possible, kept exposed to air. When the infected area must be covered, use only clean, dry coverings; change socks and underwear frequently and then wash them. The fungus can be transmitted to others via infected clothing and towels, so do not share these items. Antiseptic soaps such as pHisoHex and Betadine should be used if possible. Cream or powder containing tolnaftate (Tinaderm and Tinactin) is generally effective in clearing up the infection if washing doesn't.

PRICKLY HEAT. This is another common complaint of children. A rash develops into raised red spots, often with white heads. Once again, frequent washing (preferably with an antiseptic soap), drying, and exposure to air are needed. A powder of equal parts of boric acid, zinc oxide, and talc, with a little camphor, applied after every washing, will also help.

CUTS AND SCRATCHES. Any skin break has a tendency to become infected quite quickly, sometimes developing into a nasty abscess. Apart from being painful, an abscess may need to be drained surgically. All puncture wounds, however slight, should be cleaned with soap and water as soon as possible. Minor scrapes and scratches are best left uncovered, or lightly covered if flies are common. Watch for any sign of infection, such as redness or swelling around the wound. If seen, apply an antibiotic cream (e.g., Neosporin, Polysporin, or an ointment containing tetracycline).

If a cut becomes infected, allow it to drain. Promote healing by soaking the wound several times a day in slightly salted water that is as hot as you can stand. Change the dressing regularly and keep applying the antibiotic cream.

One particular problem sometimes experienced by sailors on long, wet crossings is the occurrence of saltwater boils on the buttocks. Regular washing with fresh water, followed by a generous application of Desitin at the first sign of pimples, will prevent this.

INSECT BITES. Bites are generally no more than a nuisance. In rare cases an acute allergic reaction occurs requiring immediate medical aid. Otherwise cold compresses with baking soda, soothing lotions (Calamine, Caladryl, Benzocaine, and various corticosteroid creams, although the latter should be used sparingly) are all that are needed. Antihistamines such as diphenhydramine (Benadryl), dymenhydrinate (Dramamine), and promethazine (Phenergan) will help to reduce itching but will also make you drowsy.

The best insect repellants are those containing diethylmetatoluamide (DET) or dimethylphthalate (DMP)—Deet, Six-Plus-Twelve, and Off. Various other "folk" remedies that may or may not help to keep insects at bay are eating large quantities of garlic (more easily taken in capsule form and also thought to help combat stomach ailments), and taking 200 mg. of vitamin B–1 daily for a month before exposure.

HEPATITIS A AND B. Both forms of hepatitis are a problem. Hepatitis A is common in Central America and easily passed on by infected food-handlers and as a result of unsanitary conditions. Hepatitis B is generally acquired only by using unclean hypodermic needles, from blood transfusions or drug use, and through sexual intercourse with an infected person. In rare cases it has developed from insect bites.

There is no cure for hepatitis other than resting, drinking a lot of fluids, avoiding alcohol (hepatitis affects the liver, which will be having a hard enough time without giving it extra work to do), and letting the body heal itself. Antibiotics will not help and may do real harm. If infected, you are likely to feel very sick for up to two weeks and to remain weak for one to three months afterward. An innoculation with immune serum globulin (see page 30) provides effective protection against hepatits A, but only for a limited period of time; booster shots are required every four to six months.

MARINE HAZARDS

Sharks, barracuda, and moray eels have been known to bite reckless swimmers, but only on rare occasions.

SHARKS. Because they have an extraordinary sense of smell and an acute sense of hearing, sharks are generally attracted by blood in the water or thrashing motions such as might be made by a wounded fish. The only time they are likely to be dangerous is when you are carrying bleeding fish when spear-fishing. Hold the fish well away from your body, and get it into your dinghy as fast as possible. If the blood attracts sharks, get out of the water.

BARRACUDA. These fish hunt by sight and are attracted by bright, flashing objects. Avoid wearing bright wristwatches or jewelry in the water. Barracuda are both curious and bold, and frequently will approach very closely, mouths open, displaying their fearsome teeth, which can be a little unnerving. In reality you need not be afraid.

MORAY EELS. These shy creatures rarely venture out of their protective caves in the coral. However, if you thrust your hand into a moray's lair, you may get bitten. The bite is not poisonous but is likely to become rapidly infected; it will need thorough cleaning with an antiseptic (e.g., Merthiolate), and treatment with an antibiotic cream (see "Cuts and scratches").

STINGRAYS. Stingrays, especially large ones, can inflict a deep and extremely painful venomous cut. Infection is very likely. You should, if possible, immediately urinate on the wound! Urine is a nearly sterile liquid, which will flush away some of the poison and probably help to alleviate the pain. Continue to flush with fresh water—as soon as possible—and an antiseptic (e.g., merthiolate). Then bathe the wound in as hot water as you can stand for 30 minutes—the heat deactivates the poison. Apply antibiotic cream and cover the wound with an antiseptic and sterile dressing. Seek medical help.

SCORPIONFISH. These fish have poisonous spines along their dorsal area. Since they are well camoflaged and generally motionless, you can easily step on or touch one accidentally. Stings, which are deep and painful, should be treated as for stingrays, above.

SEA URCHINS. Sea urchin spines are not normally poisonous; they are sharp, however. On occasion they have even penetrated sneakers and bootees, so watch where you put your feet. The spines are brittle—once embedded they tend to break off and are impossible to extract. Treat as for stingrays. Warm lime juice applied to the embedded spines is also said to dissolve them. Otherwise the body generally will absorb them over a period of time.

JELLYFISH. Sometimes seen in great concentrations, most jellyfish can sting. Only the Portuguese man of war, readily identified by its bright blue float, is particularly dangerous. If you are stung by a Portuguese man of war, bathe the affected area with ammonia, which neutralizes the venom. If ammonia is not available, use alcohol. *Do not try to wash the affected area with fresh water since this will cause remaining stinging cells to discharge their poison.*

FIRE CORAL. This coral is quite common, especially at shallow (snorkeling) depths. It is generally yellowish brown and relatively smooth. Any contact can produce a painful rash. Bathe the affected area with ammonia. This, and all other coral scrapes and scratches, should be treated with an antiseptic and watched closely for infection.

CIGUATERA POISON. Certain species of tropical marine reef fish carry this poison, although it is not as prevalent in this region as in some other areas of the Caribbean. However, you still should avoid eating any large barracuda (over 3 feet) and check with local fishermen for problems in their area.

BASIC MEDICAL KIT CHECKLIST

Along with the generic names of various medicines, I give the best-known brand names, but you will often save money by buying a generic drug.

- Sunglasses, sun hat, sunscreen or suntan lotion, Desitin, lip balm (Chap Stick).
- Adhesive tape, adhesive strip bandages, butterfly bandages to close cuts, gauze, bandage rolls, safety pins, Q-tips, cotton balls.
- Scissors and tweezers, needle and thread for stitches, thermometer.
- Merthiolate, isopropyl alcohol (rubbing type).
- Antiseptic soap (pHisoHex, Betadine).
- Antibiotic cream (Neosporin, polysporin, or creams with tetracycline).
- Boric acid, zinc oxide powder, talcum powder, and camphor, or a medicated talcum powder (Ammens).
- Anti-malaria tablets (Aralen—most easily bought when in Central America).
- Pain pills—aspirin, paracetamol (Tylenol), especially for children.
- Antihistamines—one of promethazine (Phenergan), diphenhydramine (Benadryl), or dimenhydrinate (Dramamine).
- Seasickness medication—add ephedrine to the promethazine, scopalomine patches.
- Milk of Magnesia (laxative).
- Lomotil (for diarrhea, but see the text. Use only if you need to bind up your bowels for a specific purpose such as a long bus journey).
- Ammonia (useful on some bites and jellyfish stings).

- Insect repellent—DET or DMP (Deet, Off, Six-Plus-Twelve).
- Soothing lotions—one of Calamine, Caladryl, Benzocaine, Novocain.
- Corticosteroid cream.
- Cream and powder with tolnaftate for athlete's foot (Tinaderm).
- Medi-halers and other medicine for asthma and bronchitis sufferers.
- Bleach (for sterilizing water and cleaning tanks) and water purification tablets (Halozone) to take on trips inland.

BIBLIOGRAPHY

Where There Is No Doctor, by David Werner, published by The Hesperian Foundation, P.O. Box 1692, Palo Alto, CA 94302. This book was written to encourage medical self-help among Mexican villagers with little or no access to doctors. Since this approximates the situation of cruising sailors in remote areas of the world, it has much information of outstanding value for us also. With its emphasis on illnesses common in Central America, it is particularly relevant to anyone cruising the Northwest Caribbean.

Prescription drugs are widely sold "over the counter" throughout Central America. If you cannot find a doctor, this book will help you diagnose your condition and choose appropriate drugs, if necessary, to deal with the situation. It also has an excellent first-aid section. Highly recommended.

Preservation of Personal Health in Warm Climates, by The Ross Institute of Tropical Hygiene, London School of Hygiene and Tropical Medicine, Keppel Street (Gower Street), LONDON WC1E 7HT, England. A very good little booklet.

Staying Healthy in Asia, Africa and Latin America, by Volunteers in Asia, Box 4543, Stanford, CA 94305.

Navigational Considerations

CHARTS

In many respects, considering the resources available to the U.S.A. and the U.K., the charts for the Northwest Caribbean are a disgrace.

Most of Mexico is covered in no more detail than a scale of 1:1,000,000. This is fine for passage-making but of little use for inshore work, especially around reefs. Many anchorages mentioned in this guide are not even shown as a dot!

The principal surveys of Belize were conducted by the British Navy between 1831 and 1840 and have not been comprehensively revised since then. The charted position of many cays differs by as much as a mile from fixes acquired by satnav, the differences being mostly in longitude rather than latitude. The early surveyors must have been having problems with their chronometer! There are rumors that the Royal Navy has been doing some renewed survey work lately, particularly of Lighthouse and Glover's reefs, so better charts may be in the offing. In the meantime hurricanes and humans have recontoured a number of cays since the original surveys were made, and reefs have grown and died. Many of these changes are not reflected on the existing charts. Two examples:

1. Years ago a hurricane blasted a channel through Hicks Cay in northern Belize. This has for a long time been the principal small-boat channel to and from the northern cays. While the latest U.S. chart (DMA 28167) does show the channel, it was until 1990 shown as dry land on the relevant British chart.

2. The United States recently brought out a new chart of southern Belize (DMA 28162). This chart adds at least two new substantial cays that do not now and never have existed! How, in this age of satellite mapping, can such gross errors creep in?

In fairness I must say that in spite of these inaccuracies and the age of the surveys on which the charts are based, it is surprising how many of the small details are still correct. The British charts, in particular, offer a wealth of detail and soundings, most of which are still true, whereas the U.S. charts of Belizean waters are far less detailed and contain a mass of errors. The problem lies in the cruiser's need to know what has changed and what has remained the same.

There are no detailed charts of the Rio Dulce and El Golfete, and no chart at all of Lago Izabal.

Good detailed charts of Utila and Guanaja (Bonacca), the two small islands in the Bay Islands group, do exist but are based on 150-year-old surveys; they are also quite hard to read. No detailed charts are available for Roatan, the principal island in the Bay Islands, although the U.S. has just produced two charts (DMA 28154 and 28151) that cover the region from the western end of Roatan to the east of Guanaja, southward to the Honduran mainland (including Cayos Cochinos) at a scale of 1:80,000, which is the best coverage to date. Otherwise exisiting charts contain such helpful notations as "the islands are reported to be two to four miles further apart than shown"! In fact, according to our satnav and loran, the distances are pretty much accurate.

The accompanying table lists the U.S. and U.K. charts that cover this region, noting some recent changes in the U.S. charts. I would recommend the following mix of charts (BA = British Admiralty; DMA = Defense Mapping Agency):

BA 1220—Gulf of Honduras and Yucatán Channel, 1:1,000,000. Good general coverage for planning purposes. If you can get your hands on a copy of the now obsolete DMA 28015—The

Yucatán Channel and Approaches, to a scale of 1:906,530—this provides much the same coverage of Mexico. The new DMA 28001—the Caribbean Sea: Western Part, to a scale of 1:1,300,000—covers a simlar area as BA1220, but with less detail.

DMA 27120—Yucatán Channel, 1:350,000. Useful for planning approaches to or leaving from Isla Mujeres, and for plotting the Gulf Stream Loop when deciding a strategy for crossing the Gulf of Mexico. Note however that it does not show the reef from Isla Contoy south to Isla Mujeres.

DMA 28202—Isla Mujeres, Cancún, and Approaches, 1:30,000.

DMA 28196—Isla Cozumel, 1:60,000.

BA 959—Approaches to Belize City, 1:125,000. The old (now obsolete) DMA 28167, also called "Approaches to Belize City," covered the same area to the same scale and also included a useful insert to the Cay Bokel anchorage to a scale of 1:36,000. The new DMA 28167, now called "Ambergris Cay to Pelican Cays" is to a scale of 1:150,000. It has better coverage to the north of Belize City than BA 959 (it covers the region all the way to San Pedro) but it no longer has the Cay Bokel itsert; it is inferior to the BA chart south of Belize City.

BA 522—Belize Harbour, 1:40,000.

BA 1797—Ranguana Cay to Columbus Cay, including Glover's Reef, 1:125,000, is far superior to both its old and new U.S. counterparts.

BA 1573—Honduras Gulf with the Zapotilla Cays, 1:121,000. This chart is far superior to its U.S. counterpart.

DMA 28154—Approaches to La Ceiba, 1:80,000, and DMA 28151, Approaches to Puerto Castilla, 1:80,000, are the two new charts of Honduran waters already mentioned; they are far superior to anything previously available.

BA 2988—Ports in the Gulf of Honduras: Approaches to Puerto Barrios and Santo Tomas de

U.S. CHARTS FOR THE NORTHWEST CARIBBEAN		
U.S. Defense Mapping Agency Charts		
Number	**Title**	**Scale**
28001	Formerly Punta Herrero to Cabo Gracias a Dios, 1:936,430; now Caribbean Sea: Western Part	1,300,000
28015	Yucatán Channel and Approaches (discontinued)	906,530
27120	Yucatán Channel	350,000
28202	Isla Mujeres, Cancún, and Approaches	30,000
28201	Puerto Morelos	18,241
28196	Isla Cozumel	60,000
28197	Cozumel	15,000
28167	Formerly Approaches to Belize City, 1:125,000; now Ambergris Cay to Pelican Cays	150,000
28168	Belize City Harbor	40,000
28160	Gulf of Honduras and Approaches	290,000
28166	Ranguana Cay to Columbus Cay (discontinued)	125,000
28162	Tela to Pelican Cays	150,000
28164	Approaches to Puerto Barrios	50,000
28165	Puerto Barrios	12,500
28150	Tela to Barra de Caratasca	300,000
28163	Approaches to Puerto Cortes	20,000
28143	Isla de Utila	37,420
28154	Approaches to La Ceiba	80,000
28151	Approaches to Puerto Castilla	80,000
28123	Bonacca (Guanaja)	36,481
28142	Puerto Castilla	20,000
28144	Port Ceiba	7,200
28161	Puerto de Tela and Approaches	30,000

Castilla, 1:65,000; Puerto Barrios and Santo Tomas de Castilla, 1:25,000; Approaches to Puerto Cortes, 1:30,000; and Puerto Cortes, 1:12,500. This chart consolidates information shown on four U.S. charts.

DMA 28150—Tela to Barra de Caratasca, 1:300,000. Gives an overview of the entire Honduran coastline and the Bay Islands.
DMA 28143—Isla Utila, 1:37,420.
DMA 28123—Bonacca (Guanaja), 1:36,481.

The British charts are generally more colorful and readable. They are corrected up to the date of issue, and are mostly a standard size, making them easier to stow. They are, however, expensive if bought in the United States. You can order them with a Visa or MasterCard directly from the following chart dealers in the United Kingdom:

Kelvin Hughes, 19–23 Featherstone St., LONDON EC1 Y8SL. Tel: 01-250-1010. Telex: 884934 (I have dealt with them several times; they provide an excellent service).

Brown and Perring Ltd., Redwing House, 36-44 Tabernacle St., LONDON EC2A 4DT. Tel: 01-253-4517. Telex: 263184.

Note: The British Charts of Belize were revised in late 1989 with some significant improvements. They are greatly superior to their latest American counterparts.

For a list of other official and "unofficial" publications that will help with navigation in the region, see the appendices.

SKETCH CHARTS IN

THIS GUIDE

The outlines of the land masses are generally taken from the most detailed topographical maps I could obtain—normally 1:50,000 but sometimes 1:250,000. These have been translated from the land-based grid to latitude and longitude, and corrected at times by personal observations.

Navigational data are derived from two sources: the existing charts, supplemented by soundings, and other observations made by ourselves and Peter Hancock. Reef areas and other hazards are taken from existing charts and modified according to our observations. Where we have added or modified information, we have endeavored to obtain at least

two bearings from known points to give us a reasonably accurate fix. *All soundings are in feet.* I consider anything less than six feet to be shoal water.

Since I did not wish to clutter the charts with compass roses, you will have to plot your position and lay off courses using parallel rules. This is done quite simply. Suppose you wish to plot a course of 160°M from a known position in Belize. Convert this to a true heading (by adding 3° in 1990, giving 163°T). Lay the parallel rules across the nearest line of longitude at such an angle that both "S" and 163° marks on the parallel rules lay across the line of longitude. Now "walk" the rules to the point from which the course is to be laid off.

Conversely, if you wish to measure the bearing of a course line on the chart, lay the parallel rules along the course line and then "walk" them across the chart to the nearest line of longitude. Position the "S" on the line and read off the bearing where the line of longitude crosses the other side of the parallel rules. Remember this is a true bearing and will need to be converted to a magnetic heading to steer by.

NAVIGATIONAL

INSTRUMENTS

Some years ago we were on the beach at Isla Mujeres when a sailboat came in flying its Q flag. The captain and crew dropped their hook, jumped in the dinghy, and hastened ashore. The captain was thoroughly disoriented, which was hardly surprising since he thought he was in Cozumel some 60 miles to the south. He had navigated around the reefs at Isla Mujeres using his Cozumel chart!

His loran had quit three days earlier on the way down from Florida, and he had made no allowance in his dead reckoning for the Yucatán Current, which has been known to run at seven knots and has a normal speed of two to three knots. To deal with just such emergencies, I am old-fashioned enough to believe that every yacht venturing offshore should carry a sextant and sight-reduction tables, and should have someone aboard who knows how to use them. Having said that, I must say, in all honesty, that I have only used mine once in years, however, that one time it was critical to my peace of mind in crossing the Mona Passage since our satnav had broken down.

If you are going to rely solely on electronics for navigating the open-water passages necessary to reach the Northwest Caribbean, you should have at the very least two independent systems—probably loran and satnav, but possibly GPS—and you must ensure adequate battery capacity to keep them functioning until you make landfall. In particular, do not use the engine-cranking battery for your electronics—preferably allocate a separate battery to the electronics.

One of the region's delights is that you are almost never out of sight of land; most trips are quite short, and all navigation can be done with coastal piloting techniques. In fact, especially in Belizean waters, it is best to forget about electronic position-finding and instead to rely on basic piloting skills. As noted elsewhere, many of the charts of Belizean cays and outlying reefs are in error by as much as a mile. Reliance on electronic navigation is likely to put you on a reef and could cost you your boat.

LORAN. The stations to use are the 7980/11/43 chain.

Loran coverage is generally excellent at least as far south as Isla Mujeres. We have found coverage to be fair all the way to Belize. However, as we crossed the Mexico/Belize line, the signal strength declined sharply and our machine began to give us seriously erroneous fixes without warning. Had we been sailing at night and relying on the loran, we would have ended up on a reef.

At times we obtained reasonably accurate fixes in Belizean waters, but at other times the machine was wildly inaccurate—the proximity of the mainland and the cays messes the signal up. Down in the Bay Islands, however, a good signal returned as did excellent fixes—quite remarkable considering the distances to the transmitting stations. We have heard of boats receiving accurate fixes as far south as San Andreas (St. Andrew's) Island off the coast of Nicaragua.

SATNAV AND GPS. These function throughout the region, of course, but I adamantly repeat:
Neither satnav nor GPS should be relied upon

as the primary means of position-fixing in the areas covered by this guide because of the inaccuracies in the charted positions of many reefs and cays. You must keep track of your position using basic piloting techniques rather than electronic instruments.

WHERE AM I? Once within the region you will almost never be out of sight of land. As you move along, you must maintain an updated plot of your position on your charts. In Belize, in particular, one cay looks much like another, and it is easy to forget which one you have just passed. In Roatan, from seaward, one bight also looks much like another, and the same thing is true.

One of the most important navigational tools is a good quality, accurate, hand-bearing compass. If you know which cay you have just passed and which is just ahead, with two bearings you can have your position accurately plotted within seconds. Speed of plotting is frequently critical when navigating around coral reefs, especially if the light is not adequate for judging water depths. During our cruises my hand-bearing compass seemed as if it were permanently strung around my neck, and I almost always knew exactly where we were.

NAVIGATING AROUND CORAL

There are no substitutes for good eyes, good light, and a comfortable perch aloft, either on mast-steps, ratlines, or spreaders. In many areas there are reefs that come almost straight up from the bottom—by the time a depthsounder gives an alarm, it is frequently too late to take evasive action.

The water, generally speaking, is spectacularly clear and undergoes a gorgeous change of color as depths and bottom conditions alter: a deep navy blue when off soundings; a dark turquoise in 60 to 30 feet, changing to a light turquoise as the water shoals; a reddish ochre-brown as coral nears the surface; a green-gray where the bottom is grassy, becoming lighter in shallower water; and paling to white as water shoals over sand.

Even so it is not possible to gauge depths by water coloration if the light is not right. If the sun is in your eyes, you see only reflected glare; if the day is overcast and squally, the water takes on a uniformly slate-gray appearance. If it is partly cloudy, the shadows are hard to distinguish from rock and coral. When poking around in coral, you must wait for the right light conditions—basically a sunny day with the sun behind you.

The next most important things in navigating around coral are to wear a pair of good-quality, polarized sunglasses and to get as high as possible—every foot gained increases the range of your vision and your depth perception. I like to perch just below, or on, our lower spreaders, while Terrie (my wife) takes the helm. This puts me 15 to 20 feet above the water and gives me an excellent picture of what is going on around us. If navigation is particularly tricky, we furl the headsail so that I have an unobstructed view forward. I have spent up to six hours a day like this, piloting through dangerous coral without serious mishap, so it pays to make the perch comfortable.

Those of you who have sailed the Bahamas will be well prepared to work around coral, judging depths by water color. Those of you new to this kind of sailing will need to take it slowly and carefully until your eyes are "tuned in"—after a while you will find you can judge depths in most areas with a surprising degree of accuracy.

SAILING AT NIGHT

Given the inaccuracies of the existing charts, the presence of sometimes strong currents, and the large number of small islands and reefs scattered throughout the Northwest Caribbean, night passages are unsafe in much of the region. This is particularly the case in Belizean waters. Fortunately, with the multiplicity of available anchorages, there is rarely any need to sail overnight.

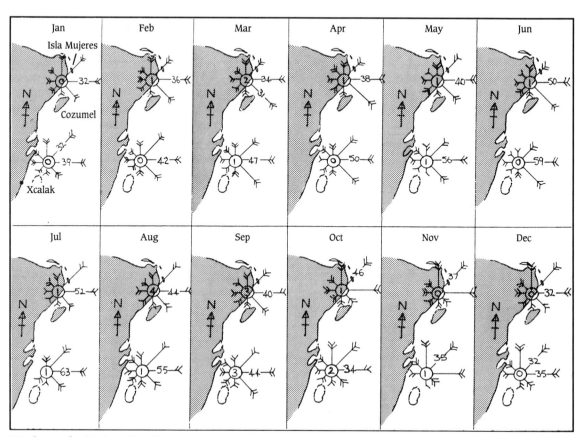

Wind roses for Mexico's Yucatán Coast.

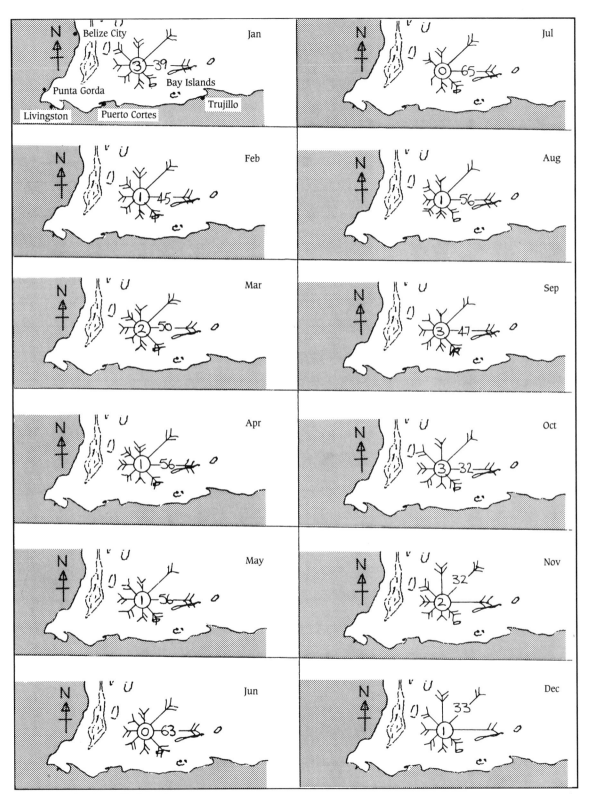

Wind roses for the Gulf of Honduras.

GENERAL WEATHER
CHARACTERISTICS

The climate throughout the entire Northwest Caribbean is remarkably equable and consistent, both along the coasts and further inland. Its main features are the dry season, the wet season, the trade winds, the impact of fronts, particularly northers, and the occasional hurricane.

Temperatures are fairly uniform year-round, with average daytime ranges between 80°F (27°C) and 90°F (32°C), and average nighttime temperatures between 65°F (18°C) and 75°F (24°C). In all the records I have gathered, the coldest coastal temperature I can find is 38°F (3°C), and the hottest 105°F (41°C), both, surprisingly, recorded at Punta Gorda in Belize.

With a relative humidity between 75 percent and 85 percent, so long as a breeze is blowing, conditions are extremely pleasant—some would say just about perfect. However, when the breeze dies, or you move inland, it becomes a little sticky.

SEASONS. The region's two distinct seasons, dry and wet, follow relatively clear annual patterns. The dry season runs from October or November to May or June, and the wet season from May or June to October or November. Rainfall varies markedly, ranging from less than 20 inches on the Yucatán penin-sula to more than 150 inches at Dangriga on the Belizean mainland. It drops to around 125 inches at Puerto Barrios in Guatemala, and to 70 inches in the Bay Islands. The cays just off the coast near Dangriga experience dramatically less rainfall than the mainland.

In areas with lower annual rainfall, the dry season is dry—it sometimes doesn't rain for months on end—but where the annual rainfall is higher, some precipitation occurs year-round, though still with a heavy concentration in the rainy season.

TRADE WINDS. The trades come primarily from the east, though with a stronger northeasterly component in the early winter months, and a tendency toward the southeast in the late spring and early summer. The wind is more forceful from December to March, with a greater incidence of calms in the summer months, particularly August, September, and October.

The wind roses on pages 42 and 43, taken from the *Atlas of Pilot Charts for Central American Waters* (DMA publication 106), show the regional average monthly wind strength and the direction from which it blows. The longer an arrow, the more frequently the wind blows from this direction. When the wind blows for more than 30 percent of the time from any one direction, the percentage figure is written in. The number of "barbs" on the arrows indicates the average wind-strength, measured by the Beaufort Scale. One barb = force 1; two barbs = force 2; etc. The accompanying table converts the Beaufort Scale to knots. The number in the circle at the center of each wind rose gives the percentage of calms (winds less than one knot) in that month.

NORTHERS. These winds are common in the winter months, particularly in the Yucatán. Their effects are felt all the way down to the Bay Islands and mainland Honduras. Frontal systems with which northers are associated may make their appearance as early as October and continue through April. The greatest incidence is from late November to the end of March, peaking in January.

CONVERTING BEAUFORT SCALE TO KNOTS	
Beaufort Number	**Wind Speed (in knots)**
0	Less than 1
1	1–3
2	4–6
3	7–10
4	11–16
5	17–21
6	22–27
7	28–33
8	34–40
9	41–47
10	48–55
11	56–63
12	64+

TROPICAL STORMS AND HURRICANES

Tropical storms, from which hurricanes develop, have been recorded in every month from June through November, with a fairly even distribution over these months.

Hurricanes also can occur in the Caribbean between June and November. However, almost all that have hit the Northwest Caribbean have occurred during just two months—September and October—with the majority of these being in September. Mexico and Belize have suffered the most; the mainland coast of Honduras and the Bay Islands have rarely been hit.

Hurricanes are not common—on average eight a year pass through the whole of the Caribbean and the Gulf of Mexico, and of these only a small percentage hit the Northwest Caribbean—but they are of such awesome destructive power that no one can afford to sail during hurricane season assuming that he or she will not encounter one. With the exception of the inland waters of the Rio Dulce, every part of the Northwest Caribbean has, at one time or another, been devastated by a hurricane.

A CLOSER LOOK AT HURRICANES

The exact mechanism that generates a hurricane is not fully understood, but certain generalizations can be made. The surface temperature of the sea must be raised to a certain critical level. This leads to the evaporation of surface water. A tropical wave—a disturbance in the atmosphere—develops a circular movement of air, drawing in the water vapor. As the level of saturation increases, water condenses back into droplets. When water vapor condenses, it releases a considerable amount of heat ("latent heat of condensation"). This heat warms the air within the system, causing it to rise, which in turn sucks in more moisture-laden air.

The system begins to feed on itself, generating greater amounts of energy and stronger winds, building first to a tropical depression, then a tropical storm, and finally a hurricane.

Once past a certain critical point, the process is likely to continue until the supply of moisture-laden air is cut off, either through the hurricane moving over colder water or onto land. When such conditions are met, the hurricane rapidly exhausts itself as torrential rainfall burns up its remaining energy reserves without any fresh moisture being drawn into the system to replenish that which was lost.

FORECASTING HURRICANES. Modern forecasting methods enable several days' advance warning of the likely entry of a hurricane into the Northwest Caribbean. All early-season hurricanes form in the Atlantic and can be tracked for some time before they threaten any part of the Caribbean. Some late-season hurricanes form in the Caribbean itself, in which case less notice can be given.

In the absence of adequate weather forecasts, there are certain tell-tale signs of an impending hurricane. The intense winds generate swells that move out in all directions from the center of the storm. If you experience an unusually long swell, there may be a storm center some way off, in the general direction from which the swells are coming. If the swell direction remains constant, the storm is approaching directly. If, when facing the storm, the direction from which the swells are coming changes clockwise, the storm center will likely pass you from left to right; if the swell direction changes counterclockwise, the storm center will likely pass you from right to left.

The nearer approach of a hurricane will be signaled by rapidly falling barometric pressure. A pressure drop of 2 millibars in 3 hours signals an impending storm; 5 millibars in 3 hours, a strong storm; 10 millibars in 3 hours, an extreme storm.

On the day before the arrival of a hurricane, the weather is likely to be clear with a few cumulus clouds. High-level cirrus will begin to fill in from the direction of the storm, followed by increasing cover of altocumulus clouds, shower activity, and strong winds. Finally, a dark wall of cloud announces the arrival of the hurricane itself.

AVOIDANCE TACTICS. In the northern hemisphere, the most dangerous quadrant, with the strongest winds and greatest tidal surge, is that to the right of the eye. Adding 115 degrees to the direction of the true wind will indicate the approximate center of the storm. If the wind veers (shifts clockwise), you are on the dangerous side; if the wind backs (shifts counterclockwise), you are on the safer (sometimes called "navigable"!) side.

In the northern hemisphere and assuming adequate sea room, if you are on the dangerous side, the best policy is to keep the wind 045 degrees off your starboard bow and make all possible speed out of the area. If on the "safer" side, keep the wind on your starboard quarter (approximately 130 degrees relative to your vessel) and once again make all possible speed out of the area. If the wind direction remains steady while building in intensity, accompanied by a falling barometer, you are on the storm track itself. Keep the wind 160 degrees relative to your vesel. Finally, if the wind direction remains steady, but decreases in speed and is accompanied by rising barometric pressure, you are behind the storm. Try to stay there!

HURRICANE HOLES. For years the fabulously well-protected bay at Ensenada Honda on the Island of Culebra, to the east of Puerto Rico, has been known as one of the best hurricane holes in the Caribbean. When the bay took a direct hit from Hurricane Hugo in 1989, well over 200 boats were crammed inside. Hardly a single one survived unscathed, and most were a total loss. In the Northwest Caribbean, the lagoon at Isla Mujeres has always been considered an excellent hurricane hole but, when it took a direct hit from Hurricane Gilbert in 1988, not a single boat came through undamaged (though to my knowledge most survived).

These recent examples prove yet again, if such proof is necessary, that there is no such thing as a "safe" hurricane hole. Both Gilbert and Hugo generated wind gusts in excess of 200 knots: How can there be safety anywhere in such conditions? The only truly safe policy is to get out of the reach of a hurricane, and in the Northwest Caribbean this can only be done by heading up the Rio Dulce. Once safely inland, you are privy to the best hurricane protection in the Caribbean, the Bahamas, or the Gulf of Mexico (including the Gulf Coast of the United States from Texas to Florida). For those wishing to hang up their cruising during hurricane season, the various marinas on the Rio Dulce offer wonderful service at very economical prices.

In addition to the Rio Dulce marinas, numerous protected lagoons and bays throughout the region offer protection (against all but direct hits) as good as or better than anywhere else in the Caribbean. In Mexico the most notable are the marinas at Isla Mujeres and Puerto Aventuras; in Belize, the marina at Cay Chapel, the channel at Mapp's Cay, Sapodilla Lagoon, and New Haven Bight; on mainland Honduras, Laguna El Diamante (sometimes mistakenly referred to as Laguna Tinto); and in the Bay Islands, the various deep bays on the south coast of Roatan. All are covered in detail in this guide.

WEATHER FORECASTS

The Coast Guard broadcasts weather information for the Atlantic, Caribbean, and Gulf of Mexico from its stations at Portsmouth, Virginia and Miami, Florida. On July 1, 1991, under the terms of a new international agreement, many of the transmission frequencies changed. The new schedule and frequencies are given in the accompanying table. All frequencies are Upper Sideband, and a general coverage or SSB receiver is needed to pick up these transmissions. I strongly advise all sailors cruising

COAST GUARD WEATHER FORECASTS AND FREQUENCIES FOR NMN (PORTSMOUTH, VA) AND WOM (MIAMI)		
Time	(GMT) Station	Frequencies (kHz)
0400	NMN	4427.4, 6502.4, 8765.4
1000	NMN	4427.4, 6502.4, 8765.4
1600	NMN	6502.4, 8765.4, 13090.4
2200	NMN	6502.4, 8765.4, 13090.4
1300	WOM	8722.0 (Ch. 802), 13092.0
2300	WOM	(Ch. 1206), 17242.0 (Ch. 1601)

in the Caribbean during the hurricane season to buy such a receiver.

If reception on one frequency is poor, you should try another. The forecasts begin with the North Atlantic and work down toward the Caribbean and South Atlantic, then cover the Gulf of Mexico and the location of the Gulf Stream. You should listen regularly to familiarize yourself with the format and terminology then, even if reception is poor, you will be able to understand what is said. The 1600 and 2200 GMT broadasts from NMN Portsmouth contain up-to-date information on the location of the Gulf Stream.

If you buy a SSB transceiver (with which you can transmit as well as receive) or have a ham-radio transceiver, you also will be able to listen to and participate in various amateur radio "nets." I must point out that a special license is required to legally transmit; to qualify for a license you must pass exams. A number of nets are broadcasting on unauthorized frequencies, and many of those participating are doing so illegally. Penalties for illegal transmissions can be quite severe.

RADIO BELIZE. Radio Belize gives a local weather forecast on 830 kHz and 93 FM. This follows the 0700 (local time) news and generally comes on at around 0710. All that is needed to pick up these forecasts is a regular AM/FM receiver (i.e., a normal radio, or automotive stereo). Other weather forecasts are given during the day, particularly at 1230 hours on 830 kHz and at 2100 hours on 93 FM.

Route Planning

Route Planning to and from

the Northwest Caribbean

There are four principal ways of sailing to and from the Northwest Caribbean (see the sketch chart):

1. Via the Yucatán Channel (to and from the Gulf of Mexico);
2. Via the Windward Passage (to and from the Bahamas and the East Coast of the United States);
3. Across the Caribbean (to and from the Virgin, Windward, and Leeward islands); and
4. To and from the Panama Canal.

COMMON

CONSIDERATIONS

Certain factors are common when considering a passage between the Northwest Caribbean and any of these regions.

HURRICANES. The Caribbean and the Gulf of Mexico are within the summertime hurricane belt. The season runs from June through November, with the greatest incidence of hurricanes in August, September, and October. In general, *extended* offshore passages should not be attempted at this time.

Given the ability of modern weather forecasters to give advance notice of hurricanes, you can make safe passage during the early part of the hurricane season. Passages of up to several days' duration ei-

ther to or from the Northwest Caribbean, and particularly within the region are perfectly safe as long as you have one ear cocked to the forecast. I would have no qualms, for example, in crossing the Gulf of Mexico in June or July, if the forecasts were favorable and contained no mention of tropical depression formation in the Atlantic and Caribbean. Within the region itself, no point is more than two days' sail from the Rio Dulce or other hurricane holes. Therefore, with due care there is no reason *not* to cruise throughout most of the hurricane season. However, any voyaging at this time of year must be done with a safe bolt-hole in mind should a tropical depression form and start to build.

TRADE WINDS. The Caribbean is dominated by the primarily easterly trade winds, which tend more to the northeast in the early part of winter and the southeast in late spring and early summer. Strong winds from December to March can generate rough conditions throughout much of the Caribbean. During summer months the winds are less predictable, interspersed with periods of calm and, of course, the occasional hurricane.

The Gulf of Mexico is far less consistent. Insofar as generalizations are valid, similar conditions exist—i.e., predominantly easterly winds tending more to the northeast in early winter and the southeast in late spring and early summer. The winter months are also characterized by numerous northers as cold fronts push down from the Arctic

SAILING ROUTES TO AND FROM THE NORTHWEST CARIBBEAN

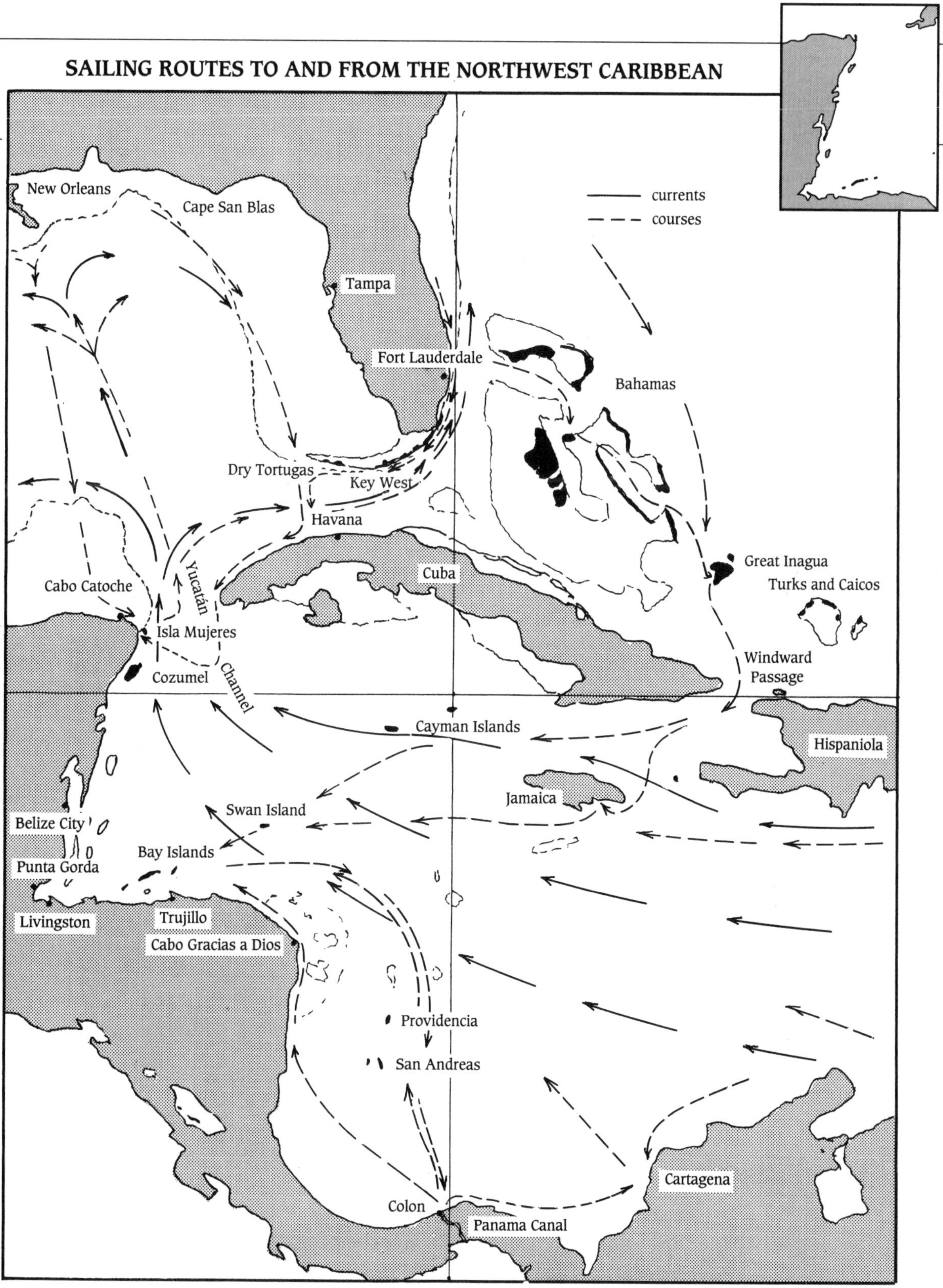

New Orleans

Cape San Blas

Tampa

Fort Lauderdale

Bahamas

currents

courses

Dry Tortugas

Key West

Havana

Cuba

Great Inagua

Turks and Caicos

Cabo Catoche

Yucatán

Isla Mujeres

Cozumel

Channel

Windward Passage

Cayman Islands

Hispaniola

Jamaica

Swan Island

Belize City

Bay Islands

Punta Gorda

Livingston

Trujillo

Cabo Gracias a Dios

Providencia

San Andreas

Cartagena

Colon

Panama Canal

over the continental United States, bringing strong northwest and northerly winds and a sharp drop in temperatures.

Where strong north winds drive against the Yucatán Current, dangerous seas can be generated, similar to those experienced along the eastern seaboard of the United States when northerly winds blow against the Gulf Stream. The greatest frequency of northers is in December and January. At times one will follow another in rapid succession for several weeks.

CURRENT PATTERNS. The general pattern of the current in this region is consistent throughout the year. The North Equatorial Current, flowing westwards across the Atlantic, comes up against South America and is deflected to the northwest, sweeping across the Caribbean. The current then bears onto the Yucatán and is funneled through the narrow slot between the Yucatán and Cuba (the Yucatán Strait). The waters fan out in the Gulf of Mexico before once again concentrating in the slot between Cuba and Florida (the Florida Strait). The Gulf Stream, as it is then known, is diverted by the Bahamas northward up the eastern seaboard of the United States.

Vast quantities of water are circulating through the Caribbean—somewhere between 12 and 25 times the total amount of fresh water in all the rivers of the world put together, according to different estimates I have read. Where the flow becomes concentrated—up the Yucatán coast, through the Yucatán Strait, and around to the Florida Strait—its rate of speed accelerates, typically to three knots but to a recorded high of seven knots.

Powerful currents of this nature always create eddies and countercurrents, and this one is no exception. While the generalized flow pattern is clear, the reality can be very different. On our last northward crossing of the Gulf of Mexico, we sailed halfway from Isla Contoy to Cuba looking for the current and never found it! On a couple of other occasions, where we had expected to find the current we found two- to four-knot countercurrents caused by bodies of water spinning off from the main stream.

Nevertheless the central part of the stream is pretty much as charted. It is when you are operating around its periphery that you must pay closest attention to your track and speed over the bottom. Many times a move of just a few hundred yards to the side of your existing track will put you in or out of currents of up to several knots with a great effect on your speed- and course-made-good.

A loran (or GPS receiver) is ideal for working among currents since it gives instant readouts of course- and speed-made-good, enabling you to gauge the current accurately. In the Gulf of Mexico another useful navigating tool is a thermometer. The Caribbean waters of the Yucatán Current are generally above 80°F (27°C), even in winter, and are warmer than the waters of the Gulf. Any sudden change in temperature indicates a move from one body of water to the other. Any time you see flying fish or sargassum weed floating by, you are in Caribbean rather than Gulf waters.

GENERAL CONCLUSIONS. From the general considerations given, you can draw the following broad conclusions.

1. It is best to passage to or from the Northwest Caribbean either in November, when the chances of a hurricane developing are slight and the northers are not yet in full swing, or in late spring/early summer (April/May/June), when the winter trades have eased in strength and before the onset of hurricane season.

2. When sailing south—i.e., coming from the north (U.S.A., Bahamas, and Gulf of Mexico) or heading down toward Panama—November offers less chance of having to beat into a southeast wind, which is why it is the preferable time to sail south. When sailing north—i.e., coming from Panama or heading up to the Windward Passage or Gulf of Mexico—April, May, and June are preferred since there is less chance of having to beat into a northeast wind.

3. At just about any time of year, the passage from the east (Virgins, Windwards, and Leewards) should be a downhill run, while any passage to the east is going to be an uphill beat. The current will almost always be a key factor in determining specific courses, needing to be sought out or avoided, depending on the direction in which you are sailing.

THE YUCATÁN STRAIT AND THE GULF OF MEXICO

Caution: The Yucatán Strait is the principal shipping lane for large vessels bound between Panama and other Central American ports and the U.S. gulf ports of New Orleans and Galveston. Keep a good watch!

Whichever side of the Gulf of Mexico you happen to be on, it is best to wait for a favorable weather pattern to cross. If heading north, you can spend a pleasant time in Isla Mujeres.

THE FLORIDA STRAIT. The dominant factor in route planning is the Yucatán Current/Gulf Stream. If bound from the Yucatán to Florida and the East Coast of the United States, you will need to head out toward Cuba until you pick up the stream, and then sit squarely in it, riding the three-knot current all the way. The current tends to loop up into the Gulf of Mexico and then hook down to the southeast, so you will need to watch your track and to make whatever course corrections are needed to counteract any offset.

If you are sailing southward, you do best to hug the east coast of Florida and the Florida Keys as far as the Dry Tortugas (which make a pleasant break in the passage). Beyond the Dry Tortugas the preferred route is to cut across the main axis of the stream at right angles until close to the Cuban shore. Off the northern coast of Cuba, a one-knot countercurrent sometimes works in your favor. You need to keep a close check on your position since there may be strong and unpredictable eddies in the current, some of which could set you onto the reefs to the northeast of Cabo San Antonio. Once off Cabo San Antonio, you should head south, perhaps as far as 20°30'N, staying out of the current, before heading due west straight across the axis of the stream once again. The current will bring you back to Isla Mujeres.

This course, however, has political perils at the present time since the Cubans are still very suspicious of all boats in their waters. You must remain outside their 12-mile limit unless you want to risk being towed in or chased off by a gunboat (as happened to us). Hopefully, the situation will improve soon.

PASSAGEMAKING VIA THE CENTRAL GULF OF MEXICO

One arm of the Yucatán Current flows broadly up the center of the Gulf of Mexico, slowing as it goes. Somewhere south of the Mississippi Delta it divides, swinging east and west along the United States Gulf Coast (see the sketch chart). If you are headed north toward any of the Gulf states, you should ride this current to at least the center of the Gulf of Mexico before setting course for your final destination.

Boats sailing south from the eastern Gulf states (Alabama to Florida) need to follow a different route from those setting out from Louisiana or Texas. Mississippi falls somewhere in between.

If you are headed south from the eastern Gulf, you should seek the eastward looping current, broadly following the 100-fathom curve around the coast of Florida and down to the Dry Tortugas; from there you follow the course outlined above.

If you are headed south from Louisiana or Texas, you need to stay west of the central arm of the Yucatán Current, heading for a point on the 100-fathom line of the Campeche Bank at approximately 24°N, 88°W. If you find yourself in a strong northward setting current, go west. Once on the Campeche Bank, the current and seas diminish. Head down toward Cabo Catoche and then work around the tip of the Yucatán, under power if necessary, following the 10-fathom line. In so doing, you make a landfall on Isla Contoy lighthouse and can then follow the seaward side of the reef down to Isla Mujeres.

LOCATING THE GULF STREAM. The National Weather Service center in Coral Gables, Florida monitors (by satellite) the temperature of the water in the Gulf of Mexico. It issues updated thermal charts at regular intervals. These charts enable you to pinpont the main thrust of the Yucatán Current—known as the "Gulf Stream loop"—and perhaps enable you to pick out major eddies, the outside of which generally provide a countercurrent to the main stream. Unfortunately, due to atmospheric conditions, the satellites can only pick up the loop current between November and May so that no picture is available in the summer months. The NWS

STRATEGIES FOR CROSSING THE GULF OF MEXICO

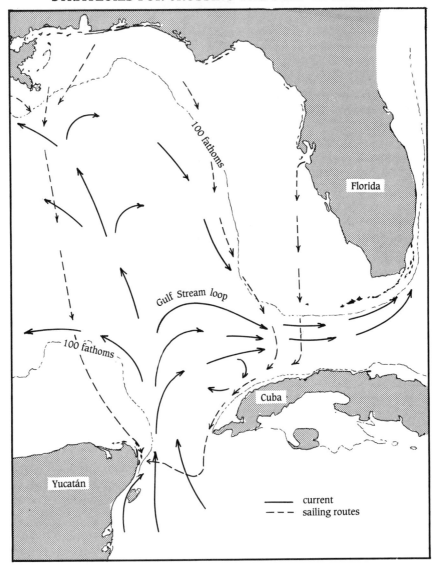

telephone number is: (305) 665-4707; the fax number, (305) 661-0738, gives access to printouts of the latest charts (see samples on pages 53 and 54).

USING A COLD FRONT WHEN GOING SOUTH.

We have passaged from New Orleans to Isla Mujeres and back three times, and from New Orleans to Key West and back once. We are atypical in that we choose to make the southward passage in the wintertime and *to leave at the onset of a moderate cold front*. As the front passes through, the wind veers

into the west and then the northwest, strengthening to 25 to 35 knots. The wind slowly eases and moves into the northeast, finally swinging back to the east or the southeast. By this time we are generally on the Campeche Bank, having had favorable winds for the entire crossing. It can be a little rough, especially when the wind blows against a westward-setting arm of the Yucatán Current that flows around the Bay of Campeche toward Texas, but our boat is well built and we make a fast passage.

Associate editor Peter Hancock made the same

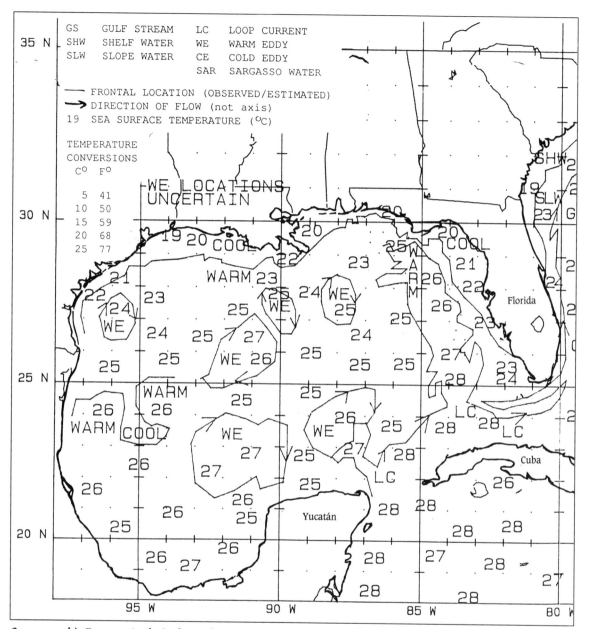

Oceanographic Features Analysis chart. This National Weather Service chart shows the location of the Gulf Stream loop in the Gulf of Mexico, and various eddies. Note that the axis of the loop current is not shown; this is indicated approximately on the relevant nautical charts. (COURTESY NOAA OCEAN PRODUCTS CENTER)

crossing in his 26-foot sailboat, *Kylie*, in late December in a 45-knot, freezing cold, norther—the strongest December cold front on record in Louisiana. From the Mississippi Gulf Outlet Canal, he made Isla Mujeres in four days, but I think he would wait for a rather more moderate front the next time!

April, May, and June offer the best prospects for favorable winds and a fair passage on the return voyage.

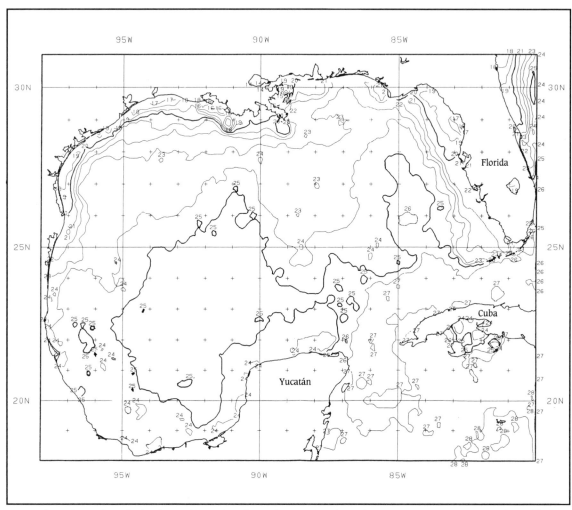

Sea Surface Thermal Analysis chart. This National Weather Service chart shows water temperatures in the Gulf of Mexico, giving a fair idea of the outer boundary of warm water in the Gulf Stream loop. (COURTESY NOAA OCEAN PRODUCTS CENTER)

THE WINDWARD PASSAGE

Most boats passaging from the East Coast of the United States want to come through the Bahamas in easy stages all the way to Great Inagua, the southernmost island in the Bahamas. From Great Inagua you should have a reach through the Windward Passage (although the winds may be light in the lee of Hispaniola) and a run across the western Caribbean with the current in your favor, enabling you to make an easy landfall on Guanaja in the Bay Islands.

The Windward Passage is an attractive route.

The United States East Coast can be traveled via the Intracoastal Waterway with a short passage, at a time of your choosing, across the Gulf Stream into the relative protection of the Bahamas. The myriad Bahamian islands have dozens of excellent anchorages where you can wait for favorable winds for the next stretch. Much of the Bahamas can be traversed on the "inside" rather than in open ocean passages.

Great Inagua is a dusty island with just one town (Mathew Town), 50,000 flamingoes (the largest colony in the Caribbean), and acre upon acre of salt evaporation ponds. It has an open roadstead for an anchorage, but just to the north of Mathew Town is a small harbor that has been scooped out of the island. This harbor affords excellent protection.

From Great Inagua it should be downhill all the way to Guanaja, except when a norther is blowing. Potential stops on this route are Jamaica, the Cayman Islands, and Swan Island. However, in 1990 Jamaica was inhospitable to visiting yachts, restricted them to one or two anchorages, and thieves were as active as ever; Swan Island was completely barred to visiting yachts by the Honduran military (with wild rumors circulating as to the reasons why). You might be better off pressing on to Guanaja. Here, at least, the reception will be friendly.

If returning to the United States, you would be better off following the current through the Yucatán and Florida straits rather than trying to buck the wind and current to regain the Windward Passage.

CROSSING THE CARIBBEAN

From the Virgins, Windwards, or Leewards at any time of year, it is a downhill run to the Bay Islands (except during northers), making a landfall on Guanaja. The first part of the passage can be taken in stages working along either the southern or the northern coasts of Puerto Rico and Hispaniola. Both islands have a number of good anchorages and a lot to offer in the way of scenery and some of the friendliest people in the Caribbean. Thereafter the route is as for the Windward Passage.

In sailing to the western Caribbean, you will be trading in as much as 1,500 miles of easting. You should make sure you have seen all that you want to of the Windwards, Leewards, and the north coast of South America (Venezuela, the ABC Islands, and perhaps Colombia) before making this passage. It is a long, hard beat back. Once in the Northwest Caribbean, I am confident you will consider the loss of easting well worthwhile. For many cruising people, this region turns out to be the high point of a circumnavigation of the Caribbean.

Probably the easiest way to return to the eastern Caribbean is via the Yucatán and Florida straits, through the Bahamas, along the northern coast of Hispaniola, through the Mona Passage, and along the southern coast of Puerto Rico. From Florida onward, this route is against the prevailing winds and

currents, but the Bahamas provide protection, and the mountains of Hispaniola and Puerto Rico modify the prevailing pattern of the trade winds.

Close inshore these high islands tend to experience a diurnal wind shift. At night it is relatively calm, with perhaps a light offshore breeze; in the morning, the trade winds begin to reassert themselves, and by mid-afternoon are blowing at full strength out of the east. To make easting you should sail at night and in the early morning, hugging the coastline, planning on being securely anchored in some protected lagoon by noon.

Well-documented anchorages on the north coast of Hispaniola are sparse—basically Cap Haitian, Puerto Plata, and Samana—while lights along the coast are unreliable, few, and far between. Night passages require careful and accurate navigation. Puerto Rico, on the other hand, is well lit with many beautifully protected lagoons along its southern coast. Then comes the island of Culebra, with several excellent anchorages, by which time St. Thomas in the Virgin Islands is in sight.

TO AND FROM THE

PANAMA CANAL

It is difficult to make easting along the northern coast of South America. Consequently, after transiting the Panama Canal, almost all boats coming from the Pacific and the U.S. West Coast choose to make a clockwise circuit of the Caribbean. There are a couple of broad choices: to make directly for the Windward Passage or points further east (Puerto Rico, the Virgin Islands) or to work around Cabo Gracias a Dios and on to Guanaja in the Bay Islands.

The eastern shore of Nicaragua is bordered by numerous dangerous and poorly charted reefs that stretch many miles out to sea, beset with often strong and unpredictable currents. Several boats have been lost in this area in recent years. Passage should be made either *inside* this reef area, close inshore up the Mosquito Channel, or the entire area should be given a wide berth. In the past decade, the former route has been unattractive due to the turmoil in Nicaragua and rumors of piracy on the Nicaraguan coast, but hopefully this is now changing for the better—it may even be possible to think of exploring this coastline, which is reputed to have a number of safe and lovely anchorages. If you choose the outside route, the journey can be broken at San Andreas and Providencia islands, or anchorage can be found on some of the offshore banks (Roncador, Serranilla).

The best time to make the northward passage is in April, May, or June when the winds are easing and there is a greater chance of a southeasterly component, before the onset of hurricane season. This puts you in the Bay Islands at the beginning of the hurricane season, but as noted earlier, with an attentive ear to weather forecasts, the Northwest Caribbean can be cruised through much of hurricane season. Alternatively you could spend the summer on the Rio Dulce—a delightful prospect to anyone who knows Guatemala.

During the winter months with the trades blowing more forcefully and with a more northeasterly set, it is likely to be a hard beat all the way from Panama to Cabo Gracias a Dios. Some boats have chosen to first make easting through the San Blas Islands, then to slog it out to Cartagena in Colombia. From here it is usually a close reach all the way around Cabo Gracias a Dios.

The San Blas Islands—a group of more than 300 coconut-clad, sandy islets—are home to the Cuna Indians, the second smallest race on earth after the Pygmies. The Cuna have managed to preserve intact much of their culture. Theirs is a matriarchal society—young men marry into the bride's family; the women run the households and allocate tasks to the men; and so on. The women wear the wealth of the family. They are gloriously adorned in gold with beautiful blouses, decorated with *molas*—a reverse appliqué technique that involves intricate patterns made from many layers of brightly colored cloth. You could easily spend weeks here, especially in the out-islands, which are the least influenced by western culture.

So far as Colombia is concerned, in spite of the internal turmoil and all the problems associated with the drug trade, I have had nothing but favorable reports on Cartagena. This is one of the most beautiful cities in the western hemisphere, with many finely preserved Spanish fortifications and, I am told, a very friendly population. As of 1990, Cartagena was largely untouched by the violence plaguing other parts of Colombia, but check the current situation before heading that way. Note that if you carry insurance on your boat, you will probably find that your policy excludes coverage while you are in Colombian waters.

The return route from the Bay Islands to Panama is best made in November when the chance of a hurricane is slight, northers are unlikely, and the trade winds tend toward the northeast while not yet at their full strength. Even in November, this is a hard beat against wind and current until you round Cabo Gracias a Dios with no safe haven on the Honduran mainland. Beyond Trujillo this is a rugged coast offering no protection. The only possible exception is Caratasca Bay, but the bay is poorly charted and has a shifting bar that has no more than six feet over it, according to recent reports. From Cabo Gracias a Dios you should have a reach to Panama.

Route Planning Within the Region

From Isla Mujeres to Punta Gorda, the mainland coast of the Yucatán Peninsula runs in a south-southwesterly direction. During the early winter months, with the trade winds from the northeast, and numerous northers, any passage south is likely to be an exhilarating reach, with the favorable wind more than offsetting the effects of the northward-setting current. Any passage to the north at this time of year is likely to be a hard beat, although the current is in your favor. During the late spring and early summer, when the wind tends more to the south of east, it should be easier to head north, while it is still generally possible to make good speed south.

From Punta Gorda to the Bay Islands, the mainland coast runs almost due east. Currents here are less predictable, with an easterly set quite common close inshore and a westerly set further out. The wind is almost always more or less out of the east, making any course to the Bay Islands a beat, whereas any course in the other direction should be a run.

LANDFALL IN

ISLA MUJERES

The best month to make a landfall on Isla Mujeres is November, whether you are crossing the Gulf of Mexico or working your way south. In November, you can make a leisurely cruise down the Mexican and Belizean coasts, taking advantage of the winds' northeasterly slant to make headway against the current. You need to keep an ear cocked to the weather forecasts and be prepared to sit out cold fronts. There are a number of protected anchorages on the Mexican and Belizean coasts in which to do this.

You can avoid much of the current by hugging the reef along the Mexican coast, staying in 40 to 60 feet of water, but this can be done only in daylight and good visibility. We found at times that just straying out to the 100-foot line would carry us from no current into two knots of adverse current.

Once off San Pedro, Ambergris Cay (Belize), you are able to enter the inshore passage. From here a six-foot draft can be carried all the way down to Punta Gorda in protected waters behind the reef. Those with more than a six-foot draft have to enter the reef at English Cay. The sailing is glorious; the current in the main channel generally sets in a southerly direction at about one knot. Livingston, at the mouth of the Rio Dulce, is an easy passage from Punta Gorda.

A problem arises when making easting from Livingston or Punta Gorda to the Bay Islands. You might be lucky enough to catch a rare west wind, or a calm might allow you to motor, but otherwise you have to choose one of two options:

1. Work back to the north behind the Belizean reef as far as Tobacco Cay or even English Cay, which then puts you on a broadly southeast course to the Bay Islands. In the winter months you should be able to make Utila in one tack, and may even be able to free the sheets a little. However, you are likely to be bucking a north-westward-setting current.
2. Work along the Honduran coastline, close inshore, taking advantage of the diurnal wind-shifts that tend to occur as a result of the high mountains interacting with the trade winds. At night there are often calms or even west winds. In the daytime the easterly trades reassert themselves, building to maximum strength in mid to late afternoon. If you choose this route, you need to sail overnight or in the early mornings and be anchored by noon. Obviously careful and accurate navigation is essential. Anchorages (sometimes rolly) can be found in the lee of

Cabo Tres Puntas, at Puerto Cortes, and in Laguna El Diamante (see the detailed notes in this guide). Thereafter there is no protection on the mainland until Trujillo and you will need to strike out for Puerto Este on Utila, some 40 miles away. I recommend commencing this crossing at dusk to allow adequate time to enter Puerto Este in daylight the following day. The current should be generally favorable. You need to keep a close watch on your position and to steer clear of the one or two shoals en route.

From Utila, depending on the wind, you might consider making for the Cayos Cochinos. Roatan is generally a reach from the Cochinos. If your plan is to return to Belize or Mexico, you might even consider making for Trujillo from the Cochinos, and then to Guanaja. From Guanaja it is an easy run back to explore the other islands.

LANDFALL ON GUANAJA

It is easy to sail to any other point in the region from Guanaja; the wind will be with you. However, once you are in the Rio Dulce or Punta Gorda, you have worked yourself into a cul-de-sac and probably will have to beat back out. The best months in which to do this are April, May, and June. Since there is generally a one-knot current setting south down the inner channel in Belize, the best strategy for going north is to work into the protected water immediately behind the reef and to remain fairly close to the reef. Here there is very little wave action and the current is neutral. There are many lovely cays behind which you can anchor, but also lots of lovely coral heads to ground on, so you need to pay close attention to the detailed information in this guide.

Once clear of the Belizean reef, to go north to the Yucatán Strait the best tactic is to stand offshore three or four miles and position yourself squarely in the current. You must check in at Xcalak, but thereafter—if you have already explored Mexico—you should make a direct run to Isla Mujeres, riding the current the whole way.

CIRCUMNAVIGATING THE BAY ISLANDS

The conventional wisdom is to circle each island in a counterclockwise direction, taking advantage of a possible easterly setting current on the south shore, a possible westerly setting current on the north shore, and the prevailing trade winds on the north shore. However, we found that the southwest to northeast axis of the islands frequently created a partial lee on the north shore. The result: The seas here, close inshore at least, generally were more subdued than on the south shore. The current was often weak on either shore. It was therefore easier to work to windward on the north shore, suggesting a clockwise circumnavigation as the better choice.

I believe that when the winds tend to the northeast (the early winter months) the conventional choice is the best one, but when the winds tend to the southeast (late spring and early summer) a clockwise circuit is easier.

What is not in question is that the winds tend to build steadily throughout the day and then subside late at night and in the early hours of the morning. Any easting is more easily made in the morning than in the afternoon, so plan on making an early start (so long as the light is adequate for any reef passages).

A SUMMARY OF LANDFALL STRATEGIES

ISLA MUJERES. Check in to Mexico at Isla Mujeres. Explore the Mexican coastline on the way south, hugging the reef to keep out of the current. Check out of Mexico at Xcalak. Enter the reef and check into Belize at San Pedro. (If you draw more than six feet, you have to stay outside the reef until English Cay and then check in at Belize City.) Explore the Belizean cays while working south behind the reef. Make sidetrips out to Turneffe Island, Glover's Reef and Lighthouse Reef at this time. From a sailing point of view, if you intend to return to the states via the Yucatán Strait, it makes more sense to visit these reefs on the way home; but since that would involve major detours to clear in and out of Belizean waters, it is best to do these sidetrips while going southward.

Check out of Belize at Punta Gorda and enter the Rio Dulce, clearing into Guatemala at Livingston. Explore the Rio Dulce, check out of Guatemala at Livingston, and head for the Bay Islands. If you choose the coastal route, clear in to Honduras at Puerto Cortes; if you choose to take the northern route through the Belize cays, you need to clear in and out of Belize once again at either Punta Gorda or Dangriga. If you have not already visited Turneffe Island, Glover's Reef, and Lighthouse Reef, this would be another excellent opportunity to do so. When leaving the Bay Islands either head north to clear into Mexico at Xcalak; or ride the current directly to Isla Mujeres; or go east for the Windward Passage, Panama, or whatever your plans call for.

GUANAJA. Clear in at Guanaja settlement. You may not be able to clear with immigration at this time, in which case clear immigration at Coxen's Hole on Roatan when you get there. Explore the Bay Islands and the Cayos Cochinos, returning to Coxen's Hole to clear out of Honduras with the immigration authorities. This is necessary since there is no immigration office on Utila; you can obtain your exit zarpe from the port captain on Utila, but not immigration stamps. Usually you may spend a few days in Utila on your way east after clearing out with immigration in Coxen's Hole.

Enter the Rio Dulce, clearing in to Guatemala at Livingston. Explore the Rio Dulce and then check out of Guatemala at Livingston. Check into Belize at Punta Gorda and work your way up inside the reef exploring the cays, with sidetrips to Turneffe Island, Glover's Reef, and Lighthouse Reef. If you draw more than six feet, check out at Dangriga rather than Belize City (this involves backtracking a certain amount but avoids a lot of hassles); if you draw six feet or less, continue inside the reef to San Pedro to check out. This cost $30 (U.S.) in 1990 but, in my opinion, was worth it. Come outside the reef for the short trip to Xcalak and check into Mexico. Continue to Isla Mujeres with as many stops as you wish to make.

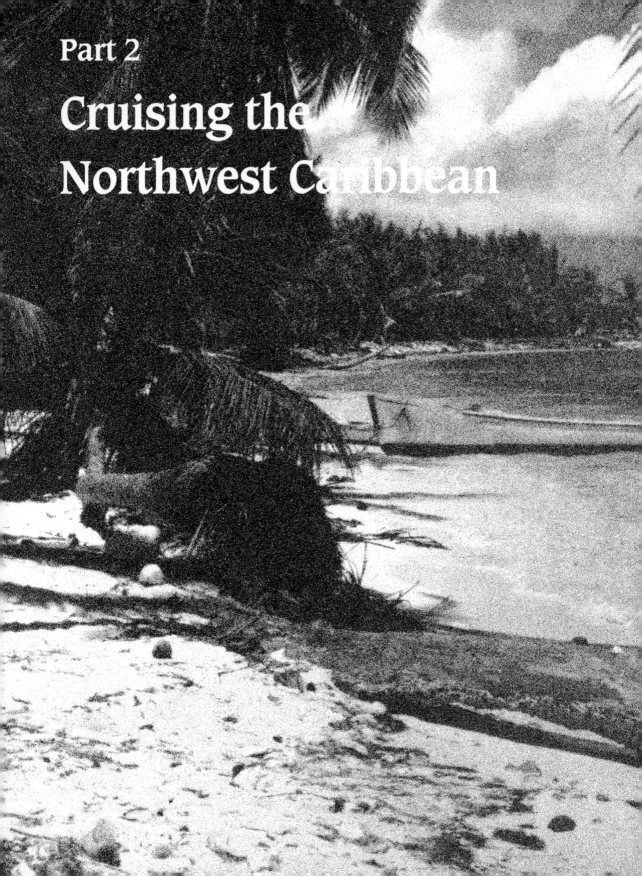

Part 2
Cruising the Northwest Caribbean

Mexico's Yucatán Coast

The Caribbean coast of Mexico stretches for approximately 200 miles, from Cabo Catoche in the north to the border with Belize. Most of the terrain is low-lying and featureless, covered with mangroves interspersed with coconut palms. Many of the palms have been decapitated—the result of a disease working its way throughout the region—but they are being steadily replaced by disease-resistant strains.

Frequently the swamps and low cliffs give way to mile upon mile of lovely white sand beaches. A couple of decades ago the Mexican government picked one such beach, on an unknown spit of land known as Cancún, and developed it into an international resort. The project was spectacularly suc-

cessful. It has spawned numerous smaller developments in the same area, but as you move south these give way to virgin beaches with infrequent, undisturbed, relatively primitive Mexican settlements.

Offshore are several islands. In the north, Contoy and Isla Mujeres. Further south, Cozumel. Close to Belize, the Banco Chinchorro, a more-or-less circular reef with one or two low-lying islets. Isla Contoy is a wildlife refuge—home to thousands of frigate birds, boobies, pelicans, and cormorants. Isla Mujeres is a popular vacation spot for Mexicans and foreigners alike, with a far more relaxed atmosphere than neighboring Cancún. Cozumel is especially popular with divers since the island is ringed

The anchorage at Tulum with the trade wind blowing in over the reef.

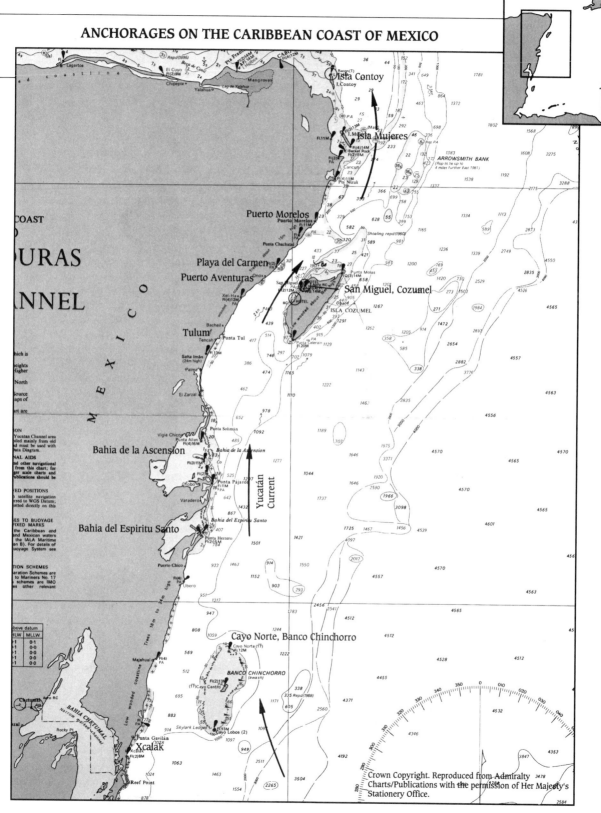

ANCHORAGES ON THE CARIBBEAN COAST OF MEXICO

Isla Contoy

Isla Mujeres

Puerto Morelos

Playa del Carmen

Puerto Aventuras

San Miguel, Cozumel

Tulum

Bahia de la Ascension

Yucatán Current

Bahia del Espiritu Santo

Cayo Norte, Banco Chinchorro

BANCO CHINCHORRO
(awash)

Xcalak

Crown Copyright. Reproduced from Admiralty Charts/Publications with the permission of Her Majesty's Stationery Office.

by spectacular coral reefs. Banco Chinchorro is uninhabited and largely virgin reef.

For much of its length the mainland is also fronted by a fringing reef, here and there merging with the shoreline, at other places up to a mile offshore. Outside the reef the bottom drops precipitously. The water is crystal clear—a deep ultramarine blue offshore, a lovely light translucent blue as you approach the reef, which is largely unspoiled and offers almost unlimited opportunities for snorkeling and diving. The waters are teeming with fish; sportfishing boats come here from near and far for some of the finest fishing in the Caribbean.

A number of protected anchorages are strung out along this coastline—Isla Contoy, Isla Mujeres, Puerto Morelos, Playa del Carmen, Puerto Aventuras, Cozumel, Tulum, the Bahia de la Ascension, the Bahia del Espiritu Santo, Cayo Norte on Banco Chinchorro, and Xcalak. All are described in detail in the following pages. Two marinas—El Paraiso at Isla Mujeres, and Puerto Aventuras—provide secure bases in which you can safely leave your boat and venture inland. You should, in particular, plan on a trip of at least a week to visit the magnificent ruins at Chichén Itzá, Uxmal, and Palenque, and also to spend a day or two in Mérida.

The prevailing winds and swells are from the east, tending to come more from the northeast in the early winter and the southeast in the spring and early summer. Northers are fairly common in winter; calms more prevalent in summer. This area is, of course, within the summertime hurricane belt.

The Yucatán Current flows up the coastline in a northerly direction, generally at two to three knots, but with some variation. Sailing south against the current can be difficult. The winter months, when the trade winds tend to be more in the northeast and there is a greater chance of northers, are the best time for heading south. If you can hug the reef, staying in 60 feet or so of water, you can escape most of the current and may even pick up a favorable countercurrent. However, you should never try to sail close inshore at night.

I have endeavored to identify a secure anchorage at least every 30 miles so as to avoid night passages. However, between the Bahia del Espiritu Santo and Xcalak, a distance of 75 miles, there is no anchorage on the mainland. Unless you traverse the current to Cayo Norte on Banco Chinchorro, you will probably have to make a night passage. Be prepared to stand off the mainland coast at least a couple of miles and to buck some of the current.

Heading north, the best plan is to stand well out into the strongest part of the stream and to just keep on going. It will be necessary to check in with the port captain in Xcalak to obtain a zarpe, but thereafter I advise sailing straight through to Isla Mujeres. The late spring/early summer months provide the best chance of a southeast wind, putting you on a fast, comfortable reach.

The Mexican coast has a number of well-maintained lights (more than are shown on the charts), which provide visual lines of position at night to supplement loran and satnav readings.

ISLA CONTOY

Charts: BA 1220; DMA 28015 and 27120.

Note: The latter chart does not show the reef extending southward from Contoy approximately inside the 10-meter line. Much of this reef is awash and clearly visible.

The lighthouse on the northern tip of Isla Contoy is usually the first landfall for boats coming south from the U.S.A., and the last for those heading north into the Gulf of Mexico. It is a solid brick Victorian structure that would not look out of place on the New England coast. Over the years it has weathered several hurricanes. It is painted white and is conspicuous from miles away, standing out above the low-lying island.

Isla Contoy is not a port of entry. If you are heading south, do not stop at Contoy without first clearing in at Isla Mujeres; if heading north, you are permitted to clear out at Isla Mujeres and then to stop overnight at Contoy.

The whole island is designated as a wildlife refuge and as such is supposed to be uninhabited except for a couple of wardens in the ranger station near the island's southern end. However, the last time we were there, a number of fishermen had established shacks on the northern part of the island, and there was a detachment of the Mexican military, which inspected our papers and made a perfunctory search of the boat.

APPROACHES. Approach the anchorage around the northern end of the island only—the southern end is beset with reefs—clearing the northernmost tip of the land by one-half mile or more. If you are coming from the south, the eastern coast of Contoy is free of obstructions, permitting you to come within one-quarter mile of the shore, but a reef extends up to one-third mile north from the lighthouse, some of it breaking the surface, so don't attempt to cut this corner.

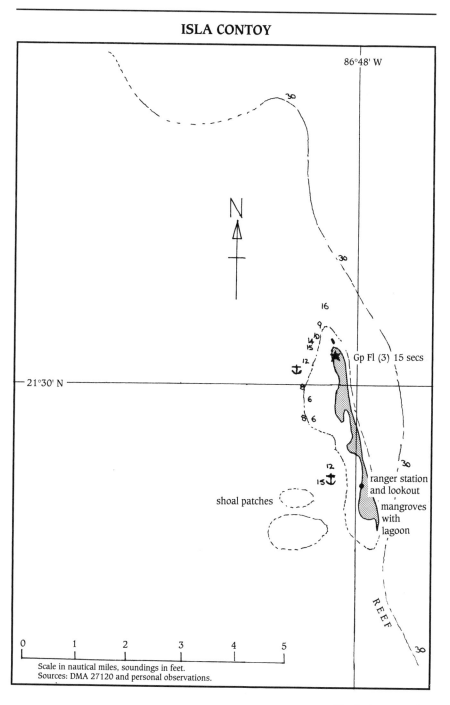

ISLA CONTOY

86°48' W

30

N

16

9

4 6
15
5
12   Gp Fl (3) 15 secs

21°30' N

8
6

8 6

12   30
15   ranger station
          and lookout

shoal patches   mangroves
                     with
                     lagoon

R E E F

30

0   1   2   3   4   5
Scale in nautical miles, soundings in feet.
Sources: DMA 27120 and personal observations.

The Migration of the Spiny Lobster

Once a year, in the late fall, thousands upon thousands of spiny lobsters—the delicious, clawless Caribbean variety of crawfish—congregate at Isla Contoy, hiding under every rock. Here they wait until the first norther after Christmas comes down across the Gulf of Mexico. This is the signal for them to move out, walking in a long line to the southeast. In spite of considerable research, nobody knows the purpose of this annual migration, or the destination of the lobsters.

The local fishermen have long known about the migration and taken advantage of it. With today's modern freezing techniques, in just two days they can catch and ship tons of lobsters to the United States. Unfortunately, in a few years this may make the once-plentiful lobster as scarce here as elsewhere in the overfished Caribbean.

As you come in around the northwestern side of the island swing wide, staying in depths of 12 feet or more. A shoal area extends one-quarter mile westward from the northern tip of the island.

The whole area between Contoy and the mainland is protected in normal trade-wind conditions but is open to northers. If looking for strictly overnight protection, you can anchor as soon as you are in the lee of the island and out of the swells hooking around from the northeast.

It is possible to carry 6 feet all the way down to the southern end of Contoy, but there are numerous shoal patches to be negotiated with depths of less than this, and the water is sometimes not clear enough to see the bottom properly. The best approach is to stand a mile or so toward the mainland where the water is a little deeper, and then to work back in toward the ranger station.

ANCHORAGE. Anchor well off the ranger station in 12 to 15 feet. There is a hard sand bottom with excellent holding. Close by there are outcrops of coral with galaxies of tropical fish which, when the water is clear, provide perfect snorkeling conditions. The roots of the mangroves support a fascinating ecosystem of their own. Just to the south of the ranger station, we took our dinghy through a tunnel

Frigate Birds (Man-O-War Birds)

The magnificent sight of frigate birds soaring high in the sky on ascending currents of air is a sure sign of land. Although the frigate bird survives on food from the sea, it has no oils in its feathers. If a frigate bird were to land in the water, it would be unable to take off and would soon become waterlogged; the sea-fishing bird would drown. For this reason the birds never stray far from land, always returning to roost in trees at night.

Frigate birds have very light bodies. This, with their huge wing spans of up to 7 or 8 feet, enables them to rise effortlessly on the hot air currents that occur over land during the day as the heat of the tropical sun is reflected back into the atmosphere. From their high vantage point, they keep a sharp eye out both for marine life on the surface of the water and also on their neighbors, for the frigate is one of nature's thieves. Although the frigate is capable of swooping down to seize a flying fish in flight, it would just as soon save itself the trouble by stealing from another species of bird, or even one of its own.

Frigate birds almost always nest in colonies with boobies (see page 162) and pelicans. Both are great fishers but less agile in the air than the frigate. The frigate will wait on high until it sees a pelican or booby struggling up from the water with its catch, and will then dive-bomb the unfortunate bird, forcing it to throw up its catch, which the frigate will seize before it hits the surface of the water. As soon as one frigate gets a fish, half a dozen others are likely to try to scare it into dropping its ill-gotten gains—there is clearly no honor among thieves! Should a booby or pelican leave its nest unguarded, the frigates will rob it of eggs and young chicks.

During mating season the male frigate birds blow up a bright-red pouch beneath their beaks to the size of a small balloon, then hang around in groups in the tops of the mangroves wooing the ladies! This is quite a sight to see. The best time to visit a frigate bird colony is between March and June.

in the mangroves into a lagoon at the southern end of the island. Inside were hundreds of nesting frigate birds and boobies, many in full mating display. Terrie was given a tremendous fright when she almost stepped on a large boa constrictor. Among the rocks on the eastern shore were several large iguanas.

Although the resident colonies of birds were hard hit by Hurricane Gilbert, Contoy is a magical place for nature lovers, especially during mating and nesting seasons (March through May). If you don't want to sail there in your own boat, you can see it by taking a day trip out of Isla Mujeres.

ISLA MUJERES

Chart: DMA 28202.

Isla Mujeres is the principal port of entry or exit for those coming from or leaving for the U.S.A. The anchorage is well protected except in really strong northers when it can get a little rolly. The officials are friendly. The island offers many services and has numerous tourist attractions. In April and May the port hosts annual sailboat races from Texas and Florida.

APPROACHES

From the North. If you approach from the north, note that a more-or-less continuous reef runs south from Isla Contoy to Isla Mujeres, much of it awash. This reef is not shown on DMA chart 27120—it runs inside the 10-meter line. Any track that stays east of longitude 86°44'W will ensure adequate clearance. As you approach Isla Mujeres, the Hotel Presidente will be conspicuous from miles away, looking like some great slab-sided Mayan temple. There is a 600-yard-wide break in the reef north of the hotel, which provides a straightforward passage around the northern end of the island and into the lagoon. The reef is traversed approximately one-third mile north of the light known as Roca El Yunque. The passage appears to be free of coral heads, and we have recorded no depths shallower than 12 feet. Beware of a shoal patch a quarter mile west of the western tip of the island. You can come inside it about 200 yards off the beach.

When the trade winds are blowing hard, you will have to ride substantial swells through this passage. In these conditions, rather than risk surfing and a potential broach, you may wish to sail around the southern end of the island, which is free of hazards. In this case, on your approach do not close the northern end of the island—stay 2 miles or more off the Hotel Presidente. Isla Mujeres lies on a northwest to southeast axis: If you close the hotel in prevailing winds, you will have to beat back to the east to round the southern tip of the island.

From the South. The approach is free of all dangers, except the clearly marked Roca la Bandera, until you are due west of the southern tip of the island. A considerable area of reef extends to the west at this point; you should hold a course for the mainland to pass west of the Bajo Pepito buoy, at which point the range (leading) light on the south side of the entrance to the lagoon will be in line with the lighthouse at the northern side of the entrance to the lagoon on a heading of 000°T. Head north and a little west until you pick up the channel buoys.

A shoal area between the leading light and the lighthouse is not shown on the charts. It is possible to carry 6 feet between the leading light and this shoal, but it is better to stay north of the channel buoys, hooking around the northern side of the lagoon. You will pass the fuel (and water) dock to port and then will see a navy dock, usually with a gunboat alongside.

ANCHORAGE. You can anchor either between the navy dock and the shoal, or else further south in the lagoon. The holding and protection are excellent except, as noted, from the northwest.

DINGHY DOCKING. You can use just about any dock or section of beach with the exception of the navy and ferry docks. We have never experienced or heard of any problem with theft in Isla Mujeres, but here as elsewhere it would be as well to at least lock your outboard to your dinghy.

CLEARANCE PROCEDURES. If entering, fly your Q flag. At all times in Mexican waters fly a courtesy flag. To clear in or out you will need five to seven copies of your crew list (I recommend seven) typed in Spanish. See the accompanying sample *lista de tripulantes* on page 70.

(Continued on page 71)

APPROACHES TO ISLA MUJERES

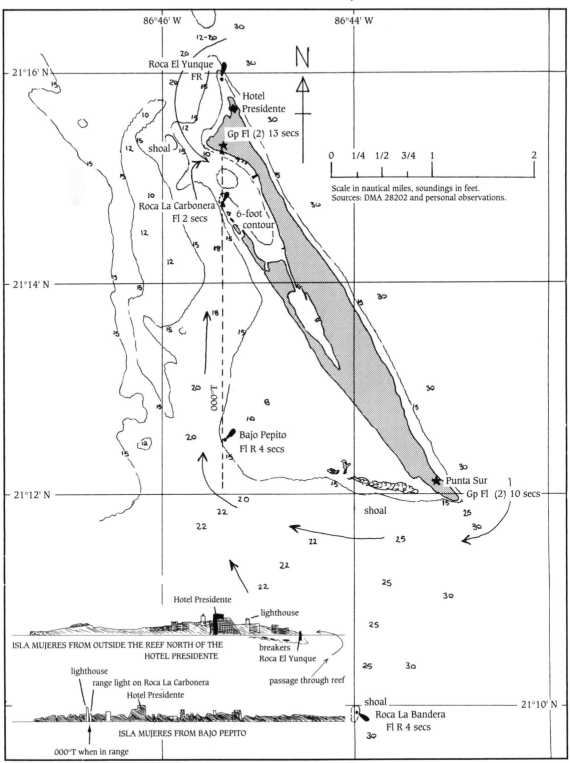

86°46' W   86°44' W

12-20

30

20

30

Roca El Yunque
FR

21°16' N

20

15

Hotel
Presidente

Gp Fl (2) 13 secs

30

N

10

12

shoal

15

10

12

15

Roca La Carbonera
Fl 2 secs

6-foot
contour

30

12

18

15

21°14' N

12

15

15

18

000°T

15

15

15

20

8

10

20

22

12

15

Bajo Pepito
Fl R 4 secs

20

21°12' N

20

22

22

22

Scale in nautical miles, soundings in feet.
Sources: DMA 28202 and personal observations.

0   1/4   1/2   3/4   1   2

30

15

30

15

Punta Sur
Gp Fl (2) 10 secs

30

shoal

25

30

22

25

22

25

30

25

Hotel Presidente

lighthouse

ISLA MUJERES FROM OUTSIDE THE REEF NORTH OF THE
HOTEL PRESIDENTE

breakers
Roca El Yunque

25

30

passage through reef

lighthouse
range light on Roca La Carbonera
Hotel Presidente

shoal

21°10' N

Roca La Bandera
Fl R 4 secs

ISLA MUJERES FROM BAJO PEPITO

30

000°T when in range

THE LAGOON AT ISLA MUJERES

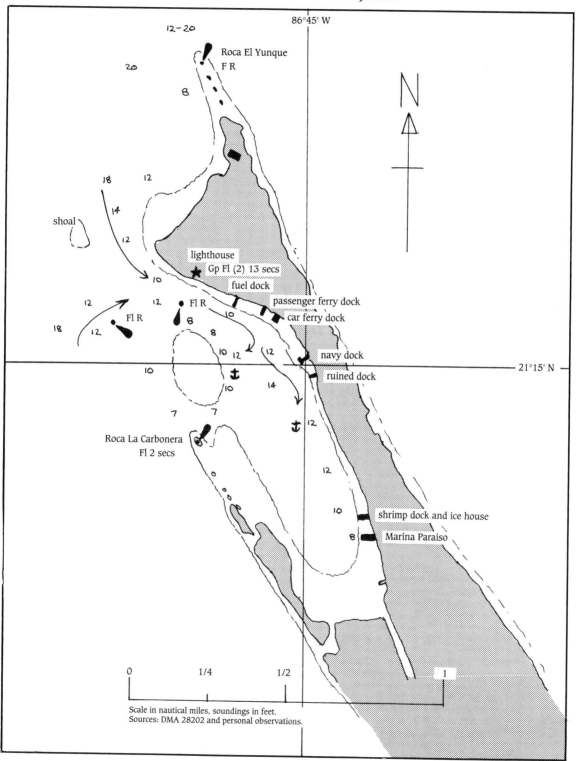

86°45' W

12-20

20

8

Roca El Yunque
F R

18   12

14

shoal

12

lighthouse
Gp Fl (2) 13 secs
fuel dock

passenger ferry dock

12   12   Fl R
car ferry dock

18   12   Fl R
8
10

8

navy dock
10   12   12
ruined dock   21°15' N

10   10   14

10   7   7

Roca La Carbonera
Fl 2 secs

12

10

12

10   shrimp dock and ice house

8   Marina Paraiso

N

0   1/4   1/2   1

Scale in nautical miles, soundings in feet.
Sources: DMA 28202 and personal observations.

LISTA DE TRIPULANTES

DE LA EMBARCACION (name of your boat), NO. DE REGISTRO (registration number of your boat—state, coast guard, or whatever), DE BANDERA (your flag—"Norteamericana," "Brittanico," etc.), CAPITAN (the full name of the captain), DE (the weight of your boat, in tons) TONELADAS NETAS, Y (its length, in meters) METROS DE LONGITUD, QUE ZARPARA DEL PUERTO DE (if clearing in, the name of the last port you cleared from, and the country if other than Mexico; if clearing out, the name of the port you are currently in), CON DESTINO AL PUERTO DE (if clearing in, the name of the port you are currently in; if clearing out, the name of the next port at which you wish to clear in, and its country if other than Mexico), CON PUNTOS INTERMEDIOS (if clearing from one port in Mexico to another, list the places you wish to visit before clearing out again; if clearing out, omit this section):

#: NOMBRE Y APPELLIDOS	NACIONALIDAD	EDAD	CARGO A BORDO
1 (Full names)	(Nationality)	(Age)	(Position on board)

EL SUSCRITO CAPITAN DE LA EMBARCACION (name of your boat) DECLARA SOLEMNEMENTE QUE LA LISTA DE TRIPULANTES QUE ANTECEDE CONTIENE TODOS LOS NOMBRES DE LOS INDIVIDUOS QUE COMPONEN LA TRIPULACION DEL MENCIONADO BARCO Y SE OBLIGA AL EXACTO CUMPLIMIENTO DE CUANTO DISPONEN LAS REYES Y REGLAMENTOS VIGENTES DE LAS AUTORIDADES PORTUARIAS DE LA REPUBLICA MEXICANA.

_____   _____
(Last sailing port and date)   (Captain's signature)

This last paragraph says that the captain of the boat solemnly declares that all the crew members are on the crew list and the vessel is committed to obeying the laws and regulations of the Mexican port authorities.

Example 1: Clearing in from Abroad

LISTA DE TRIPULANTES

DE LA EMBARCACION "NADA", NO. DE REGISTRO: LA 2739AX, DE BANDERA NORTEAMERICANA, CAPITAN NIGEL CALDER, DE 12 TONELADAS NETAS, Y DE 12 METROS DE LONGITUD, QUE ZARPARA DEL PUERTO DE NEW ORLEANS, USA, CON DESTINO AL PUERTO DE ISLA MUJERES, MEXICO:

#: NOMBRE Y APPELLIDOS	NACIONALIDAD	EDAD	CARGO A BORDO
1. Nigel Calder	Ingles	42	Capitan
2. Terrie Calder	USA	38	Piloto

EL SUSCRITO CAPITAN DE LA EMBARCACION "NADA" DECLARA SOLEMNEMENTE QUE LA LISTA DE TRIPULANTES QUE ANTECEDE CONTIENE TODOS LOS NOMBRES DE LOS INDIVIDUOS QUE COMPONEN LA TRIPULACION DEL MENCIONADO BARCO Y SE OBLIGA AL EXACTO CUMPLIMIENTO DE QUANTO DISPONEN LAS LEYES Y REGLAMENTOS VIGENTES DE LAS AUTORIDADES PORTUARIAS DE LA REPUBLICA MEXICANA.

NEW ORLEANS: (Date)   CAPITAN: (Signature)

Example 2: Moving Within Mexico

LISTA DE TRIPULANTES

DE LA EMBARCACION "NADA", NO. DE REGISTRO: LA 2739AX, DE BANDERA NORTEAMERICANA, CAPITAN NIGEL CALDER, DE 12 TONELADAS NETAS, Y DE 12 METROS DE LONGITUD, QUE ZARPARA DEL PUERTO DE ISLA MUJERES CON DESTINO AL PUERTO DE XCALAK, CON PUNTOS INTERMEDIOS PLAYA DEL CARMEN, BAHIA DE LA ASCENSION, BAHIA DEL ESPIRITU SANTO, Y CAYO NORTE (BANCO CHINCHORRO): (etc., etc.).

Sample crew list. The sample uses lower case letters for the variable terms and explanations. When you do your list, type the entire document in capital letters.

(Continued from page 67)

You go first to the port captain's office (see the map); he will stamp your crew lists and, if you are entering, charge you according to the net tonnage of your boat. You then take the road along the waterfront past the ferry dock to the immigration office on the right-hand side. Here you must present your passports and you will be issued a tourist card if entering (there is a charge), or your card will be collected if you are checking out. Customs is next, two doors back toward the port captain. There is no charge. You may be required to go to the hospital to obtain a health clearance: The receptionist will place the appropriate stamp on your paperwork.

Make sure that all officials *stamp and sign* all copies of the crew list. At each stop they will retain one or two copies. If you used a typewriter and carbon paper in making up the crew list, keep the top copy (the best one) which now goes back to the port captain. He will issue you a zarpe.

If you are entering Mexico draw up a list of all the places you may wish to visit—e.g., Puerto Morelos, Playa del Carmen, Puerto Aventuras, San Miguel (Cozumel), Tulum, Bahia de la Ascension, Bahia del Espiritu Santo, Cayo Norte (Banco Chinchorro), Xcalak—and try to have them all listed on the zarpe as *puntos intermedios*. By doing this, you may be able to avoid any further paperwork until checkout time, especially if you stay clear of Puerto Morelos and Cozumel (more on these places later).

PROVISIONS/FACILITIES. Marina Paraiso, located toward the southern end of the lagoon, can accommodate boats of up to 10-foot draft. There is water and electricity (110 and 220 volts) in the slips, with baths, showers, a swimming pool, a laundry, and rooms for visiting guests ashore. Security is good. The marina will hold mail, and its office has one of only two international phones on the island. Use of the phone is restricted to those staying in the marina. The rates are very reasonable. This is the best place to leave a boat to venture inland to see the sights of the Yucatán. Mañuel Gutierrez is the owner/manager. Tel: 2-02-52. Address: Marina Paraiso, Isla Mujeres, Quintana Roo, Mexico.

Diesel fuel, gasoline, and water are all available on the fuel dock, which has a controlling depth of 8 feet on its outer end. The water is piped from the mainland and is reputed to be the safest in Mexico.

ISLA MUJERES

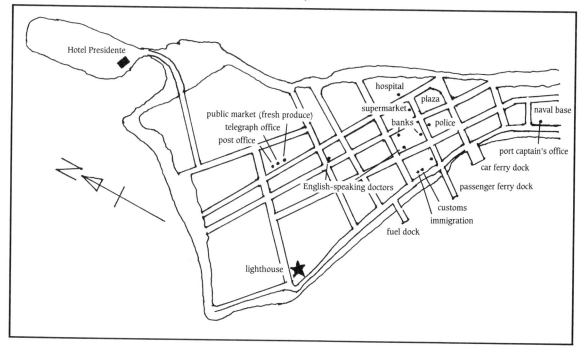

Ice can be bought in enormous blocks (up to 220 pounds, or 100 kilograms) very cheaply from the ice house on the shrimp-boat dock. Dinghy over and take your own tote bag to haul away as much as you want. Post office and bank locations are given in the accompanying map. A well-stocked supermarket (the best this side of Belize) is on the north side of the plaza, and there is a market for fresh produce two blocks farther north.

Two English-speaking doctors have consulting rooms in town. Dr. Antonio Salas Torres, Calle Hidalgo #8 (across the street from the Gomar Restaurant), tel: 2-04-77 and 2-01-95; and Dr. Antonio Torres Garcia, Hidalgo Ave. & Abasolo, tel: 2-03-83. You can contact the U.S. Consular Agent at 30 Coba Ave., Cancún; tel: 4-24-11 or 4-63-99.

The airlines at Cancún airport include AeroMexico (tel: 4-27-28 and 4-26-39); Aero-Caribe (4-36-83); American Airlines (4-29-47 and 4-26-51); Continental (4-25-40 and 4-27-06); Mexicana (4-27-40); United (4-28-58 and 4-25-28); and Lacsa (3-01-03 and 4-12-76).

Passenger ferries run to and from Puerto Juarez. The car ferries, which also take passengers, run to and from Punta Sam, which is just a little farther north along the coast. The ferries run throughout the day from 6:00 a.m. to early evening. In 1990 the fare was less than a dollar.

A #8 bus takes you from either Punta Sam or Puerto Juarez to the main bus terminal or into downtown Cancún. There are always taxis. No bus runs to and from the airport, which is some 12 miles the other side of Cancún; you need a taxi to get there. The standard fare in 1990 was $20, but with haggling it was possible to ride for less than $10. Regular buses go from the main bus terminal to all the major tourist attractions in the Yucatán. Alternatively, there are several car rental agencies in downtown Cancún.

THINGS TO DO. The town of Isla Mujeres itself is pretty, with cobbled streets and many small, tourist-oriented shops and restaurants. To the north is an excellent beach stretching around to the Hotel Presidente, with relatively protected snorkeling on the reef by the hotel. Farther south, on the western side of the island, are several lovely beaches, the best known at El Garrafón with protected snorkeling right off the beach. At the southern tip of the island is a small Mayan temple ruin, which was, unfortunately, further eroded by Hurricane Gilbert in 1988. There are several dive shops in town. The reef to the east of Isla Mujeres provides a great drop-off, though with heavy swells at times and considerable currents. The "sleeping shark caves," discovered by a local fisherman freediving for lobster and subsequently made famous by Jacques Cousteau, are a short boatride away.

PUERTO MORELOS

Chart: DMA 28201.

APPROACHES.

From Isla Mujeres. Once clear of the reef at the southern end of Isla Mujeres, you will encounter no offlying dangers along the mainland coast as far as Punta Nizuc. The high-rise buildings of the hotel district of Cancún are strung out along the beach. From Punta Nizuc an almost continuous breaking reef runs south to Puerto Morelos. Staying close to the reef keeps you out of the northward flowing current. Since the reef is mostly awash, it is easy to follow. North of Puerto Morelos stands a conspicuous building resembling an aircraft hanger. It comes into view before you lose the hotels on Punta Nizuc. Next the lighthouse stands out clearly. You need to sail approximately 2 miles past the lighthouse to round the southern end of the reef.

Unfortunately we were navigating on a photocopy of a photocopied chart with the latitude and longitude lines wrongly labeled. Our cross-bearings and fixes of the various buoys are suspect, and so I have omitted them from the sketch chart. You need not be concerned, however: The channel into Puerto Morelos is clearly marked with a sea buoy (Fl (2) 10 secs) well to the southeast, farther north a buoy close to the East Channel, and then buoys lining both sides of the channel up to the ferry dock. Keep the lighthouse on a bearing of approximately 026°T.

From the South. The approach is free of hazards. Head past the sea buoy and into the channel, then 026°T on the lighthouse.

ANCHORAGE. It is best to anchor north of the

APPROACHES TO PUERTO MORELOS

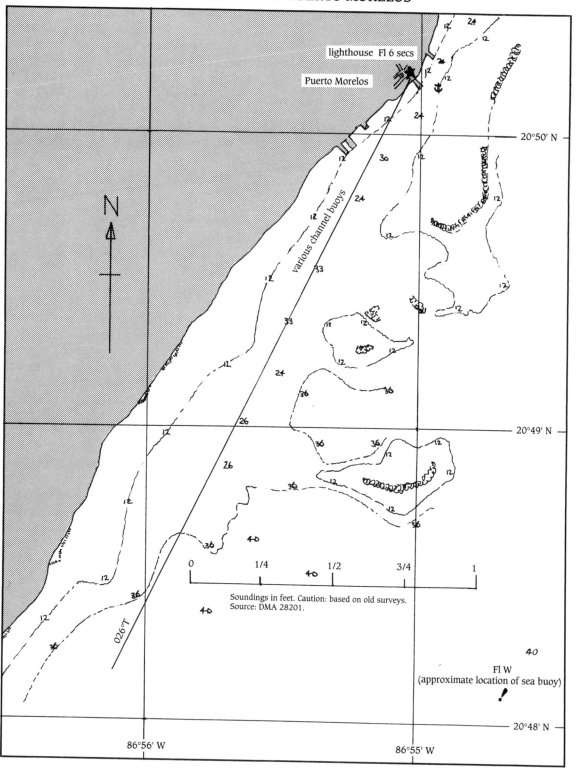

lighthouse Fl 6 secs

Puerto Morelos

20°50' N

N

various channel buoys

20°49' N

| 0 | 1/4 | 1/2 | 3/4 | 1 |

Soundings in feet. Caution: based on old surveys.
Source: DMA 28201.

026°T

Fl W
(approximate location of sea buoy)

20°48' N

86°56' W

86°55' W

PUERTO MORELOS

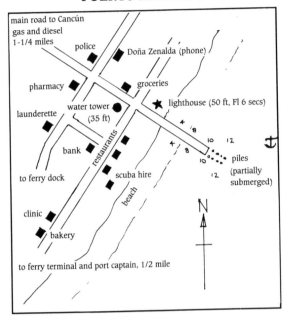

main road to Cancún
gas and diesel
1-1/4 miles

police

Doña Zenalda (phone)

pharmacy

groceries

water tower
(35 ft)

★ lighthouse (50 ft, Fl 6 secs)

launderette

bank

restaurants

to ferry dock

scuba hire

piles
(partially
submerged)

beach

clinic

bakery

N

to ferry terminal and port captain, 1/2 mile

PROVISIONS/FACILITIES. This is a quiet, dusty little town with few facilities of interest to visiting yachts. Water (of unknown quality) is available from a faucet at the base of the town's water tower (in the plaza); fuel can be hauled in jerry cans from a gas station outside of town. The grocery store has a limited selection of goods. Close by are a bakery and a number of seafood restaurants.

Note: During one night someone tried to steal the outboard from our dinghy; fortunately we disturbed him. Be sure to securely lock outboards and dinghies.

PLAYA DEL CARMEN

Chart: Not shown on any chart; use BA 1220 or DMA 28015. Location approximately 20°36.5'N; 87°04.5'W.

APPROACHES.

From the North. You will see that the reef from Puerto Morelos south to Playa del Carmen hugs the shoreline. It is submerged and does not break. The Yucatán Current runs strongly up the channel between the mainland and Cozumel but can be avoided by hugging the reef, keeping in 40 to 60 feet of water. Straying out into 100 feet can put you into 2 knots of adverse current. Just north of Playa del Carmen, the reef is awash. Behind it is a holiday village of Mayan *palapas* (small, palm-thatched huts). At this point the ferry dock farther south will be clearly visible—stay offshore until south of it, when two orange/yellow buoys will come into view. Turn between the buoys and head 001°T for the tip of the ferry dock. Depths coming through the reef and up to the dock shoal gradually from 30 to 8 feet. A lighthouse (Gp Fl (2) 12 secs.) stands at the end of the dock toward the land.

From the South. You will find no offlying dangers. Come north until you pick up the channel buoys and then head in between them, 001°T, for the tip of the ferry dock.

ANCHORAGE. The best anchorage is south of the dock in 9 feet of water over a sand bottom. Anchor well clear of the dock to avoid passenger ferry traffic (to and from Cozumel). At night there may be an

---

commercial dock (which is the vehicle ferry terminal to and from Cozumel) to keep out of the ship traffic. There is 10 feet on the outer end of the dock off the lighthouse, and you can anchor anywhere in this area. The anchorage is an open roadstead with some protection from the reef. The bottom is mostly grassy, with patches of clear sand and some rock. We had no trouble setting an anchor; the holding is good. Anchorage can also be made farther north behind the reef where there is reputed to be excellent snorkeling.

CLEARANCE PROCEDURES. All boats are supposed to clear in and out with the port captain whose office is near the commercial dock. He is extremely bureaucratic and inclined to try to extract bribes. If you have Puerto Morelos listed as a *punto intermedio* on your zarpe, you would be better off trying to get away with not clearing. However he may send a detachment of soldiers down to the dock to tell you to report in. Then he probably will not recognize your existing zarpe and will insist on issuing a new one. *On no account clear into or out of Mexico at Puerto Morelos*—the port captain will fly in various customs and health officials at your expense (it cost one boat $250). While anchored here our boat was thoroughly searched.

APPROACHES TO PLAYA DEL CARMEN, PUERTO AVENTURAS, AND SAN MIGUEL, COZUMEL

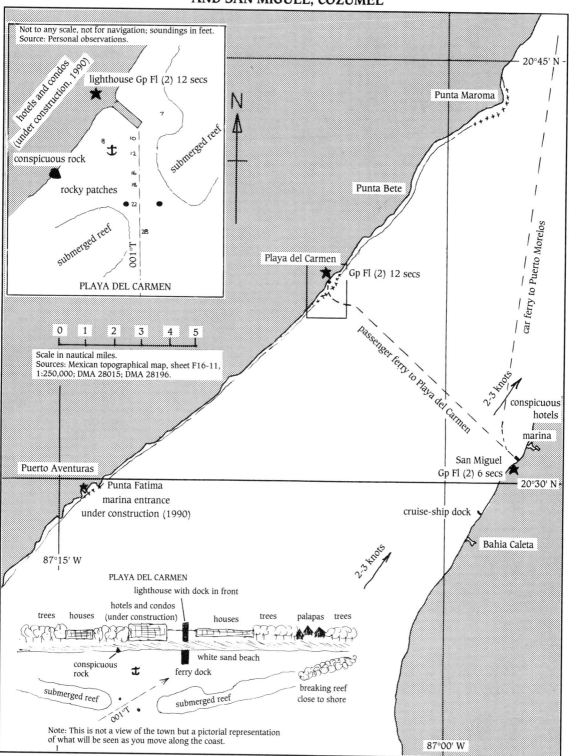

Not to any scale, not for navigation; soundings in feet.
Source: Personal observations.

hotels and condos (under construction, 1990)

lighthouse Gp Fl (2) 12 secs

conspicuous rock

rocky patches

submerged reef

submerged reef

001°T

PLAYA DEL CARMEN

N

Scale in nautical miles.
Sources: Mexican topographical map, sheet F16-11,
1:250,000; DMA 28015; DMA 28196.

0 1 2 3 4 5

Punta Maroma

20°45' N

Punta Bete

Playa del Carmen

Gp Fl (2) 12 secs

passenger ferry to Playa del Carmen

car ferry to Puerto Morelos

2-3 knots

conspicuous hotels

marina

San Miguel
Gp Fl (2) 6 secs

20°30' N

cruise-ship dock

Bahia Caleta

2-3 knots

Puerto Aventuras

Punta Fatima
marina entrance
under construction (1990)

87°15' W

PLAYA DEL CARMEN

lighthouse with dock in front

hotels and condos
(under construction)

trees houses   houses   trees palapas trees

conspicuous
rock

ferry dock

white sand beach

submerged reef

001°T

submerged reef

breaking reef
close to shore

Note: This is not a view of the town but a pictorial representation
of what will be seen as you move along the coast.

87°00' W

Mexico's Yucatán Coast   75

offshore breeze so allow adequate swinging room or use a running moor. Some swells and boat wakes are likely to come in over the reef, so this anchorage can be rolly, especially when the night breeze holds your boat broadside to the waves. Protection is adequate.

DINGHY DOCKING. There appears to be a dinghy dock on the main dock but *it not safe to use it* since one of the ferries ties up here. In heavy swells, there may be some breakers on the beach making it difficult to land.

CLEARANCE PROCEDURES. The port captain's office is at the head of the ferry dock but often he is not there. In any case, no one seems bothered about whether you clear or not.

PROVISIONS/FACILITIES. Playa del Carmen has a very picturesque beach with palm trees and beautiful clear water. The town has a considerable variety of shops including small tourist-oriented arts and crafts stores, boutiques, supermarkets (with mediocre stocks), and fresh-produce stands. There are many restaurants, a municipal market, banks, a post office (which will hold mail), an international phone (in the Hotel Molcas), and propane refills at the Super Plomeros. Allow several days for propane refills since the bottles are sent to Cancún. No water is available, and the only fuel is outside of town.

Playa del Carmen has a large bus terminal with excellent service all over the Yucatán. Cars can be rented in town. The nearest airport is at Cancún.

PUERTO AVENTURAS

Chart: Not shown on any chart; use BA 1220 or DMA 28015. Location approximately 20°29.5'N; 87°13.5'W.

Note: The marina monitors channel 70. No clearance procedures.

Puerto Aventuras is a multimillion-dollar resort development consisting principally of condominiums with associated facilities—swimming pools, bars, restaurants, tennis courts, an 18-hole golf course, an exercise center, and so on. The resort is being built around a large marina and numerous artificial canals. Two more marinas are planned. Everything is first class, with prices to match.

APPROACHES. The coastline is free of offlying dangers at this point. As you close the shore, you will see some moderately high-rise developments and, about a mile to the south of them, a light structure. Just south of the light is a bay that looks like it might be the marina but it is not. Do not try to enter here; it is shallow with coral. There is a substantial rock breakwater in front of the high rises. The marina is entered by the narrow channel that cuts through this wall.

The marina channel currently is marked by red (to starboard, when entering) and green structures, with one or two stakes along the western side. A lighthouse and various other lighted buoys and structures are planned for the near future. Enter on a course of almost due north (357°T), between the markers. Once you have identified the markers, the course is straightforward—clear up the center of the channel. In certain swell conditions, however, it can be hair-raising. The channel is narrow with least depths of 8 feet (dredging to 10 feet is planned). To starboard there is the rocky seawall; to port a reef awash. Problems arise if sizable swells are running. In such conditions the seawall sometimes causes the swells to hook around into the channel and break. Boats can broach and be driven either into the wall or onto the reef. If the swells are running, you must get the entry path absolutely clear in your mind while you are still a couple of hundred yards out. Then come in with sufficient speed to maintain steerage. If you follow these instructions, you should have no problems. Once inside, take the first left and moor up immediately on the left (there are one or two shoal areas a little farther in).

PROVISIONS/FACILITIES. The marina has water (albeit brackish tasting) and electricity (110 and 220 volts) available in all slips; fuel on the fuel dock; telephone and cable TV hook-ups; free ice; showers; a laundry; a couple of small supermarkets; and you may use the other resort facilities (swimming pool, golf course, etc.). Propane refills can be organized from Cancún. Security, even from hurricanes, is excellent with Cancún airport reasonably close by; this would be a good place to leave a boat.

PLAYA DEL CARMEN

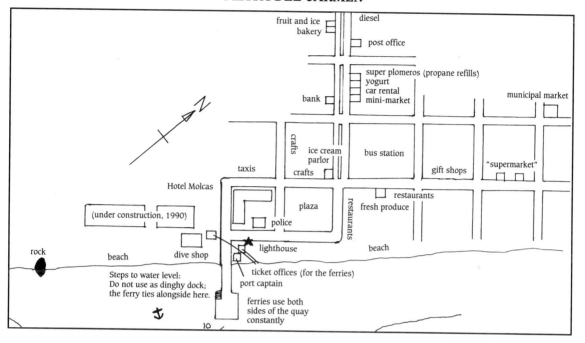

fruit and ice
bakery
diesel
post office

super plomeros (propane refills)
yogurt
car rental
mini-market
bank
municipal market

crafts
ice cream parlor
bus station
crafts
taxis
gift shops
"supermarket"

Hotel Molcas
restaurants
(under construction, 1990)
plaza
restaurants
fresh produce
police

rock
beach
dive shop
lighthouse
beach

Steps to water level:
Do not use as dinghy dock;
the ferry ties alongside here.
ticket offices (for the ferries)
port captain

ferries use both
sides of the quay
constantly

10

PUERTO AVENTURAS

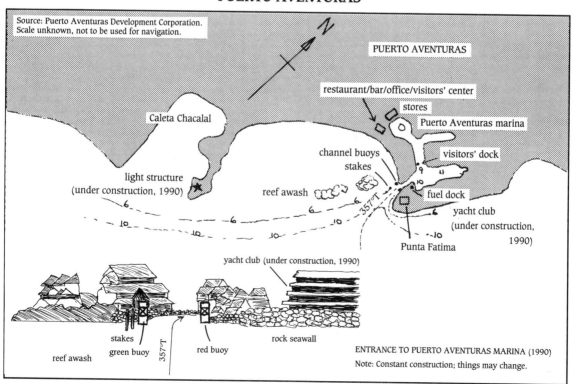

Source: Puerto Aventuras Development Corporation.
Scale unknown, not to be used for navigation.

PUERTO AVENTURAS

restaurant/bar/office/visitors' center
stores
Puerto Aventuras marina

Caleta Chacalal

channel buoys
stakes
visitors' dock

light structure
(under construction, 1990)
reef awash
fuel dock

6
yacht club
(under construction,
1990)
10
6
6
10
10
357°T
10
Punta Fatima

yacht club (under construction, 1990)

stakes
green buoy
357°T
red buoy
rock seawall

reef awash

ENTRANCE TO PUERTO AVENTURAS MARINA (1990)
Note: Constant construction; things may change.

A substantial yacht club was nearing completion in 1990. The beach is lovely with excellent snorkeling. You can charter dive and fishing boats out of the marina to take you to some of the best diving and fishing in the Caribbean. The resort has an interesting Museum of Nautical Archeology (established by CEDAM—a nonprofit diving organization). All in all, an impressive development with impressive prices.

ISLA COZUMEL

Chart: DMA 28196.

Note: Weather Information is found on VHF Channel 06, at 0930, 1300, and 2000 hours, local time.

Cozumel is Mexico's largest island, approximately 25 miles long and 10 miles wide. It is mostly low-lying and relatively featureless—not very interesting in fact—but the island is ringed by coral reef with some of the best diving in the Caribbean. Every year 150,000 scuba enthusiasts dive Palancar, its most famous reef. The entire western coast, out to the drop-off into the ocean depths, is a protected region in which it is illegal to fish or remove any marine life.

With the tourists have come tourist-oriented shops, restaurants, and hotels. San Miguel, the principal town, has numerous boutiques and small gift shops. It is also one of the few places on the Yucatán coast of Mexico with good-quality seafood restaurants. The prices match its popularity.

In normal trade wind conditions, the entire western coast affords adequate protection where the bottom conditions permit anchoring. Depending on the direction of the prevailing swells, the northern or southern end of the island is likely to prove uncomfortably rolly. There is little protection from northers and no protection at all on the eastern shore.

San Miguel is where the ferry boats dock and where it is necessary to clear in and out. From San Miguel to San Francisco beach (Punta Piedras), the shoreline is low-lying, rocky, and uninteresting, with sporadic construction. The water is deep and there are no offlying dangers. From Piedras southward for 3 miles are attractive sandy beaches—the Playa San Francisco—with reasonable depths for anchoring close inshore. Just south of Punta Piedras you can almost run up on the beach; as you come in, the water shoals to 10 to 12 feet some way out and then becomes deeper once again (16 to 20 feet) until close to the beach. The bottom consists of sandy patches over rock with isolated coral heads—pick a spot free of coral—and the holding is not particularly good. Snorkeling is good about one-quarter mile southwest of Punta Piedras. Playa Palancar is south of Playa San Francisco, with a beach enclosed by the most famous reef on Cozumel. No anchorage exists off this beach because of the reef, which drops off precipitously on its outer edge. To snorkel or dive this reef, you have to visit by dinghy. South of Palancar, reef areas extend up to one-half mile offshore, and the swells are likely to be hooking around the southern end of the island. We have been told there is an anchorage off the light at the southern tip of Cozumel, but have not been there in calm conditions to check it out.

APPROACHES. There are no offlying dangers, but as you approach San Miguel, you have to allow for the Yucatán Current, which runs northward just off the coast, generally at 2 to 3 knots. The hotels at the northern end of the island are visible 10 miles out.

ANCHORAGES. At San Miguel a conspicuous lighthouse (Gp Fl (2) 6 secs) stands toward the southern end of town. North of the light is a dock for the passenger ferries from Playa del Carmen. Anchor north of this dock in 15 to 20 feet of water. The holding is thin sand over rock, in which it took three attempts to set the CQR. The Danforth bit right away. Be sure to check the set of your anchor since the wind blows hard through here at times. This anchorage, an open roadstead, can be quite rolly and is wide open to northers. You can take your dinghy to the beach at the head of the ferry dock, choosing the most protected side to land in order to avoid the swells.

Club Nautico marina entrance is a mile north of San Miguel and looks like a break in a wall with a lighted steel post on either side (green to port, red to starboard, when entering). Inside you probably will be able to see plenty of sportfishing boats. The entrance is narrow but not difficult—stay in mid-chan-

SAN MIGUEL, COZUMEL

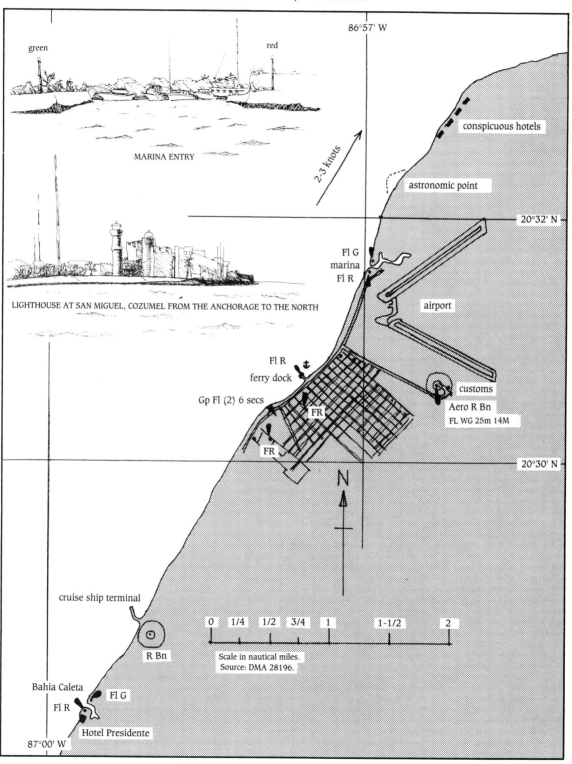

86°57' W

green

red

MARINA ENTRY

2-3 knots

conspicuous hotels

astronomic point

20°32' N

Fl G
marina
Fl R

airport

LIGHTHOUSE AT SAN MIGUEL, COZUMEL FROM THE ANCHORAGE TO THE NORTH

Fl R
ferry dock

Gp Fl (2) 6 secs

FR

customs

Aero R Bn
FL WG 25m 14M

FR

20°30' N

N

cruise ship terminal

R Bn

0   1/4   1/2   3/4   1   1-1/2   2

Scale in nautical miles.
Source: DMA 28196.

Bahia Caleta

Fl G

Fl R

Hotel Presidente

87°00' W

SAN MIGUEL

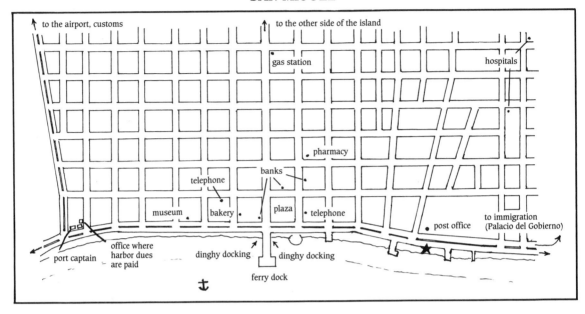

nel and make whatever allowance is necessary for the current. Protection is good, though it is surprising how deflected swells sometimes run up into the inlet. The marina is often crowded and maneuvering space somewhat limited. Berthing is expensive, especially during the sportfishing season, which runs from March through June, and the facilities are

BAHIA CALETA

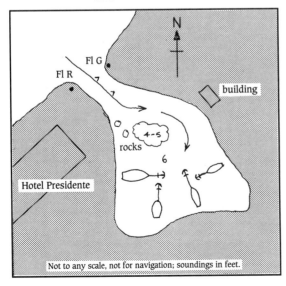

Not to any scale, not for navigation; soundings in feet.

somewhat rundown. Water is available at the fuel dock, and electricity in all the slips.

Bahia Caleta, the only natural harbor on the island, is 3 miles south of San Miguel. It has a narrow inlet opening into a small lagoon, which offers excellent protection. Immediately south of the Bahia Caleta is the Hotel Presidente, a conspicuous landmark. The entrance to the bay is marked by lighted pylons. A maximum of 7 feet can be carried inside, if you stay in the center of the channel. The channel has a sandy bottom but is narrow with numerous rocks on either side—take it slowly and maintain a bow lookout (I do not recommend entering if there are heavy swells running). Once inside you must hook to the north to avoid a large rock with 4 to 5 feet over it; the bay then opens up. Bahia Caleta is generally crowded with local boats and sportfishermen so there may be no spot to moor up. Before visiting you should call the Hotel Presidente and check on the availability of space (tel: 2-03-22).

CLEARANCE PROCEDURES. The officials at San Miguel are extremely bureaucratic and one or two are given to extracting bribes (*mordida*). The various offices are widely scattered and sometimes unoccupied, necessitating more than one visit. It can take hours, even days, of frustrating foot-slogging, or expensive taxi rides, to clear in and out. Unless you particularly want to visit Cozumel, I recommend you seriously think about forgoing the island—it offers nothing that can't be found elsewhere.

There are two simple ways to clear. One is to find an "agent"—if you anchor off San Miguel and then dinghy ashore you almost certainly will be approached by more than one as soon as you set foot ashore. The other is to book into the marina for a night and let the yacht club agent deal with the formalities. The cost will vary from a low of $25 to as high as $90, depending upon whom you get and what kind of a deal you strike.

To clear in you first must go to the port captain's office—a white house with arches, which is on the waterfront north of the passenger ferry dock (see the map)—with your last zarpe and seven new copies of your crew list. You will be sent next door to pay your port dues (which, strictly speaking, should not be levied if you have already paid elsewhere), and then to the customs office, which is at the airport a good mile away, to have the crew lists stamped and signed. From there you go to the immigration office with your passports (and tourist cards if you have already entered elsewhere—once again, strictly speaking, this visit should not be necessary) to have the crew lists stamped and signed. Immigration is downtown past the lighthouse in a white government-style building (the Palacio de Gobierno) on the left-hand side of the street as you head out of town. From immigration you return to the port captain's office.

To clear out you take seven copies of a new crew list to the immigration office for stamping and signing, together with passports and tourist cards. Then proceed to the customs office at the airport, where you must not only have the crew lists stamped and signed but also obtain a *solvencia aduanal* (customs clearance) for which officials probably will try to extract a bribe. Finally you go to the port captain's office for a new zarpe.

PROVISIONS/FACILITIES. San Miguel is a major tourist city and has all the facilities you would expect—bars, restaurants, hotels, nightclubs, international phones, banks, grocery stores, fresh produce, and so on. An excellent museum is located on the seafront close to the ferry dock (see the map).

TULUM

Charts: BA 1220; DMA 28015. On DMA 28015 the lighthouse is shown (approximately 20°12.0'N; 87°26.7'W) but with no name (the charted light position is about a mile out). Just north of the light, the chart contains the notation: "Tower (ruins)." Tulum is named on DMA chart 411 (The Gulf of Mexico, scale 1:2,160,000).

Note: No clearance procedures.

Tulum was the only known Mayan seaport and has impressive ruins perched on top of a cliff. South of the ruins, the reef encloses a stretch of coastline providing reasonable protection. Entry to the anchorage is via a break in the reef.

APPROACHES. When approached **from the north or the west**, the ruins stand out as a square mass in a small indentation in an otherwise low-lying and featureless coastline; **from the south**, the white lighthouse on top of a low cliff is clearly visible. The passage through the reef is about 1 1/2 miles south of the lighthouse, perhaps as much as 2 miles. Moving south from the lighthouse, you will see two groups of palapas on the beach separated by scrubby vegetation. Beyond them a sandy bluff is followed by a stand of coconuts, In 1990, this stand could be differentiated in that most of the trees still had their tops while the surrounding palms had been decapitated by disease; this may no longer hold true. South of these coconuts the rocky shoreline is indented by a small bay. The bay opposes the break in the reef. From offshore, outside the cut, a tall, straggly tree is visible behind the healthy coconut stand—it is conspicuous not so much for its size, but because it is a different species (an Australian pine, I was told). Entry is made on a heading of 312°T for this tree.

As you close the reef, beware a flat-topped rock that looks like the top of a pillar; it is barely awash and you must leave it about 100 yards to port. When you are coming in, it is important to constantly check the bearing of the tree since the current may set you off. Once inside you must hook around to the north behind the reef.

We have made this entrance in rough seas with swells breaking in the pass, causing momentary

TULUM

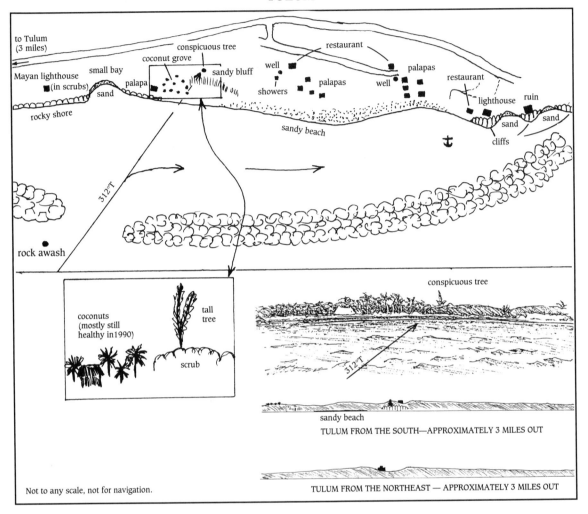

coconuts
(mostly still
healthy in1990)

tall
tree

scrub

Not to any scale, not for navigation.

conspicuous tree

312°T

sandy beach

TULUM FROM THE SOUTH—APPROXIMATELY 3 MILES OUT

TULUM FROM THE NORTHEAST — APPROXIMATELY 3 MILES OUT

surfing. It is essential in such conditions to keep your stern square to the breakers and to keep up sufficient speed to maintain steerage. If not, you risk a broach. Once committed, there is no turning back so you must be absolutely certain you are in the right place!

ANCHORAGE. The anchorage is off the beach, south of the lighthouse. The holding is poor—thin sand over rock—and try as we might we could not get a CQR to set, although Peter Hancock did finally manage to set his. Our Danforths, however, bit well. Although the protection is generally good, even during northers, if heavy seas are running outside the reef, the residual swells enter the anchorage

making it quite uncomfortable. The trade winds also whistle through the rigging, so make sure your anchors are well set. Other boats have reported isolated coral heads in this anchorage, so you should check your swinging room, or lie to a running moor.

PROVISIONS/FACILITIES. In heavy swell conditions there may be a moderate surf, making it difficult to dinghy to the lovely beach and three somewhat primitive restaurants. The palapas are rented out to tourists (no Indians live here). Drinking water can be drawn from a couple of wells, but otherwise there are no facilities. The town of Tulum, which has limited groceries and a gas station, lies 3 miles to the south. You can usually catch a taxi.

Drawing water in Tulum.

THINGS TO DO. The major attraction is the ruins, a short walk away. A trail, leading up past the back of the restaurant that overlooks the anchorage, links up with a road about one-quarter mile inland. Turn right on this road and the ruins are about one-half mile ahead. They are not as grandiose or spectacular as those at Chichén Itzá and Uxmal but nevertheless impressive. These ruins are lent a special charm by their cliff-top location, overlooking the crystal clear, blue waters of the Caribbean. Definitely a recommended stop.

BAHIA DE LA ASCENSION

Charts: BA 1220; DMA 28015.
  Note: No clearance procedures.

The Bahia de la Ascension is a large bay approximately 30 miles south of Tulum. The barrier reef stretches across much of its mouth, but with a substantial break that allows access. Inside are sev-eral small islands, the most notable being the Culebra Cays. The bay is sparsely inhabited with a small fishing settlement near Punta Allen on the north side. The waters are teeming with fish and lobster. The fishermen set large concrete doors on blocks on the bottom. The lobster hide under these doors, which the fishermen then flip over so they can grab lobsters by the handful!

APPROACHES. White sandy beaches both to the north (around Punta Soliman) and the south (Punta Pajaros) can be seen from offshore. The white lighthouse on Punta Allen (Gp Fl (4) 14 secs) is also conspicuous. As you close the bay, the Culebra Cays become clearly visible in the center.

Hart and Hayes (*A Cruising Guide to the Caribbean*) locate a position bearing 286°T on Punta Allen and 244°T on the northernmost shoulder of the Culebra Cays, and then come in on a westerly heading, "but beware a dangerous rock about 1.5 cables southwest of the drying reef to starboard of the entrance."

We followed the same course. Coming from the

BAHIA DE LA ASCENSION

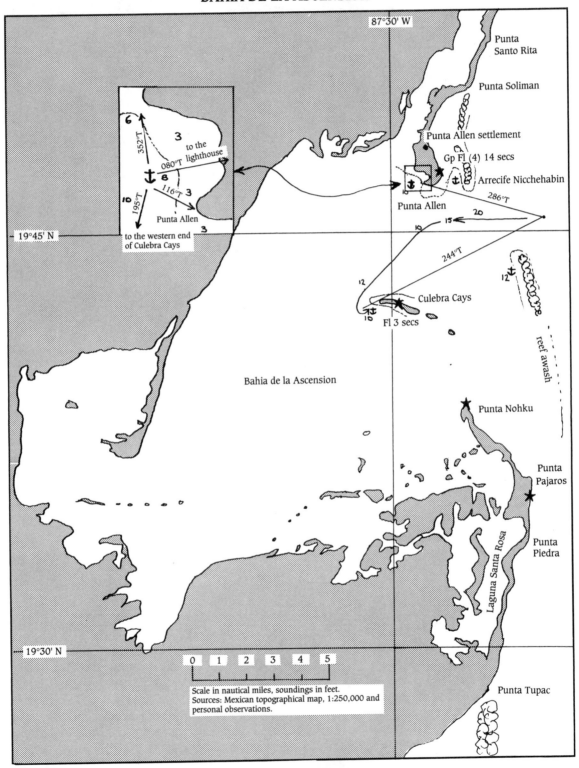

Scale in nautical miles, soundings in feet.
Sources: Mexican topographical map, 1:250,000 and
personal observations.

A mangrove from the Bahia de la Ascension.

north, it is safe to come farther inshore than indicated, which helps in identifying the Culebra Cays, but from the south it is as well to stay offshore since the reef comes out quite a way. We found no depth shallower than 12 feet coming through the reef. We never did see the rock, though we did find shoal patches up toward Punta Allen, and I have no doubt the rock is there.

ANCHORAGES. Once south of Punta Allen light, we made for a point one-quarter mile or so north of the Culebra Cays, swinging around a shoal that extends 200 yards northwest of the cays. We anchored behind the shoal off a lovely little beach on the northern end of the cays—coconut trees and much bird life (from the boat we saw great blue herons, white ibis, kingfishers, terns, ospreys, hawks, boat-tailed grackles, white herons, cormorants, and plovers!). The no-see-ums were irksome on the beach, but not a problem on the boat. Least depths were 10 feet; holding was good in a sandy bottom; the protection, excellent. In the evenings the fish were jumping all around—we caught some barra-

cuda by trolling with a spoon. An uninhabited lighthouse (Fl (3) secs) is in the center of the island. It was working in 1990. (Note: Its position is on the northernmost Culebra Cay as opposed to farther south, as shown on the charts.)

Protected anchorages also can be found behind the breaking reefs on either side of the bay's entrance, and in the lee of Punta Allen, as shown on the sketch chart. In the latter case, take care to avoid various shoals.

BAHIA DEL ESPIRITU SANTO

Charts: BA 1220; DMA 28015.
Note: No clearance procedures.

Bahia del Espiritu Santo is another large bay 20 miles or so south of the Bahia de la Ascension. It too has a barrier reef with an almost 2-mile–wide break giving access to the bay and sheltered anchorages behind the reef. Inside the bay is an island—Isla

BAHIA DEL ESPIRITU SANTO

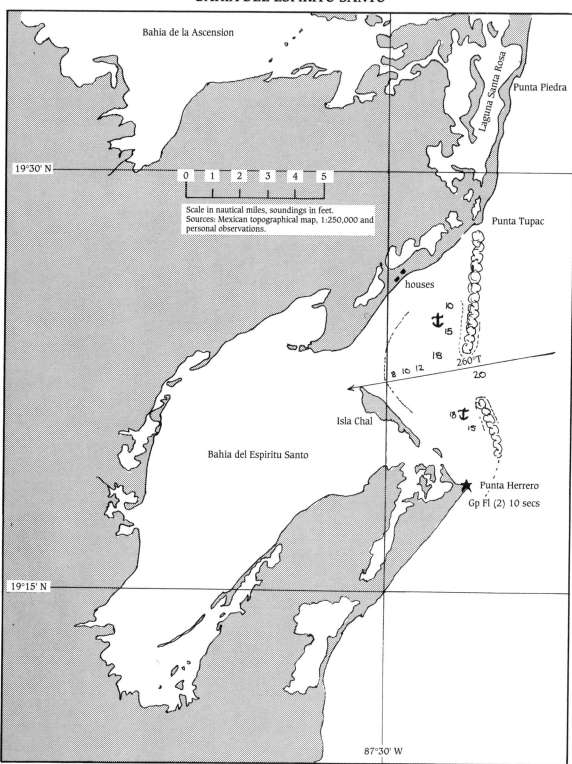

Bahia de la Ascension

Laguna Santa Rosa

Punta Piedra

19°30' N

0 1 2 3 4 5

Scale in nautical miles, soundings in feet.
Sources: Mexican topographical map, 1:250,000 and
personal observations.

Punta Tupac

houses

10

15

18

260°T

20

8 10 12

Isla Chal

18

15

Bahia del Espiritu Santo

Punta Herrero
Gp Fl (2) 10 secs

19°15' N

87°30' W

Chal—but it is not possible to carry 6 feet into its lee since a narrow shoal extends across the bay to the northeast side of the island.

APPROACHES. From the north, once clear of the reef off Punta Pajaros, stay outside of an imaginary line drawn between Punta Pajaros and Punta Herrero; this will keep you clear of all reefs north of the entrance to the bay. **From the south** sail a mile or so farther east to round the reef to the northeast of Punta Herrero. The break in the reef is wide with depths of 18 to 20 feet. Enter with the northern tip of Isla Chal (shown as Owen Island in Hart and Hayes) bearing *not less than* 260°T.

ANCHORAGE. Once inside, you can anchor behind the breaking reef either to the north or the south. You can come in quite close to the reef but will need to find a patch of sand in which to drop the hook. The holding is poor—thin sand over rock—a Danforth sets better than a CQR or Bruce. Excellent snorkeling, fish life, and lobsters.

CAYO NORTE

(BANCO CHINCHORRO)

(see maps pages 88/89)

Charts: BA 1220; DMA 28001 (old version).
Note: No clearance procedures.

Banco Chinchorro is a large, kidney-shaped reef, 25 miles long and 10 miles wide, lying 18 miles off the southern Mexican coast. The reef rises straight up from the depths of the ocean. Very strong currents affect this area, setting onto the reef's eastern side, which is a graveyard for many ships. Within the reef is a large, shallow, lagoon which the chart shows to have depths of $1^1/_2$ to 4 fathoms ($7^1/_2$ to 24 feet). However, after entering through a wide break in the reef at its northwest extremity, we were unable to find a passage for our 6-foot–draft boat around Cayo Norte into the rest of the lagoon.

Cayo Norte is uninhabited and rather desolate, covered in scrubby vegetation with a few coconuts. At its northern end is the ruin of an old lighthouse with a new lighthouse just to the south. The water shoals to a foot or less some way out from a sandy beach and you have to drag a dinghy in through eel grass. The anchorage is reasonably well protected and therefore offers a useful stopover if headed either north or south, but otherwise we found little of interest. I understand, however, that spectacular diving can be found along the reef.

There are other breaks in the reef, particularly in the south around Cayo Lobos, but we have not, as yet, had the opportunity to explore them.

The Mexican government has made Banco Chinchorro a national park: it is illegal to pick up or remove anything (shells, coral, fish, etc.). Gunboats patrol the reef to enforce the regulations.

APPROACHES. The Yucatán current sets strongly northward in the channel between the mainland and Banco Chinchorro. Allowance must be made when setting any course. The reef rises abruptly along its outer edge with no offlying dangers. The break in the reef is approached on a heading of anywhere from 125°T to 135°T on the new lighthouse.

When you enter, the southern end of the break in the reef is marked by a steel tank on the reef; the northern end is awash and is clearly visible. The gap is wide, with 10 to 20 feet of water, and appeared to be free of coral heads when we sailed up most of its length. We then came in on a heading of 130°T on the new lighthouse.

ANCHORAGE. The bottom shoals gradually and evenly. The 6-foot depth contour forms a wide arc around to the reef on both sides, and about a mile off Cayo Norte. Once inside the reef you can anchor just about anywhere—there are no coral heads in this area. Protection is good, but holding poor—thin sand over rock. If the wind is blowing hard from the east, a rough chop will build up, for the wind has a 2- to 3-mile fetch. In a norther you would need to move as far as you could into the lee of the reef.

XCALAK

(see maps pages 90/91)

Charts: BA 1220; DMA 28001 (old version). The light at Xcalak (approximately 18°16.3'N;

BANCO CHINCHORRO

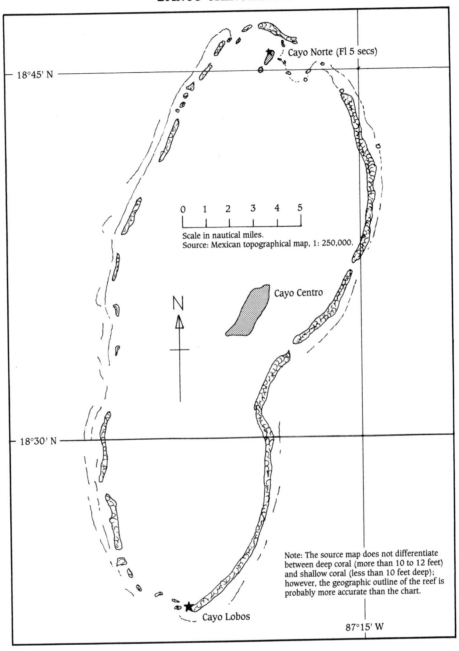

0 1 2 3 4 5

Scale in nautical miles.
Source: Mexican topographical map, 1: 250,000.

Cayo Norte (Fl 5 secs)

— 18°45' N

Cayo Centro

N

— 18°30' N

Note: The source map does not differentiate between deep coral (more than 10 to 12 feet) and shallow coral (less than 10 feet deep); however, the geographic outline of the reef is probably more accurate than the chart.

87°15' W

Cayo Lobos

CAYO NORTE, BANCO CHINCHORRO

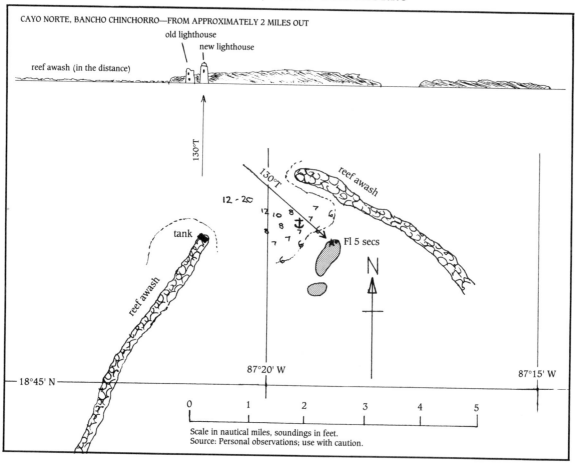

CAYO NORTE, BANCHO CHINCHORRO—FROM APPROXIMATELY 2 MILES OUT

old lighthouse

new lighthouse

reef awash (in the distance)

130°T

130°T

12 - 20

tank

reef awash

Fl 5 secs

N

reef awash

18°45' N

87°20' W

87°15' W

0   1   2   3   4   5

Scale in nautical miles, soundings in feet.
Source: Personal observations; use with caution.

87°50.2'W) is shown on DMA 28001, but not named.

Xcalak is the end of the line in Mexico, the last stop at the end of a dirt road. The town was once a flourishing center of coconut production and a resort for Mexicans, with a number of substantial two-story homes, bars, and restaurants. In the 1950s a hurricane wiped it out. No trace of its former glory exists. Today it is a sleepy little settlement with just a few hundred inhabitants and nothing much going on. We rather like its laid-back atmosphere. In particular, clearance procedures here are more relaxed than in any other port on this coast—this is definitely the place to clear out or in if you are headed out of, or into, Mexican waters.

APPROACHES.

From the North. The barrier reef runs all down this coast, sometimes converging with the shore, sometimes moving a mile or so out. Since there are no secure anchorages between here and Cayo Norte or the Bahia del Espiritu Santo, an overnight passage is almost certainly required, which means you must stay well off the coast to keep clear of the reef. On no account try to hug the reef at night since there are strong and unpredictable currents. You will find lighthouses at both Mahaqual (Fl (4) 20 secs) and north of Gavilan (Fl 5 secs), neither of which is shown on chart DMA 28001, although both are shown on BA 1220.

From the South, or Belize. The same considerations apply. The reef at times is a mile offshore. It is beset with strong and unpredictable currents. In

APPROACHES TO XCALAK

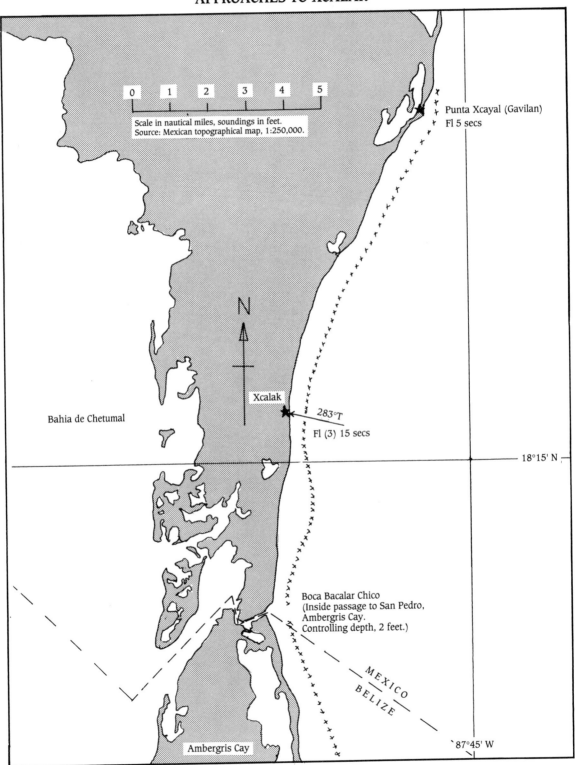

0　1　2　3　4　5

Scale in nautical miles, soundings in feet.
Source: Mexican topographical map, 1:250,000.

Punta Xcayal (Gavilan)
Fl 5 secs

N

Xcalak

Bahia de Chetumal

283°T

Fl (3) 15 secs

18°15' N

Boca Bacalar Chico
(Inside passage to San Pedro,
Ambergris Cay.
Controlling depth, 2 feet.)

MEXICO
BELIZE

87°45' W

Ambergris Cay

XCALAK

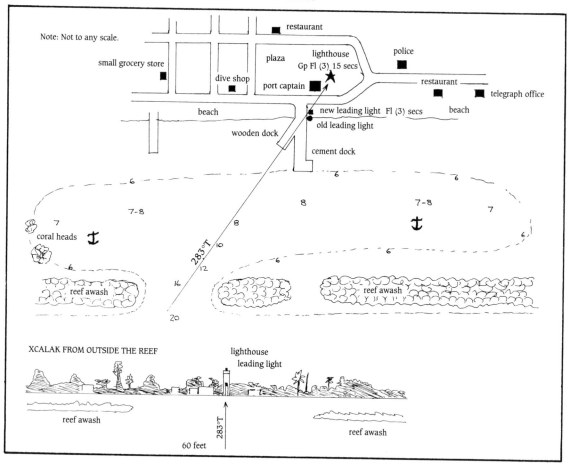

Note: Not to any scale.

small grocery store

dive shop

plaza

port captain

restaurant

lighthouse
Gp Fl (3) 15 secs

police

restaurant

telegraph office

beach

wooden dock

new leading light Fl (3) secs
old leading light

beach

cement dock

283°T

7-8

8

7-8

7

coral heads

reef awash

reef awash

XCALAK FROM OUTSIDE THE REEF

lighthouse
leading light

reef awash

283°T

reef awash

60 feet

---

particular, be sure to stand out far enough to clear Reef Point, 10 miles south of Xcalak (you will, in any case, want to stay offshore to work the favorable current).

The pass through the reef at Xcalak is narrow, but entry is easy since there is a leading light in front of the lighthouse. All you have to do is to keep the two structures exactly in line (283°T), in particular, do not stray to the south of the channel. There are actually two leading-light structures. Hurricane Gilbert wrecked the old one and another one to replace it was built right alongside. They are close enough together to appear more or less as one from offshore. As you come through the pass in the reef, you need to make allowance for the current (which may well be a countercurrent at this point). If it is rough you must keep up enough speed to maintain steerage and avoid broaching in the entrance. There

is 12 feet in the cut, and thereafter the bottom shoals steadily.

ANCHORAGE. There is no more than 6 feet of water at the very tip of the new (cement) dock, and only 3 feet on the old (wooden) dock. You can anchor either northeast or southeast of the docks in 7 to 8 feet. The holding is poor: thin sand over rock, with some eel grass. You will want to get far enough north or south of the break in the reef to avoid the swells that roll through, especially since the current is likely to hold you at least partially broadside to the waves. To the north, however, the bottom shoals to less than 6 feet within one-half mile and, to the south, there are coral heads almost breaking the surface less than one-half mile from the entrance.

DINGHY DOCKING. Take the dinghy to the lee-ward side of either dock.

CLEARANCE PROCEDURES. The port captain's office is at the head of the dock. The procedures are very relaxed. The port captain—Jorgé, who speaks English—will type the necessary documents at no charge. You should also check in at the police station (see the map).

PROVISIONS/FACILITIES. A surprising number of people speak English, owing to the presence of Belize just to the south. A couple of restaurants and a small grocery store, supplemented by a visiting vegetable truck from time to time, are about all there are in the way of supplies. There are no phones, but there is a telegraph office (the operator had never heard of England!). Two dive shops are intermittently open. A bus leaves once a day for Chetumal, but you won't be able to get back the same day.

Belize

The Belizean coastline stretches for approximately 120 miles south-southwest from the Mexican border. The barrier reef, which hugs the mainland throughout Mexico, maintains a north-south axis, steadily diverging from the coast until, at the Gladden Entrance, it is 25 miles from Placencia. South of Gladden Entrance, the reef hooks to the south-southwest, paralleling the coastline. The reef ends at the Sapodilla Cays, leaving a 20-mile–wide stretch of open water between it and Honduras.

The coastal regions of mainland Belize are generally low-lying, swampy, and uninviting, with only a few good anchorages. Toward the south, the Cockscomb and Maya Mountains rise in the distance. The settlements—Corozal, Belize City, Dangriga, Placencia, Monkey River, and Punta Gorda—are few and far between with limited facilities. Outside these towns the country is sparsely inhabited: Total population is less than 180,000, almost one-third of which lives in Belize City. A paved road leads westward from this city to Belmopan, the new capital established after Hurricane Hattie caused extensive damage to Belize City in 1961. From Belmopan the road continues to the border with Guatemala. The highway to the north is also paved, but the one to the south deteriorates before Dangriga. It is possible to sail from Dangriga to Belize City in little more time than the bus takes! If it is fancy restaurants and chic tourist shops you are looking for, you are in the wrong country.

A quiet anchorage off West Snake Cay.

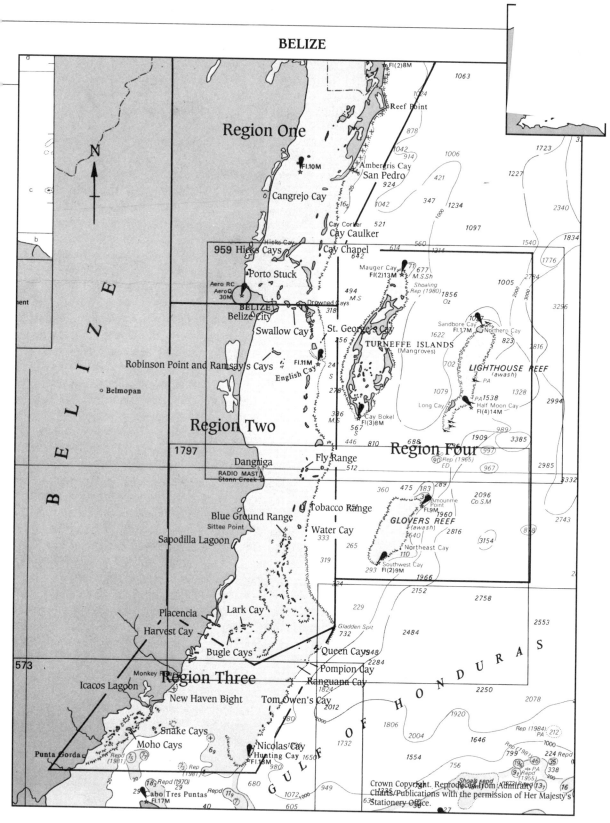

Region One

N

1063

Fl(2)8M

1024

Reef Point

878

1042 *914*

1006

1723

Ambergris Cay

San Pedro

924

421

1227

2340

Cangrejo Cay

16₉

347 *1234*

1042

521

1000

1097

Cay Corker

Cay Caulker

1540

1834

959 Hicks Cays

Hicks Cay

Cay Chapel

614 *560* *1214*

642

Porto Stuck

Mauger Cay 71 677
Fl(2)13M M.S.Sh

1776

1005

2784

Aero RC
Aero Q
30M

494
M.S

Shoaling
Rep (1980)

1856
Oz

1622

3000

3296

BELIZE
Belize City

Drowned Cays

318

Sandbore Cay 1017
Fl.1.7M Northern Cay

823

2816

Swallow Cay

St. George's Cay

156

TURNEFFE ISLANDS
(Mangroves)

702

LIGHTHOUSE REEF
(awash)

Robinson Point and Ramsay's Cays

Fl.11M

24
S

278

PA

Belmopan

English Cay

Long Cay

1079

PA 1538
Half Moon Cay
Fl(4)14M

1328

2994

Region Two

386
M.S

Cay Bokel
Fl(3)8M

567
S

1909

989

3385

446 *810*

688

997

1797

Dangriga

Fly Range

512

90 Rep (1965)
ED

967

2985

RADIO MAST
Stann Creek

Region Four

3332

360 *475* *183*
3₆

289

Blue Ground Range

Tobacco Range

Amounme
Point
Fl9M

2096
Co.S.M

2743

Sittee Point

Water Cay

1960

GLOVERS REEF
(awash)

638

Sapodilla Lagoon

333

265

640

2816

3154

319

Northeast Cay

110

Lark Cay

Southwest Cay
Fl(2)9M

293

1966

24

2152

2758

2553

Placencia

229

Harvest Cay

Gladden Spit

732

2484

2250

2078

573

Bugle Cays

Queen Cays

48

2284

Icacos Lagoon

Monkey R

Region Three

Pompion Cay

Ranguana Cay

1824

GULF OF HONDURAS

New Haven Bight

Tom Owen's Cay

2012

980

2000

1806

1920

Rep (1984)
PA 212

Snake Cays

980

1732

2004

1646

1000

Moho Cays

6₉

Nicolas Cay
Hunting Cay
Fl.11.5M

1650

1554

799 Repd

756

35

Punta Gorda

Repd
(1981) 7₅ 7₇

7₃ Rep

980

19₅ PA *22₇*
9₁ Repd
(1955)

338
200

20

18₃ Repd (1970)
29

680

1072 *1000*

949

13₇

16

29

Cabo Tres Puntas
Fl.17M

Repd
(1981) 11₉
7

605

63₈

27

The Belizean reef is the major attraction for most cruisers. From north to south it is studded with dozens of little islands (*cays*—pronounced keys) with hundreds more just to the west in its lee. With the exception of San Pedro, a bustling tourist town on Ambergris Cay, the majority of cays are uninhabited. Here and there you find a primitive fishing community, while one or two cays are experiencing some low-level tourist development, but the cays have no infrastructure to support any extensive growth—they are likely to remain essentially unchanged for many years to come.

Most of the northern cays and those behind the reef are little more than clumps of mangroves, sometimes quite dense, rooted to coral outcrops. The cays on the reef are coconut-clad, sandy islets increasing in beauty as you move south to the crown jewels—the Queen Cays, Pompion Cay, Ranguana Cay, Tom Owen's Cay, Nicolas Cay, and Hunting Cay—each one a pearl set in crystal-clear azure water and surrounded by some of the finest snorkeling and diving in the Caribbean.

Between the reef and the mainland lies the Inner Channel. The trade winds blow across the reef from the east but little wave action develops. The sailing conditions could not be more perfect—you will experience some of the most exhilarating reaching of your life. The West Indies has no equal to this, with the possible exception of the Sir Francis Drake Channel in the Virgin Islands.

Just east of the barrier reef, rising from the depths of the ocean, lie Turneffe Island, Glover's Reef, and Lighthouse Reef. Turneffe is mostly mangroves, but Glover's and Lighthouse are classic, South Pacific–type coral atolls—protected lagoons inside a ring of coral with coconut-clad sandy islets clinging to the rim. The diving on all three is reported as spectacular. Turneffe is also one of the principal remaining habitats for the American crocodile, and Half Moon Cay (a wildlife sanctuary on Lighthouse Reef) is a major nesting ground for the endangered booby.

Ecologically Belize is one of the most important countries in Central America. Though small, it contains key habitats for a number of endangered species. As well as the crocodiles, its waters are home to three turtle species—the Hawksbill, Green, and Leatherback—and also a sizable population of manatees. Ashore the low population density has helped the jaguar to survive.

Various government and international organizations are making considerable efforts to protect these and other species, and to promote environmentally sensitive tourism as an economic alternative to slash-and-burn agriculture and other destructive fishing and farming practices. The world's first jaguar preserve has been established in the Cockscomb Mountains in southern Belize. Ocelots and margays (two smaller members of the cat family) are also found in this region along with Baird's tapirs and scarlet macaws—all endangered. In the north the Community Baboon Sanctuary protects the howler monkey, while the nearby Crooked Tree Wildlife Sanctuary—a network of inland lagoons, swamps, and waterways—is home to many, many species of birds (Belize has more than 500) as well as howler monkeys, crocodiles, and turtles.

Numerous Mayan ruins are scattered throughout the interior. According to one estimate, at the height of the Mayan civilization one million Indians lived in the area now included in Belize. A few ruins are partially excavated but only one or two are accessible to tourists. The best known, Xunantunich, is close to the Guatemalan border in the Mountain Pine Ridge district and could, perhaps, be seen as part of an exploration of this region from San Ignacio (a "resort" town) on the way to Tikál (see page 184).

Jaguar.

NAVIGATIONAL AND
ANCHORAGE INFORMATION

The cays of Belize contain a multiplicity of anchorages and offer almost unlimited opportunities for gunkholing in mostly protected waters. It would take a large guidebook devoted solely to Belize to cover all these cays in detail; therefore I have limited myself to the principal anchorages and most attractive cays—there is still plenty of exploring left for those with adventurous spirits.

Only two anchorages (Moho Marina and Cay Chapel Marina) are really secure and accessible enough from the mainland to permit a cruiser to leave a boat for an extended trip ashore or to fly back home.

For anchoring overnight in settled trade-wind conditions, almost any section of reef to windward provides protection. In the winter months, however, you must always be on guard for northers, which can come down with almost no warning, blowing at 20 to 30 knots or more from the northwest, sometimes for several days at a stretch. They make most trade-wind anchorages uncomfortable and sometimes untenable. From November to April you should anchor with this possibility in mind, staying well off the reef, shore, or mangroves, or setting a running moor.

In the summer months, occasional violent winds out of the southwest (*biamas*) can strike with little warning (normally they are preceded by a glassy, breathless calm with a line of dark clouds advancing from the southwest) and then blow at up to 60 knots for an hour or two.

Most aids to navigation (channel markers and lights) are in place as shown on the charts, but many have changed light characteristics. The majority of the lights have been converted to solar power but without an understanding of the need for

(Continued on page 98)

Coral Reefs

Coral reefs, and the fishes found on them, are nature at its most flamboyant and spectacular. There is nothing in the animal or bird kingdoms that can compare to the riot of colors, shapes, and textures. The excitement of that first encounter with a dazzling school of fish in a gorgeous coral garden just cannot be described. I know of no one who has snorkeled a coral reef who has not been hooked for life.

Coral reefs fall into three broad categories: fringing, barrier, and atoll. The Northwest Caribbean has all three in abundance.

- Fringing reefs are composed of corals building out from the mainland coast itself. Much of the reef along the Caribbean coast of Mexico is of this type.
- A barrier reef lies several miles offshore, with a deep-water channel between itself and the mainland. Belize's barrier reef is the finest example in the Western Hemisphere.
- An atoll is a circular reef enclosing a lagoon. Atolls can form around the craters of submerged volcanoes (as in many cases in the South Pacific), or can occur as a result of a barrier reef around an island steadily building upward as the island within subsides, or the sea level rises—Lighthouse Reef, Glover's Reef, and Banco Chinchorro are all examples of the latter.

Living corals are composed of millions of tiny *polyps*, members of the same family as jellyfish and anemones. The polyps have a fringe of tentacles surrounding a digestive tract, which in turn is protected by a stony core. The core is composed of calcium carbonate extracted from the seawater. The tentacles strain nutrients from the water and catch tiny prey. Corals also harbor microscopic plant cells that are necessary for growth. These cells require light for photosynthesis. As a result, corals cannot survive at depths greater than 100 feet. New polyps grow (or "bud") from old ones, or from fertilized eggs which, if they survive, settle on rocks and begin a fresh colony.

The great reefs we see today are composed of countless billions of minute limestone skeletons, together with broken bits of coral, and other detritus, capped with living coral. The living corals are divided into two broad categories: (1) hard corals, such as elk, staghorn, sheet, star, pillar, and brain coral and (2) soft corals, such as sea fans and sponges. Both types occur in profusion in the Northwest Caribbean.

(Continued from page 97)
deep-cycle batteries. (The solar panel charges the battery daily while the light discharges it every night—the battery is cycled once a day.) As a result many of the batteries have failed and will not hold a charge, so that the lights work for an hour or two after a sunny day and then die.

Small-boat channels are often marked by stakes, but these are knocked down or washed away quite frequently. I mention any stakes we found in place, but by the time you get there they may have gone, or been moved. Do not trust blindly in such impermanent markers. There are many, many more stakes with no navigational significance whatsoever; these are used to mark the location of fish traps and lobster pots.

WEATHER INFORMATION

Weather and tides are given on Radio Belize, 830 kHz and 93 FM, after the 0700 (local time) news broadcast, at about 0710 hours, but sometimes as late as 0725. Other broadcasts during the day occur at 1230 hours on 830 kHz, and at 2100 hours on 93 FM. The tides are fairly regular with an ebb and flow every 6^1/$_2$ hours and a tidal range of a little over a foot. Tide times in the outer cays are obviously a little different from those at Belize City, but do not vary by more than an hour.

CLEARANCE PROCEDURES

You need to clear in within 24 hours of arriving in Belizean waters, and to clear out just before leaving. Once cleared in, you are free to sail anywhere without further procedures. Clearance procedures can be carried out only in San Pedro, Dangriga, Punta Gorda, or Belize City. The specific procedures are covered in the relevant sections below. I recommend avoiding Belize City since it is oriented toward big-ship traffic and the offices are far apart.

Region 1: San Pedro to Belize City

Passage can be made through the barrier reef at San Pedro, but between here and Belize City all the water inside the reef is relatively shoal. The controlling depth in this northern region is 6 feet 6 inches—and even a boat with this draft can expect to bump from time to time. If you draw more than 6 feet, you therefore are advised to enter or exit the reef through the big-ship channel at English Cay and to stay out of this area.

SAN PEDRO

Charts: Not shown on any chart; use charts BA 1220 and DMA 28001 (old version) or 28167 (new version). Location approximately 17°56'N; 87°57'W.

Note: Chart DMA 28001 does not show the barrier reef running south of Ambergris Cay to the east of Cay Caulker ("Corker" on the chart), Cay Chapel, and Long Cay down to the reef east of the Drowned Cays. This reef is almost continuous and is awash in most places.

San Pedro is an attractive little town with pretty beaches, coconut trees, clapboard houses, and an interesting mix of people. It is in a transitional stage, moving toward becoming a tourist mecca, but as yet is largely unspoiled and the pace of development is slow. There are no high-rises or paved streets. The people are friendly and, as elsewhere throughout the Northwest Caribbean, there is no hustling of visiting "yachties" (in contrast to most of the West Indies). You will find numerous pleasant restaurants (the best in all Belize) and tourist shops (in all likelihood the only ones in all Belize). One sight not to be missed is the sand barges—gaff-rigged sloops without motors—sailing in at hull speed, loaded to the gunwales, and luffing up alongside the town dock to unload (by hand, using shovels). The sand is used in new construction on the island.

APPROACHES. The reef runs in an almost unbroken line to both the north and the south between one-half mile and one mile off the coast of Ambergris Cay. San Pedro is the only settlement of any size along this coast and has several substantial buildings (two and three stories high) and a conspicuous radio mast. You should have no problems locating it. There are several small breaks in the reef off San Pedro with little to differentiate them. The navigable one is just to the south of the radio tower. It has 12 feet of water and is free of coral heads whereas the others contain dangerous heads. Until recently there was a substantial channel marker but it has gone. Currently (1990) a 4-foot–high stake with a red ball impaled on the top is set a little inside the entrance, but it is very difficult to see this stake from outside. The entry is not quite straightforward since there is a slight dogleg. On your first visit, unless the conditions are calm and the visibility good, it would be best to follow a guide-boat in. If you sail up and down outside the reef, someone will soon come out to lead you in. The reef is entered on a heading of 312°T for the stake with the red ball on top of it. Once inside the main reef, you come around to the north for the radio mast (357°T), leaving the stake to port.

When substantial swells are running onto the reef against a strong tidal current, conditions in the passage can be chaotic and rough, with a chance of broaching. (A friend of ours actually had his spreaders in the water and was very lucky not to be driven onto the inner section of the reef.) In these circumstances you would do better to enter farther south, either through the wide break south of St. George's Cay or through the main ship channel at English Cay (both are covered later).

ANCHORAGE. As soon as you are inside the reef, the bottom shoals to 7 to 8 feet. Thereafter it gradually shoals to 7 feet about 100 yards or so off the series of small wooden piers in front of the town.

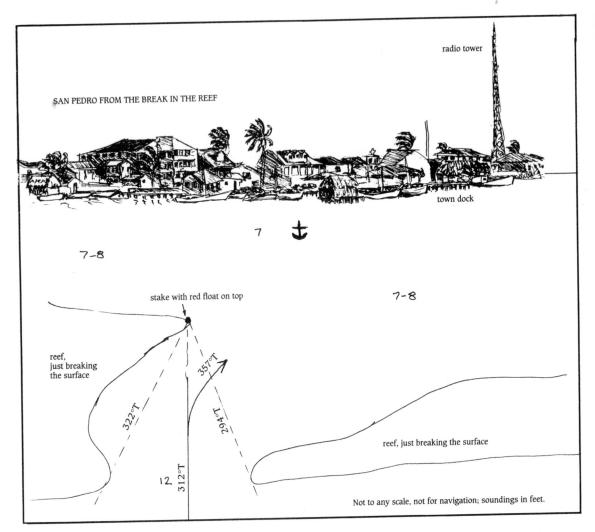

SAN PEDRO FROM THE BREAK IN THE REEF

radio tower

town dock

7

7-8

7-8

stake with red float on top

reef,
just breaking
the surface

357°T

322°T

294°T

12 312°T

reef, just breaking the surface

Not to any scale, not for navigation; soundings in feet.

The protection is adequate, even in a norther, but the holding is poor—thin sand over rock. You probably need two anchors, with Danforth-types setting the best.

DINGHY DOCKING. You can use many of the piers or run up onto the beach, but stay away from the town dock since this has a lot of traffic.

CLEARANCE PROCEDURES. San Pedro is not a port of entry. However, if you wish to clear in here, check in with the police (see the town map). They will telephone the customs office in Belize City so that you can arrange to fly an officer out for $60 ($30 U.S.—these are 1990 prices). This is the cost of the return airfare for the customs officer and does not represent any payment to the official.

The Belizeans are quite strict about clearance procedures: If you do not bring the officer to you, you will have to sail immediately to Belize City to clear in, without stopping at any of the cays en route. Clearance procedures in Belize City are a hassle due to distances between offices, and officials used to dealing with big ships, not small yachts. I consider it worthwhile to pay the extra money to clear in at San Pedro. If you enter with other boats, you can split the cost of the airfare. Try to get to the police station early in the day to give the customs officer plenty of time to fly in and return to Belize City the same day. Otherwise officials may attempt to charge you for an overnight stay in a hotel plus meals ($60 U.S.); you should strongly resist this.

The local health officials also will want to inspect your boat. Their office is in the town hall

The Preservation of Coral Reefs

Coral is extremely delicate as well as vulnerable to bacterial and fungal infections. The slightest touch—or even sand stirred up by an anchor or snorkeler's flipper—can kill coral polyps. Coral is also extremely slow growing—in one unthinking moment we can do damage that will take years to repair.

In other areas of the Caribbean, an influx of pleasureboaters, snorkelers, and divers has spelled death for many a formerly beautiful reef. All of us have a responsibility to see that the same does not occur in the Northwest Caribbean. The following are a few of the more obvious measures that can be easily taken to protect coral reefs:

- Do not anchor on coral.
- Do not throw trash overboard in the area of coral reefs.
- Do not touch coral.
- Never take living samples from a coral reef. Out of water they will in any case soon fade to a dull white, and you will find plenty of this dead coral on beaches wherever you go.
- Avoid stirring up sand around coral.
- Spearfishing is banned on many reefs. Where permitted, generally only Hawaiian slings are allowed (this is the kind of spear gun fired by a large rubber band).

More general measures for the preservation of coral reefs include pressure on governments to clean up their act by reducing effluent and industrial waste discharges into the oceans of the world; to ban the manufacture and export of items made from coral; to regulate fishing and lobstering on reefs; to establish more marine parks; and to continue to educate the public on the importance of, and care of, coral reefs.

---

above the police station. They are likely to require a list of all the groceries on board (dried, canned, frozen, and fresh).

To clear out, if you are headed north to Mexico, it is probably more convenient to fly the customs officer to San Pedro rather than sail to Belize City to check out.

Belizean officials have an abrupt, seemingly rude manner, which has upset visiting sailors. In general, however, they have no intention of being rude—in fact, we found officials everywhere (with the exception of the police on Cay Caulker, discussed later) to be courteous and correct. Their abruptness is something of a national mannerism. If you observe men talking to each other in the street, you will notice the same pattern of behavior, so do not take offence! Officers of the Belize Defense Force are the only officers of any nationality (including the U.S. Coast Guard) who have ever asked Peter Hancock or ourselves formal permission before stepping aboard.

PROVISIONS/FACILITIES. The town map indicates most of the services available. You can get water, which you have to haul in jerry cans, from a faucet outside the police station. There are two hardware stores in town. The post office will hold mail. The airport has regular flights to and from Belize City. Out toward the airport is a clinic and Jack's Propeller Shop where you can get all kinds of welding done. (Another welder lives on the north end of town.)

SAN PEDRO, AMBERGRIS CAY

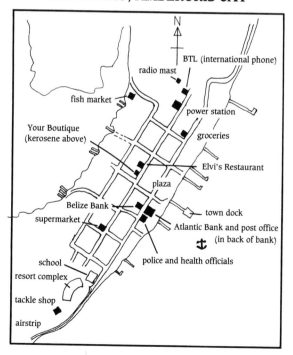

N

- BTL (international phone)
- radio mast
- fish market
- power station
- Your Boutique (kerosene above)
- groceries
- Elvi's Restaurant
- plaza
- Belize Bank
- town dock
- supermarket
- Atlantic Bank and post office (in back of bank)
- police and health officials
- school
- resort complex
- tackle shop
- airstrip

SAN PEDRO TO CAY CAULKER

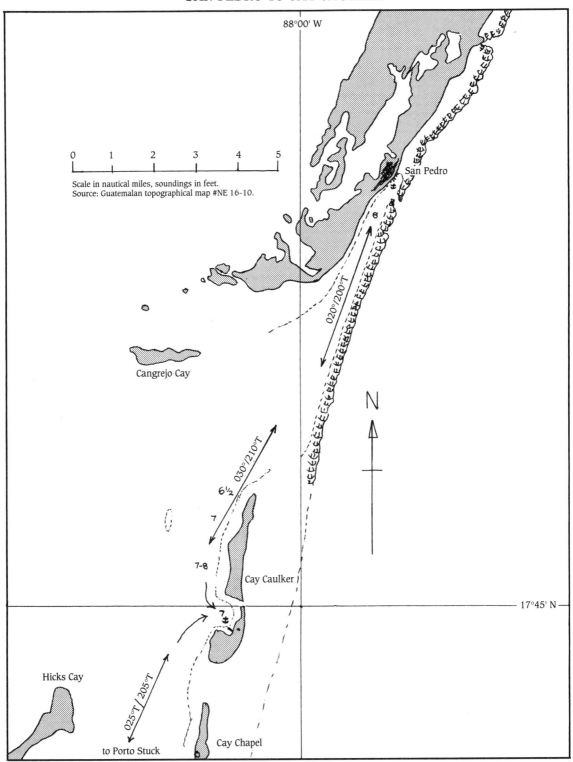

88°00' W

0   1   2   3   4   5

Scale in nautical miles, soundings in feet.
Source: Guatemalan topographical map #NE 16-10.

San Pedro

020°/200°T

Cangrejo Cay

N

030°/210°T

6½

7

7-8

7

Cay Caulker

17°45' N

Hicks Cay

025°T / 205°T

to Porto Stuck

Cay Chapel

Top left: *Guatemalan girl.* **Top right:** *Man in marketplace, Guatemala. The men from different villages also at times wear distinctive clothing — this man is from Nahuala.* **Bottom:** *Women of Santiago de Atitlan filling water jugs from Lake Atitlan. In the foreground are the prows of the dugout canoes used by the fishermen on the lake.*

Top left: Toucan, seen throughout inland areas of the Northwest Caribbean.
Top right: Scarlet macaw, also seen in many areas.
Bottom: Jungle tree at Tikál.

Top: *A primitive fishing settlement, reminiscent of those in the South Pacific, on Lower Monitor, one of the islands in the Cayos Cochinos.*
Bottom: *Beach scene in the Cayos Cochinos, a spectacularly beautiful group of islands off the coast of mainland Honduras.*

Top: A dugout canoe ("cayuco"), powered by an inboard diesel engine, runs through a mangrove-lined canal on Roatan, the principal island in the Bay Islands of Honduras. These canals link many of the settlements scattered along the north and south shores of the island.

Bottom: Sunset at Diamond Cay, a tiny coral islet southwest of Utila, itself the southwesternmost island in the Bay Islands.

Top: The Mayan temple of Tulum, looking south toward the anchorage. **Bottom:** Sand barges, San Pedro, Belize. All the sand used in construction on the island is shipped from the mainland in a fleet of these gaff-rigged sailing vessels. The sand barges, racing hull-down in a stiff trade wind, and then luffing up on the dock at the last minute, are a spectacular sight, clearly visible from the anchorage in front of the town.

Facing Page, Top:
Hunting Cay.
Bottom: View from the lighthouse on Hunting Cay, Belize, looking north toward Nicolas Cay.
This Page, Top: Typical West Indian-style house in Belize City with ornate gingerbread wood trim — a survivor from a more prosperous past.
Bottom: Flower ladies on the church steps, Chichicastenango, Guatemala. In the background a Mayan priest is letting off a mortar bomb to scare away evil spirits.

Top left: *A market scene in Guatemala's Central Highlands. The women from different villages weave and embroider their clothes to different patterns. After a while you can tell the home town of a woman simply by the clothes she is wearing.* *Top right:* *Easter week in Antigua, Guatemala. These carpets ("alfambras"), laid on the bare cobblestones of the street, are made entirely of dyed sawdust. Each takes a full night of hard work by several families. In a short while they will be trampled to dust by thousands of feet in one of the many spectacular Easter processions that take place in this old colonial city.* *Bottom:* *One of the many Easter processions in Antigua, Guatemala.*

CAY CAULKER

CHARTS: BA 1220; DMA 28001 (old version) and 28167 (new version). DMA 28001 does not show the barrier reef to the east of Cay Caulker (spelled "Corker" on the chart).

Cay Caulker.

Cay Caulker, a sandy, coconut-clad island, is home to a mix of fishermen, tourists, and expatriate Americans. When compared with San Pedro, it seems to be a sleepy little town with just a couple of restaurants, bars, dive shops, and a tiny grocery store. Nevertheless Caulker is the most heavily populated cay from here southward and the last one to have any kind of groceries for sale, or even a bar.

A speedboat calls by at 0600 hours each morning to take people to Belize City. This trip takes about one hour and the cost (1990) is $12 (Belize) each way. The return trip is made in the early afternoon. This trip can be a convenient way to stock up on groceries and other supplies, since the anchorage off the Fort George Hotel in Belize City is uncomfortable most of the time.

While anchored off Cay Caulker, we were boarded after dark by armed plainclothes policemen, who pushed their way aboard after crashing their aluminum flatboat into our *Nada*. Since initially they did not show us any identification, they gave us quite a fright. They had with them another couple—liveaboards from the only other boat in the anchorage—whom they had quite arbitrarily ordered into their flatboat. After a fruitless search for drugs, they left, shortly afterward releasing the other couple. These Belizean officials were definitely rude!

APPROACHES.

From San Pedro. Hold a course of approximately 200°T southward, staying in the deeper water behind the reef to avoid the shoals off the southeast tip of Ambergris Cay. When abeam of Cangrejo Cay, come around to a heading of approximately 210°T to clear the northwestern tip of Cay Caulker by no more than 1/3 to 1/2 mile. This stretch is the controlling depth for this passage with 6 feet 6 inches of water. Follow the western coastline of Cay Caulker until the town dock becomes visible in the bay, then head for the dock.

From Porto Stuck. Head approximately 025°T to give the shoal water between Cay Chapel and Cay Caulker a wide berth—one-half mile or more—and then swing east into the bay on Cay Caulker.

ANCHORAGE. Anchor northwest of the dock in 7 to 8 feet of water, over eel grass with a sandy bottom. The holding is good once an anchor is set. This

CAY CAULKER

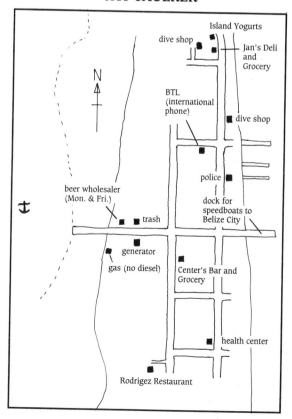

anchorage offers excellent protection in trade-wind conditions but is open to northers.

CAY CHAPEL

Charts: BA 959; DMA 28167. Note that pre–1990 BA 959 does not show Porto Stuck, the small-boat channel through Hicks Cays.

Cay Chapel is privately owned by the Pyramid Island Resort (P.O. Box 192, Cay Chapel, Belize, Central America. Tel: 44-409), which also owns the hotel and landing strip on the island. The bar and restaurant are open to visiting sailors, but make reservations for meals (VHF channel 68).

A marina has been scooped out of the west side of the cay. This is the best place in Belize to leave a boat unattended for any length of time. The protection is excellent and security very good. All the slips have 110/220 VAC power and water. There is a fuel dock. The marina manager, "Smitty," monitors channel 68. A speedboat runs to Belize City and back daily. Alternatively you can fly into Belize airport on the hotel's plane.

APPROACHES. From Cay Caulker, follow the

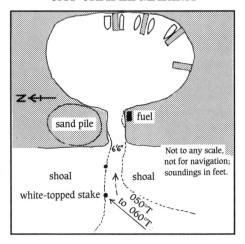

CAY CHAPEL MARINA

sand pile

fuel

6'6"

shoal

shoal

white-topped stake

Not to any scale, not for navigation; soundings in feet.

050°T to 060°T

coastline south, staying one-half mile off to avoid shoals between Cay Caulker and Cay Chapel, and shoals off the coast of Cay Chapel. **From Porto Stuck** head 040°T.

The entrance to the marina can be seen from miles away since there is a large spoil-heap of white sand on the north side of the channel. There are shoals one-quarter mile offshore; the narrow channel, which is marked with a couple of stakes, has

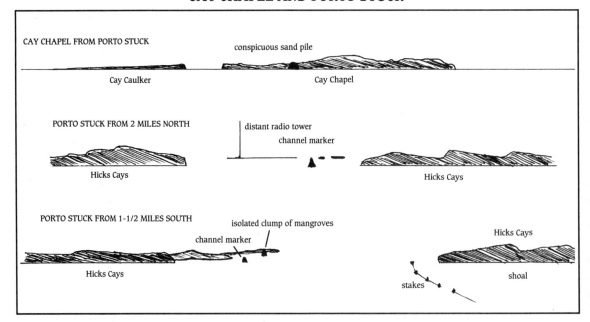

CAY CHAPEL AND PORTO STUCK

CAY CHAPEL FROM PORTO STUCK

conspicuous sand pile

Cay Caulker

Cay Chapel

PORTO STUCK FROM 2 MILES NORTH

distant radio tower

channel marker

Hicks Cays

Hicks Cays

PORTO STUCK FROM 1-1/2 MILES SOUTH

isolated clump of mangroves

channel marker

Hicks Cays

Hicks Cays

Hicks Cays

stakes

shoal

just 6 feet 6 inches of water. From one-half mile out approach is made on a heading of 050°T to 060°T on the outer (white-topped) stake; both stakes are then left immediately to port.

PORTO STUCK

Charts: BA 959; DMA 28167. Note that pre–1990 BA 959 does not show Porto Stuck.

Years ago the Porto Stuck channel was blasted straight through Hicks Cays by a hurricane. It provides waterborne access inside the reef between Belize City and the northern cays and is relatively busy with small-boat traffic. The controlling depth in the cut is 10 feet, although no more than 6 feet 6 inches can be carried through to the north and south.

APPROACHES.
From the North. Once you are clear of the bay at Cay Caulker head 205°T, or 220°T when clear of the marina at Cay Chapel. From about 2 miles out Porto Stuck appears much as in the sketch. The channel marker is, in fact, a tripod with a light. Head for this and then leave it about two boat lengths off the starboard bow, coming around onto a heading of 183°T. Keep the line of stakes just to port as you head south.
From the South. The two approaches are from the Swallow Cay Bogue channel and St. George's Cay. From Swallow Cay Bogue channel an appropriate course would be 012°T; from just off the southwest tip of St. George's Cay steer 345°T. At about 1½ miles out Porto Stuck will appear much as in the sketch. When passing through your heading will be approximately 003°T, with the line of stakes just to starboard and the tripod at the north end of the channel passing to port.

ST. GEORGE'S CAY

Charts: BA 959; DMA 28167.

Tiny St. George's Cay was the capital of the Brit-

ish settlement in Belize from 1650 to 1784, and the site of a 1798 naval engagement with the Spanish, in which the Spanish retreated. This is regarded in Belizean history as a great naval victory and celebrated with a public holiday on September 10. The island consists of little more than a string of well-kept, substantial, private homes and a rest and recreation center for British troops stationed in Belize. (These troops have been present since 1981 when Guatemala threatened to invade Belize. Guatemala has not relinquished its claim to Belize and shows it as a region of Guatemala on all maps).

APPROACHES. The cay is beset with shoals, particularly to the southwest and the east.
From Porto Stuck or Swallow Cay Bogue, stay one-half mile south of the island until the large white house with the windmills (this is the St. George's Lodge hotel), bears 348°T. Come in toward the end of the hotel dock.
If approaching **from outside the reef** (see below), once through the pass head directly for the houses on the cay.

ANCHORAGE. You will not be able to come closer than 300 yards southeast of the hotel dock, anchoring in 6 feet 6 inches to 7 feet over a sand-and-grass bottom.

PROVISIONS/FACILITIES. You can dinghy into the hotel dock and use the bar and restaurant (expensive, reservations needed for meals, channel 68). The island has a post office and gift shop but no other facilities. Snorkeling is excellent at the northern end of the southern side of the break in the reef.

REEF ENTRY,

ST. GEORGE'S CAY

Charts: BA 959; DMA 28167.
Note: If entering Belizean waters for the first time, you will need to proceed to Belize City to clear in.

There is a 2-mile break in the barrier reef be-

PORTO STUCK TO SWALLOW CAY BOGUE

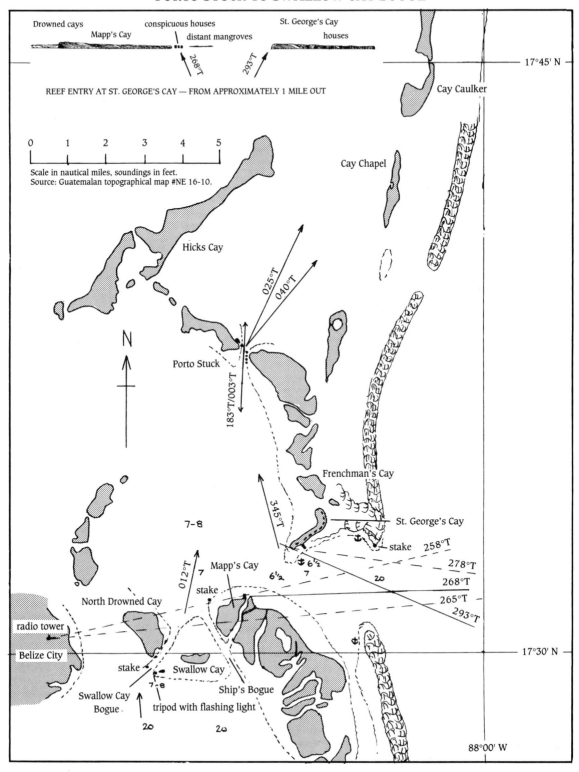

Drowned cays

Mapp's Cay

conspicuous houses

distant mangroves

268°T

293°T

St. George's Cay

houses

Cay Caulker

17°45' N

REEF ENTRY AT ST. GEORGE'S CAY — FROM APPROXIMATELY 1 MILE OUT

0 1 2 3 4 5

Scale in nautical miles, soundings in feet.
Source: Guatemalan topographical map #NE 16-10.

Cay Chapel

Hicks Cay

025°T

040°T

N

Porto Stuck

183°T/003°T

Frenchman's Cay

345°T

7-8

St. George's Cay

stake 258°T

278°T

012°T

7

Mapp's Cay

stake

6½

6½

7

20

268°T

265°T

293°T

North Drowned Cay

radio tower

Belize City

17°30' N

stake

Swallow Cay

stake

7-8

Swallow Cay
Bogue

tripod with flashing light

Ship's Bogue

20

20

88°00' W

tween St. George's Cay and the Drowned Cays, with depths in the pass of 8 to 20 feet. We sailed up and down the break and could find no coral heads with less than 8 feet. This provides an excellent entry channel if conditions are too rough at San Pedro. There are plenty of reference points for making your entrance. Once inside, controlling depth between St. George's Cay and Mapp's Cay is 6 feet 6 inches.

APPROACHES.

From the North. The northern end of the entry channel is marked by a stake, which is topped with a white can, set on the reef. When the southern end of St. George's Cay bears 278°T or more, you are clear of all obstructions and can head in on a westerly course. You often can see a very tall radio mast in Belize City from outside the reef. When the mast is in line with the prominent house on the northern tip of Mapp's Cay (258°T), you are clear to head in.

From the South. The same radio mast can be seen above the Drowned Cays. When it bears 265°T or less, you are clear to enter on a westerly course. If the radio mast is obscured by haze, you will know you are centered up in the break when the conspicuous house on Mapp's Cay bears 268°T.

To enter you initially want to hold a westerly course for the noticeable house on Mapp's Cay in order to give the southern end of St. George's Cay a wide berth (unless you intend to stop there, in which case head up toward the houses and anchor—see above). Then continue approximately midway between Mapp's Cay and St. George's Cay to keep clear of extensive shoals to the north of Mapp's Cay. The depth between Mapp's Cay and St. George's Cay will shoal to a maximum of 6 feet 6 inches.

SWALLOW CAY BOGUE

(CHANNEL)

Chart: BA 522; DMA 28168.

This is the principal channel inside the reef linking Belize City and the southern cays with Porto Stuck and the northern cays. Least depths are around 12 feet in the channel, but 6 to 7 feet north of the channel.

Extensive shoals surround Swallow Cay, extending farther north than shown on DMA chart 28168. Pay careful attention to water color and courses. In particular, you need to take back bearings and adjust for current set where necessary.

The channel markers change from time to time! In 1990 a tripod with a flashing light stood at the southern end of the channel with a stake opposite it on the western side of the channel. Only two other small and hard-to-spot stakes lined the channel, both of them on the western side. Another more substantial stake marked the western edge of a shoal off Mapp's Cay. These were the markers on my last cruise before writing this guide; they may or may not still mark the channel.

APPROACHES.

From St. George's Cay. Stay north of the stake off the northwest tip of Mapp's Cay.

From Porto Stuck and St. George's Cay. Make toward the eastern point of North Drowned Cay until the channel marker (the tripod) at the southern end of the Swallow Cay Bogue bears 210°T and the northern tip of North Drowned Cay bears 303°T. The stake to the northwest of Mapp's Cay will be centered on the gap between St. George's Cay and Frenchman's Cay, bearing 048°T. Make for a point just to the west of the channel-marking tripod, keeping an eye out for the two small stakes and the final stake opposite the tripod, all of which should be left just to starboard. The tripod is on a shoal, whereas the last stake is in 10 feet of water, so stay over toward the stake.

From the South. Hold a course for the westernmost tip of North Drowned Cay until the tripod bears 038°T, then come around onto this heading. Leave the tripod to starboard and hold over toward the stake on the other side of the channel, leaving it to port. Continue up the channel on an initial heading of 038°T, curving gradually to northward (033°T) and leaving the other two stakes to port. If you are making for St. George's, wait until the prominent house on the northern tip of Mapp's Cay bears 070°T before heading toward the southern tip of St. George's. Leave the stake to the northwest of Mapp's Cay to starboard. Stay one-half mile south of St. George's Cay to avoid the shoal to the southwest of this cay.

From Belize City. Make toward a point a

SWALLOW CAY BOGUE

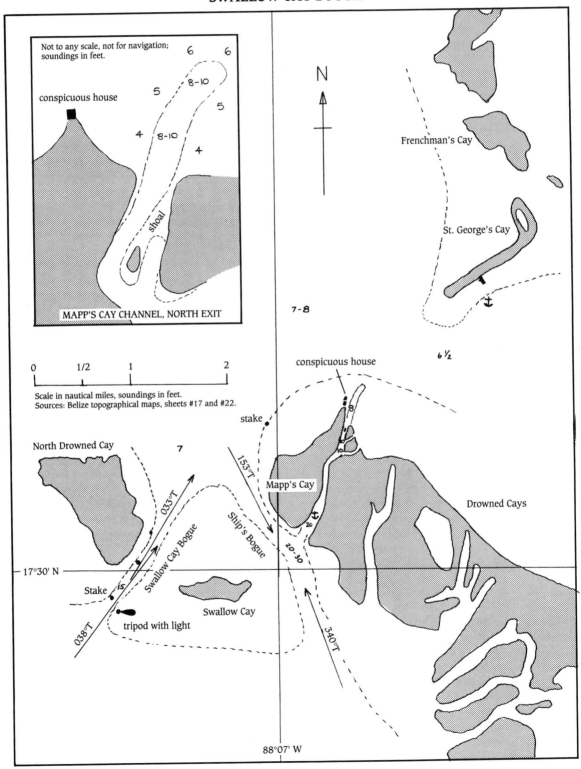

Not to any scale, not for navigation; soundings in feet.

conspicuous house

6   6
8-10
5
5
4   8-10
4
shoal

MAPP'S CAY CHANNEL, NORTH EXIT

N

Frenchman's Cay

St. George's Cay

7-8

6½

0   1/2   1   2

Scale in nautical miles, soundings in feet.
Sources: Belize topographical maps, sheets #17 and #22.

conspicuous house

stake

North Drowned Cay

7

153°T

Mapp's Cay

Drowned Cays

035°T

Swallow Cay Bogue

Ship's Bogue

17°30' N

Stake

038°T

Swallow Cay

tripod with light

20-30

340°T

88°07' W

couple of hundred yards south of the tripod at the southern end of the channel. When it is to the northeast (045°T) come through the channel as above.

SHIP'S BOGUE (CHANNEL)

Charts: BA 522; DMA 28168.

The Ship's Bogue is a deep-water (20 to 30 feet) channel between the Drowned Cays and Swallow Cay.

If approaching **from the north**, enter to the west of the stake off the northwest tip of Mapp's Cay, heading south at approximately 153°T.

If approaching **from the south**, when the western edge of Mapp's Cay bears 347°T, a course of 340°T carries you into the channel. It curves a little to the northwest about midway through. You should be able to differentiate between the color of the deeper water in the channel and the shoals on either side of it.

MAPP'S CAY

Charts: BA 522; DMA 28168.

Note: This anchorage could be included in Region Two since it is accessible, via the Ship's Bogue, to boats with greater draft than 6 feet; geographically, it makes better sense to place it here.

Mapp's Cay provides a very sheltered and secure anchorage among the mangroves, but it offers little to do or see and you are likely to be bothered by mosquitoes and no-see-ums. The channel is entered from the Ship's Bogue, hooking to the south on entry to avoid a shoal on the north side of the entrance and then immediately making up to mid-channel. Inside, depths are 20 to 30 feet and here you may be lucky enough to see manatees, which are regular visitors.

You can pass right through Mapp's Cay, taking the left fork whenever the channel divides; the other channels end in a bar on the eastern side of Mapp's Cay. You will come to a small island, which you leave to starboard, and then will emerge just to the east of the conspicuous house on the northern tip of Mapp's Cay. A narrow channel continues with 8- to 10-foot depths for another one-quarter mile, but then abruptly lessens to 6 feet.

Region 2: Belize City to Placencia

For more than 60 miles, the barrier reef runs more or less parallel to the mainland, less than 15 miles offshore, with both on a north-south axis. With the notable exception of the cays on the reef (Rendez-vous Cay, Tobacco Cay, South Water Cay), the cays along this stretch are not the prettiest, but they provide a number of excellent anchorages to break the journey when sailing north or south. In normal trade-wind conditions the sailing in either direction is spectacular, whether in the Inner Channel or just in the lee of the reef. Southward you are on a broad reach, coming north on a close reach, with your boat racing along at hull speed and not a drop of water over the decks! Toward the southern end of this area, where the reef hooks out into the ocean near Gladden Cays, the snorkeling and diving inside the reef are outstanding.

BELIZE CITY

Charts: BA 522; DMA 28168.

Note: Give the Stake Bank wide clearance from any direction; it is conspicuous because of the tall mangroves, but is surrounded by extensive shoals.

Belize City has a major problem with thieves, who will snatch purses and bags in broad daylight anywhere in the city.

Belize City is no longer the capital of Belize—the extensive damage caused by Hurricane Hattie in 1961 finally drove the government to move inland to the new purpose-built capital, Belmopan—but it is still the only really substantial population center in Belize with 50,000 inhabitants, about one-third the country's population. Belize City is somewhat rundown and dirty, with a scattering of faded, rather ragged West Indian-style, gingerbread-decorated homes that still evoke some of the glory of more prosperous days.

APPROACHES.

From the North and Inside the Reef. You can approach either via Swallow Cay Bogue (the more usual passage) or Ship's Bogue (see pages 107–109).

From Outside the Reef. You can enter in daylight or darkness via the well-marked and lit big-ship channel at English Cay. You do not have to follow the twists and turns of the channel. Once past Northeast Spit you can head directly for the Baron Bliss Lighthouse (320°T). You will have depths of 12 feet or more until you close the city, with the exception of one small shoal patch charted at 5 feet just outside the northern edge of the ship channel and bearing 303°T from the Northeast Spit channel marker. Be sure to give this adequate clearance.

From the South Up the Inner Channel. You will want to stay west of Robinson Point to avoid hazards, unless you are coming from the southern cays; in this case you can safely cross the Twelve Feet Bank at any point between Middle Long Cay and the Triangles so long as you do not stray west of Spanish Cay Spit or east onto the extensive shoal north of Middle Long Cay. Once again, watch out for the shoal patch that is northwest of Northeast Spit.

ANCHORAGE. Anchor just north of the Baron Bliss Lighthouse, 100 yards or more off the end of the dock at the Fort George Hotel (this is a prominent modern building). The anchorage is generally uncomfortably rolly, but has excellent holding in thick mud. It is calmer in the mornings than the afternoons.

Mooring to the dock can be difficult. You must drop an anchor about 100 yards out and back down. However, the tide sets across the end of the dock while the wind generally blows straight onto it, making it tricky to hold your alignment when you are backing down. Check anchored boats to gauge the strength and direction of the drift so that you

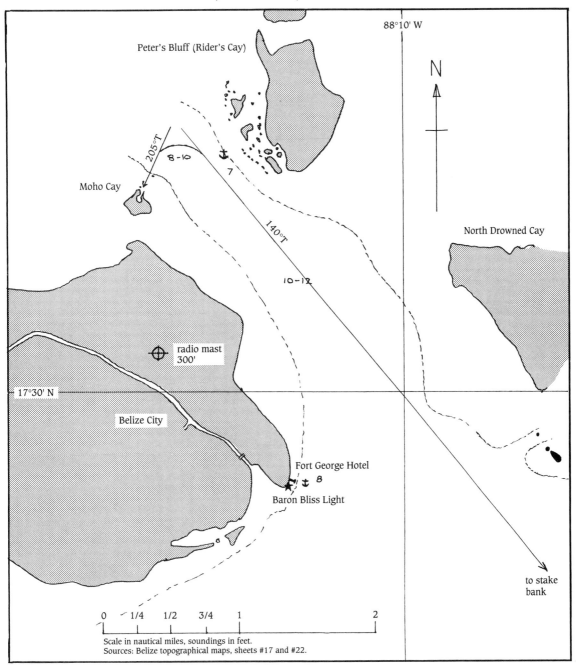

Peter's Bluff (Rider's Cay)

88°10' W

N

205°T

8 - 10

7

Moho Cay

140°T

North Drowned Cay

10 - 12

radio mast
300'

17°30' N

Belize City

Fort George Hotel

8

Baron Bliss Light

to stake
bank

0   1/4   1/2   3/4   1   2

Scale in nautical miles, soundings in feet.
Sources: Belize topographical maps, sheets #17 and #22.

can make an adequate allowance when dropping the hook. The surge against the dock is sometimes fierce—a number of boats have been damaged—so be sure to allow sufficient scope and set the anchor hard before easing back the last few feet to the dock.

When the tide changes you may still be set onto the dock, so it is best just to take on fuel and water, then pull off and anchor out. You can dinghy back to take care of other business.

Security, especially during the daytime, is good

here, but not elsewhere around Belize City. I would not leave a boat anchored out and unattended overnight anywhere near the city. In any case, if you need to lay over a night you will find far more comfortable anchorages just a short distance away in the lee of Peter's Bluff, at Bannister Bogue (our favorite), and at Robinson Point (the most popular stop for cruisers but not the best). See below for a description of all three.

DINGHY DOCKING. You can dinghy to the dock to clear in and out, or go shopping. Check in with the dockmaster and ask him to keep an eye on your dinghy.

CLEARANCE PROCEDURES. Checking in and out at Belize City can be a time-consuming hassle since the procedures are not set up for small boats. To clear in, first visit the customs office close to the Fort George Hotel (around the waterfront to the southwest). Officials here may call around to gather up the other necessary officials, but expect to wait some time. A party of officials probably will want to come aboard to check the boat.

To clear out you must visit the Port Authority at the deep-water port to the south of the city, the immigration office at 115 Barracks Road in the city, and customs. You may have to pay various charges and will incur taxi fares in the neighborhood of $20 (Belize) or more for the necessary running around. It is much easier, and may be no more expensive, to fly the customs officer into San Pedro (see page 100). Alternatively, try to arrange your travel plans such that you can clear in or out at Punta Gorda or Dangriga (see pages 122 and 152).

BELIZE CITY

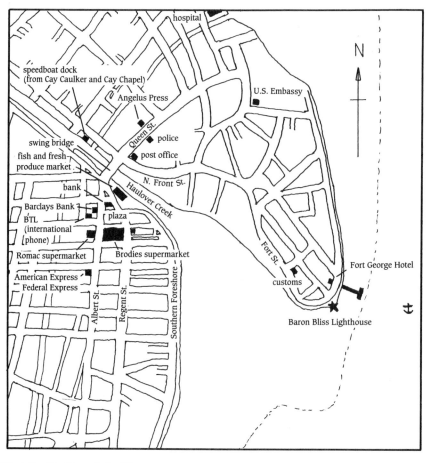

PROVISIONS/FACILITIES. Come onto the end of the dock at the Fort George Hotel for fuel and water—depths are just over 6 feet, shoaling farther inshore. Belize City has all the usual big-city services—banks, telephones, post office (which will hold mail), travel agents, an American Express office, and an international airport with direct flights to Houston, New Orleans, Miami, and London as well as other cities. Three supermarkets (Brodies, Romac, and U-Save) offer the best grocery shopping in the Northwest Caribbean south of Isla Mujeres. There are numerous hardware stores. Propane tanks can be refilled (15 W. Collett Canal and 6428 Marigold Lane). The Angelus Press has a few charts of Belizean waters, the *Belize Cruising Guide*, and likely will stock this book as well! All stores close at 1200 (noon) on Wednesdays (an old British custom) but are open on Saturday mornings.

Arthur Hoare has a marine railway up Haulover Creek; it is capable of handling just about any size of pleasureboat. Hoare is an experienced boatbuilder, but has limited supplies—bring your own bottom paint and other goods. The controlling depth off the mouth of Haulover Creek used to be 5 feet but has reportedly been dredged to 9 feet. You should check with local sailors and probably get a guide since the water is muddy and it is not possible to tell the channel. After you pass through a swing bridge, you are in the creek, which has plenty of water.

MOHO CAY AND PETER'S BLUFF (RIDER'S CAYS)

(see map page 111)

Charts: BA 959; DMA 28167.

Moho Cay is the base for Belize Marine Charters. A marina has been scooped out of the northern side of the island. It is a secure place to leave a boat to travel inland or to return home for a spell. The marina will shuttle guests to and from the mainland. The office monitors channel 78 on the VHF; the telephone numbers are 457-98 and 310-63.

APPROACH. Come northwest past Belize City on a heading of approximately 320°T with Stake Bank at your stern; this keeps you about 1 mile off the mainland. At the present time (1990) three substantial stakes mark the channel into the marina. The outer one is about 200 yards offshore. The stakes become visible when you are off Peter's Bluff (Rider's Cays). Hook around in a broad arc on a heading of 205°T to leave the first stake to port and the other two to starboard. The channel has just 6 feet at low water, but dredging to 10 feet is planned (at which time the stakes will almost certainly get disturbed).

ANCHORAGE. In normal trade-wind conditions, settled anchorage can be found in the lee of Peter's Bluff (Rider's Cay). The bottom shoals gradually toward the mangroves with less than 6 feet a couple of hundred yards out. You do not, in any case, want to get closer because of the bugs! This is a far more comfortable spot to spend the night than off the Fort George Hotel dock, which is just 2 miles away.

PROVISIONS/FACILITIES. Transient slips are available with 110/220 VAC and water. The marina has an international phone, a fax machine, and a laundry.

BANNISTER, FARL'S, AND GORING BOGUES

Charts: BA 522; DMA 28168.

There are three passages through the Drowned Cays. Depths are as shown on the charts. You can pass right through, staying in mid-channel.

APPROACHES. Farl's Bogue is the most straightforward since it is wide open at its eastern end with a stake marking the reef to the southeast—stay north of this stake. The navigable channel through Goring Bogue becomes quite narrow—good light is needed to watch for coral. Bannister Bogue requires a slight dogleg. It is transited on a heading of 083°T, continuing out the east side until you are in line with the most distant points of the Drowned Cays to north and south, at which point you need to head 113°T to keep clear of a shoal patch to the north.

BANNISTER, FARL'S, AND GORING BOGUES

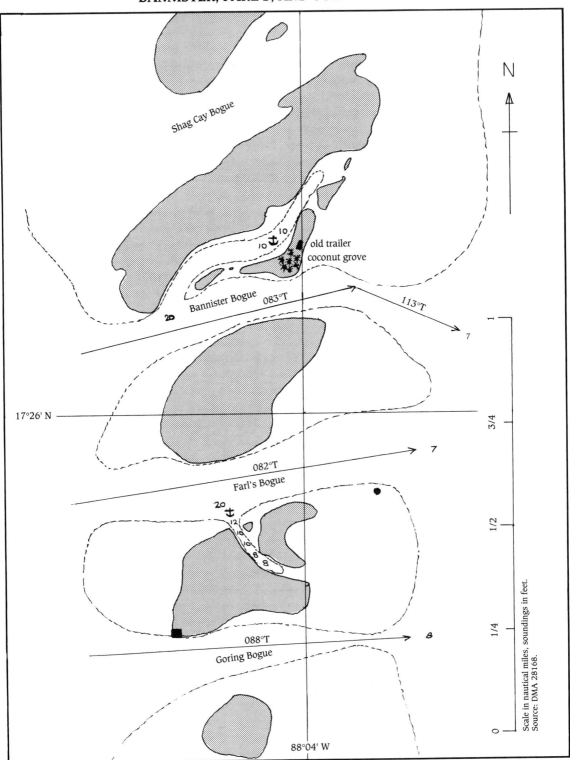

Shag Cay Bogue

old trailer
coconut grove

Bannister Bogue   083°T

113°T

7

N

17°26' N

082°T

7

Farl's Bogue

088°T

8

Goring Bogue

88°04' W

Scale in nautical miles, soundings in feet.
Source: DMA 28168.

Take back-bearings and make any necessary allowance for crosscurrents. To the east, all three passages have depths of at least 7 to 8 feet.

ANCHORAGES. Bannister Bogue has an excellent all-weather anchorage to the north of the small mangrove islets. Entry is straightforward from the west, keeping in center channel, with no depth less than 10 feet. Keep going until almost to the eastern end, then anchor off the abandoned trailer and co-conut grove. The holding is good, with a nice breeze funneling in from the east to keep the bugs at bay. This is a very good spot in which to anchor over-night, whether you are coming from or going to Belize City.

Farl's Bogue also has a pleasant anchorage about midway through, off the small islet on the southern shore. The anchorage is less protected than Bannister Bogue and has a strong breeze blowing through it. Depth is 12 feet shoaling slowly to 6 feet up against the mangroves in the channel that is to the west and south of the tiny islet.

GALLOWS POINT TO
ENGLISH CAY

Charts: BA 522; DMA 28168.

APPROACHES. A passage runs behind the barrier reef from St. George's Cay to the Ship Channel at English Cay. It narrows off Gallows Point and shoals to a little over 6 feet, then broadens again. Off Shag Bluff the chart indicates one or two shoal patches, so keep a good lookout. The water is clear and, in good light, you should have no problem navigating the channel: just stay in the blue water and keep a lookout posted in the ratlines to watch for isolated coral heads. South of Shag Bluff are numerous breaks in the reef through which you should be able to pass with care in calm conditions.

ANCHORAGES. Paunch Cay is no more than a sandbar, but provides reasonable protection for day-time anchoring. Sergeant's Cay is another dot of sand, but it has 3½ coconut trees! The anchorage is rather exposed, with swells hooking around from

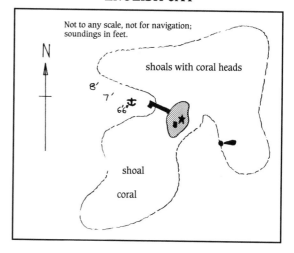

ENGLISH CAY

Not to any scale, not for navigation; soundings in feet.

the gap in the reef to the north. The snorkeling is excellent to the north of the cay. Goff's Cay provides considerably more protection than Sergeant's with good snorkeling behind the reef just to the south.

English Cay is substantially larger than Goff's and Sergeant's and has a number of palm trees, a lighthouse, and two lighthouse keepers in residence. A dock extends to the west-northwest. Six feet can be carried onto the tip of the dock, coming straight in for it. Coral heads will be just to the north of you, and an extensive shoal to the south. This anchorage can be uncomfortable owing to swells hooking around the island. It is wide open to the northwest and should not be used overnight in the winter months. The lighthouse keepers will let you climb the light, affording a fine view of the surrounding cays.

ROBINSON POINT AND
RAMSAY'S CAY

Charts: BA 522; DMA 28168.

The anchorage south of Robinson Cay is a popular overnight stop before or after a trip to Belize City. Bannister Bogue, however, offers better protection, has more reasonable depths, and is closer to the city.

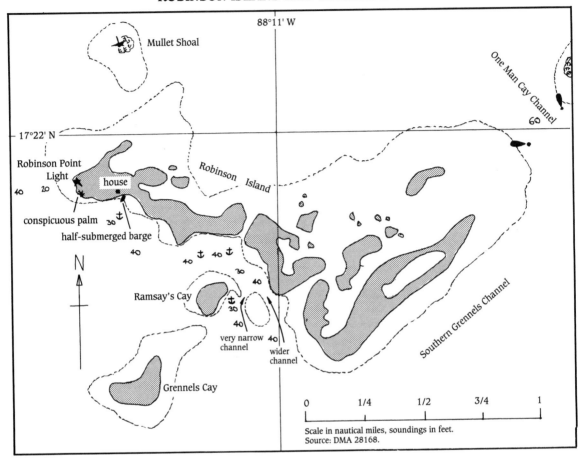

Scale in nautical miles, soundings in feet.
Source: DMA 28168.

APPROACHES. On approaching Robinson Island, you will see a conspicuous palm tree just to the southeast of the light structure before you see the light itself.

ANCHORAGES. The holding behind the island is good but deep (40 feet), so you need plenty of scope. The anchorage is wide open to the west and exposed during the early stages of a norther. Better protection can be had by tucking in to the northeast of Ramsay's Cay, or around on the southeast side of Ramsay's Cay where you find deep water almost up into the mangroves (not the shoal shown on the charts)—but come in slowly as the bottom comes up suddenly from 30 feet. Beware the shoal east of Ramsay's Cay: It is possible to pass either side of it, but the western channel is very narrow. You need good light for both passages.

MIDDLE LONG CAY

Charts: BA 959; DMA 28167.

Numerous shoal patches exist along the western shore of Middle Long Cay. Most have 7 feet over them, except for a few, very isolated coral heads. With good light and a lookout you can carry 6 feet almost to the mangroves.

ANCHORAGE. Protection is good in normal trade-wind conditions, especially when tucked in down toward Negro Head where there are some very pretty patches of coral ferns. However, the holding is poor and you need to find an area free of coral. The anchorage in the lagoon at the Bluefield Range, immediately to the south, is much to be preferred.

THE BLUEFIELD RANGE

Charts: BA 959; DMA 28167.

The lagoon in the Bluefield Range is our favorite anchorage in this part of Belize. It has good holding in a well-protected lagoon inside a group of mangrove islands, and pleasant breezes keep it bug-free. The islands are prettier than most mangrove cays with one being home to a frigate bird and pelican rookery. The lagoon is frequented by manatees.

APPROACHES. The entry from both north and south can be a little tricky since there is extensive coral off both ends of the island.

From the North. Entering is not quite as intimidating as you might suppose from the chart. The large coral patch shown has groups of coral heads with 2 feet of water over them, interspersed with depths of 7 feet—you could thread through much of it in good light, though I do not recommend it. Instead I advise working around to the north and east of this coral or through a channel to the south. The latter is narrower but more direct. Come south, staying west of an imaginary line drawn between the western extremities of Negro Head and the Bluefield Range, until you see a stake that marks the northern end of the reef off the Bluefield Range. When the northernmost point of the Bluefield Range bears 098°T, come in on this heading just to the north of the stake. With the stake 100 to 200 yards astern, come around onto a heading of 183°T for the eastern edge of the western cay in the Bluefield Range. Hold this course until past the gap between the two eastern cays. This will keep you clear of a very shallow coral patch in the anchorage. Anchor over toward the eastern shore.

The passage around to the north of the coral patch between Middle Long Cay and the Bluefield Range is wider but has least depths of 7 feet. You follow the outer edge of the shoal around the southern end of Middle Long Cay in 7 to 8 feet of water until Rendezvous Cay (out on the barrier reef) bears 090°T. Hold a course for Rendezvous Cay until the eastern cay in the Bluefield Range obscures the entrance to the lagoon. Now head 195°T; if the lagoon entrance opens up, go farther east until it is once again obscured—this keeps you clear of the coral in

depths of 7 to 10 feet. When Rendezvous Cay bears 073°T, come around to a heading of 243°T—you then are one-quarter to one-half mile off the Bluefield Range. You will see the stake on the reef at the northern end of the Bluefield Range one-quarter to one-half mile ahead. Depths increase to 10 to 20 feet. When the eastern edge of the western cay bears 183°T, head into the lagoon as above, staying 100 to 200 yards east of the stake.

From the South. Stay in the deep water until you are past Alligator Cay; there are a number of uncharted coral heads to its northwest. When Rendezvous Cay (out on the barrier reef) is in line with the southern tip of the Bluefield Range (049°T), come in more or less on this heading but keep a tiny gap between Rendezvous Cay and the Bluefield Range. Do not stray to the north. You will be crossing an extensive shoal with fairly uniform depths of 7 feet. In our several passages we have seen no coral heads on this track. When the eastern edge of the channel into the lagoon at Bluefield bears 020°T, come in on this heading, staying 100 yards off the mangroves. Do not stray west toward the group of mangroves in center channel since you will hit a shoal patch with 2-foot depths.

Leaving to the South. Once again stay over toward the mangroves on the eastern side of the channel. Immediately south of Bluefield, come around to a heading of 200°T and hold this until you can differentiate Rendezvous Cay from the Bluefield Range, at which point you head southwest for deeper water.

RENDEZVOUS CAY (#1)

Charts: BA 959; DMA 28167.

Rendezvous is a lovely little cay, sand with coconuts, surrounded by reef patches and gorgeous water colors—quite the prettiest cay and water on this northern half of Belize's barrier reef. Although it provides reasonable protection in normal trade-wind conditions, Rendezvous Cay is in a somewhat exposed location and should be treated as a daytime anchorage only; retreat to Bluefield Lagoon at night (or leave your big boat in Bluefield and dinghy over to Rendezvous). You can enter and exit the reef at

BLUEFIELD RANGE AND RENDEZVOUS CAY #1

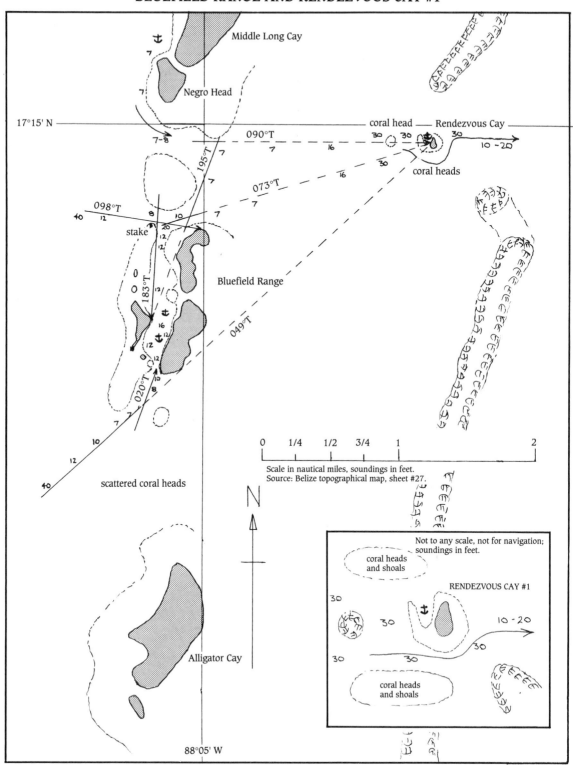

Middle Long Cay

Negro Head

17°15' N

coral head — Rendezvous Cay

090°T

195°T

7-8

7

7

16

30

30

30

10-20

coral heads

073°T

16

098°T

16

stake

Bluefield Range

049°T

183°T

020°T

scattered coral heads

N

Alligator Cay

| 0 | 1/4 | 1/2 | 3/4 | 1 | | 2 |

Scale in nautical miles, soundings in feet.
Source: Belize topographical map, sheet #27.

Not to any scale, not for navigation;
soundings in feet.

coral heads
and shoals

RENDEZVOUS CAY #1

30

30

10-20

30

30

30

coral heads
and shoals

88°05' W

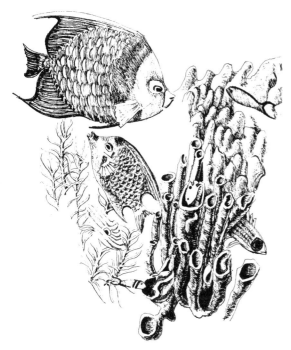

Underwater life is especially beautiful in this region.

Rendezvous, making this a good jumping off point for Turneffe Island and Lighthouse Reef, but this passage should be attempted only in good light and settled weather. The cay is surrounded with uncharted coral. In any but calm conditions, you should head up to the Ship Channel at English Cay to pass through the reef.

APPROACHES. Follow the shoal around the southern edge of Middle Long Cay until Rendezvous Cay bears 090°T, then head straight for it. Alternatively come around the stake to the north of the Bluefield Range (see the notes on the Bluefield Range), holding an easterly course until north of the eastern island in the Bluefield Range, and then head directly for Rendezvous Cay.

Both approaches have depths of just 7 feet for considerable distances. As you close the cay, water depths increase steadily to 30 feet, and the color changes to a spectacular light translucent blue, but there are a number of coral patches. We sailed over several to gauge the depths and all appear to have at least 6 to 7 feet, but you had better dodge around them. In front of the cay is a shoal—hook around its northern end to come in behind the cay, close to the beach.

To Exit the Reef. At Rendezvous Cay, come around to the south of the cay and then head northeast between the reef that extends eastward from the cay (not shown on the charts) and the substantial reef area to the east-southeast. When due east of Rendezvous, head east. You will cross an extensive shoal area of sand and rocks with depths of 10 to 20 feet (also not shown on the charts) but which, so far as we could see, is free of coral heads. However, exercise extreme caution because, if substantial swells are running, crossing will be rough, and since your course is dead to windward you will have no option but to crash into the waves without being able to maintain a proper watch for coral heads. *Do not do it!* Play it safe and go to the Ship Channel at English Cay instead.

RENDEZVOUS CAY TO THE FLY RANGE VIA THE INNER CHANNEL

Charts: BA 959 and 1797; DMA 28168 and 28166.

Note: The shoal patches between the Colson Cays and Southern Long Cay are more extensive than shown on the charts so good light and a lookout are essential in these waters. South from Southern Long Cay there are numerous shoal and coral patches, both charted and uncharted.

ANCHORAGES. Although you can work in close to the mangroves, Alligator Cay has several uncharted coral heads to the northwest and west with nothing much to see ashore: It is not worth the trouble to visit it.

The Colson Cays are also rather uninteresting, except for a frigate bird and pelican rookery at the northwest tip. We worked our way almost into the mangroves and anchored in 6 feet 6 inches so that Terrie could sketch the birds. We found a grassy bottom with no coral, but coral lies to both the southwest and the north. There is deeper water in the gap between the two cays—approach on a heading of 063°T—with a fairly well-protected anchorage over a grassy bottom.

Southern Long Cay has a gently shoaling grassy bottom on its western side. Once again you can work in quite close to the mangroves for good protection in normal trade-wind conditions, but there is little to see ashore.

Columbus Cay has a gently shoaling, coral-free shelf on its western side, with 6 feet fairly close to the mangroves. The holding is poor—thin sand over rock—with numerous sponges that you should avoid tearing up. There is no reason to stop here.

BEHIND THE REEF
BETWEEN RENDEZVOUS AND
SOUTH WATER CAY

Charts: BA 959 and 1797; DMA 28167 and 28166.

You can carry a 6-foot draft behind the barrier reef all the way from Rendezvous Cay to South Water Cay and on to the south. In the northern stretch you have to dodge coral patches through much of the passage—good light and a good lookout are essential. East of Columbus Cay the channel narrows and shoals to 7 feet. Between Columbus Cay and Tobacco Cay you will have a wonderful sail in 10- to 12-foot depths free of coral heads. The water is sparkling clear with almost no wave action and the trade wind blows in over the foam-drenched reef to the east. Immediately south of Tobacco Cay you must head west for one-half mile to round an extensive sandbar (see page 125), but then the same glorious conditions prevail on past South Water Cay (see page 126).

THE FLY RANGE

Charts: BA 1797; DMA 26166 and 28167 (new edition). The charts contain one or two little inaccuracies noted below.

The Fly Range is essentially two parallel reefs with a 40-foot deep-water channel in between. On the western reef are Sandfly Cay and Hutson's Cay; on the eastern reef Mosquito Cay and Garbutt's Cay. In spite of their off-putting names, these cays have a number of protected spots in which to anchor and, with a breeze, the bugs here are no worse than anywhere else!

APPROACHES.

From the North. Stay 1 1/2 miles west of Mosquito Cay in the deep water of the Inner Channel until the northern tip of Mosquito Cay is in line with the southern tip of Columbus Cay (100°T), then come in while you keep the two in line. When the southern tip of Mosquito Cay is in line with the western tip of Cross Cay, come around onto a heading of 135°T, keeping the two in line once again, until inside the channel. As you enter there will be two isolated clumps of mangroves to your north. You will find a least depth of 10 feet coming out of the Inner Channel, steadily increasing to 40 feet. This is an easy entrance with these two ranges.

From the South. If you are making passage to or from Tobacco Cay, you have to give a good clearance to the shoals to the southwest of Garbutt's Cay, and the northeast of the Tobacco Range. Note that there is also a shoal south of Hutson's Cay where the chart reports 2 1/2 fathoms, so don't cut across here if you are coming from Dangriga.

As you make your final approach from the southwest, Garbutt's Cay breaks up into two islands (both are actually clusters of mangroves). A course of 083°T on the house at the northern tip of the southern cluster runs up the center of the channel in 50 feet of water. There is a shoal in front of the house, but otherwise the channel is deep almost into the mangroves (this is another point on which the chart is wrong).

ANCHORAGE. The most protected anchorage is tucked in to the south of the house—a small beach will be to your southeast. Depths are 30 feet until quite close to the mangroves but they then come up suddenly. The holding tends to be poor due to a generally rocky bottom, but there must be something more clay-like down there because once in a while an anchor will set hard. You may need to make a number of attempts to get a good bite.

We got caught out here when a squall blew up from the west in the night. We were blown up toward the mangroves but the bottom comes up so steeply that rather than being aground we were laid up against the edge of the shelf! Once we got a

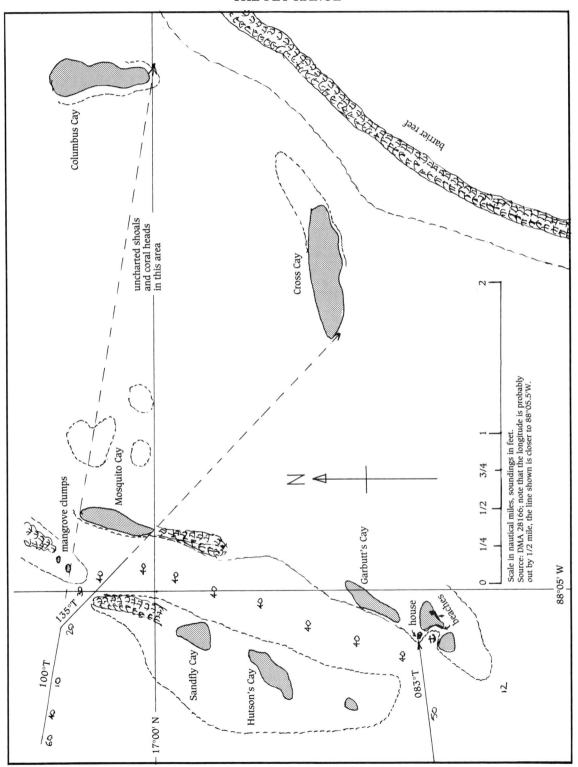

Columbus Cay

barrier reef

uncharted shoals and coral heads in this area

Cross Cay

2

1

3/4

1/2

1/4

N

0

Scale in nautical miles, soundings in feet.
Source: DMA 28166; note that the longitude is probably out by 1/2 mile, the line shown is closer to 88°05.5'W.

88°05' W

mangrove clumps

Mosquito Cay

Garbutt's Cay

house

beach

135°T

100°T

17°00' N

Sandfly Cay

Hutson's Cay

083°T

12

Fishing in the Inner Channel is not always successful!

kedge anchor to bite (the third attempt) we had no trouble getting off.

Some people consider this to be one of the best anchorages in this area, but the Blue Ground Range, 10 miles to the south (see below) combines better all-around protection with far superior holding.

DANGRIGA (STANN CREEK)

Charts: BA 1797; DMA 26166 and 28167 (new edition).

There is little reason to go to Dangriga except to clear in and out of Belize, which is much easier here than at Belize City. The anchorage is an open roadstead and is generally rolly and uncomfortable, so if you need to visit Dangriga plan on making an early start to give yourself enough time to return to a comfortable overnight anchorage in the Fly Range.

APPROACH/ANCHORAGE. As you approach Dangriga you will see a tall radio tower from miles

out, and later a water tower just to the south. The town dock is a little farther south and is distinguished by the outhouse on its end! The bottom shoals a good way off so you have to drop the hook when in 8 to 10 feet of water and dinghy in. Note that the shoals extend farther offshore a couple of hundred yards south of the town dock where the Stann Creek flows out. The holding is good but if the swells are running hard you might want to put out two anchors for added security. Stann Creek has a very narrow and shallow sandbar across its mouth, but then plenty of water once inside. If you care to drag your dinghy over the bar, you can run up to the bridge in town and tie up there.

CLEARANCE PROCEDURES. The customs office is in the administration building next to the court house, which is just up from the town dock. The immigration officer is in the police station at the top of the same street. Opposite are the supermarket and telephone office.

PROVISIONS/FACILITIES. The town has limited facilities—a reasonable supermarket, an interna-

DANGRIGA TO COMMERCE BIGHT

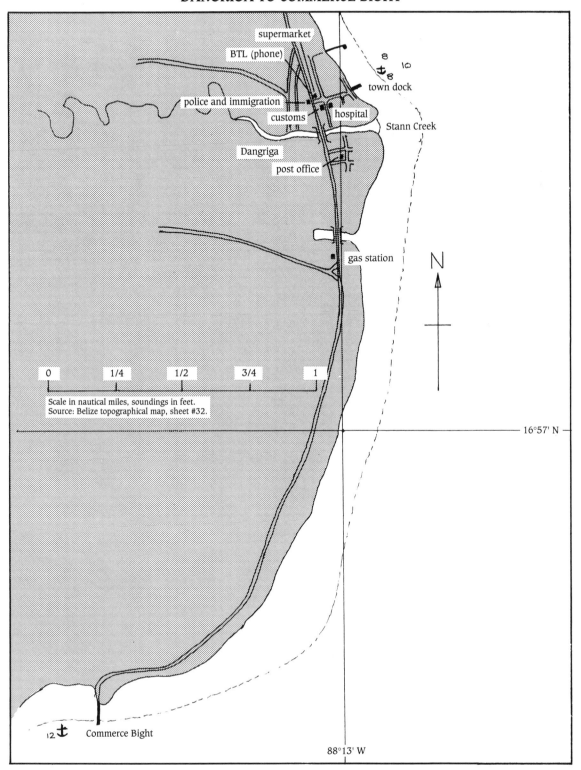

supermarket

BTL (phone)

town dock

police and immigration

customs

hospital

Stann Creek

Dangriga

post office

gas station

N

0   1/4   1/2   3/4   1

Scale in nautical miles, soundings in feet.
Source: Belize topographical map, sheet #32.

16°57' N

Commerce Bight

88°13' W

View from the anchorage at the Pelican Cays (see page 128).

tional phone and fax machine, a post office (which holds mail), and a gas station that has diesel but is one-half mile from the center of town.

COMMERCE BIGHT. Three miles south of Dan-

Grouper Mating Frenzy

Groupers are some of the larger fishes to be found around the reefs. Once a year a great congregation occurs in valleys in Belize's barrier reef. Tens of thousands of groupers converge to participate in a huge mating frenzy and spawning session. The groupers, which can change sex, becoming alternately male and female, separate into pairs and circle close to one another, changing color from the more normal brown to silvery white and purplish red, releasing millions of fertilized eggs into the currents to be carried away.

The local Belizean fishermen eagerly await the grouper runs. They build temporary fish pens in the roots of mangroves and in shallow spots on the reef. When the grouper come, in just a few days, using hooks and line, they catch tons of fish. These are kept alive in the pens and sold according to market demand.

---

griga stands a large commercial pier. When visiting Dangriga some people like to anchor out in the "lee" of this pier, dinghy ashore, and walk or catch a taxi to town. However, unless the wind is in the north, the pier provides little protection. In normal easterly trade-wind conditions, you might just as well anchor off Dangriga and save yourself the added trouble and expense.

COCOA PLUM CAY TO

TOBACCO CAY

Charts: BA 1797; DMA 28166 and 28167 (new edition).

ANCHORAGES. Cocoa Plum Cay is little more than a long, but attractive, sandspit with patches of mangroves and coconut trees. A hurricane has blown a channel through the sand, dividing the island in two, and several gaps exist between the trees so that from a distance it looks like a number of smaller cays. In settled conditions you can anchor anywhere off its western shore.

Man of War Cay is conspicuous because of its

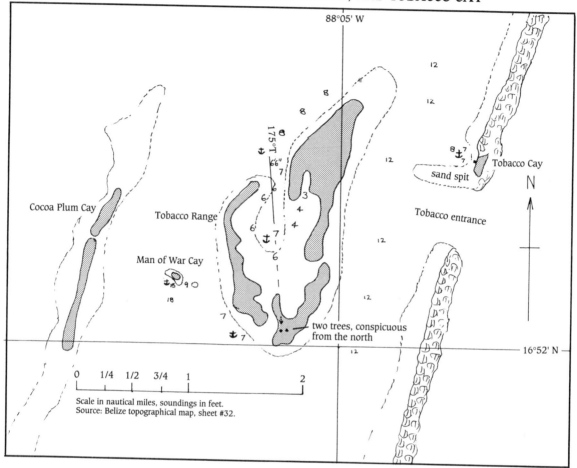

88°05' W

Cocoa Plum Cay

Tobacco Range

Man of War Cay

175°T
66"

8

8

8

3
4

4

7

6

6

6

6

7

7

7

9 O

18

two trees, conspicuous
from the north

12

12

12

12

8 7

8 7

Tobacco Cay

sand spit

Tobacco entrance

N

12

12

16°52' N

0   1/4 1/2 3/4   1   2

Scale in nautical miles, soundings in feet.
Source: Belize topographical map, sheet #32.

tall mangroves. It is home to a sizable colony of frigate and booby birds and is worth a stop during mating and nesting seasons (February to April). You
can anchor fairly close to the mangroves after approaching from the southwest (there are shoals to
both the northwest and southeast) and watch the
bizarre courtship rituals from the comfort of your
boat.

TOBACCO RANGE. In the lee of the cays of the
Tobacco Range, you can find sheltered water in just
about any wind conditions, but why anchor here
with the Fly Range to the north and the Blue
Ground Range to the south? The chart shows 3 feet
inside the lagoon. We found 7 feet going in, favor-
ing the north side of the entrance, with 7 feet in the
center of the lagoon shoaling gradually toward the

shore. The bottom is eel grass—a Danforth sets better than a plow or Bruce. When rounding the northern end of the Tobacco Range, be sure to give the
shoal to the northeast good clearance.

Tobacco Cay stands sentinel over a substantial
break in the barrier reef, making it a good jumping-
off point for Glover's Reef. Entry and exit are
straightforward, but between the cay and the reef
entrance lies a substantial sandspit that stretches almost half way across to the Tobacco Range. There is
a narrow cut through the sand close to Tobacco Cay
(not the wide channel shown on the charts) but it is
better to go around to the west.

Protected anchorage can be found in normal
trade-wind conditions off the dock on the west side
of Tobacco Cay, but this is wide open to northers.
You will find 6 to 8 feet within 200 yards of the

dock, with a grassy bottom in which anchors do not set or hold too well. Excellent snorkeling can be found at the north end of the south side of the break in the reef.

Tobacco Cay and South Water Cay to the south are pretty coconut-clad islands almost on the reef with a number of friendly inhabitants (and maybe by the time this is published a restaurant/bar on Tobacco Cay). As with other outlying settlements, they are spotlessly clean—much of the cay is freshly raked every day!

BLUE GROUND RANGE

Charts: BA 1797; DMA 28166 and 28167 (new edition).

The Blue Ground Range is a collection of scattered mangrove cays that more or less enclose a deep-water (40-foot) lagoon. The protection and holding are both excellent. There are shoals and reef patches between most of the cays: The lagoon can be entered only from the west or the north.

APPROACHES.

From the West. Stay in the deep water of the Inner Channel until Carrie Bow Cay, a clump of palms out on the barrier reef, can be seen bearing 099°T through a gap in the mangroves. Come straight in for Carrie Bow—least depths crossing the bar are 13 feet.

From the North. There are numerous shoal patches just north of a line drawn from the Twin Cays to the northern end of the Blue Ground Range. While most shoals appear to have at least 7 feet over them, and you should not need to stray up into this area anyway, keep a good lookout. Approach is made to the north of the Blue Ground Range on a heading of 273°T with the southern tip of the Twin Cays on a back-bearing of 093°T. This brings you a mile or so north of the northeastern cays of the Blue Ground Range in 30 feet of water with reefs to port, starboard, and ahead! Hook around to the south onto a heading of 190°T, following the curve of the reef to the west and coming around onto a heading of 183°T for the center of the gap between the

northern cays, which you enter in mid-channel. In spite of the 1½ fathoms (9 feet) shown on the chart, you are never in less than 30 feet of water.

BLUE GROUND RANGE TO WATER CAY

Charts: BA 1797; DMA 28166 and 28167 (new edition).

ANCHORAGES. The Twin Cays can be entered from the southwest by dodging shoals. You will find 12 feet inside with excellent protection but are likely to be joined by an army of bugs at dusk since the cay breaks the breeze.

South Water Cay (known simply as "Water Cay") is another exceptionally pretty, inhabited, sand and coconut cay. Approach from the west to anchor in 8 feet over eel grass (avoid the shoal area extending toward the northwest). Holding is not good and you may experience problems setting an anchor—a Danforth-type will bite better than a plow or Bruce. Protection is good in normal trade-wind conditions but wide open to a norther.

Water Cay is a good jumping off spot for Glover's Reef.

Carrie Bow Cay is a gorgeous little privately owned island with reasonable shelter in 8 to 10 feet close in. Swells do tend to hook around from the Ellen Cut just to the south but a small shoal extending southward from the cay breaks most of them.

Curlew Cay has been all but washed away, leaving just a 200-yard spit of sand.

BLUE GROUND RANGE TO THE PELICAN CAYS

Charts: BA 1797; DMA 28166 and 28167 (new edition).

A deep-water channel runs to the east between the Blue Ground Range and the barrier reef. The sailing is great and the water colors are wonderful.

BLUE GROUND RANGE TO WATER CAY

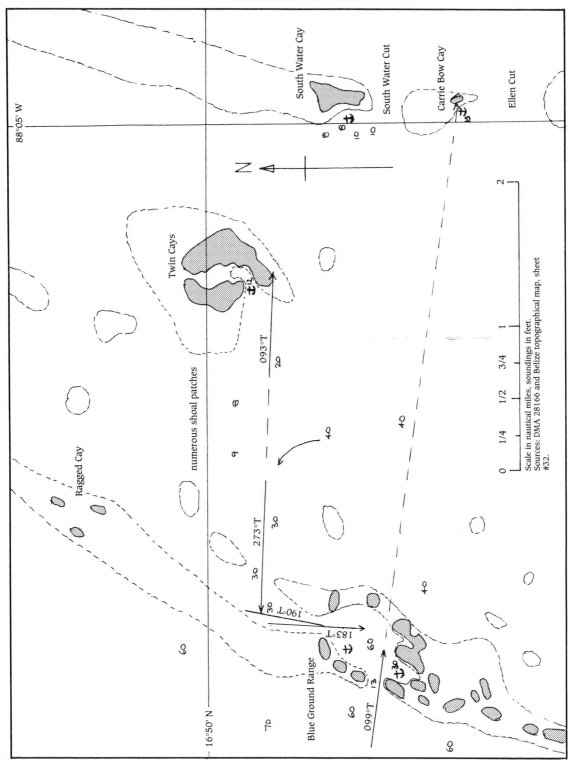

Scale in nautical miles, soundings in feet.
Sources: DMA 28166 and Belize topographical map, sheet #32.

You need to stay in the deep blue water and keep a good watch; although the channel is basically free of obstructions, there are one or two coral patches and sand bores close by (shown on the charts) and one shallow sandy shoal, which is not shown on the charts, 1½ miles northeast of Spruce Cay, in the middle of the channel.

Wee Wee Cay is a mangrove cay with a wildlife station and a live-in caretaker. Anchorage can be found on the western side in 25 feet fairly close to the dock (which has 5 feet on its outboard end). Approach is made from either the north or the south, rounding the shoal areas immediately to the northwest and southeast of the island, but staying inside the reef areas one-third mile to the northwest and the southwest.

Spruce, Norval, and Douglas cays are mangrove islands, surrounded by shoals as indicated on the charts. All provide poor protection. The Elbow Cays enclose a protected lagoon, but shoals obstruct all channels and no entry is possible.

THE PELICAN CAYS

Charts: BA 1797; DMA 28166 and 28167 (new edition).

The Pelican Cays are another group of mangrove islets enclosing a deep-water (60-foot) sheltered lagoon with excellent holding and protection.

APPROACH. You can enter the Pelican Cays only from the west—all other channels are obstructed by shoals. Coming down the Inner Channel, you pass a sandy beach with a house on the southern end of the northern cay, then a gap with a clump of mangroves in it, followed by another cay. After this is a half-mile-wide gap through which you can see two cays inside the lagoon (they may appear as one) and another couple of cays on the far side of the lagoon. When the southern edge of the northernmost of these two eastern cays bears 101°T to 103°T, head for it. You cross a bar with depths of 10 feet. If you stray any farther south the water shoals to 7 feet. Inside the lagoon depths are mostly 60 feet—including to the west of the two inner cays where the chart shows shoal water.

ANCHORAGE. The most protected anchorage is off the fishing camp in the northwest corner. The breeze funnels through, pelicans dive around you (the cays are aptly named), the water colors are lovely, and to the west you have a beautiful view of the Cockscomb Mountains—a very pleasant spot indeed.

THE PELICAN CAYS TO
THE GLADDEN CAYS

Charts: BA 1797; DMA 28166 and 28162.

From the Pelican Cays southward the main channels diverge. The Inner Channel continues to Placencia; the Victoria Channel branches off to the southeast but then curves back to the southwest to rejoin the Inner Channel; and a third, unnamed, channel works its way down, also southeastward, toward the Queen Cays entrance. This third channel runs to the east of the Pelican Cays. If anchored at the Pelican Cays, you have to exit to the west and then come around to the north, staying off the coral at the north end, before coming down to the west of the Elbow Cays. The various possible channels working to the southeast are deep and free of obstructions but narrow in places. At times you will be in 60 feet with reefs or sandbars breaking the surface less than 100 yards off on either side. The bottom comes up suddenly—our bow has been touching coral when our depthsounder was reading 30 feet! The play of light over the water and the colors are indescribable. Good light and a good lookout are essential.

ANCHORAGES. The Lagoon Cays sound and look like an ideal anchorage, but the lagoon, on the northern of the two cays, is barred by a shoal across its mouth. You can anchor off its mouth in 10 to 12 feet and take the dinghy inside, but there is not much to see except mangroves.

The Channel Cays provide no anchorage. To the south there is an enticing sandspit-enclosed lagoon, but we could find no entry. The shoals appear to be continuous all the way south for almost 2½ miles to what shows on the chart as a reef but is in fact a shoal.

THE PELICAN CAYS TO THE LAGOON CAYS

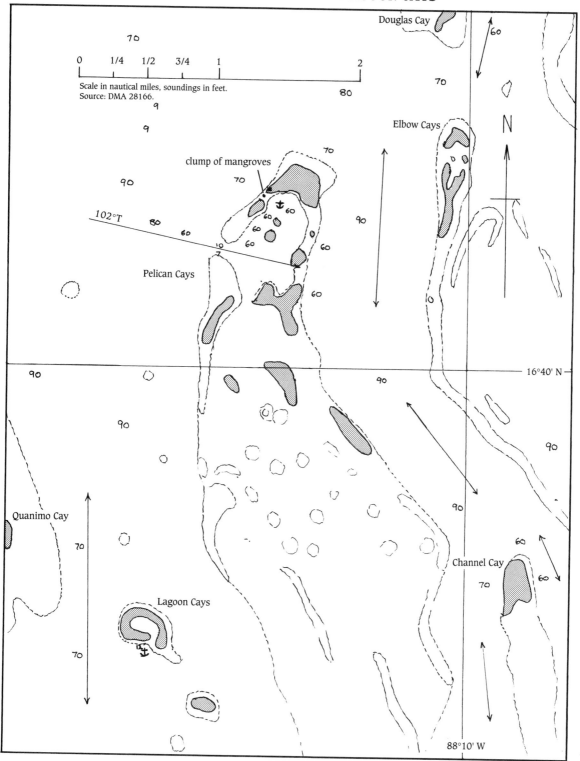

Douglas Cay

60

70

70

Elbow Cays

N

70

clump of mangroves

90

70

90

102°T

80

60

Pelican Cays

60

60

60

60

90

16°40' N

90

90

90

90

90

Quanimo Cay

70

Channel Cay

60

60

70

70

Lagoon Cays

70

Scale in nautical miles, soundings in feet.
Source: DMA 28166.

0   1/4   1/2   3/4   1   2

80

9

9

90

88°10' W

LONG COCOA CAY TO THE GLADDEN CAYS

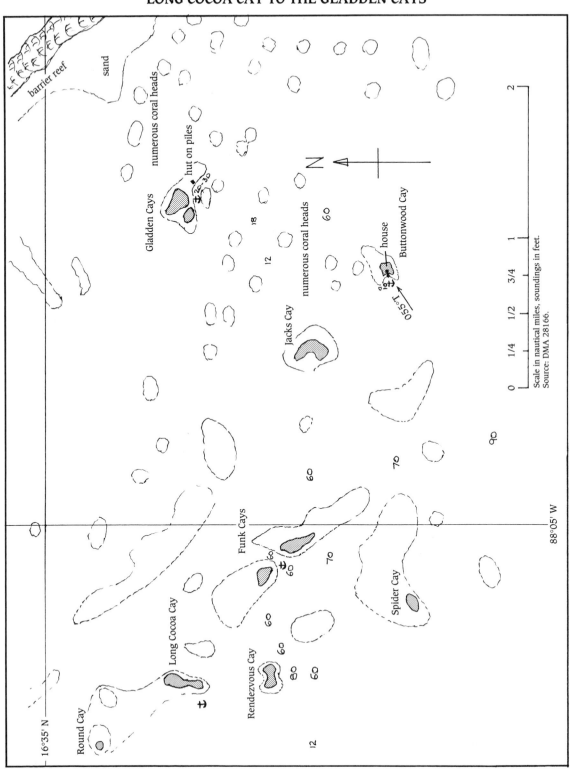

barrier reef

sand

numerous coral heads

Gladden Cays

hut on piles

numerous coral heads

Buttonwood Cay

house

Jacks Cay

N

2

1

3/4

1/2

1/4

0

Scale in nautical miles, soundings in feet.
Source: DMA 28166.

Funk Cays

Long Cocoa Cay

Rendezvous Cay

Spider Cay

Round Cay

16°35' N

88°05' W

Tarpum Cay is a mangrove cay with many pelicans but no decent anchorage. The lagoon is shallow with many coral heads, and anchoring is only possible on the outside to the southwest.

Long Cocoa Cay, an attractive sandy island with coconut trees, offers reasonable protection in normal trade-wind conditions in 10 to 12 feet just to the southwest.

Rendezvous Cay (#2, not the same cay described on page 117) is not as charted. There is a gradually shoaling shelf along the southern shore which, at about 12 feet, suddenly drops off into 80 feet. The shelf is predominantly thin sand over rock with quite a bit of scattered coral. The holding is poor and your attempts to anchor will tear up the coral. Should your anchor drag, it will go off the edge of the shelf and hang uselessly. The deep water continues around to the north of the coral patch, which the charts show to the southeast of Rendezvous Cay, but which is not as extensive as shown. If you do wish to anchor at Rendezvous, you should drop your hook in the deep water. The holding is good in a clay-like deposit, but you need a tremendous amount of scope.

The Funk Cays are similar to Rendezvous with a gradually shoaling, coral-encrusted shelf suddenly dropping into 60 feet; the deep water reaches between the two cays. Once again, anchor in the deep water to spare the coral and find good holding. We weathered a strong norther here for five days (not out of choice—it was not forecast and we got caught). The protection here was fine, but the necessary scope left us alarmingly close to the coral. Coral heads broke the surface 10 feet off our stern with the wind blowing in excess of 30 knots—not a very relaxing situation. We finally lost an anchor when the wind shifted and we dragged our rode across a coral head. The anchor is still down there—we couldn't find it.

Buttonwood Cay has an anchorage to its southwest in 10 to 12 feet, but the bottom is thin sand over rock with only fair holding. A small reef to the south provides some protection, but swells tend to hook in from the southeast. Numerous coral heads with depths of less than 6 feet are sprinkled north and west of Buttonwood Cay. This is strictly a good-light area; in the right conditions, however, you will have no problem picking your way through since there is plenty of water between the heads.

The Gladden Cays have a surprisingly good anchorage immediately south-southeast of the gap between the two islands. Although the anchorage appears to be wide open, reef areas to the east and the south break any wave action, and a cool breeze blows in from the barrier reef, which is just 1¹/₂ miles to the east. Depths are 20 to 30 feet over a sandy bottom with good holding. Swinging room is a little restricted—if you intend to stay overnight you should set a running moor.

THINGS TO DO. The Gladden Cays are some of the prettier mangrove cays, but their real beauty is below the surface. All around, especially up toward the northeast (see below) is wonderful snorkeling in perfect conditions.

INSIDE THE REEF BETWEEN
SOUTH WATER CAY AND
THE GLADDEN CAYS

Charts: BA 1797; DMA 28166 and 28162.

There are a number of navigable breaks in the barrier reef between South Water Cay and South Cut, but between South Cut and the Gladden Entrance the reef forms a solid wall. In its lee a broad band of shallow sand gradually deepens to 9 to 12 feet. Patches of gorgeous living coral are scattered all over the deeper water, almost breaking the surface, but with plenty of navigable water in between.

You can sail the full length of the reef, but first you should get some experience of judging water depths by color—at times the maze becomes quite intricate. Good light is absolutely essential; ideally you need the sun high in the sky and behind you, on a day with no clouds. In the winter months the sun is to the south and the passage should be made from south to north, but in the summer months the midday sun is a little to the north and it may prove easier to come south.

Once you have started and are into the fields of coral heads there will be no turning back into the sun. Should the light deteriorate, you can anchor just about anywhere in sand and await better conditions. You may need to set a running moor if swinging room is restricted. In any case, it is worth anchoring to snorkel some of the heads: The finest coral is in the stretch closest to the Gladden Cays.

If you start northward from the Gladden Cays, aim broadly for a wreck on the reef to the northeast. Ten miles farther north sandspits extend westward a mile or so on either side of South Cut, but these have navigable gaps in places—you will need to detour around the sand and, once across the South Cut channel, follow the curve of the sand back toward the reef. Similar sandspits occur off some of the other unnamed cuts to the north of South Cut. From Water Cay up past Tobacco Cay the channel is unobstructed (see page 120). This is a spectacular passage with indescribable water colors, crystal clear water, and outstanding coral. In normal trade-wind conditions, a fresh breeze blows in across the reef but it brings no wave action. If you are able to relax this close to so much coral, it is well worth the effort and concentration required to pick your way through.

THE PELICAN CAYS TO

LAUGHING BIRD CAY

Charts: BA 1797; DMA 28166 and 28162.

The Victoria Channel leads southeast from the Pelican Cays, on its western side is a series of cays. Quamino Cay, Crawl Cay, and Bakers Rendezvous are all surrounded by extensive coral, which drops off into deep water. This provides little opportunity for anchoring.

APPROACHES/ANCHORAGES. Cary Cay is best approached from the southwest on a heading of 075°T for the midpoint of the island, then hooking around toward the gap between the cay and the small islet immediately to its south. This track stays in deep water, avoiding the shoal area to the west of the cay. Depths will be 80 feet until fairly close in, then the bottom—grass over sand—comes up suddenly. Anchor in 10 to 20 feet. Cary Cay has a small beach with some excellent snorkeling on the nearby reef. To gain the western side of Cary Cay from the

Victoria Channel, the sandspit between Cary Cay and Long Cocoa Cay can be crossed with care one-quarter mile or more south of Cary Cay.

Long Cocoa Cay #2 (not the same Long Cocoa Cay described on page 131) has an extensive area of coral to the northwest. You can pick your way between the heads, but the reef hooking out from the island to the northwest, which borders this coral, is almost continuous with just one very narrow, 20-foot-deep cut about one-quarter mile offshore. The island has a well-protected anchorage in normal trade-wind conditions.

Mosquito Cay is privately owned with a considerable amount of development underway.

Laughing Bird Cay is a pretty little sand-and-coconut island, reputed to be the nesting ground for laughing bird gulls. We saw no sign of a nest and very few gulls. A shallow area of coral extends to the southwest of the southern half of the island, but north of this the bottom is free of coral heads. You can tuck in close to the northern tip of the island in 12 feet with a small reef to the north providing a measure of protection. Nevertheless this can be a rolly anchorage and should be treated as a daytime stop only.

There is good, shallow snorkeling on the reef.

LARK CAY TO COLSON CAY

Charts: BA 1797; DMA 28166 and 28162.

The cays in this area form a rough circle approximately 3 miles in diameter. The water within this ring of cays is generally well-protected, while the surrounding islands have a number of reasonable anchorages.

The sand bore between the Bugle Cays and Lark Cay has a couple of small mangroves and extends farther to the southeast than charted. We also found one or two other uncharted shoals within the broad circle formed by the cays in this area.

APPROACHES/ANCHORAGES. Lark Cay has the best anchorage in the bight formed by its southern shore. The protection and holding are both good. The anchorage can be entered from the north with care around both the east and west ends of the is-

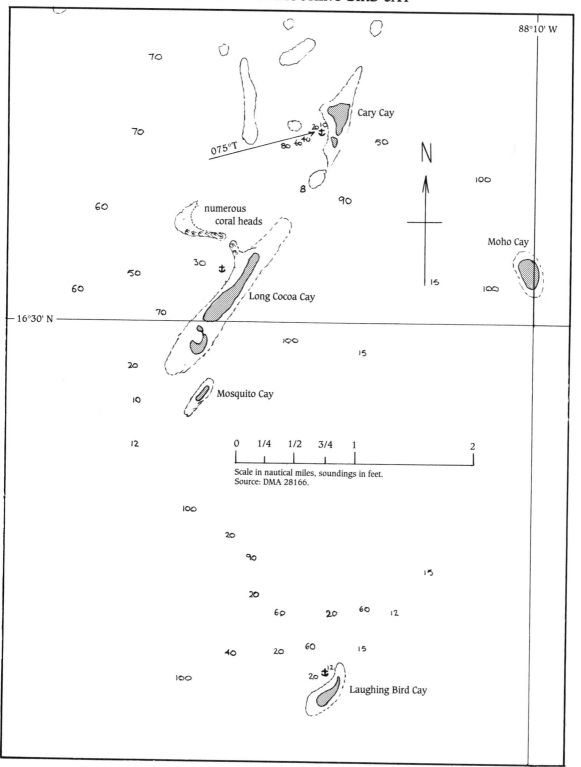

88°10' W

70

70

075°T   80 to 10

Cary Cay

50

N

100

60

numerous
coral heads

Moho Cay

50

15

60

Long Cocoa Cay

100

— 16°30' N

70

100

15

20

10   Mosquito Cay

12

| 0 | 1/4 | 1/2 | 3/4 | 1 | | 2 |

Scale in nautical miles, soundings in feet.
Source: DMA 28166.

100

20

90

15

20

60   20   60   12

40   20   60   15

100   20   12   Laughing Bird Cay

LARK, BUGLE, SCIPIO, AND COLSON CAYS

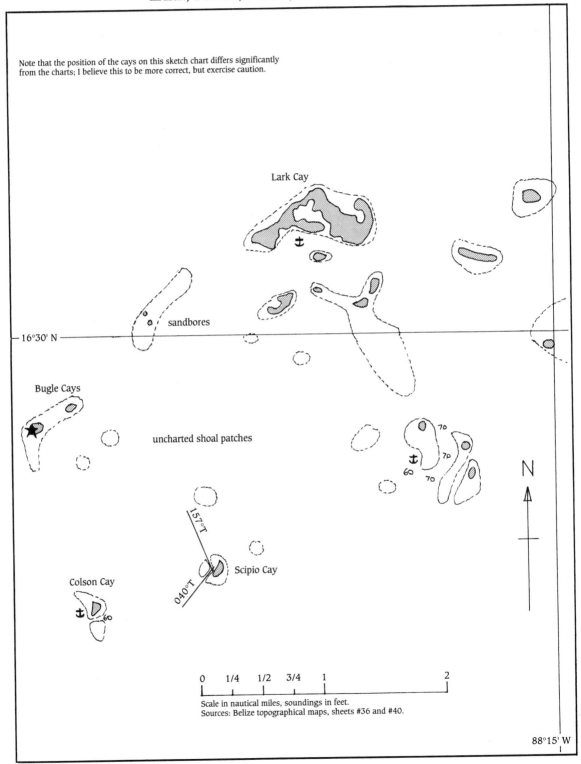

Note that the position of the cays on this sketch chart differs significantly from the charts; I believe this to be more correct, but exercise caution.

Lark Cay

sandbores

— 16°30' N

Bugle Cays

uncharted shoal patches

70

70

60

70

N

157°T

040°T

Scipio Cay

Colson Cay

60

0   1/4   1/2   3/4   1   2

Scale in nautical miles, soundings in feet.
Sources: Belize topographical maps, sheets #36 and #40.

88°15' W

land, or from the south. Note that the channel shown on the chart between the cays to the southeast is in fact completely blocked by coral.

The reef area 2 miles to the southeast of Lark Cay consists of three separate cays with deep water between them. The westernmost island has a frigate bird and booby colony with a convenient anchorage for bird lovers on its south side.

Scipio Cay has an anchorage almost on the beach on its western shore. Approach is made either from the southwest on a heading of 040°T for the northern tip of the island, or from the northwest on a heading of 157°T for the southern tip of the island. Only attempt this entry, which is in 40-foot-deep channels between reefs, in good light.

Colson Cay has a pretty mix of coconut and other trees. In normal trade-wind conditions, a reasonable anchorage can be found to the southwest. An uncharted 70- to 80-foot-deep channel cuts through the extensive shoal on the southern side of the island about one-quarter mile off the coast.

The Bugle Cays are predominantly mangroves with the lighthouse on the southern tip of the southern cay. Both islands are surrounded by coral and without a decent anchorage.

SITTEE RIVER TO
SAPODILLA LAGOON

(see map page 136)

Charts: BA 1797; DMA 28166 and 28162.

This short stretch of mainland coastline is low-lying and generally featureless. It would be of little interest to cruisers were it not for Sapodilla Lagoon, which is, arguably, the best-protected anchorage in Belize. If we were to get caught out in a hurricane in these waters, this is the spot I would head for.

Sittee River has a 4-foot-deep bar across its mouth. The bight formed to the southwest by its estuary affords protection from northers with good holding in 12 to 15 feet over a mud bottom. However, with Sapodilla Lagoon just 3 miles to the southwest, there is little point in anchoring here.

Sapodilla Lagoon is easy to enter. Just follow the coastline from the north or the south staying about

one-half mile off until the channel into the lagoon opens up, then enter in mid-channel. The depth going in is about 14 feet, slowly decreasing to 10 just inside the entrance and to 8 feet as you work around to the western shore. On entering you will see an island to the southwest (just one—not two as shown on the charts). Come around to the north of this island, holding over toward the north shore of the lagoon to avoid a shoal.

ANCHORAGE. You can anchor anywhere from here on around to a point midway between the island and the western shore of the lagoon. You should not attempt to go farther south, or to work around to the east of the island, since the water shoals to less than 6 feet. The holding is good in a mud bottom with a lovely view across pine-clad hills to the mountains in the west. We had a good breeze and no problems with bugs.

PLACENCIA

(see map page 137)

Charts: BA 1797; DMA 28166 and 28162.

Placencia is a fishing village on a sandy spit, with Placencia Cay immediately to its east. Several hundred people live here and a steady trickle of tourists come and go, staying in town or at a couple of low-key "resort" hotels on the bay to the north.

Placencia has an airport with regular flights to

Placencia.

SITTEE RIVER TO SAPODILLA LAGOON

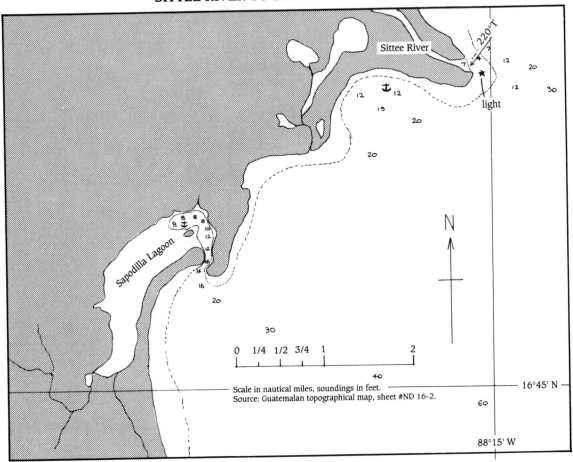

Belize City (and which now boasts a brand-new, modern hotel), another small hotel in town, very limited groceries, two or three restaurants and bars, a post office (with a phone), and a police station.

This is a pleasant spot in which to take a break in your exploration of the cays and to get a little taste of "civilization." The settlement is well placed to serve as a base from which to explore the outer cays.

APPROACHES. From the north, a relatively narrow, 20-foot-deep channel runs between the settlement and Placencia Cay. Shoals extend one-quarter mile or more to the north-northeast of Placencia Cay: Stay one-half mile north of the cay until the channel is south of you, then come through in mid-channel.

From the south, come straight up into the anchorage between the cay and the settlement, staying west of the shoal that extends south of Placencia Cay. The approach is so straightforward that it is one of the few Belizean entries that is feasible after dark.

ANCHORAGE. Usually, several boats are anchored off Placencia, either south of the town jetty or in the lee of the cay. When one anchorage gets a little rolly, the other is almost always calm. The anchorage off the town is usually the most convenient. Both areas have good holding in about 16 feet of water. The protection, even in a norther, is excellent.

Big Creek to the southwest of Placencia is being developed to handle commercial traffic. The entry

PLACENCIA

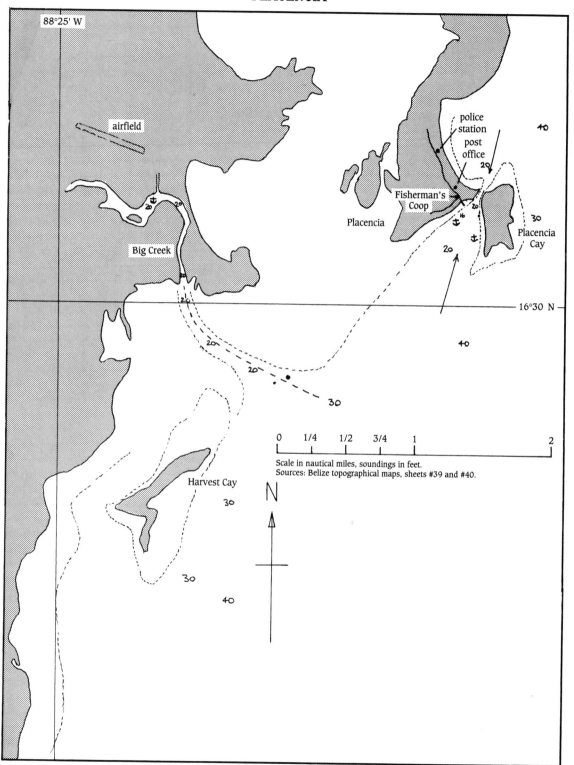

88°25' W

airfield

police
station
post
office

Fisherman's
Coop

Placencia

Placencia
Cay

Big Creek

16°30 N

Harvest Cay

30

30

40

0   1/4   1/2   3/4   1   2

Scale in nautical miles, soundings in feet.
Sources: Belize topographical maps, sheets #39 and #40.

N

channel is now exceptionally well buoyed and lit, with the IALA system of red to starboard, green to port, when going in. The channel, which has a minimum depth of 20 feet, runs past a new shipping terminal (where you can obtain water but nothing else). A shallow branch (dinghies only) runs up toward the airport. You could anchor anywhere above the shipping terminal; it is extremely well protected but very dull! This would be another good spot to weather a hurricane, but I suspect it is likely to get crowded.

HEADING NORTH

FROM PLACENCIA

Charts: BA 1797; DMA 28166 and 28162.

If you are heading north from Placencia and the wind is in the northeast, which it frequently is, you will have a hard beat against an average 1-knot current in the Inner Channel all the way to the Fly Range. After this point the coastline tends more to the north, and you should be able to ease the sheets. The best approach is to tack out from Placencia straight across the Inner Channel into the lee of the cays on the other side. Here you can avoid most of the wave action and the current. Pass through the sheltered water south of Lark Cay, keeping a close watch for uncharted shoals. Then tack north in the lee of the reef from Long Cocoa Cay to Quamino Cay; here again, a good watch is needed. From Quamino Cay either stay in the deep water of the Inner Channel, hugging its eastern shore, or come to the north of the Pelican Cays into the channel that runs between the Blue Ground Range and the barrier reef (see previous comments on page 126), working your way over to South Water Cay and on to the north in the immediate lee of the barrier reef—generally a glorious sail.

Region 3: The Outer Cays and

Routes to and from Punta Gorda

A surprising number of cruisers come to Belize and never explore this interesting southern region. There is less written about it, the distances between anchorages are greater, and the sailing conditions are not as ideal as farther north. Here, however, are unquestionably the most attractive of all the Belizean cays, and they should not be missed.

The cays on the outer reef are all sandy islands, covered in coconut trees, surrounded by living coral, and increasing in beauty the farther south you go all the way down to the Sapodilla Cays. In normal trade-wind conditions, the barrier reef ensures protected waters in which to sail north and south. If you stay one mile inside the reef, the water is deep and free of coral heads. In general, the navigational difficulties in cruising these cays are no greater than you already will have experienced in the more sailed waters of Belize.

Over toward the mainland are many protected mangrove-cay anchorages, which are at least as good as most of those up north, and a couple of really lovely sand-and-coconut islands (West Snake and the Moho Cays). Punta Gorda is a relaxed town in which to check in and out and to stock up on groceries.

HATCHET CAY AND

LITTLE WATER CAY

Charts: BA 1797; DMA 28166 and 28162.

Hatchet Cay is surrounded by reef—it is not possible to anchor close in. The island is mangrove-covered and not very interesting, but the snorkeling

and diving are excellent. If you follow the western edge of the encircling reef, staying in 40 to 60 feet of water, you will see a sandy shoal area to the northwest. You can either anchor on this in 10 to 12 feet over a grassy bottom, or on a 10- to 12-feet-deep shelf that extends northward from the reef. These anchorages are not as exposed as they appear; the White Bank to the north affords a measure of protection. Nevertheless both anchorages are likely to be uncomfortable at times. When the wind is in the northeast, a calmer anchorage can be found in the lee of the White Bank.

Little Water Cay is surrounded by coral and does not provide protection for a decent anchorage. The bay on the south side is rolly, has poor holding on a rocky bottom, and contains a number of large coral heads.

THE QUEEN CAYS

Charts: BA 1797; DMA 28166 and 28162.

The Queen Cays are three little gems set in gorgeous water with excellent snorkeling, cool breezes, and no bugs.

APPROACHES. You can approach from the north (Buttonwood Cay), the west (Hatchet Cay), and the southwest (Little Water Cay or Round Cay). No approach is difficult, but all demand that you watch carefully for coral heads near each cay named. The water nearing the Queen Cays is deep and free of obstructions. The chart shows a reef just to the west of the two southern Queen Cays, extending to the southwest. This reef does not exist as charted—we

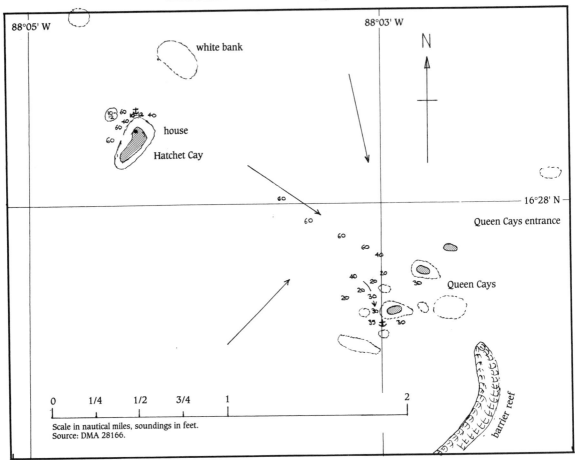

88°05' W

88°03' W

white bank

house

Hatchet Cay

16°28' N

Queen Cays entrance

Queen Cays

barrier reef

0 1/4 1/2 3/4 1 2

Scale in nautical miles, soundings in feet.
Source: DMA 28166.

sailed over much of it and found no water shallower than 15 to 20 feet. There are a number of reef patches around the three Queens, but all are clearly visible in good light and have 30-foot-deep channels between them.

ANCHORAGE. Southwest of the southernmost cay, you can anchor in 30 feet of water over a sandy bottom with good holding. This area is reasonably well protected in normal trade-wind conditions. If the wind veers into the southeast, this anchorage will be rolly. However, the water will be smooth in the lee of the middle cay.

FROM THE QUEENS TO

RANGUANA CAY

Charts: BA 1797; DMA 28166 and 28162.

Note: The little cay shown on the charts to the north of Round Cay is now just a sandbar.

APPROACHES/ANCHORAGES. Round Cay is approached on a heading of 085°T to 090°T for its small sandy beach. You can come almost to the beach, anchoring over a grassy bottom with sandy patches. The anchorage affords reasonable protection in settled weather but not in other situations.

Pompion Cay has a reef area to the north with excellent snorkeling. White Rock has deep water all around it (60 feet), so you can pass to the north or

ROUND CAY

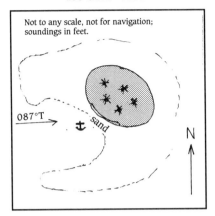

POMPION CAY

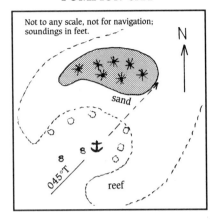

RANGUANA CAY

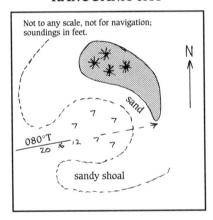

TOM OWEN'S CAY

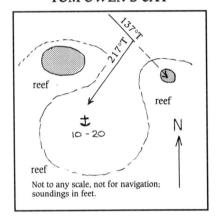

south. Make your final approach into the small lagoon at Pompion on a heading of 045°T for the eastern edge of the island. Keep Ranguana away off in the distance a little to starboard of your stern. When just inside the arms of the reef, anchor in 8 feet in a patch of sand (the bottom is mostly grass). Do not hook around to either side of the anchorage since there are rock and coral patches. The island and reef provide good protection in normal trade-wind conditions and northers, though the anchorage may be rolly. Dozens of pelicans were diving all around us on our two visits.

Ranguana Cay stands sentinel over a half-mile-wide break in the barrier reef. This entrance is very clear from the inside, but difficult to locate from the outside since the cay is a mile inside the reef. The island itself has a lovely beach tapering off to a sandspit at its eastern end. Approach is made on a heading of 080°T for the tip of this spit which brings you into a small, sheltered lagoon with 7 to 8 feet of water over a grassy bottom. There is 20 feet in the mouth of the lagoon where you can anchor and still enjoy a fair measure of protection. The bottom is eel grass with sandy patches, so you may take a couple of attempts to get an anchor to set. (Danforth-types will bite best.)

TOM OWEN'S CAY

Charts: BA 1573; DMA 28162.

Note: The tiny cays shown on the chart a mile to the southwest of Tom Owen's Cay no longer exist.

North Spot is a low sandy islet with three coconut trees. It is visible from both Ranguana Cay and Tom Owen's Cay, making it a useful reference point in the journey south or north. It provides no protection. Tom Owen's Cay has, I think, the most spectacular water colors in all of Belize. The reef encloses a small, reasonably protected lagoon, though it is open to the north and can be rolly at times.

APPROACH. Approach is made on a heading of 137°T for the little islet to the east of the cay. Once the blue-water channel into the lagoon is clear, you enter on a heading of 217°T, hugging the reef to the west of the entrance. The lagoon has 10 to 20 feet of water but is quite small and is surrounded by shallow coral. Use a running moor and make sure the anchors are well set.

Northeast Cay and Grass Cay (French Cay) are surrounded by shoals.

NICOLAS CAY

(see map page 144)

Charts: BA 1573; DMA 28162.

Nicolas Cay has a well-protected anchorage to the northeast behind the barrier reef. The reef breaks all swells at this point. Two or three mooring buoys have been placed in 12 feet of water and you should use one of these if possible. The entry is tricky and requires good light since you will be threading through much coral.

APPROACHES/ANCHORAGE.
From the North. Make your approach on a heading of 175°T for Hunting Cay.
From the West. Approach on a heading of 082°T for the southern tip of Nicolas Cay.
You will be in 60-foot-deep channels between reefs on both approaches. Now come to the southwest of Nicolas Cay in the deep water between it and Hunting Cay. When there is no more than a slight gap between Tom Owen's Cay and Grass Cay to its east, head for Tom Owen's Cay, keeping Grass Cay just open to the east—i.e., making any course corrections necessary to compensate for leeway or tidal

set. As you come abreast of the northern end of Nicolas Cay, beware the reef to the west, but stay close to its eastern edge (this is the trickiest part). When past it, gradually hook around to the east in the clear blue water. When the gap between Nicolas Cay and Hunting Cay is about to close, watch for a rocky area in mid-channel and pass either side of it.

HUNTING CAY

(see map page 144)

Charts: BA 1573; DMA 28162.

Hunting Cay is another pretty island with a lighthouse, a lighthouse keeper, an immigration officer, and a detachment of British soldiers! (Its ownership is somewhat disputed.) If coming from Honduras or Guatemala, you should check in with the immigration officer. This does not excuse you from completing formal clearance procedures in Punta Gorda. The trees have grown up around the light, obscuring it from the west when close in. In 1990 a new and taller light structure was nearing completion. Its 75-foot tower provides a commanding view over the whole area.

APPROACH. Entry to the anchorage is made on a heading of 132°T for the conspicuous outhouse toward the southern end of the western side of the island. You will have a distant cay dead astern on a back-bearing of 312°T. The bottom shoals to 6 feet at low tide for a stretch—it has small rocks but is free of coral heads.

ANCHORAGE. The anchorage is right off the outhouse in 9 feet of water; the bottom is eel grass over a sandy bottom so a Danforth-type anchor will bite better than a Plow or Bruce but may still prove hard to set. The protection is good in normal trade-wind conditions, but the wind often hooks around the island and back-winds the anchorage, so you will need to set a running moor to avoid being driven onto the beach. This would be no place to get caught in a norther, especially since you would be likely to bottom out in wave troughs when trying to escape from the anchorage.

THE SAPODILLA AND
NICOLAS CUTS

Charts: BA 1573: DMA 28162.

Note: The shoal area extending southwestward from Sapodilla Cay is poorly charted so stay out of it and in the deep water.

Low Cay, another lovely sand-and-coconut island, has 10 feet of water to the west. A reef extends one-quarter mile or so to its northeast, but immediately north of this you could enter or exit the barrier reef with depths of at least 9 feet. However, the Sapodilla Cut just to the south of Low Cay provides a much better channel.

The Sapodilla Cut is a half-mile wide and free of obstructions. From the east Nicolas Cay, Hunting Cay, and Low Cay are all clearly visible to the north, and Sapodilla Cay to the west (there is very little of it left, it has two conspicuous palm trees).

The Nicolas Cut is narrow and involves a dogleg; regardless of the light on Hunting Cay and other visual reference points, I would not advise entering here but would go instead 2 miles south to the Sapodilla Cut.

THE SNAKE CAYS

Charts: BA 1573; DMA 28162.

It is possible to anchor off all four Snake Cays (West, South, Middle, and East).

West Snake has the prettiest and most secure anchorage and is well worth a visit. A hurricane has blasted a channel through the western tip of the island; there is now a tiny islet to the west, connected to a lovely sandspit on the main island by a stretch of white sand with shallow water over it. The sandspit is backed by coconut palms with interesting bird life (egrets, pelicans, and frigate birds). Excellent snorkeling can be found on the reef beside the anchorage.

APPROACH/ANCHORAGE. The routine approach is from the west. The reef to the southwest of the cay extends farther than shown on the chart. To give it a good clearance you need to come in on an easterly heading for a point midway between West Snake and South Snake. Hold this heading until Middle Snake is entirely visible to the south of West Snake—i.e., a gap has opened up between the two. Now head for the southern tip of West Snake until the little islet is due north of you, at which point you must come in toward the anchorage on a heading of 350°T, a little to the west of the islet. This heading brings you within the arms of the reef. When abeam of the southern end of West Snake, curve around to starboard and aim for a point midway between the islet and the sandspit, heading directly for the white sand shoal between the two. Anchor shortly before the shoal in 8 to 20 feet of water on a grassy bottom. Part of the reason for giving such detailed entry instructions is to enable you to find this grassy patch—it is the only area of bottom free of coral. Search it out both to avoid doing damage and to find reasonable holding.

It would be as well to set a running moor to hold you off the shoal if the wind should shift into the south. The anchorage offers good protection in a norther but may prove rolly when the wind is in the southeast. In this case you can go around to the north side of the sandspit.

There is a more direct channel into the anchorage, coming in on a heading of 053°T on the islet through a narrow passage in the reef, but only in good light and calm conditions.

THE MAINLAND
BETWEEN PLACENCIA AND
ICACOS LAGOON

Charts: BA 1573; DMA 28162.

Note: There is a shoal to the southeast of Icacos Point, which is shown on BA 1573 but not on DMA 28162. You can come inside this shoal, staying close to the mainland in 20 to 30 feet of water.

APPROACHES/ANCHORAGES. Harvest Cay has

(Continued on page 146)

THE SAPODILLA CAYS AND SAPODILLA CUT

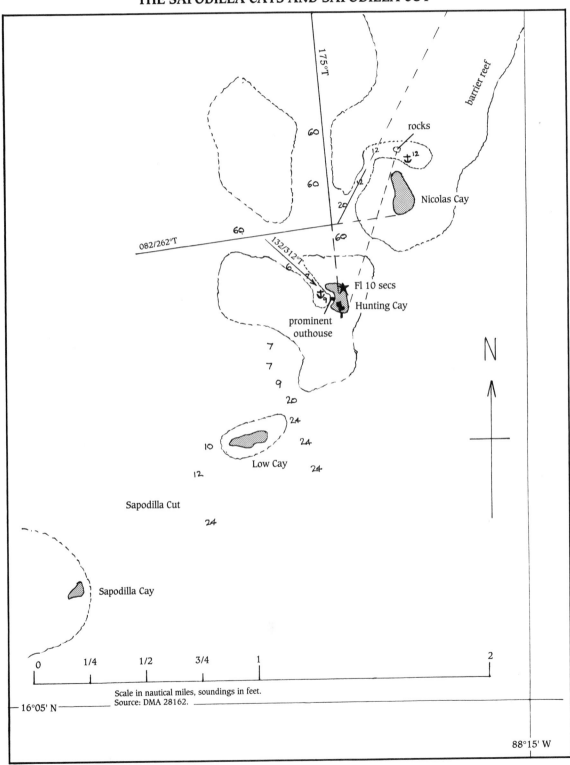

175°T

60

60

rocks

12

12

12

⚓ 12

Nicolas Cay

20

60

082/262°T   60   60

132/312°T

6

barrier reef

Fl 10 secs

Hunting Cay

prominent
outhouse

7

7

9

20

24

24

10

24

Low Cay

24

12

Sapodilla Cut

24

Sapodilla Cay

N

0   1/4   1/2   3/4   1   2

Scale in nautical miles, soundings in feet.
Source: DMA 28162.

16°05' N

88°15' W

THE SNAKE CAYS

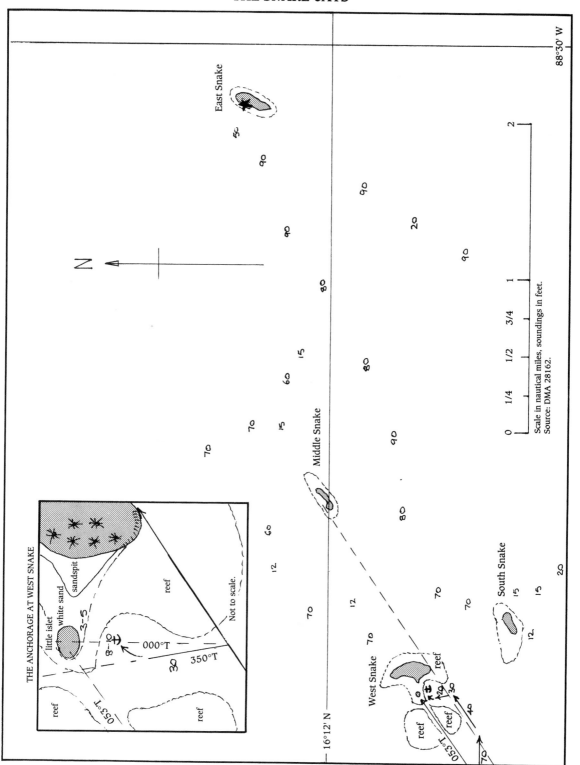

Scale in nautical miles, soundings in feet.
Source: DMA 28162.

A typical fishing camp.

(Continued from page 143)
a protected anchorage to the west. Approach from the south since the northern area is now the dumping ground for the dredgings from Big Creek.

Monkey River is a fishing settlement. A bar restricts entry to the river to vessels drawing less than 3 feet, while anchoring in the lee of Little Monkey Cay is generally uncomfortable since it is too small to offer much protection. You can find shelter to the west of Great Monkey Cay—when coming in avoid the shoal areas extending both south and northwestward from the cay, and work in toward the northern half of the cay. It is a 2-mile dinghy ride to town.

An unnamed cay to the northeast of Icacos Point provides good protection in normal trade-wind conditions, while the mainland breaks northers. Shoals extend to the southwest and northeast of the cay, but there is plenty of water in its lee when approaching either from the north or the south.

New Haven Bight is a well-protected anchorage with good holding and lots of bugs! Entry is straightforward; just stay clear of the shoal water off the eastern side of the entrance. The lagoon has 12 to 15 feet of water in the center, shoaling slowly toward the shore. Charley "Haul-Out" Carlson has a marine railway on the western shore. He can accommodate boats to 40,000 pounds and 6-foot draft. He and his mate are skilled shipwrights, but this is a very primitive facility. Bring all your own supplies and lots of bug spray.

Icacos Lagoon can be entered with a 6-foot draft but not easily. Once inside you will find 7 to 10 feet all the way into the lagoon. To enter, identify the stake just south of the eastern side of the channel. Leave this stake immediately to starboard, then curve in to hug the eastern shore as you enter, coming gradually across to mid-channel once inside. We did not explore the lagoon itself; having grounded three times coming in, we had had enough for one morning!

Deep River is reputed to have 6 feet on the bar at high tide and to be navigable for 10 to 15 miles. This should provide us with some interesting exploration on a future trip.

ICACOS LAGOON TO

THE MOHO CAYS

Charts: BA 1573; DMA 28162.

Between the mainland at Icacos Lagoon and the Moho Cays, you find deep water free of obstructions as indicated on the sketch chart, with the exception of the small half-fathom patch well to the west of the Mangrove Cays. In this area you have numerous anchoring possibilities—in the Bedford Cays and Mangrove Cays in particular, and in the lee of Wilson's Cay.

The Bedford Cays are distinguished by a tall stand of palms on their southern end. The anchorage is entered from the south. The Mangrove Cays have far less land mass than charted (and less than shown on my sketch chart, which is based on the chart) with much deep, protected water between the cays, but with nothing to do or see ashore.

THE MOHO CAYS

Charts: BA 1573; DMA 28162.

Note: The relative positions of the cays are wrongly charted. I have corrected them on my sketch charts. Note also that the most recent edition of DMA 28162 shows some cays in this area that do not exist, and never have!

There are five small islands in the Moho group, of which only the southernmost one is of particular interest. In its lee is a lovely little, well-protected anchorage off a sandy beach backed by coconut trees. The cay immediately to the north is home to a colony of frigate birds and pelicans, which can be watched from the comfort of the anchorage.

Punta Gorda is 8 miles to the southwest. Since the anchorage off Punta Gorda is an open roadstead, and tends to be uncomfortable, we always spend our last night before checking out of Belize, or the first night after checking in, at the Moho Cays. When leaving Belize, with an early start we can be cleared out and into Livingston before dark; coming from Livingston, we obtain our Guatemalan clearance papers the afternoon before departure so that,

with an early start, we can be cleared into Belize and gain the shelter of the Moho Cays before dark.

APPROACHES.

From the North. The easiest approach is to stay in the channel that comes southwest between the mainland and the Snake Cays, continuing until a mile past the Moho Cays and then rounding up into the lee of the shoal that extends south of the southernmost Moho cay.

Approach can also be made south from Icacos Lagoon/New Haven Bight (see above) or between the Mangrove and the Moho Cays, standing over toward the Mangrove Cays to avoid an extensive shoal to the north of the northeastern Moho Cay. Keep a good watch on this latter passage since there are one or two uncharted coral heads along the southern coast of the Mangrove Cays. Come south between the two northernmost cays in the Moho group, initially holding over toward the western cay but then aiming for a point 200 to 300 yards west of the little cay just to the north of the southern cay. You will be in 40 feet of water. When the water begins to shoal to the southwest of this little cay, follow the edge of the shoal, staying 200 to 300 yards off the cay in 15 to 20 feet. This is the tricky part of the approach—there is another shoal immediately to the southwest and the channel is narrow, often with indifferent water visibility.

From Punta Gorda. Moho Cay will be the easternmost cay on the horizon (it is reasonably conspicuous). The easiest approach is to come east into deeper water and then simply head for the southwest tip of the southern Moho Cay, coming up to the west of the reef and shoal area that extends almost 1 mile south of the cay.

A more protected and direct approach can be made inside the extensive shoals to the northeast of Punta Gorda, but this requires precise navigation. Head first for Stuart Cay (approximately 058°T) until the southernmost of the Moho Cays bears 070°T—it will be the easternmost cay on the horizon—and then head straight for it. You must maintain this track; if the tide sets you off such that the 070°T bearing on Moho changes, you must make suitable adjustments to your heading to maintain this relative bearing.

The shoal to the southeast of the Rio Grande has extended southward, as has the shoal to the south

ICACOS POINT TO THE MOHO CAYS

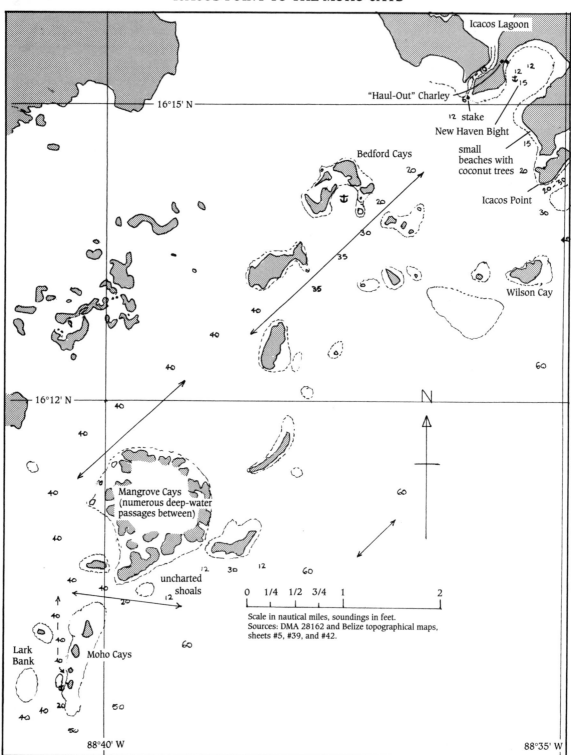

Icacos Lagoon

"Haul-Out" Charley

12 stake
New Haven Bight

small
beaches with
coconut trees 20

Icacos Point

16°15' N

Bedford Cays

Wilson Cay

16°12' N

N

Mangrove Cays
(numerous deep-water
passages between)

uncharted
shoals

0   1/4   1/2   3/4   1   2

Scale in nautical miles, soundings in feet.
Sources: DMA 28162 and Belize topographical maps,
sheets #5, #39, and #42.

Lark
Bank

Moho Cays

88°40' W

88°35' W

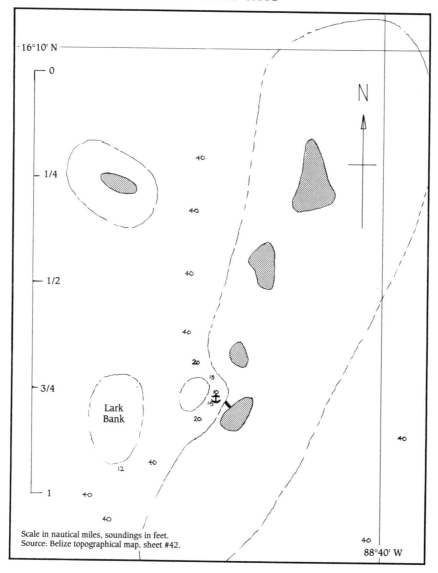

16°10' N

N

0

1/4

40

40

1/2

40

40

20

15

3/4

Lark
Bank

15

20

20

12

40

40

40

40

40

40

40

40

Scale in nautical miles, soundings in feet.
Source: Belize topographical map, sheet #42.

88°40' W

of Stuart Cay. If you stray north, you will foul both; if you stray south, you will run up on another shoal to the south of Stuart Cay. You are never in less than 12 feet of water (except possibly right off Punta Gorda), deepening to 20 feet south of Stuart Cay, and then to 40 feet, with one 12-foot patch 1½ miles before Moho. The bottom comes up quite sharply on the various shoals, while the water is generally too cloudy to judge depths by color, so keep a sharp watch on the depth sounder in the relevant areas.

Finally, the Lark Bank also extends farther south than charted—the 070°T course line clips its southern edge. One mile short of Moho bear away 20 degrees (090°T) until the dock on the west side of the cay is northeast of you, at which time you head for the tip of the dock between a couple of reef areas. The water is clear here so you can see trouble before you run into it.

ANCHORAGE. Anchor no more than 100 yards off the tip of the dock in 10 to 15 feet of water over a

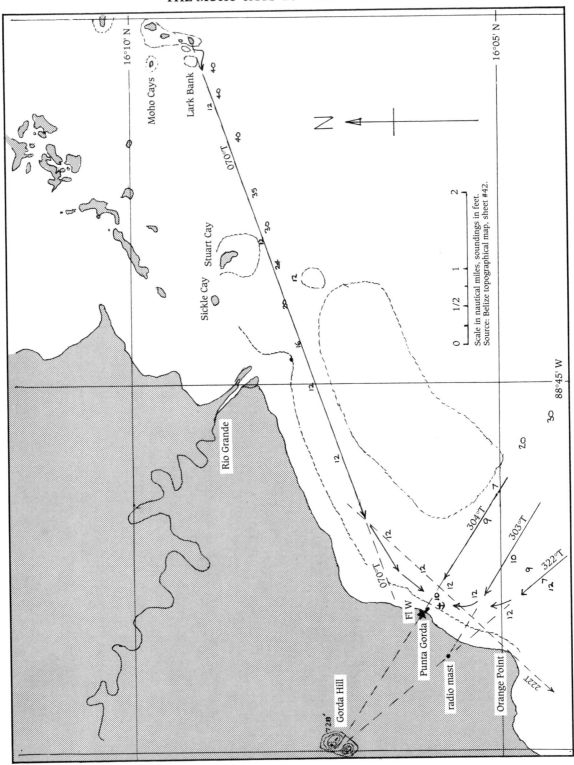

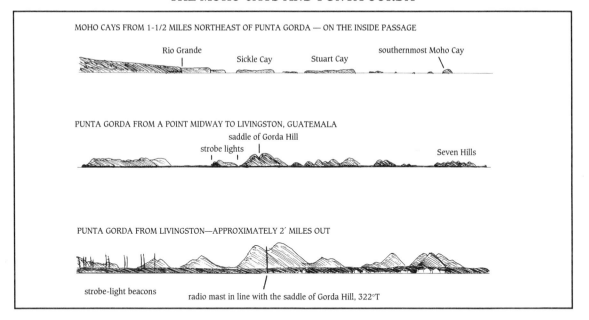

MOHO CAYS FROM 1-1/2 MILES NORTHEAST OF PUNTA GORDA — ON THE INSIDE PASSAGE

Rio Grande   Sickle Cay   Stuart Cay   southernmost Moho Cay

PUNTA GORDA FROM A POINT MIDWAY TO LIVINGSTON, GUATEMALA
saddle of Gorda Hill
strobe lights   Seven Hills

PUNTA GORDA FROM LIVINGSTON—APPROXIMATELY 2´ MILES OUT
strobe-light beacons   radio mast in line with the saddle of Gorda Hill, 322°T

grassy bottom, or a little southwest of this area. There is 6 feet of water on the tip of the dock so don't be nervous about approaching too close to it— the greater danger is a shoal 200 yards to the west of it. The reef areas to the south of the cay, and between this cay and the little one to the north, break all swells in normal trade-wind conditions, while a pleasant breeze funnels through the gap between the two cays.

PUNTA GORDA

Charts: BA 1573; DMA 28162 and 28164. The latter is a 1:50,000 chart of the Bay of Amatique which has Punta Gorda in its northwest corner. It accurately shows the water depths immediately off Punta Gorda, but the lighthouse is, I believe, one-third mile southwest of its actual position.

Punta Gorda is a port of entry and a medium-size town. Clearance procedures are simple and trouble-free, while the town has the best grocery shopping between Belize City and the Bay Islands.

APPROACHES. Gorda Hill, 2 miles to the northeast of town, is conspicuous from miles out at sea both because of its height (728 feet) and because of its twin peaks enclosing a "saddle" that distinguishes it from other hills in the area. Just to the south of Punta Gorda is a series of very powerful strobe lights, visible at night (and sometimes in daylight) from 20 miles out to sea.

From the North and the Moho Cays. The simplest approach is to head southwest from the Moho Cays, staying in the deep water to the east of the extensive shoals northeast of Punta Gorda. When the saddle of Gorda Hill bears 304°T, you are just clear of the shoals and can come in on this heading. The town dock and lighthouse are very hard to spot from offshore but will be immediately in line with the hill. This track crosses a shoal area of 7 feet; if you stray north, you will be in 6 feet. Greater depth (a minimum of 10 feet) can be assured by coming three-quarters of a mile farther south until the radio tower bears 303°T, then heading for the tower. When one-quarter to one-half mile offshore, come north toward the town dock.

The inside passage from the Moho Cays is more direct but requires precise navigation. After leaving the anchorage at the Moho Cays hold a course to the southwest for one-quarter mile and then come west until clear of the Lark Bank. When Moho Cay is on a back-bearing of 070°T, hold a course of 250°T to maintain this back-bearing; make whatever allowance necessary for leeway and tidal set. When southeast of Stuart Cay, watch your depthsounder closely. If the bottom comes up, hook south to stay in at least 20 feet of water, but then return to the 070°T back-bearing to avoid shoals farther south. When southeast of the Rio Grande, keep another close watch on the depthsounder—although here you can expect the channel to start shoaling toward 12 feet in depth. When Orange Point obscures the point farther south (it will bear 222°T), head for the prominent radio tower at Punta Gorda until the dock is visible, then make for a point 200 yards off the end of the dock.

From Livingston. You will be able to pick out Gorda Hill (and the strobe lights) from miles out. Hold a course approximately 10 degrees to the north of the hill. As you close the coast you will see the radio tower; keep this in line with the saddle of Gorda Hill (322°T). This approach passes over one small shoal with 7 feet of water over it. Immediately to the north and south of that shoal, depths go to 8 or 9 feet—a couple of degrees of deviation from the track will find this deeper water. Alternatively come north until the radio tower bears 303°T, then come in on this heading with water depths of at least 10 feet (see above). When one-quarter to one-half mile offshore, head northeast along the coast until you see the dock.

ANCHORAGE. The water is barely 6 feet deep at the end of the dock. Anchor a little to the southeast in 8 feet with good holding. Note that immediately to the northeast of the dock, the bottom is rocky with shallow coral heads and poor holding. The anchorage is likely to be somewhat uncomfortable in normal trade-wind conditions.

CLEARANCE PROCEDURES. Go first to customs, which is on the left-hand side immediately at the top of the track leading from the dock. The immigration officer is in the police station on the other side of the main street.

PROVISIONS/FACILITIES. You can refill propane cylinders and buy kerosene. The post office will hold mail and the BTL office next door has an interna-

tional phone. The airport provides regular flights to Belize City.

HEADING NORTH FROM PUNTA GORDA

Charts: BA 1573; DMA 28162
Note: Small Cay northeast of Negro Head has been washed away, leaving a hard-to-see shoal.

If you are heading north from Punta Gorda and the wind is in the northeast or the east (which it is most of the time), you will have a hard beat against an average 1-knot current all the way to Placencia. The wind is often lighter in the mornings, so make an early start. You can find sheltered water all the way to Icacos Point by taking the inside passage to the Moho Cays, then making up to the west of the Mangrove Cays and the east of the Bedford Cays (see previous notes). From Icacos Point you can avoid some of the current by working up the coast, tacking into the various bays and inside the unnamed cay north of Icacos Point and Great Monkey Cay. The other approach is to make a long tack to the east all the way to the Sapodilla Cays and to come north in the lee of the barrier reef where there will be far less wave action and little or no adverse current. If you have not visited the outer cays, this is definitely the recommended route.

Even with the wind in the east, if you first work up to Icacos Point as above, you should just about be able to make the barrier reef in one tack, and have a broadly favorable current for some of the way. Take care passing through the Snake Cays and check your position regularly in the vicinity of Lawrance Rock. The conspicuous Seal Cay is the one labeled "cocoas" on BA 1573, which is at the northern end of this group. It is not the cay 2¼ miles south described as having "cocoas and huts." To avoid the extensive shoals in this area, tack around the northern end of the Seal Cays, or, if already set to the south, you may come east and enter the reef through the Sapodilla ("Zapotilla" on the old British charts) Cut. The shoal area to the southwest of Sapodilla Cay is poorly charted so stay south of it in deep water until you enter Sapodilla Cut (see the previous notes).

Region 4: Belize's Coral Atolls

TURNEFFE ISLAND

Charts: BA 959; DMA 28167. Caution: There is some doubt as to the accuracy of the charted perimeter of Turneffe Island. The interior lagoon has not been surveyed at all.

Turneffe Island consists of hundreds of small mangrove cays enclosing a shallow lagoon, and is surrounded by an almost continuous reef that rises straight up from the ocean floor. In some places the reef is awash, but in others it is sufficiently submerged to allow passage over the top. The reef extends for 30 miles north and south, and is 10 miles across at its widest part. Strong currents set onto the reef and great caution needs to be exercised when sailing in this area, especially at night. The islands themselves are no more interesting than other mangrove islands, although the lagoon is home to American crocodiles. We made no attempt to explore Turneffe Island in detail. We did establish a reasonably protected anchorage in the south and also found a way into the lagoon for those who would like to explore further.

APPROACHES.
From the West. You can exit Belize's barrier reef at either the Ship Channel by English Cay or through the break at Rendezvous Cay. The former is recommended (see the notes on page 119). Lay a course for the channel on Turneffe Island that is named "Joes Hole" on the charts. This is, in fact, Blue Creek; Joe's Hole is 2 miles farther north (see the sketch chart). Both English Cay and Rendezvous Cay remain in sight until you close Turneffe Island so that at all times you can accurately fix your position by hand-bearing compass. The mangroves immediately to the north of Blue Creek are taller than those to the south, forming a distinct shoulder. In fact they are visible all the way to Ren-

dezvous Cay and give the impression that this is the southern tip of Turneffe. Head for this shoulder, which is a useful visual reference point in an otherwise featureless coastline. As you get closer the mangroves to the south will come into view. You will come onto soundings when about three-quarters of a mile offshore. With the exception of the southern tip of Turneffe Island, there is no visible or breaking reef in this area. The bottom comes up suddenly to 30 feet or so; then for 1 to 2 miles north of Blue Creek, it shoals relatively gradually with no apparent coral heads. South of Blue Creek lie several shallow reef areas (see below). The water is so clear that the bottom is visible at depths of greater than 80 feet.

From the South. You will see that a breaking reef runs down the eastern shore of Turneffe Island extending more than 1 mile south-southwest beyond the southern tip of the mangroves. It includes a sandy, treeless spit that was once Cay Bokel. Two lighthouses are set well inside this reef (one ruined; one new). The reef curves around and extends an additional 1 1/2 miles to the west-northwest, becoming partly submerged, with strong rip tides at times around its tip. You should give this whole area a wide berth. Once you are around the western extremity of the reef, and if trade-wind conditions are normal, you will be in the lee of Turneffe Island and in reasonably calm water—some swells do still hook around the island at this point. You can either work in toward the mangroves and anchor to snorkel the reef areas, or continue farther north for Blue Creek Channel (see below), or anchor north of Blue Creek (near the real Joe's Hole). The water here is generally calmer, but the snorkeling is nowhere near what it is in the reef areas. If heading north maintain your distance off the coast since another area of shallow coral extends southwest of Blue Creek. Once around this you can close the mangroves and head for a point south of the shoulder in the mangroves (discussed above) if you are looking for Blue

TURNEFFE ISLAND

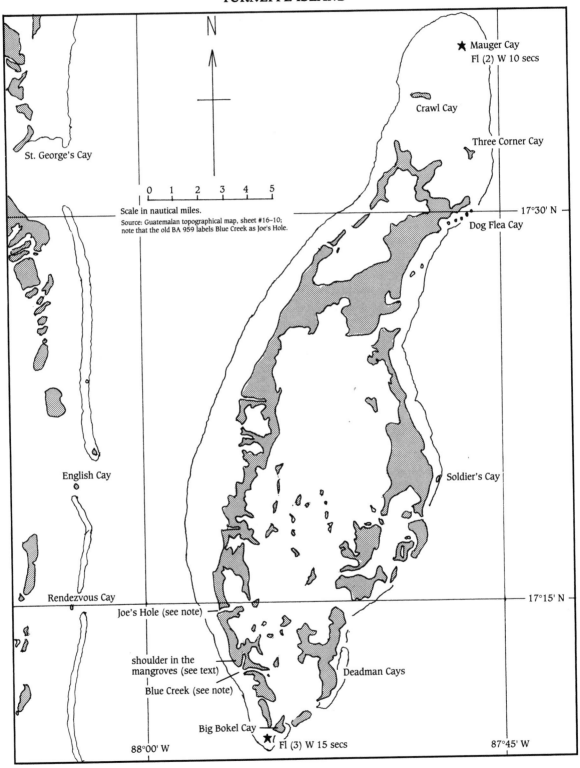

★ Mauger Cay
Fl (2) W 10 secs

Crawl Cay

Three Corner Cay

St. George's Cay

—— 17°30' N

Dog Flea Cay

Scale in nautical miles.
Source: Guatemalan topographical map, sheet #16–10;
note that the old BA 959 labels Blue Creek as Joe's Hole.

0 1 2 3 4 5

Soldier's Cay

English Cay

Rendezvous Cay

—— 17°15' N

Joe's Hole (see note)

shoulder in the
mangroves (see text)

Deadman Cays

Blue Creek (see note)

Big Bokel Cay
Fl (3) W 15 secs

88°00' W

87°45' W

Creek, or north of it if you are looking for a quiet anchorage.

ANCHORAGES. For the best snorkeling, work into the area behind the reef that runs to the southwest of the tip of the island; for smoother waters in typical trade-wind conditions, but not a norther, anchor on the shelf a mile or so north of Blue Creek. In both

TURNEFFE ISLAND: BLUE CREEK CHANNEL TO CAY BOKEL

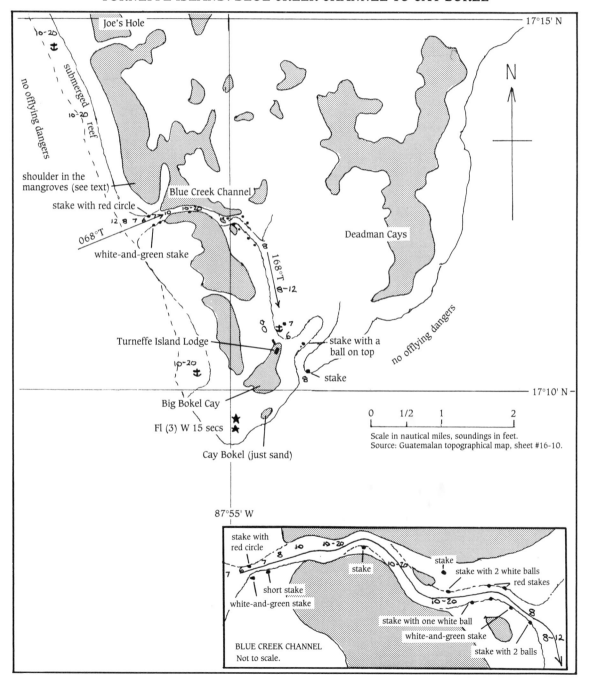

areas you should seek out a patch of sand in about 20 feet of water.

LAGOON ENTRANCES. Blue Creek Channel (Joe's Hole on the charts) is easily located by referring to the shoulder in the mangroves. South of this shoulder the coastline recedes, having one small inlet before opening to a broad, 200-yard-wide channel that leads straight into the mangroves. This is Blue Creek. Final approach is made on a heading of 068°T for the channel. In 1990, three stakes marked the entrance to the channel, but they employ the British system of buoyage (red stake to port entering, green and white stakes to starboard). The bottom shoals to barely 6 feet between the two outer stakes, with the deepest water over toward the red (port) stake. Once past the stake, the channel steadily deepens to 10 to 20 feet through the mangroves. The channel twists and turns with various curious markers, which are shown on the sketch chart. When passing through the mangroves at certain times of the year, you may be plagued by horseflies and other bugs. The channel leads into the lagoon, which is shallower, with depths of 8 to 12 feet on a heading of 168°T toward Turneffe Island Lodge. The water shoals to less than 6 feet off the lodge proper. Anchor to the northeast in 7 feet over eel grass. The wind sometimes whistles in over the reef to the east so check the set of your hook. You will find little wave action and no bugs. In a norther you could find excellent protection back in Blue Creek.

East Entry. A second channel leads more directly into the lagoon through a break in the reef to the southeast of the lodge. The reef is awash along this side of the island, and the break is reasonably obvious, at least from the inside, with a stake on the northern side of the entry. The pass is reported to have 8 feet of water and to be free of coral heads. Once inside, however, the channel twists through extensive shoals and is not easy to follow. I have shown its approximate location on the sketch chart, but I would not recommend using this entrance without a local guide.

PROVISIONS/FACILITIES/THINGS TO DO. There is excellent fishing both in the lagoon and around the reefs on the outside, and the diving is said to be spectacular. Two hotels cater to fishermen and divers. The Turneffe Island Lodge is in the extreme south on Cay Bokel (not the Cay Bokel shown on the chart—this has been washed away); food and drinks are available here, but you should check in before going ashore (VHF channel 16) and prior

The fishing is excellent near Turneffe Island, both in the lagoon and outside the reef.

reservations generally are required for meals. The Turneffe Flats Hotel is about midway along the eastern shore. Turneffe Lodge monitors channel 16 on the VHF; Turneffe Flats channel 68.

LIGHTHOUSE REEF

Charts: BA 959; DMA 28167. Caution: There is considerable doubt about the charted position of Lighthouse Reef, particularly its southwest portion, which almost certainly lies as much as 1 mile farther west than indicated. Sandbore Cay in the north bears little resemblance to its charted appearance.

Note: My sketch charts have been developed from a map derived from computer-enhanced satellite photographs. This map was kindly made available by Dan Thompson and CEDAM International. However, the satellite photos gave no indication of true north, latitude, or longitude. Initially I determined these by reference to the position of the lighthouses on Sandbore Cay and Half Moon Cay, as printed in the latest Light List for Belize. The ensuing lines of longitude and latitude corresponded to BA 959. I assumed a magnetic variation of 3°E (in 1990 it was 2°40'E) but found that none of the 60 to 70 bearings we took at Lighthouse Reef fitted the chart. To make sense of these bearings, I had either to assume a magnetic variation of 1°E or move true north 2°W. I moved true north 2°W of its indication on BA 959. Since the northern end of the reef is reported to be where it is charted, I used the lighthouse on Sandbore Cay as my point of reference for lines of latitude and longitude. The rest of the reef is charted from this perspective. This has had the effect of moving the southern end of the reef a little more than one-half mile to the west of its charted position on BA 959. This fits with other reported data. Assuming 3°E variation (1990), almost all of our relative bearings fitted within this framework. *But please note:* I may have got it all wrong! On no account rely on the latitude and longitude coordinates on these sketch charts for detailed navigational purposes, especially when using electronic aids to navigation. When you are laying off courses, assume 3°E variation (1990) as in other Belizean waters.

The reef at Lighthouse forms a perimeter 22 miles long and 5 miles across at its widest point. Most of it is awash, but here and there breaks afford access to the sheltered lagoon within. In all this area there are just five, sandy, coconut-clad islands—tiny Hat Cay in the southwest, Long Cay a mile to its north, Half Moon Cay in the southeast, and Northern and Sandbore Cays at the northern end.

The lagoon can be navigated from east to west, and north to south, but these are good-light passages only—you will be dodging coral patches the entire way. More or less in the center is the "Blue Hole" made famous by Jacques Cousteau—a circular reef with precipitous coral encrusted walls enclosing an almost 500-foot-deep pool. The diving here and elsewhere on the outside of the barrier reef is world-renowned, while the snorkeling on just about any of the coral patches is excellent.

APPROACHES. The reef is all low-lying and hard to see from more than 1 or 2 miles distant. Strong currents frequently set onto it. Several wrecks along the eastern shore are vivid evidence of the dangers of navigating in this area. This is no place to be sailing at night, and a close watch needs to be kept in the daytime.

From the West. You should aim to make your landfall on Long Cay.

From the North. Aim to make your landfall on Sandbore Cay.

From the South or Southeast (the Bay Islands). Aim to make your landfall on Half Moon Cay.

All of these are visible from several miles out. The reef can be entered northwest and north of Long Cay, to the west of Half Moon Cay, to the northeast and northwest of Sandbore Cay, and to the northwest of Northern Cay. We have used all these entries except the one to the northeast of Sandbore Cay.

LAGOON ENTRANCES.

Northwest of Long Cay. A break in the reef affords access to an anchorage in the lee of Long Cay, which is well protected in normal trade-wind conditions but open to the north (although the reef would break some of the wave action). The approach is made from the west on a heading of 098°T for the northern tip of Long Cay. You will be able to

LIGHTHOUSE REEF

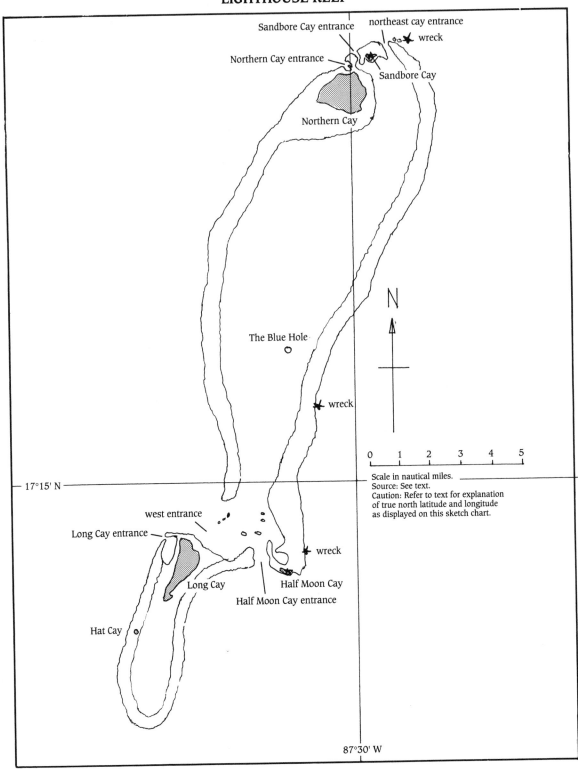

Sandbore Cay entrance

northeast cay entrance

wreck

Northern Cay entrance

Sandbore Cay

Northern Cay

N

The Blue Hole

wreck

0 1 2 3 4 5

Scale in nautical miles.
Source: See text.
Caution: Refer to text for explanation
of true north latitude and longitude
as displayed on this sketch chart.

17°15' N

west entrance

Long Cay entrance

wreck

Long Cay

Half Moon Cay

Half Moon Cay entrance

Hat Cay

87°30' W

ENTRANCES TO LONG CAY, WEST, AND HALF MOON CAY

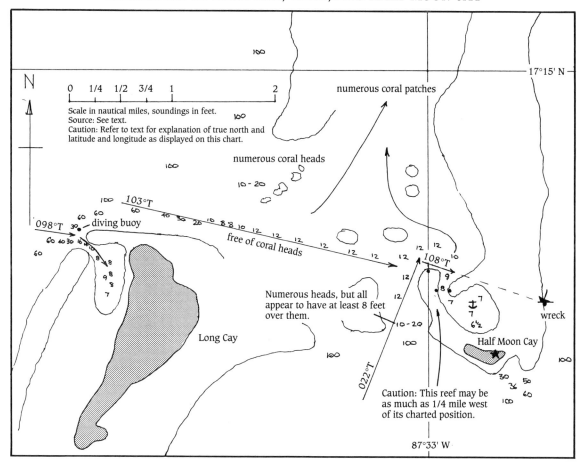

pick out a conspicuous wreck north of Half Moon Cay (itself obscured) on the eastern (far) side of the lagoon. If you can't see the wreck, go north until it is visible. Once the wreck is in view, close the reef, keeping the wreck just visible to the north of Long Cay (098°T). A diving buoy is outside the reef at this point; the channel is immediately to its south. Once within the reef passage, come slightly to the south so that Long Cay just blanks off the wreck. Coming in no depth will be less than 10 feet. When inside the reef, arc gently southward toward the northernmost white sand beach on Long Cay, then find a patch of sand in 7 to 9 feet in which to anchor. Do not approach too closely to Long Cay; the water shoals farther south between the island and the reef, and to the north so that there is no passage around the island into the main lagoon. You must

go back outside the reef and in the next entry (see below).

North of Long Cay. The barrier reef runs east/west for about 1 1/2 miles before returning to a north/south axis. At the point where it curves back to the north, it is submerged for a mile. The southern half of this break is free of coral heads, whereas the northern half has many. A heading of 103°T to 105°T on the conspicuous wreck to the north of Half Moon Cay keeps you on the southern side of the channel and out of the heads. The bottom shoals to 8 feet (it looks shallower because the water is so clear) over white sand. Farther north (107°T on the wreck) the water is deeper but with some coral heads. On the heading of 103°T, you can come three-quarters of the way across the lagoon without encountering any coral. Depths are around 12 feet.

ENTRANCES AT SANDBORE AND NORTHERN CAYS

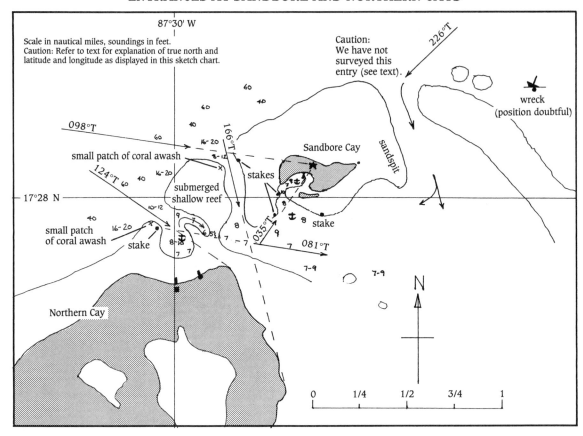

The heading of 107°T, on the other hand, crosses a substantial patch of shallow coral about halfway across. On any heading, as you approach to within 1¹/₂ miles of Half Moon Cay, you have to negotiate a considerable amount of coral in order to enter the anchorage (see below).

West of Half Moon Cay. Approximately 1 mile to the west of Half Moon Cay is an entrance. From outside you should be able to pick out a wreck (in two parts) 5 miles to the north. Make your entry on a heading of 022°T for this wreck. The first part of the passage through the reef crosses an extensive field of coral heads, but all seem to have 8 to 10 feet over them (we deliberately motored around in circles over several to confirm this). Continue north for a mile or more before working into the anchorage at Half Moon Cay (see below).

Northeast of Sandbore Cay. I hesitate to include this entry because we have never tried it. It looks to be perhaps the easiest entry of all, whereas the other two entries at this end of the reef have some problems associated with them. The information here is based on my observations made from atop the Sandbore Lighthouse and conversations with local fishermen and dive-boat operators.

The passage appears to be wide, deep, and free of coral. The remains of a wreck are on the reef to the southeast of the entrance. From the Sandbore Light the western edge of the entrance bears 036°T (216°T from outside) and the eastern edge 056°T (236°T from outside). A heading of 226°T on Sandbore Light therefore should bring you into center channel, at which point you would need to head south southeast, keeping over to the sheltered water on the inside of the barrier reef now to the east. Do not maintain the heading for Sandbore Light since there is a substantial sandspit between it and the channel (see the sketch charts), which extends southward as far as a heading of 283°T on the light. You can continue all the way south to Half

Moon Cay in the lee of the reef (this we have done), or come around the sandspit to Sandbore and Northern Cay (see below for notes on all these options).

Northwest of Sandbore Cay. Both this entrance and the next are difficult because the reef between the two passages is for the most part just submerged and not breaking. Unless you approach it with care, you risk running onto it. This Sandbore Cay northwest entry is narrow and tricky; only attempt it in calm conditions and good light. What is more, the water inside shoals to 6 to 8 feet—deeper-draft vessels have to use the northeast entrance.

Approach is made on a heading of 098°T for Sandbore Light until almost on the reef. At this time you should be able to pick out a stake on the reef immediately to the southeast; leave this to port. In any event, when the eastern tip of Northern Cay bears 166°T, head for it, maintaining this heading until Sandbore Light bears 035°T or less. This channel through the reef is narrow in places, and you will need to make minor course adjustments to avoid coral outcroppings. When Sandbore Light bears 035°T, or less, you can head east into Lighthouse Lagoon, or work into the Sandbore anchorage (see below). A shoal area with a maximum depth of 5 feet 6 inches blocks passage to the west into the anchorage at Northern Cay.

Northwest of Northern Cay. This entry is straightforward but, for most cruising yachts, provides access only to the anchorage at Northern Cay since the maximum draft that can be carried to the east into the main lagoon is 5 feet 6 inches.

Entry is made on a heading of 124°T for the tip of the vegetation on the northeastern tip of Northern Cay. An area of reef awash is immediately to your south, with a stake just inside it, and an area of barely submerged reef to the north. There are coral heads in the channel but all appear to have at least 7 feet of water over them. The water between heads is 10 to 12 feet deep. The course line leads you into a lagoon that is bounded on its northern side by a conspicuous white sandspit covered by just 3 feet of water. See below for details on the anchorage.

ANCHORAGES. The bottom shoals well to the north of Half Moon Cay. A reef extends northward from the western end of the island. Another reef extends west from the barrier reef in the vicinity of the conspicuous wreck, almost intersecting the first reef. You can work down to within one-half mile of the cay through a narrow gap between these two reefs.

Coming from either Long Cay or the entrance west of Half Moon Cay, head north until the wreck bears at least 108°T. You now come around the northern reef, following its arc to the southeast. You will see the narrow gap straight ahead with a stake on either side. The water shoals from 12 feet deep off the northern reef to 9 feet by the gap and 7 feet south of it. Once through the gap, make over to the east slightly and anchor. Find a patch of sand in which to drop your hook and make sure it is set—the holding is poor. This would be no place to get caught in a norther since you would be banging the bottom in wave troughs, and unable to find your way out at night.

Half Moon Cay is a wildlife sanctuary for a large colony of endangered booby birds, together with pelicans and frigate birds. A trail along the northern side of the island cuts in toward an observation tower in the center. From here you have a fabulous view over the rookery with nesting birds just a few arm-lengths away. This is a worthwhile stop, particularly during mating and nesting seasons (February to June).

Sandbore Cay is a lovely spot; 7 feet of water can be carried into a tiny, well-protected anchorage which has room for only one boat. The final approach is made from the south when Sandbore Light bears less than 028°T (this keeps you out of the reef area to the west), heading north for the western tip of the island. You will see some stakes on the reef to the west, and another marking the edge of a shoal and reef area to the northeast. You enter a "funnel" with the shoals to the east closing in. Ahead will be a stake on another reef patch. This stake must be left immediately to port (20 feet or so—the channel is very narrow at this point). You continue until almost on the beach, then hook around and anchor off the end of the dock (which has 8 feet on its western tip, but a pile of conch shells and a shoal immediately to the east). You may need to run a line to the dock to hold you off the shoals. This anchorage affords excellent protection in a norther. Sheltered anchorage can also be found in the mouth of the "funnel" in 7 to 9 feet over a grassy bottom. A couple of friendly lighthouse keepers live on the is-

The Half Moon Cay Natural Monument

The Half Moon Cay Natural Monument was established in March of 1982. It is an area reserved specifically for the protection of the nesting colony of red-footed boobies, as well as parts of the surrounding reef and lagoon area. Damaging, removing, or catching any flora, wildlife, or fish is prohibited.

The western half of the cay is covered with a dense forest of ziricote, gumbo limbo, fig, and other trees. It is here that the red-footed boobies nest. This colony has been in existence for well over 100 years. In the early 1860s, biologist Osbert Salvin visited the cay and reported that the boobies nesting there numbered several thousand. In the 1950s a thorough study was made by an ornithologist who counted some 1,400 nests and estimated a population of more than 4,000 birds. Hurricane Hattie in 1961 swept away the nesting trees and killed many birds, but those remaining came back the next year, nesting on the few broken stumps left and on the low new growth. Since then the trees have grown back and the number of nesting birds has increased.

The birds begin arriving at the cay in November, seeking their old nests, which they renovate for egg-laying. The nests are rough structures of sticks and twigs, often many to a tree. Both parents share the task of incubating. At the end of six weeks or so, the baby chicks break out of their shells. They are covered with a thick, white down and look like little fluffy balls with bare black faces and big black bills.

The work of the parents then begins; they must feed the hungry youngsters. One parent usually flies off to fish while the other remains to guard the chicks from predators, mainly frigate birds (see page 66) and rats. The food-gathering parent brings back partially digested fish and the baby booby sticks its bill, and often its whole head, into the parent's throat, while the parent regurgitates the fish.

The red-footed booby has two adult phases of plumage. Young boobies are dull grayish brown and take three years and several molts to achieve adult plumage. One adult phase is brown with a white tail. The other is a beautiful, golden-tinged white, with black wing tips and edges. Studies have shown that most of the adult birds in the Caribbean are brown. But practically all the nesting birds at Half Moon Cay are white-phase adults—beautiful birds with bright red feet and blue-and-pink bills. This coloring is what makes the red-footed boobies so special.

(COURTESY OF THE BELIZE AUDUBON SOCIETY.)

---

land. They will let you climb the light tower, which affords a wonderful view of the surrounding cays and reef.

The lagoon at Northern Cay shoals well out from the beach. The best anchorage is behind the sandspit in 8 to 10 feet. Drop your hook in the edge of the sand since the bay is rocky with poor holding. Ashore a brand new divers' resort (Lighthouse Reef Resort) is being developed, complete with airstrip. A marina is planned! Good fresh water is available on their dock, but the dock has only 4 feet of water alongside. Drinks can be bought at the bar, and meals in the restaurant (prior reservations needed—VHF channel 68). The interior of Northern Cay is low-lying and swampy with two shallow lagoons. These are home to crocodiles and many species of birds—endangered white-crowned pigeons, reddish and white egrets, ospreys, frigate birds, sandpipers, and others.

WITHIN LIGHTHOUSE LAGOON. Sailing up and down the lagoon is generally an exhilarating broad reach in calm seas with a strong trade-wind blowing over the reef. The deeper water is toward the eastern side of the lagoon, immediately to the west of the shallow sandy apron behind the reef. Numerous coral patches are scattered around. In the right light all are clearly visible. The water is at least 12 feet deep almost everywhere, with the exception of the area to the southwest of Northern and Sandbore Cays where the bottom shoals to 7 to 9 feet with numerous shallower patches. Saddle Cay no longer exists. The shoal area behind the eastern reef extends one-quarter mile or so farther west in the region where the chart shows it to have been.

The Blue Hole is easily found with any of the following bearings: 153°T on the wreck in two parts on the eastern reef; 177°T on the conspicuous wreck just to the north of Half Moon Cay; 213°T on the northwestern tip of Long Cay; or 008°T on the western tip of Northern Cay. You can anchor in numerous clear patches of sand between the coral patches surrounding the Blue Hole. You can even take your boat inside through breaks in the coral rim on the north and east sides!

GLOVER'S REEF

Charts: BA 1797; DMA 28166. Caution: The exact boundaries of Glover's Reef are uncertain, so much so that a note alongside the eastern edge of the reef on DMA chart 28160 reads "Reported to lie 1.5 miles eastward (1966)." The lagoon at Glover's Reef has never been surveyed.

Glover's Reef is the third of Belize's major offshore reefs, once again consisting of a perimeter wall of coral rising straight out of the ocean to enclose a shallow lagoon. Diving and snorkeling on the reef and the coral within the lagoon are world

class. A few small, but beautiful, sand-and-coconut cays cling to the southeastern rim of the reef. I have included directions for entering the reef in the area of these islands, but we made no attempt to do any further exploration.

APPROACHES/ANCHORAGES.

From Belize. Glover's Reef is best approached from Tobacco Cay or South Water Cay. A 15- to 17-mile open-water passage separates the entry at the southern end of Glover's Reef from Belize's barrier reef, but in normal trade-wind conditions this can be made on a fast close reach. On a clear day Tobacco Cay, South Water Cay, and Carrie Bow Cay will all still be clearly identifiable when the Southwest Cays on Glover's Reef come into view. This enables you to get precise fixes with a hand-bearing compass. The reef comes up very suddenly, but is partly submerged on much of this western shore so you need to keep close watch to avoid running onto it. It extends southward to a line almost due west of the southern tip of the Southwest Cays. Once this tip bears 093°T, you are just clear to head east.

From the Bay Islands. Between Northeast Cay and the light at the northeast point of Glover's Reef (a distance of almost 10 miles), there are no landmarks. The reef is low-lying, hard to spot from more than 1 or 2 miles out to sea, and may be as much as 1 1/2 miles east of its charted position. The current generally sets in a northwest direction from the Bay Islands toward Glover's Reef. The distance is something greater than 60 miles. *What this all adds up to is that any approach from the Bay Islands must be made with extreme caution* and planned so as to ensure a landfall in daylight. Precise navigation is required. You should make for the light on Southwest Cay since the entry there is the easier of the two.

LAGOON ENTRANCES. The usual entry to Southwest Cay is on a heading of 035°T just to the west of the cay. You will see a stake marking the end of the reef to the south of the cay. This is left to starboard. As you come into the shelter of the island, you will be in 10 to 20 feet of water with a long shoal off to port.

An alternative entry, especially if coming from Belize, is to line up the western edges of Middle Cay and Long Cay and to come in on this heading. This

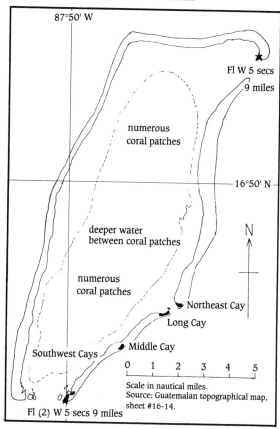

GLOVER'S REEF

87°50' W

Fl W 5 secs
9 miles

numerous coral patches

16°50' N

N

deeper water between coral patches

numerous coral patches

Northeast Cay

Long Cay

Middle Cay

Southwest Cays

0   1   2   3   4   5

Scale in nautical miles.
Source: Guatemalan topographical map, sheet #16-14.

Fl (2) W 5 secs 9 miles

ENTRANCES TO SOUTHWEST AND NORTHEAST CAYS

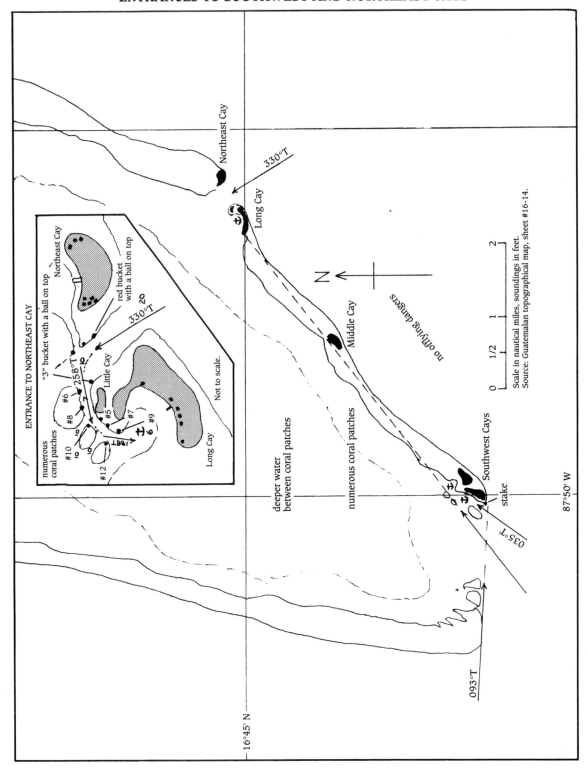

Northeast Cay

330°T

Long Cay

N

Middle Cay

no outlying dangers

Southwest Cays

stake

035°T

093°T

16°45' N

87°50' W

Scale in nautical miles, soundings in feet.
Source: Guatemalan topographical map, sheet #16-14.

0   1/2   1   2

deeper water
between coral patches

numerous coral patches

ENTRANCE TO NORTHEAST CAY

Northeast Cay

red bucket
with a ball on top

"3" bucket with a ball on top

330°T

258°T

Little Cay

#6

#8   #5   #7

#10   #9

188°T

#12

numerous
coral patches

Not to scale.

Long Cay

track is free of all obstructions until you are broad off Southwest Cay; at this time you will see an obvious shoal ahead which can be rounded to the north or south. Anchor anywhere in the lee of the cays in 10 to 12 feet with good holding in grass over sand. The bottom shoals gently toward the beach.

Northeast Cay and Long Cay comprise the windward side of the reef, so at times there may be considerable swells driving up into this entrance. It is preferable to come in at Southwest Cay and reserve this pass for leaving. The reef is awash in front of both Long Cay and Northeast Cay. In between a 20- to 40-foot-deep shelf shoals steadily for one-quarter mile out to sea before dropping off into the depths of the ocean.

Approach is made on a heading of 330°T for a point midway between Northeast Cay and Little Cay—the islet to the north of Long Cay. Once you are inside the arms of the reef, any swell will subside rapidly. Ahead you should see a strange collection of channel markers, but since the dive resort on Northeast Cay has closed, these will likely disappear over time. In 1990, the two principal ones were (1) a stake surmounted by a red bucket and ball, numbered "4," which is left to starboard, and (2) a stake surmounted by a bucket, number "3," which is left to port. Beyond the red bucket and ball on the starboard side of the channel are two more stakes that help delineate a very narrow channel leading to the dock on Northeast Cay. Do not attempt this channel. Come around the port-side bucket (#3) onto a heading of 258°T; this leads you clear of the western tip of Little Cay by 200 yards. You will leave two more markers to starboard (#6 and #8) and then come between #10 (to starboard) and #5 (to port) just beyond Little Cay. You must now curve to the south onto a heading of 188°T, leaving markers #10 and #12 to starboard, and #7 and #9 to port. This brings you into a protected little anchorage. At all times, keep a sharp lookout for coral heads jutting into the channel: A little bit of weaving may be required. The controlling depth is just over 6 feet. A deeper, 10-foot channel can be found by working around the coral heads to the west, but since the anchorage has just 6 feet of water, deeper-draft vessels have to anchor off in a clear patch between the numerous shoals in this area.

WITHIN THE LAGOON. You can pick your way through the coral between the Southwest Cays and Long Cay. The water is generally calm and crystal clear. Immediately in the lee of the reef it is very shallow, but one-quarter to one-half mile to the west, the channel deepens to 12 feet for most of the way, with some really deep channels farther west. There is a superabundance of living coral, most of it just breaking the surface! However, deeper water surrounds almost all the heads, with one or two relatively clear channels for several hundred yards. Making your way through is a matter of picking the right light conditions, positioning someone in the ratlines to keep a good watch, and taking your time.

You can enter or exit the anchorage at Long Cay from or to the west, dodging shoals. The channel is barely 7 feet deep for much of the last one-half mile. Deeper water can be found by working around the heads to the northwest into the channel between Long Cay and Northeast Cay.

Guatemala

The Caribbean coast of Guatemala is short and has little of interest to offer the visiting cruiser. Were it not for the Rio Dulce, most sailors would happily pass by the Bahia de Amatique en route from Belize to the Bay Islands or vice versa. Even the Rio Dulce system is not large—from the mouth of the river at Livingston to the westernmost navigable limits of Lago Izabal, it is less than 40 miles.

Yet Guatemala and the Rio Dulce provide a cruising experience quite unlike any other in the Caribbean and one that can rapidly become addictive. For many sailors, a stay on the Rio Dulce is the high point of a circumnavigation of the Caribbean. Others keep coming back and some never leave. There is a steadily growing community of cruisers on the river, and expatriate Americans are building homes along its banks.

What makes this experience unique? Here is some of what impressed us most: the 300-foot jungle-clad towering walls of the Rio Dulce canyon; the fresh water, which both we and the boat loved; the exhilarating protected sailing on El Golfete and Lago Izabal; the forever-pleasant climate in which some flower is blooming year-round (Guatemala is

Cast-net fishermen in a cayuco on Lago Izabal.

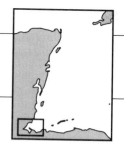

GUATEMALA

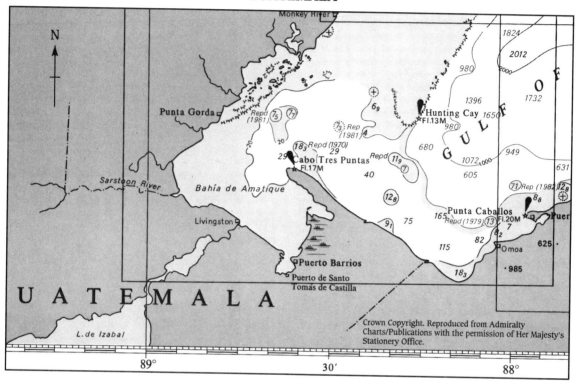

Crown Copyright. Reproduced from Admiralty Charts/Publications with the permission of Her Majesty's Stationery Office.

known as the "land of eternal spring"); sailing through a carpet of water hyacinths; exploring jungle rivers replete with water lilies, dense tropical vegetation, flowering trees, bromeliads and orchids, dripping vines, monkeys swinging through the branches, parrots flying overhead, and almost no bugs; but above all, the people, the color, and the spectacular sights to be seen inland.

Half of Guatemala's population is still purebred Mayan Indian. The people have preserved their lifestyle and traditions as have no other group of Mayans in Central America. They are shy but friendly, hardworking, and unbelievably cheerful and honest in the midst of often grinding poverty and harsh persecution. They hand-weave the most

intricately patterned cloth, dyed every color of the rainbow, and spend months hand-embroidering the clothes made from this cloth. Then they wear these clothes every day while working in the fields and shopping in the marketplace, just as their ancestors have done for hundreds, and perhaps thousands, of years.

Guatemalan markets, especially in the populous central mountain region, are an unforgettable sight. Every village has its own particular pattern of cloth and style of ornamentation. On market day the Mayans come together, packed in their thousands, in riotous color with an overall uniformity of dress but an infinite variety of detail, a feast for the eye (and the camera) to the point where it becomes

Fetching water from the town well, Santa Maria de Jesus.

nominally Catholic, in many ways they have taken over the Catholic Church and under its umbrella continued their own religion. On this day the local Mayan priesthood, clothed in wonderful outfits, sallied forth from the church carrying an image of San Pedro to make a round of the town, letting off mortar bombs every 100 yards or so to scare off the evil spirits, and then afterward got drunk.

We spent Easter Week in Antigua. We saw one procession after another, each one involving thousands of splendidly garbed acolytes carrying an enormously heavy, ornately carved wooden platform surmounted by an image of Jesus, through the narrow colonial streets of the city. The processions continued for 12 hours, late into the night. The final processions passed over an almost continuous carpet of dyed and intricately patterned sawdust that the populace had spent all the previous night laying

(Continued on page 170)

overwhelming; frequently some towering volcanic peak in the background adds to the dramatic effect. Huge cast-iron pots bubble over smoky open fires; men stagger to market carrying enormous loads in woven reed baskets on their backs, suspended from leather straps around the forehead in the time-honored Mayan fashion. Almost every woman has a bundle on her head, and every other one has a baby on her back, wrapped in yet more brightly colored, hand-woven cloth. This is what the marketplaces must have been like in medieval Europe, minus the glorious colors.

And then there are the feast days. . . . Our stay in Chichicastenango, one of the more colorful towns with lovely colonial architecture, coincided not only with the market day but also a feast day. The town is a great religious center. Although the Mayans are

Dancers in the Peten province. The mask on the left represents a conquistador, that on the right a deer.

A Guatemalan market.

The Central Highlands

Nowhere in Central America can you find such a concentration of Mayan Indians with such an adherence to tradition as in the Central Highlands of Guatemala. Thanks to modern roads and the buses, this region is readily accessible to tourists. The scenery is often spectacular, with the steep slopes of numerous volcanoes, some still periodically active, terraced and highly cultivated, forming an intricate mosaic of colors and geometric designs. Now and then as the bus twists and turns on steep mountain roads you catch an enticing glimpse of Lake Atitlan through a break in the encircling volcanoes.

You should certainly try to spend at least a week savoring some of the towns in this region. Refer to pages 182 and 184 for information on how to travel to Guatemala City, and within Guatemala.

Most towns have a weekly open-air market and you should make an effort to be in town on this day. The rest of the week, the towns can be awfully quiet and the streets almost deserted. Here are a few of our favorite stops:

- Chichicastenango combines a huge market, with a heavy emphasis on native crafts, and beautiful colonial architecture. The sight of the flower ladies on the church steps is a memorable one. Market days are Thursdays and Sundays. The local Catholic church has an auxiliary Mayan priesthood organized in a complicated and powerful series of brotherhoods (*cofrades*). Each brotherhood is responsible for organizing a celebration on a particular saint's day. We were in town for just a minor procession, which we found riveting. The most important celebration is on December 21 in honor of Santo Tomas—the patron saint of the town. This is preceded by six days of processions, dancing, and native folk arts. The next most important dates are March 19 (San Jose) and January 20 (San Sebastian). Other dates to watch for are January 1; Good Friday; April 29; May 3; June 29; August 18; September 14, 29, and 30; No-

(Continued on page 170)

(Continued from page 169)

vember 1; and December 8. There are two or three expensive, western-style hotels in Chichi. The best of the budget hotels is the Hospedaje Salvador, two blocks from the square.

- San Cristobal has a market on Sundays spread out along the banks of a river with volcanic peaks in the distance. There is nowhere to stay, but a few miles up a mountain road is San Francisco El Alto where the Hotel Hermoza Vista offers excellent value and a lovely view. San Francisco has a large market on Fridays. The surrounding countryside is beautiful.

- Salcaja is an uninteresting town to look at, but its weaving industry is fascinating. As you drive in, you will see long skeins of cotton staked out by the roadside. Walking around town, peeking through windows and into courtyards, you see people spinning, dyeing, and weaving. The whole town is devoted to the cloth-making business. Numerous stores sell weavers supplies and finished material. You should walk down to the bridge and cross the river—on the far side more yarn is staked out along the riverbank. Knock on a couple of doors and ask if you can watch the weavers—they are normally happy to oblige. Market day is Wednesday. There are two hotels in town, one at each end of the main through-road (Hotel Salcaja and Hotel Mansion).

- Solala overlooks Lake Atitlan. It has a huge market on Saturdays. We saw more variety of native dress here than anywhere else in Guatemala. There are several hotels in town.

- Santiago de Atitlan is reached by passenger ferry across Lake Atitlan from Panajachel. The boatride is worth taking just to see the lake. The clothes in Santiago have a very different style of ornamentation to others elsewhere in Guatemala: Both men and women wear garments heavily embroidered with flowers and birds. The church, dating back to 1568, is impressive and has a large collection of carved statuary. Market day is Friday. The Hospedaje Chi-Nim-Ya just up from the ferry dock is clean and cheap.

Quetzal bird. The national bird of Guatemala.

through the streets of the city, knowing the procession would trample it to dust in a few seconds.

Lastly there are the Mayan ruins. Tikál, in particular, is an experience not to be missed by anyone. In the cool early morning light or the last orange glow of sunset, the enormous ruins, thrusting up through the canopy of jungle, take on a mystical and mythical quality. You can sit marveling on top of a temple and watch the sun sink in the west, with spider monkeys peering shyly out of the trees and coveys of brightly plumaged tropical birds flying by to roost for the night. There can be few finer places in the world for bird watchers—there are hundreds of species in this small region. I could continue in this vein for some time. As you can see, we liked Guatemala! You can judge it for yourself. . . .

LIVINGSTON

(see map page 172)

Charts: BA 1573; DMA 28162 and 28164. The latter is a chart of the Bahia de Amatique with excellent detail on the approaches to Livingston and Puerto Barrios, and on Cabo Tres Puntas.

Tikál

The great Mayan ruins at Tikál are awe-inspiring, one of the world's major archeological wonders, while the surrounding jungle is alive with birds and wildlife. You see spider monkeys, parrots, toucans, and much, much more at relatively close quarters. Tikál is hot and sometimes crowded in the middle of the day. It is best seen early in the morning and in the evening. (The latter requires special passes but these are easily obtained.) Sunrises and sunsets seen from atop a temple are magical. Two days are needed to do the ruins even minimal justice.

The hotels close to the ruins are moderately expensive. Cheaper and quite pleasant accommodations can be found in Flores, a town perched on a small island in Lake Peten Itza about 40 miles away. Flores is connected to the mainland by a causeway, at the end of which is Santa Elena, a dirty little town where pigs root in open sewers. Regular buses run from here to Tikál, commencing at 0600 hours. The bus to Guatemala City also departs from here (Fuente del Norte), leaving nightly at 2300 hours (see page 184).

The ruins at Tikál.

The people of Livingston are mostly Black Caribs with a distinctly West Indian flavor in contrast to the Mayan presence in the rest of Guatemala.

APPROACHES. From Punta Gorda, head 167°T for the sea buoy off the mouth of the Rio Dulce—a distance of a little more than 16 miles, which is free of hazards. Most of the time you are on a broad reach or a run.

All other approaches bring you around Cabo Tres Puntas, a low-lying headland to the northeast of Livingston. If necessary, you can anchor in the lee of the cape and await daylight to enter Livingston. From Cabo Tres Puntas to the Livingston sea buoy is a little more than 10 miles, bearing 218°T. This course line clips the tip of Bajo de Ox Tongue (Ox Tongue Shoal) in the middle of the bay, but this is of no concern to cruisers since there is a minimum

LIVINGSTON AND THE RIO DULCE BAR

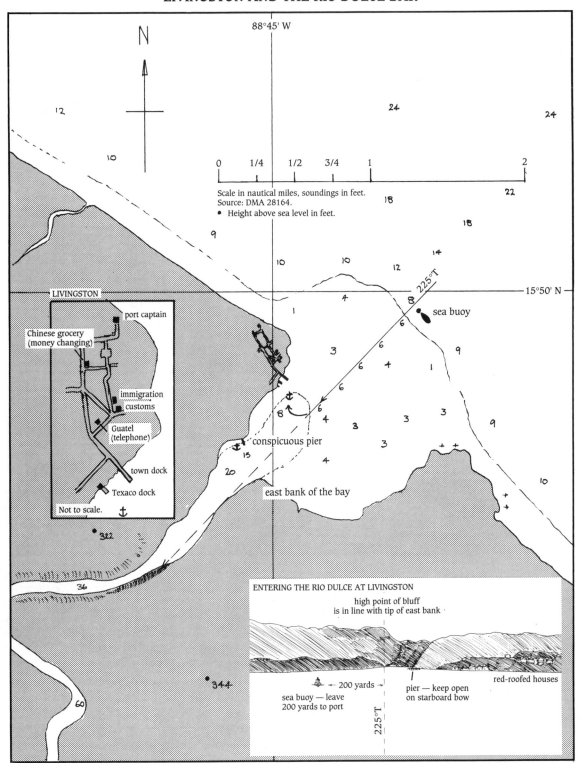

88°45' W

N

12

10

24

24

0   1/4   1/2   3/4   1   2

Scale in nautical miles, soundings in feet.
Source: DMA 28164.
● Height above sea level in feet.

18

22

9

18

18

10

10

10

12

14

LIVINGSTON

port captain

Chinese grocery
(money changing)

immigration
customs

Guatel
(telephone)

town dock

Texaco dock

Not to scale.

4

1

225°T

15°50' N

8

6

sea buoy

3

6

6

4

9

1

6

8

6

4

3

3

3

9

8

3

4

conspicuous pier

15

4

3

+ +

20

east bank of the bay

10

+
+

● 322

36

● 344

ENTERING THE RIO DULCE AT LIVINGSTON

high point of bluff
is in line with tip of east bank

red-roofed houses

⚓ ← 200 yards →
sea buoy — leave
200 yards to port

pier — keep open
on starboard bow

225°T

68

of 10 feet of water over the shoal, with 15 feet toward this western end, which is marked by a lighted buoy. Another buoy 3 miles to the south marks the Heredia Shoal, which has 18 feet of water over it.

From seaward the mouth of the Rio Dulce tends to get lost in the surrounding hills. Since the saddle of Gorda Hill, the tip of Cabo Tres Puntas, and Sarstoon Hill are all visible, a bearing on any two provides an accurate fix, enabling you to determine your final approach.

CROSSING THE BAR AT LIVINGSTON. A shallow bar more than one-half mile wide extends across the mouth of the Rio Dulce and out to sea. We poled it extensively close to low tide on the entry path outlined below and recorded fairly uniform depths of 6 feet 3 inches. High tide adds about a foot. In the afternoons strong onshore winds blowing against the water flowing out of the river will frequently back up the flow and add a few more inches.

The tide tables tell us that high water at Livingston is 1 hour 25 minutes before Key West, with 0.92 of the range at Key West. However local conditions may cause considerable deviation from the predicted pattern. If your vessel draws more than 6 feet, you should try to radio the port captain on approach (VHF channel 16) to check the time of the tide (but note that you will probably be answered by a Spanish-speaking enlisted man). Alternatively try to raise a yacht anchored off the town (there are normally one or two) and ask someone onboard it to eyeball the level against the town dock. Boats with more than a 7-foot draft have made it into the river, but only with a tow. There are a couple of reasonably powerful "tugboats" based in Livingston that will do this for you. I would not advise this if your boat has an externally bolted fin keel or a spade rudder—the bottom is hard sand and shale with very little give to it. With *Nada's* 6-foot draft, we enter and leave without paying too much attention to the tide, but have bumped lightly on occasion. Stay in the channel (see below) since in places the bottom shoals quite suddenly just a little to either side (particularly the east). Many a boat has run aground and spent several uncomfortable hours banging the bottom; some, caught in choppy seas, have suffered quite extensive damage.

To enter the Rio Dulce first locate the sea buoy, which is just off the edge of the bar in 8 feet of water, and take up a position 200 yards to the west (i.e., with the buoy to port). Looking into the river's mouth, you will see the town of Livingston to starboard, behind it a headland (the west bank of the Rio Dulce canyon), and straight ahead (on a heading of 225°T) a steep bluff on the first major bend in the river. This bluff will be in line with the tip of the relatively low-lying east bank of the bay that leads into the canyon. If the bluff is obscured by clouds, look for the large pier that extends from the western bank in front of the mouth of the canyon. The tip of this pier is reasonably conspicuous and should be kept just off the starboard bow when entering. Come in on a heading of 225°T, keeping the tip of the east bank in line with the bluff, making any necessary course corrections for leeway; this is where people sometimes get caught out since, in our experience, the current tends to set you onto the shoals immediately to the east. If you are confident you are in the right place and on the right heading, then come in fairly fast so that if you touch bottom you don't stick! If you do get stuck and need a tow, call the port captain on VHF channel 16.

ANCHORAGE. Maintain the heading of 225°T until you are in 9 feet broad off the Texaco fuel dock, a little to the south of the town dock, then swing around toward the town. Anchoring southeast of the Texaco dock in 8 feet keeps you out of the ferry traffic that uses the town dock. The holding is good. This anchorage can be somewhat rolly, particularly in the late afternoons since an onshore wind tends to build during the day and then die at night. The river current sometimes holds you at an uncomfortable angle to the swells. Although the lee of the minor headland just south of Livingston looks inviting, you cannot tuck into it since the water shoals too far out, but we have found protection immediately upstream of the large pier by the mouth of the canyon, anchoring in 20 feet.

CLEARANCE PROCEDURES. When checking in, fly your Q flag and wait for the officials to come out. You may be able to hurry things along by calling the port captain on channel 16. If, after an hour or two, no one has showed up, *the captain only* can take a dinghy to the town dock and seek out the officials (see the map for the location of their offices).

The fish market at Livingston, Guatemala.

The boat will be boarded by the customs officer, who will take your zarpe from your last port of call and the ship's papers (including, sometimes, a bill of sale); the immigration officer, who will collect all passports; the port captain, who will take all firearms; the police, who probably will search the boat; and maybe a health official. Depending on your time of arrival, you can pick up your passports and cruising permit later the same day, or the next morning. In the meantime you should take down the Q flag; you are free to go ashore. When you pick up the papers, various charges will be levied; in 1990 these totaled $30 to $40 (U.S.). Payment is in quetzals, which you can obtain by changing money in the Chinese grocery store on the right-hand side at the top of the street leading up the hill from the town dock. A customs official will come back aboard to paste a blue sticker to your vessel. Visas and cruising permits are generally issued for 90 days but can be extended in Guatemala City (ask about the current procedure at one of the marinas—see page 179). Once cleared in you are free to cruise Guatemalan waters for as long as the permit lasts.

When you check out go first to customs for a zarpe and then take this and your passports to the immigration office (next door) and the port captain for stamping (at which time you can pick up any firearms), then return to customs for the final stamp. The cost in 1990 was about $10 (U.S.).

PROVISIONS/FACILITIES. The town is quite small, with a few bars and restaurants, limited grocery supplies, and fuel available on the Texaco dock. The water alongside the dock is only 4 feet deep. On one side of the fuel dock is a *cayuco* builder, who is worth visiting. (Cayucos are the dugout canoes used almost universally by the fishermen on the Rio Dulce.) On the other side is the communal town laundry—you will see one of these in every Guatemalan town. A little farther up the riverbank is a shipyard.

THE RIO DULCE CANYON

Charts: BA 1573; DMA 28162.

The trip upriver from Livingston is a memorable one. A little more than one mile from town, the walls of the canyon close in, rising almost sheer in places for 300 feet, covered in luxuriant tropical vegetation. In the early mornings hundreds of egrets, pelicans, and cormorants take flight at your approach and fly ahead of you up the canyon. Indians paddling tiny dugout canoes hug the riverbanks to keep out of the current, often almost hidden from view by vines and creepers trailing down from overhanging precipices high above. The river is deep, as much as 80 feet deep, and in many places you can come close enough to the banks to tangle your mast in the vines! We dodged a few creepers while I tried to photograph elusive snowy egrets in their gorgeous mating plumage, standing sentinel over dark, rocky pools beneath the cliffs.

Stay over toward the outside of bends since a couple shoal on their inner banks. The hairpin bend requires slightly different tactics. You need to stay on the outside when approaching, since there is a shoal to starboard immediately before the turn, but then cut across sharply to come onto the inside bank just around the corner, since there is a substantial shoal area to port. The island off the mouth of the Rio Lampara has an extensive shoal extending down river, so you need to favor the right-hand bank when passing. Otherwise the passage to El Golfete is straightforward.

You can carry 6 feet into the mouth of the Rio Tatin, keeping in mid-channel and continuing for about one-quarter mile, but thereafter the river shoals to less than 6 feet. This pretty little river is worth exploring in a dinghy. It forks after one-half

THE RIO DULCE CANYON

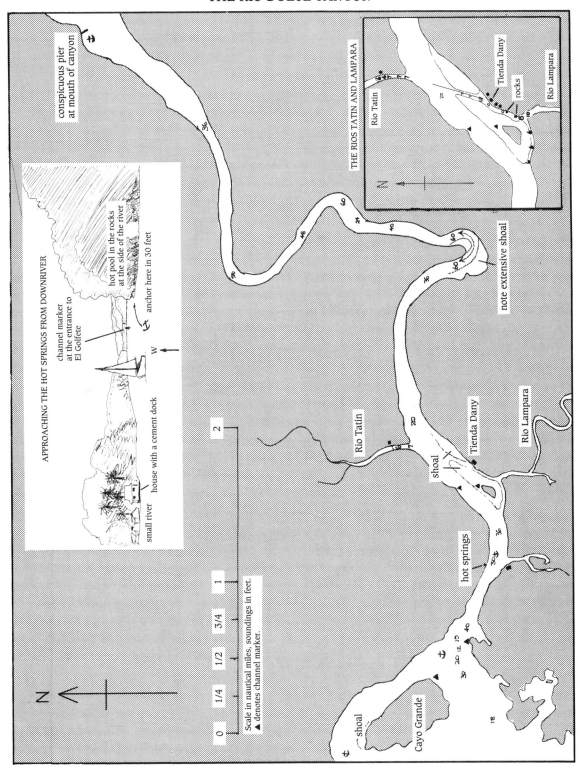

conspicuous pier at mouth of canyon

THE RIOS TATIN AND LAMPARA

Rio Tatin

Tienda Dany

rocks

Rio Lampara

N

20

APPROACHING THE HOT SPRINGS FROM DOWNRIVER

channel marker at the entrance to El Golfete

hot pool in the rocks at the side of the river

anchor here in 30 feet

W

small river   house with a cement dock

Rio Tatin

note extensive shoal

shoal

Tienda Dany

Rio Lampara

hot springs

Cayo Grande

shoal

N

0   1/4   1/2   3/4   1   2

Scale in nautical miles, soundings in feet.
▲ denotes channel marker.

mile, the left fork ending in a series of crystal-clear rocky pools, the right fork in a stream issuing from a cave.

The Rio Lampara is navigable for almost 4 miles until it is blocked by the overhanging branches of a tree. The river runs through jungle, but then the land rises and opens out into ranchland with scattered palms, and mountains in the background. The entry into the river is tricky—the island off its mouth is beset with shoals—but once you are inside, the water is 10 or more feet deep all the way to the overhanging tree. Just below the mouth of the Rio Lampara is a small store called "Tienda Dany," distinguished by its cement river frontage. You need to come in for this store with the Rio Tatin dead astern. The water shoals to 7 to 8 feet before deepening to 10 feet close to the riverbank. Hug the bank, about 20 to 30 feet off but no closer since there are rocks just 4 feet below the surface, jutting out 10 to 15 feet in a couple of places. In particular, watch for rocks as you make the turn into the Rio Lampara.

It is also possible, though not easy, to carry 6 feet around from the other side of the island, which is off the mouth of the Rio Lampara, keeping about 50 feet off the southern bank of the Rio Dulce.

THINGS TO DO. One-half mile upstream from the Rio Lampara, a scalding-hot sulphur spring bubbles up out of the rocks on the northern bank of the Rio Dulce. Some boulders form a little pool that has vegetation hanging overhead. This is a relaxing bathing stop on the way up or down the river, but it can be hard to find since the rocks around the pool are almost indistinguishable from other rocks in this stretch of riverbank. The key to finding them is the house and small river opposite. The house has a cement river frontage. You can anchor in the Rio Dulce opposite this house in about 30 feet of water (good holding), or continue to Cayo Grande at the eastern end of El Golfete, anchor there, and dinghy back. If you run your dinghy close to the north bank of the river, trailing a hand in the water, you will soon feel the hot springs. The river opposite the pool is short but worth a quick trip in the dinghy.

EL GOLFETE

Charts: BA 1573; DMA 28162.

El Golfete is a shallow lake almost 9 miles long and 2 to 3 miles wide. It has fairly uniform depths of 12 to 15 feet over much of it, but there are a couple of sizable shoal areas, one to the southwest of the Rio Chacon Machaca delta, and the other to the east of Cuatro Cayos.

In the mornings the wind is generally calm. During the day it builds steadily from the northeast and by mid-afternoon is likely to be blowing at 15 to 20 knots along the lake from northeast to southwest. Any anchorage on the southern shore will be uncomfortable until well into the night. If you are heading upstream, an afternoon run should be wonderfully fast without any of the rolling and yawing experienced at sea since the waves are quite small. If heading downstream, make an early start to avoid the wind.

APPROACHES/ANCHORAGES. Cayo Grande is an island at the northeast extremity of the lake. It can be passed to north or south, avoiding one small shoal off its northern coast. A pleasing, well-protected anchorage lies to the northwest in the lee of the mainland. From here you can dinghy to the hot springs in one direction, or the Biotopo Manatee Preserve in the other. The water is too cloudy to permit you to see any manatees, which tend to stay on the bottom anyway. (Manatees are most active early in the morning.) The preserve has an interesting half-mile-long nature walk through the jungle.

Laguna Salvador is approached via the river whose delta thrusts out to the southwest of the manatee park. Entry is straight up the center of the channel with no water shallower than 10 feet. The eastern end of the lagoon has 9 feet and provides excellent protection. It is also windless, and therefore likely to be buggy at night. We explored no farther—the other lagoon and the river running southwest to the Rio Chacon Machaca may well be navigable.

The Rio Chacon Machaca is navigable for 10 to 12 miles. Enter to the west of the channel marker, staying in mid-channel between tall reeds. Once inside you can swing to port or starboard; the water

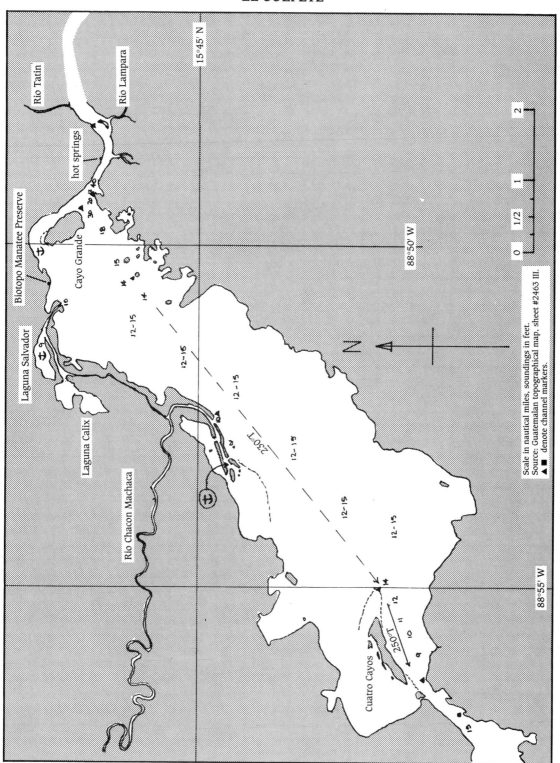

Rio Tatin

Rio Lampara

hot springs

Biotopo Manatee Preserve

Cayo Grande

Laguna Salvador

Laguna Calix

Rio Chacon Machaca

Cuatro Cayos

15°45' N

88°50' W

88°55' W

12-15

12-15

12-15

12-15

12-15

12-15

250°T

230°T

Scale in nautical miles, soundings in feet.
Source: Guatemalan topographical map, sheet #2463 III.
▲ ■ denote channel markers.

N

0   1/2   1   2

THE NORTHERN END OF EL GOLFETE

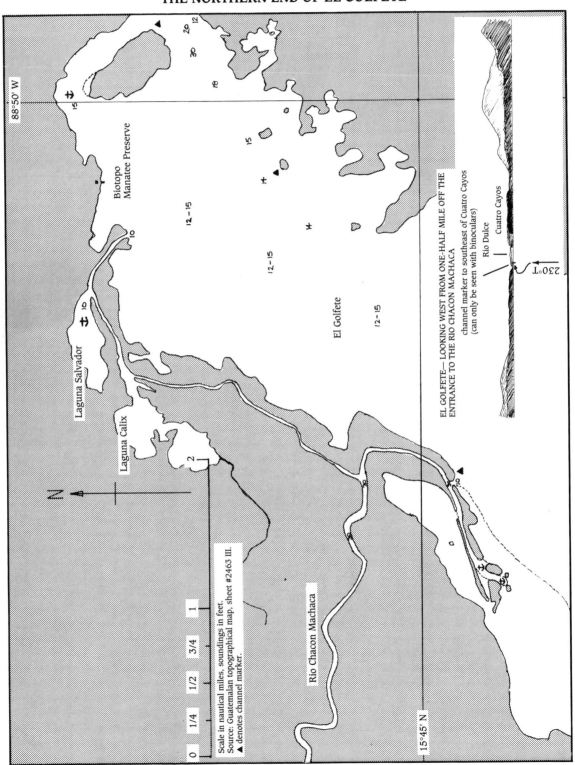

Biotopo Manatee Preserve

88°50' W

El Golfete

12–15

12–15

12–15

Laguna Salvador

Laguna Calix

Rio Chacon Machaca

N

| 0 | 1/4 | 1/2 | 3/4 | 1 |

Scale in nautical miles, soundings in feet.
Source: Guatemalan topographical map, sheet #2463 III.
▲ denotes channel marker.

15°45' N

EL GOLFETE— LOOKING WEST FROM ONE-HALF MILE OFF THE
ENTRANCE TO THE RIO CHACON MACHACA

channel marker to southeast of Cuatro Cayos
(can only be seen with binoculars)

Rio Dulce

Cuatro Cayos

230°T

on entering is at least 10 feet deep. The main river is the starboard fork. It twists and turns through rather uninteresting jungle for 4 or 5 miles before emerging into open savannah. Here you find cattle grazing in the fields and green hills on the horizon, a very peaceful scene. If you turn to port after entering, you come upon another opening to starboard, into a lagoon. This, however, has a shallow bar across its mouth. Next is an opening to port that leads back into El Golfete; beyond this lie two or three mangrove cays. Various shoals block all paths into the lake, but you can find a very pleasant anchorage in either of the spots indicated on the sketch chart. Cool breezes blow through the breaks in the mangroves while water hyacinths and other tropical vegetation surround the boat.

The northeast shore of El Golfete, immediately south of Cayo Grande, contains a number of small cays and sheltered bays with a considerable amount of deep water in a very pretty setting. A cruiser could easily spend a day or two gunkholing here.

EL GOLFETE TO

LAGO IZABAL

Charts: None.

APPROACHES. A course of 230°T down the center of El Golfete will find the channel marker east of Cuatro Cayos. A shoal lies between the island and the marker, which must be rounded to the east. The mouth of the next section of the Rio Dulce is clearly visible from here. The river in this next stretch runs through a mixture of tropical jungle and pleasant green rolling hills covered in pastureland and dotted with palms. In places cattle come to the water's edge, but most of the river frontage is steadily being developed into fancy estates for the rich elite of Guatemala. Palatial homes sit behind manicured lawns and gardens, and often a large sportfishing boat is moored to a substantial dock out front. The local Indians paddling by in their cayucos are rocked by the wake of motorboats and water-skiers.

The channel is clearly marked. The sketch chart tells you on which side to take the various markers.

There is generally 20 to 30 feet of water midstream.

MARINAS/FACILITIES. Almost 20 years ago Kevin and Louisa Lucas bought a little island in the river and began developing the Catamaran Hotel. From the outset they were hospitable to visiting yachts and soon put in some boat slips. Slowly the word got around and a steady trickle of cruisers came upriver, but for years the Guatemalan government made life difficult for visiting boats (2-week visas; requiring expensive bonds to be put up; etc.). All that has changed and the popularity of the area is mushrooming, bringing with it a surge in facilities for boaters. Clyde Crocker and the Mañana Marina were the next on the scene, tucked into a little bay immediately across from the Catamaran Hotel. Then in 1989, Susanna's Laguna Restaurant, in an almost completely enclosed lagoon a mile or so farther south, put in substantial docks and boat slips, to be followed in 1990 by Mario's Marina, one-half mile downstream from the Catamaran Hotel. A fuel dock has been built. In 1990, electricity was brought to the marinas; in 1991, there should be phones. The pace of development is accelerating, rather than diminishing.

What this means for the visiting yacht is that a wide choice of excellent facilities now exists. All the marinas have good water, dockside power, excellent security, attractive bars and restaurants, and prices that are very low by U.S. standards. You can leave your boat here for months with equanimity—the boat will be opened up to air and the bilges will be checked daily, and, if you so desire, the machinery will be run every week. The marinas will give you a cayuco ride to Fronteras to catch the bus to Guatemala City (see "Trips to Guatemala City" on page 182). Without a shadow of doubt, there is no better place to leave a boat in the whole of the Northwest Caribbean (and probably the entire Caribbean).

Various cruisers who have settled to a more-or-less permanent degree on the Rio Dulce can offer skilled services in canvas-making and sail repairs, woodworking, electronic and refrigeration repairs, and mechanical repairs. Ask at the marinas if you need help. The Hotel Catamaran and marinas standby on VHF channel 68. At 0730 hours each morning, there is a general exchange of information

(Continued on page 182)

THE RIO DULCE BETWEEN EL GOLFETE AND LAGO IZABAL

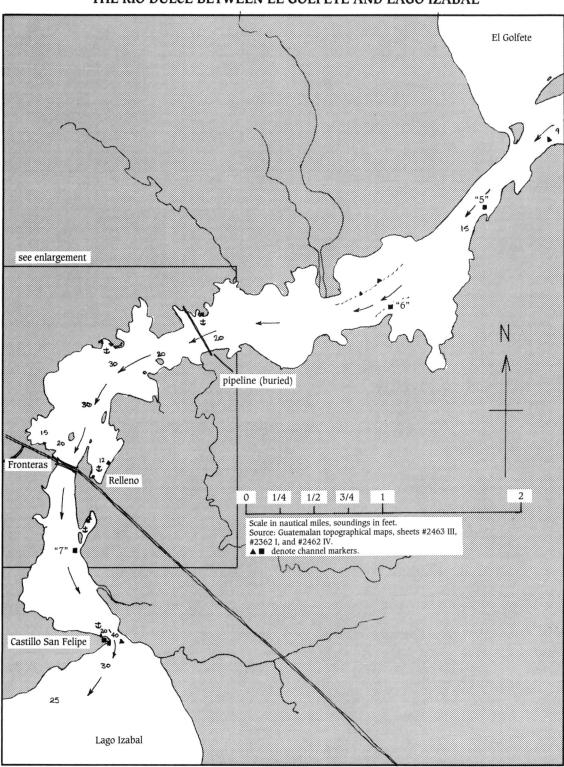

El Golfete

"5"

15

"6"

N

see enlargement

pipeline (buried)

30

20

30

15

20

Fronteras

12

Relleno

"7"

Castillo San Felipe

30

25

Lago Izabal

0   1/4   1/2   3/4   1   2

Scale in nautical miles, soundings in feet.
Source: Guatemalan topographical maps, sheets #2463 III,
#2362 I, and #2462 IV.
▲ ■ denote channel markers.

THE MARINA AREA/THE RIO DULCE

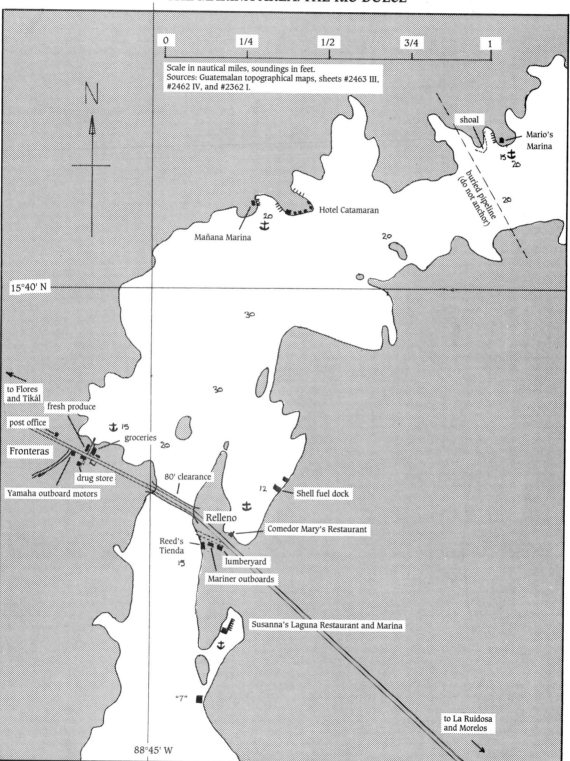

0   1/4   1/2   3/4   1

Scale in nautical miles, soundings in feet.
Sources: Guatemalan topographical maps, sheets #2463 III,
#2462 IV, and #2362 I.

shoal

Mario's
Marina

⚓ 15
20

buried pipeline
(do not anchor)

20

Hotel Catamaran

⚓ 20

Mañana Marina

20

15°40' N

30

30

to Flores
and Tikál

fresh produce

post office

⚓ 15

groceries

Fronteras

20

80' clearance

drug store

Yamaha outboard motors

12

Shell fuel dock

⚓

Relleno

Comedor Mary's Restaurant

Reed's
Tienda

15

lumberyard

Mariner outboards

Susanna's Laguna Restaurant and Marina

⚓

"7" ■

to La Ruidosa
and Morelos

88°45' W

(Continued from page 179)

on this frequency. All marinas will hold mail. The address is: Hotel Catamaran (or Mañana Marina, Susanna's Laguna Restaurant, or Mario's Marina), Frontera Rio Dulce, Morales, Izabal, Guatemala, Central America. The telephone number of the Hotel Catamaran is: (502) 232-4829.

ANCHORAGE. We prefer to anchor out here since there is a pleasant breeze on the river, whereas the marinas tend to become stifling. You can anchor off any of the marinas and are still welcome to use the facilities.

PROVISIONS/THINGS TO DO. A short dinghy ride from the marinas is a huge new concrete bridge with a clearance of 80 feet in center span. On the north side is the small town of Fronteras; on the south side, Relleno.

Fronteras has a number of small grocery stores and excellent fresh produce, together with a post office, a drug store, and a Yamaha outboard motor dealer. When you tie your dinghy to the town dock, a crowd of little boys will ask to watch it for you. You don't really need a watcher, but we always pick a boy and give him a quetzal (25¢) when we return from shopping. The bus stop is in the middle of town. From here you can catch a local bus to Morelos (Bananera) or to the crossroads (La Ruidosa) intersecting the main Guatemala City-Puerto Barrios highway. At this intersection you can catch an express (Greyhound-type) bus to the city (see sidebar).

Upstream from the bridge, on the other side of the river, is Rellenos, with Reed's Tienda, whose owner is an expatriate American married to a Guatemalan woman. They cater to the yachting community with such hard-to-find items as yogurt. They also will arrange to have propane cylinders refilled. Once a week, on Wednesdays, a refrigerated meat truck comes from Guatemala City and takes orders for the following week while handing out the previous week's orders. The meat is inexpensive and of outstanding quality. Just up the track from Reed's is a Mariner outboard motor dealer (who also sells teak); next door is a lumberyard where you can get wooden items fabricated at absurdly low prices.

Morelos (Bananera) is the regional center. It has

(Continued on page 185)

TRIPS TO GUATEMALA CITY

Frequent local buses run from Fronteras to Morelos. These will drop you off at La Ruidosa, the crossroads with the main road from Guatemala City (called "Guate") to Puerto Barrios. Here you can catch a local bus all the way to the city. The ride is long, cramped, and uncomfortable. You would do much better to time your arrival at La Ruidosa to coincide with one of the special buses, known as *Liteguas*, which run between Guate and Puerto Barrios. These are Greyhound-type buses with reclining seats (and no one sitting on your lap!). The marinas will have the current timetable. Seats can be booked in advance by calling the bus company in Puerto Barrios, but this is not normally necessary since the buses do not fill up until closer to Guate. The ride to the city takes four to five hours over sometimes atrocious roads but mostly paved highway.

Guatemala City is laid out in 13 zones, each one with grid-like streets. The *avenidas* run from north to south, and the *calles* from east to west. When giving an address the zone number is crucial since all zones have the same streets and avenues. The Litegua will drop you in zone 1, 15th calle, avenida 10-40, which is to say you will be on the 15th street, between avenidas 10 and 11, at building #40 (the building numbers restart at zero on each block).

Close to the Litegua depot are a couple of good-value budget hotels—the Hotel Spring and Lessing House—which are clean, inexpensive, and secure, and also the Ritz Continental, one of the better and more expensive hotels in the city, with a telephone and TV in every room. The Spring Hotel is at 8th avenida, calle 12-65 (i.e., on 8th avenue, between streets 12 and 13, building #65); the Lessing House is at 12th calle, avenida 4-35 (on 12th street between avenues 4 and 5, #35); and the Ritz Continental is at 6th avenida "A," calle 10-13 (the "A" denotes an extra street midway between 6th and 7th avenues).

In the same district you will find the Bank America, which will advance cash against a Visa or MasterCard, and the black market money-changers, who hang out by the post office. Zone 1 also contains the cathedral and other tourist attractions; a major underground crafts market in front of the cathedral (with prices as good as anywhere in Guatemala, but bargaining is mandatory—you should be able to buy most things at around half the initial asking price); a wonderful delicatessen shop; and numerous restaurants (including the Picadilly, an American-style pizza and hamburger fast-food joint with good prices).

GUATEMALA CITY CENTER

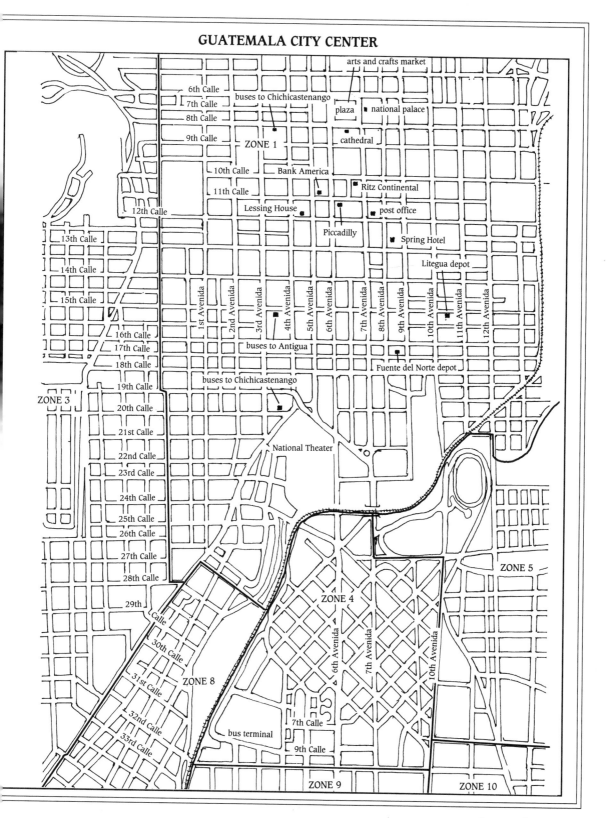

Traveling in Guatemala

You can rent a car in Guate but it is expensive; the bus service is unbelievably cheap with frequent buses to just about every major city and tiny hamlet. Some of the larger cities are also served by Litegua-style, reserved-seating buses (but with a different name, since this will be a different company). Otherwise you will have to squeeze into a bus with up to 80 Guatemalans! If you don't mind doing this, buses are definitely the way to go.

The buses, though licensed by the government and with set fares, are all privately owned and operate from a dozen different depots in Guate. This can make it hard to find the right bus for a given city. Asking people is generally not too much help. The Guatemalans apparently feel embarrassed if they cannot give you the directions you are asking for, and so will give you an answer anyway. You can ask three people in succession for the same directions and get three completely different answers, all of them wrong!

Buses for Antigua leave from 15th calle between 3rd and 4th avenidas. Buses for Chichicastenango can be caught at 20th calle, between 3rd and 4th avenidas (Transportes Rebuli) or 8th calle, between 3rd and 4th avenidas (Rutas Lima), but most leave from a depot in zone 4, known as the *terminal*, between 7th and 9th calles and 1st and 4th avenidas. From zone 1, buses 2, 5, or 6 to "El Triangulo" will drop you at a modern high-rise development just a short walk from the terminal. Other buses go right to the terminal (they normally display the word "terminal" somewhere on the front). Other towns in the Central Highlands are mostly served by buses from the terminal.

Tikál is a special case. The only road branches off from the Guatemala City to Puerto Barrios highway at La Ruidosa, crossing the Rio Dulce by the bridge at Fronteras. Some miles farther north the pavement ends, leaving a rutted, potholed, bone-jarring trail for the 100 miles or more to Flores. From Flores, the road is good for the last 40 miles.

The road to Flores is almost impassable for cars—few get through without some damage to tires, wheels, or suspensions—and if you should break down almost no help is available. *Under no circumstances attempt to drive a private or rental car to Tikál* (and I'm not easily put off). Neither would I take a local bus since the journey from Fronteras alone will comprise more than 12 hours of acute discomfort. The way to travel is to take an assigned-seat special bus. This takes 12 hours from Guate, or 6 if you can board at Fronteras. The bus leaves Guate around midnight, passing through Fronteras generally between 6:00 and 7:00 a.m. (but nothing is certain!). The bus line is Fuente del Norte, and their depot in Guate is in zone 1, 17th calle, between the 8th and 9th avenidas. They also have an office in Morelos.

If you should catch a local bus from Fronteras, you can break the journey midway at the Finca Ixobel, $2^{1}/_{2}$ miles south of Poptun. This is a farm with simple accommodations for guests in a beautiful rural setting, with swimming, horseback riding, and cave explorations. It was run for many years by Mike and Carole De Vine, but Mike was murdered in 1990. I understand Carole intends to continue the business alone.

Traveling to Tikál by road can be complicated by sporadic guerrilla activity. The bus ahead of us on our return was stopped at gunpoint, emptied, and burned! However, so far as I know, no tourists have been harmed in these actions, which are infrequent. You should carry a flask of water and snacks since you may have a long wait by the roadside for this or other reasons (the transmission went out in our bus—it took hours to get a replacement bus). The U.S. Embassy in Guatemala City can give you the latest "travel advisory" on this and other "active" regions in Guatemala.

Whether in a private vehicle or a bus, *do not attempt the trip to Tikál in the rainy season* (June through October). Even the buses have been known to take three days getting through.

There are two other ways to get to Tikál. If you can afford it, fly from Guatemala City to Flores. The other approach is to drive on the paved road from Belize City through Belmopan to the Guatemalan border and on to Tikál. If on a bus, you will have to disembark at the border and walk one-half mile to the first town on the Guatemalan side in order to catch another bus.

Hotels throughout Guatemala are primitive but correspondingly cheap. Most are clean and pleasant enough. Antigua, Chichicastenango, and Flores are exceptions since they are used to tourists. They all have at least one modern (and relatively expensive) inn, along with the usual mix of cheaper *hospedajes*. Some of the rural towns have no rented accommodations at all.

Antigua

In 1541 the early Spanish conquistadors established their capital in a cool mountain valley at the foot of a perfectly symmetrical extinct volcano whose crater contained a lake. Two years later, following torrential rains, the lip of the crater gave way and a massive mud slide buried the town. A new capital was built just three miles away at Antigua, beneath El Volcan de Agua (the volcano of water). Over the next two centuries, Antigua developed into one of the largest cities in Central America, becoming a great cultural center with numerous churches, monasteries, private palaces, and a university. Then in 1773, the city was practically leveled by an earthquake. Three years later the capital was moved to Guatemala City.

Antigua has never recovered its former size and glory. Today it is a quiet and charming colonial city still littered with the monumental ruins of the 1773 earthquake. A dozen or more language schools operate in the city. In 1990, for $22 per person per week we enjoyed one-on-one tuition with a Spanish teacher for four hours a day, five days a week. For an additional $22 per person per week we were boarded out with a local family, receiving three meals a day. The bed was horsehair with more peaks and valleys than the Central Highlands, and our diet was rice and beans, but at that price we could hardly complain!

Antigua is well worth a visit at any time of the year, but during Holy Week (*Semana Santa*) the city is absolutely unique. Every Sunday in Lent, and then on numerous occasions during Semana Santa, the local populace carry enormous platforms (*andas*), surmounted by a statue of Jesus, through the streets of the city for up to 12 hours at a time, sometimes late into the night. It takes 80 men to lift an anda. The carriers are changed every block or so—during the day up to 5,000 people will carry a platform. All the carriers are garbed in elaborate robes, normally purple and white, which look like something handed down from the Spanish Inquisition. The platform is preceded by squads of acolytes swinging incense burners until the entire street is blotted out in pungent smoke. The effect is quite medieval.

For several of the final processions, almost every able-bodied soul in the city spends the night before carpeting the streets with spectacular and elaborate designs (*alfambras*) in brightly dyed sawdust. The largest procession (on Good Friday, commemorating the Crucifixion) is preceded by a phalanx of Roman soldiers on horse and foot, and two genuine thieves carrying crosses (freed from the local prison early that morning), as well as the usual thousands of anda-carriers and dozens of incense-swinging acolytes. This spectacle has to be seen to be believed. By Easter Sunday, when most of Christendom is celebrating Jesus' resurrection, the emotional and physical energy of Antigua is spent: The streets are deserted and the churches of this highly religous city are half empty!

(Continued from page 182)

a much larger range of stores and supplies. The bus ride to and from the town is quite an experience, as are all local bus rides in Guatemala, with anywhere from three to six people in each two-person seat and the aisles packed solid!

A mile above the bridge, the river narrows and deepens before opening out into Lago Izabal. The Spanish used to assemble one of their treasure fleets at this end of the lake, after hauling the gold and silver overland from Central America. In order to ward off the predations of pirates, privateers, and buccaneers, they built a small fort, Castillo San Felipe, on the point where the river narrows, and suspended an enormous chain across the river to bar access to the lake. Some years ago the Guatemalan government discovered the original plans for the fort and reconstructed it. Behind it is a small grassy park studded with attractive trees. This is a beautiful picnic spot, while the fort, replete with cannons and redolent of so much stirring history, is fascinating. You can anchor your boat immediately to the north in 20 feet with good protection and holding, and take a dinghy to the fort's dock.

LAGO IZABAL

Charts: None.

Note: Local fishermen lay out extensive nets at night, and sometimes during the day. In particular, the channel into the lake at the Castillo San Felipe is all but closed off most nights and considerably

Castillo San Felipe.

blocked many days. Many nets are put out north of Mariscos and at the western end of the bay in the regions close to El Estor. A close watch needs to be kept at all times since these nets are frequently difficult to spot, having just a plastic jug or two holding them up. Do not sail at night: These nets are the livelihood of the local fishermen, and if you plow through one you will be taking the food directly out the mouths of his family.

Lago Izabal is a little more than 25 miles long and 10 miles across at its widest point. It is relatively deep—40 or so feet over much of its central area—shoaling gradually toward the shore. The bottom is soft mud in which an anchor sets readily but may not hold too well in a stiff blow (more on this later).

APPROACH. The lake lies between two mountain ranges, the Sierra de Santa Cruz, rising to almost 4,000 feet in the north, and the Sierra de las Minas, which rises to almost 7,000 feet in the southwest. This topography determines the wind pattern on the

lake. At night it is generally calm, but during the day the onshore trade winds from the Bahia de Amatique are funneled up the Rio Dulce and southwestward along the length of the lake between the mountains. By midafternoon it is not unusual to have a 20-knot wind whipping up steep-sided 3- and 4-foot waves. The wind drops quite suddenly toward evening and the waves subside overnight. Once in a while a norther will come whistling down with little warning from the Sierra de Santa Cruz, bringing with it short-lived winds of up to 50 knots.

You will have an exhilarating sail toward the head of the lake in the afternoons, but should make the return passage in the early morning. Because of the afternoon and evening wave action, there is not a single comfortable anchorage anywhere on the southern shores of the lake with the exception of Puerto Refugio and the bays at the western extremity of the lake (see below). On the north shore reasonable shelter can be found in normal conditions in the lee of the headland to the east of El Estor, but nowhere else.

At certain times of the year you will see large clumps of hyacinths floating down the lake. This can be disconcerting since it gives the impression that you are about to run up on a shoal. In fact the hyacinths are being washed out of all the local rivers and have no significance regarding the depth.

ANCHORAGES/PROVISIONS/FACILITIES. Puerto Refugio offers excellent protection in almost any conditions. When approaching, note the shoal immediately to the north of the peninsula that forms the bay. Ten feet can be carried between the shoal and the peninsula. Puerto Refugio is a lovely anchorage with dramatic mountains to the southwest, reeds and jungle vegetation to the north, and a considerable amount of bird life (snowy egrets, parrots, and others). You can take your dinghy up the Rio Balandra, although the Zarquita and Palochic are more interesting.

The Rio Oscuro and the Rio Zarquita are two rivers to the southwest of Puerto Refugio. They are best explored in the mornings since a bar with 3 feet of water over it will prevent your taking the big boat in, and the anchorage outside the bar (in 7 to 8 feet, good holding) is exposed to the afternoon winds and wave action. On approach note the extensive shoal area to the northeast, shown reasonably accu-

LAGO IZABAL

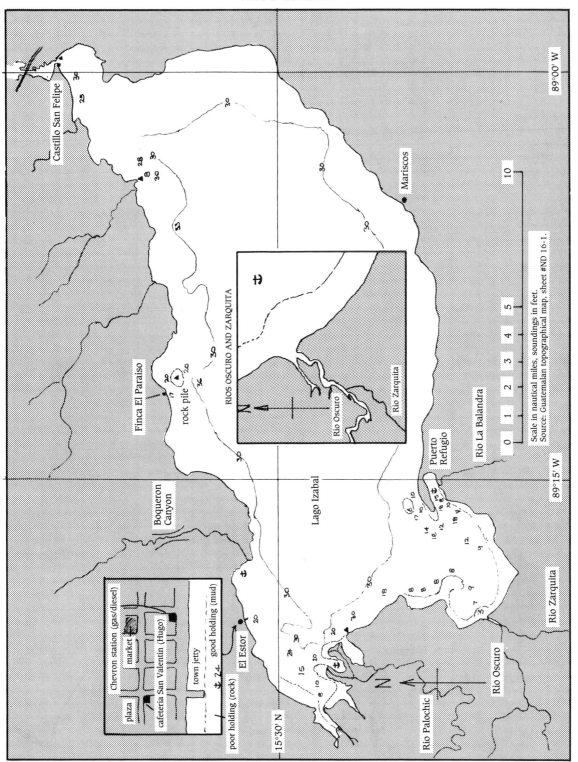

Castillo San Felipe

Finca El Paraíso

rock pile

Boqueron Canyon

RIOS OSCURO AND ZARQUITA

Rio Oscuro

Rio Zarquita

Mariscos

Lago Izabal

Puerto Refugio

Rio La Balandra

Rio Zarquita

Rio Oscuro

Rio Palochic

15°30' N

El Estor

Chevron station (gas/diesel)
market
cafeteria San Valentin (Hugo)
plaza
town jetty
good holding (mud)
poor holding (rock)

89°00' W

89°15' W

Scale in nautical miles, soundings in feet.
Source: Guatemalan topographical map, sheet #ND 16-1.

0 1 2 3 4 5   10

Guatemala   187

THE RIO PALOCHIC AND ENSENADA LAGUNA, LAGO IZABAL

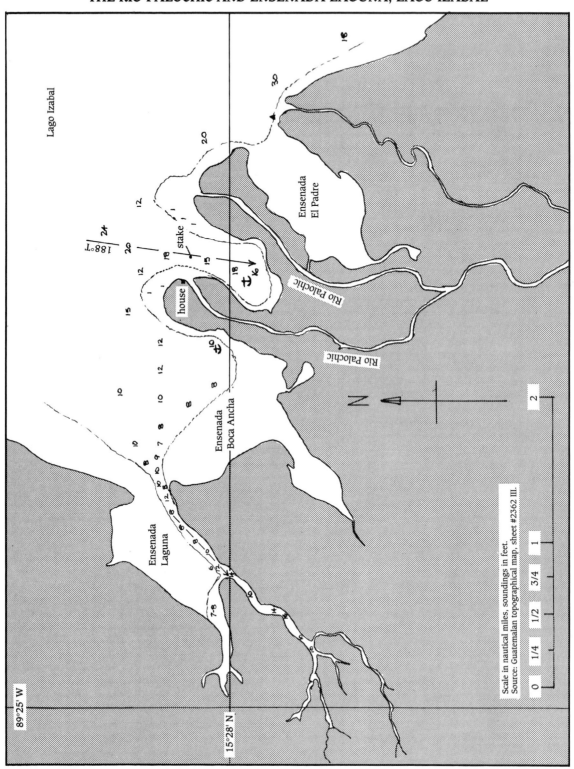

Lago Izabal

Ensenada El Padre

Rio Palochic

Rio Palochic

stake

house

Ensenada Boca Ancha

Ensenada Laguna

N

Scale in nautical miles, soundings in feet.
Source: Guatemalan topographical map, sheet #2362 III.

| 0 | 1/4 | 1/2 | 3/4 | 1 | 2 |

89°25' W

15°28' N

rately on the sketch chart. Take your dinghy into the left fork at the entrance to the Rio Oscuro past thick pads of water lilies and hyacinths. The Oscuro is a wide river that meanders for miles through swampy land. The Zarquita, which branches off through a narrow channel to the left about one-half mile up the Oscuro, is more interesting. This river is quite narrow and fast-flowing as it descends from the foothills of the Sierra de las Minas. The tree branches interlace overhead with vines and creepers hanging down—a wonderful jungle experience, with almost no bugs!

The Rio Palochic is a sizable, meandering river with small Mayan maize plots hacked out of the jungle along the banks of its lower reaches. Here we saw the hanging nests of the orependula birds and encountered several bands of noisy howler monkeys (which roar rather than howl, sounding like some much larger and more ferocious beast). We were able to step onto the riverbank and approach the monkeys quite closely; the males, far from backing off, would climb out to the extremities of branches to glare down at us, chattering angrily. I am told that if you come too close they will throw feces at you!

The Rio Palochic delta has a number of exit channels, all obstructed by shallow bars. Exploration is only possible in a dinghy. By far the best anchorage is in the unnamed bay between Ensenada El Padre and Ensenada Boca Ancha. Shoals extend to the north of this bay one-half mile on both sides. Once you are around these shoals, entry is straightforward; head 188°T for the center of the head of the bay. In 1990 a large, almost submerged stake, which you can take on either side, poked up in the center of the channel. The bay has 16 feet of water over much of it with excellent protection throughout. The mosquitoes are a problem for a short period at dusk but not otherwise. The Rio Palochic can be entered through channels both to the east and the west of this anchorage, the west entry being easier since it is deeper. After approximately 2 miles, the river forks. If you take the left channel, you come back out on the east side of the anchorage, but you may have to drag your dinghy over the bar. The deeper water is found by heading out to the east, then swinging right around the shoal to come back into the bay from the north.

The Ensenada Boca Ancha is predominantly

shoal water, although deep water extends down its eastern shore as shown on the sketch chart. Sheltered anchorage can be found here in most conditions.

The Ensenada Laguna is almost completely shoal, except for a narrow channel that hugs the southern shore on entering, then heads 225°T directly for the entrance to the southern river. Once inside the river, the water deepens and is navigable for a little more than a mile until the river is completely blocked by water hyacinths. We nosed up into the hyacinths and have a picture of our boat in a flower bed surrounded by jungle! We found a few biting flies—more a nuisance than a major problem.

El Estor is a sizable town with 8,000 inhabitants in and around it. As recently as a few years ago, the population was twice as large, supported by the now-closed International Nickel Mine just to the west. Some groceries can be bought, and fresh produce is available in the market, with diesel at the gas station. The anchorage is off the town dock in 20 to 30 feet of water. Give the dock a good clearance since a regular ferry runs to and from Mariscos. You should anchor to the east of the dock where you will find good holding in mud. To the west the bottom is rocky with poor holding. This anchorage is exposed to the afternoon swells. The best overnight anchorage is in the unnamed bay cradled in the arms of the Rio Palochic delta (see above). Otherwise the headland to the east of El Estor affords reasonable protection.

THINGS TO DO. Hugo Fajardo, at the Cafeteria San Valentin, is a bilingual guide who organizes local trips. One trip I recommend is an excursion to Boqueron Canyon, where you can paddle up the Rio Sauce as it cuts through limestone hills to form a dramatic, sheer-sided gorge. Hugo can show you some exciting swimming through natural waterslides.

The Rio de Agua Caliente is another notable excursion, this one to a steaming-hot waterfall. The river is about midway along the northern shore of the lake, close to the Finca El Paraiso. The Finca is easily spotted; it is the only two-story house for miles around and has a channel marker just offshore. *This marker sits on top of a rock pile that comes up quite suddenly*—I once cut too close and hit it hard! Anchor a couple hundred yards off the

Nada in a sea of hyacinths.

beach and dinghy ashore. This should be a morning excursion to avoid the afternoon winds since the anchorage is exposed. Set two anchors and make sure they bite well. We put down our plow, set it hard, and went ashore. While we were gone a 40- to 50-knot norther sprang up out of nowhere and blew our boat a mile or more out into the lake. The anchor was still set but simply "plowing" through the bottom. I understand we are not the first boat to have had this happen. The Finca El Paraiso is private. You should ask for Señora Blanca, who, for 5 quetzals per person (1990), will provide a guide to take you to the hot falls. It is a 2-mile hike, initially through open farmlands and then gently uphill through light tropical rain forest. You pass a Mayan village where bare-breasted women wash clothes in the river and naked children and pigs run in and out of the palapas. One-half mile farther the falls cascade into a lovely little jungle-enclosed, rocky pool with vines and creepers spanning the river.

LOS SIETE ALTARES

Charts: BA 1573; DMA 28162 and 28164.

At Los Siete Altares a small river cascades down a series of waterfalls into rocky pools. During the dry season the flow may be reduced to a trickle, but during the rainy season (June through October) this is a delightful spot for swimming in the pools and climbing the falls. The first three falls are readily accessible, but the higher ones are a difficult scramble up the riverbed or through the surrounding thick tropical jungle. The best time to visit is in the morning before the afternoon winds kick up, but if any serious swells are running, landing a dinghy on the beach beside the falls at any time of day becomes impractical. The falls themselves are not visible from seaward and can be a little hard to find.

APPROACH. From Livingston, clear the sea buoy and follow the coastline westward. A more-or-less uninterrupted beach comes from Livingston, backed

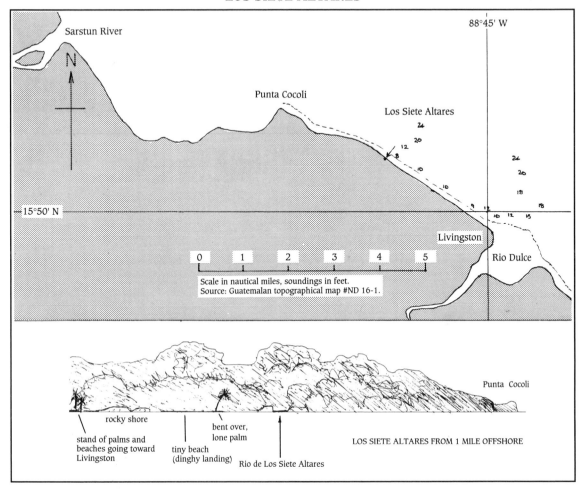

Scale in nautical miles, soundings in feet.
Source: Guatemalan topographical map #ND 16-1.

LOS SIETE ALTARES FROM 1 MILE OFFSHORE

by a number of coconut palms and the odd house or two (a couple have fences running along the beach). Moving westward, the beach ends in a rocky section of shoreline, with higher ground behind and thick vegetation (no palms). Next is a tiny beach with one lone, bent-over, palm, followed by another short stretch of rock and the river outlet, which is hard to see. The rock then runs all the way to what appears to be a headland before Punta Cocoli, although in fact the coastline curves gradually at this point. The falls are one-half mile or so east of this "headland." When you are within a mile or so, the sketch should enable you to identify the approximate location. The tiny beach is the place to land the dinghy. Immediately behind the beach is a trail to the falls.

PUERTO BARRIOS

Charts: DMA 28164 and 28165. The latter is a very detailed chart of Puerto Barrios and Santo Tomas de Castilla, which is not needed.

Santo Tomas de Castilla, to the south of Puerto Barrios, is Guatemala's principal east-coast port. As such it handles a considerable amount of large-ship traffic. The approach channel runs past Puerto Barrios and is clearly marked and free of dangers. Since the development of modern facilities at Santo Tomas, Puerto Barrios has fallen on hard times. The main dock is in a state of disrepair—the end sections have collapsed, leaving some jagged ironwork.

PUERTO BARRIOS

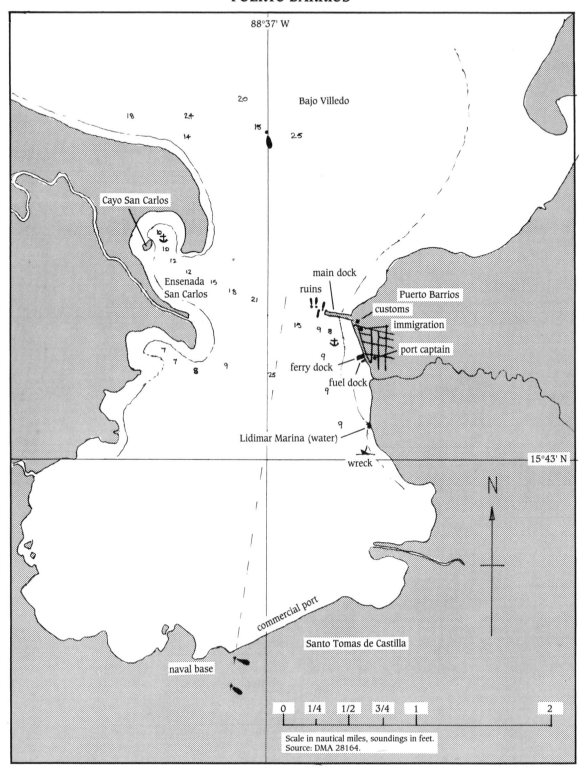

88°37' W

Bajo Villedo

20

18   24

14   15   25

Cayo San Carlos

10
10

12

12

Ensenada   15
San Carlos   18   21

main dock

ruins

Puerto Barrios

customs

immigration

15

9   8

port captain

9

7   9

7   8   9

25

ferry dock

fuel dock
9

Lidimar Marina (water)   9

wreck   15°43' N

N

commercial port

Santo Tomas de Castilla

naval base

| 0 | 1/4 | 1/2 | 3/4 | 1 | | 2 |

Scale in nautical miles, soundings in feet.
Source: DMA 28164.

APPROACH/ANCHORAGE. When approaching Puerto Barrios give the ruins extending out from the dock a wide berth and then come in to anchor in the lee of the dock. You will be just to the northwest of the municipal dock, which is used by the ferries from Punta Gorda and Livingston. The holding is good in 8 to 10 feet. This anchorage can get rolly in the afternoons and problems have been reported with thieves. At night you will find far better protection if you retreat across the bay and anchor in Ensenada San Carlos. This spot has 10-foot depths in the center of the bay and pelicans diving all around. Even in this isolated spot, you should lock up.

CLEARANCE PROCEDURES. You can check in and out at Puerto Barrios but you would be better advised to go to Livingston. Puerto Barrios officials are not as well organized as those at Livingston, and you have to do a lot of walking. We were subjected to several attempts to extract bribes.

To clear in, first go to the port captain's office. He will organize a boarding party, which you will have to ferry out to your boat. As at Livingston, the customs will take your zarpe, the immigrations your passports, and the port captain any firearms. Later you go to the various offices to pick up your paperwork (see the town plan).

To clear out, go first to customs, then the immigration and port captain, and finally back to customs.

PROVISIONS/FACILITIES. The Marina Lidimar has water on the sunken barge that serves as its dock (7 feet alongside). Fuel is available next to the municipal dock, but you will have to haul it in jerry cans. The town has various grocery stores and a fresh-produce market. It is about a one-half-mile walk from the municipal dock.

Honduras and the Bay Islands of Honduras

The mainland coast of Honduras is not hospitable to sailors. In the 300-mile stretch from the Laguna de Caratasca in the east to the Guatemalan border in the west, there is only one truly protected small-boat anchorage, a mangrove-lined lagoon called Laguna El Diamante, but it gives no access to the shore. Headlands at Trujillo and Puerto Cortes provide a measure of protection from the prevailing trade winds, but the high mountains, just a short distance inland, tend to generate offshore or westerly winds at night, making both of these harbors uncomfortable. In the winter months, they are wide open to northers. As a result, there is not a single anchorage on the mainland where you could feel secure about leaving your boat to go inland.

As if to make up for this, the Bay Islands, 20 to 30 miles off the coast, have a surfeit of wonderfully protected anchorages that compare favorably to any other anchorage in the Caribbean. I have included some notes on mainland Honduras in this guide, but I have emphasized the Bay Islands. Steer clear of the mainland in your boat—unless you are using its partial lee to work eastward from Belize and Guatemala to Utila; see page 57. If you wish to visit Honduras, particularly to see the Mayan ruins at Copán, your best option is to leave your boat at the French Harbor Yacht Club and catch one of the frequent flights from Coxen's Hole to San Pedro Sula, where you will be able to rent a car or catch a bus.

The Bay Islands consist of three principal is-

A secluded anchorage in the Cayos Cochinos.

HONDURAS AND THE BAY ISLANDS OF HONDURAS

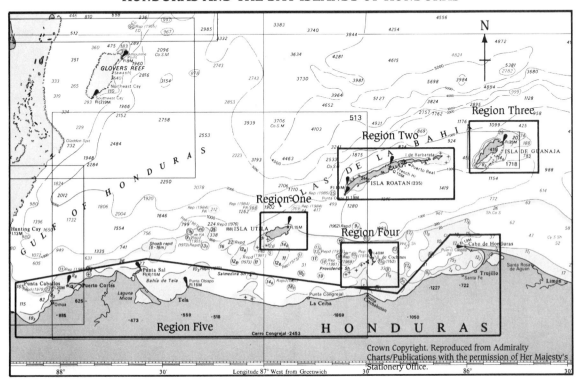

Crown Copyright. Reproduced from Admiralty Charts/Publications with the permission of Her Majesty's Stationery Office.

lands—Utila, Roatan, and Guanaja—with numerous smaller cays. Except for Utila, which is perched on the edge of the 100-fathom contour, the islands rise straight out of the depths of the ocean, with a fringing barrier reef in many places (particularly on the north shores of Roatan and Guanaja). Utila is low-lying and swampy, with just one 250-foot-high hill (Pumpkin Hill) in its extreme northeast corner. Roatan and Guanaja each have a hilly backbone, sometimes quite steep. Roatan's backbone rises to more than 700 feet; Guanaja's to more than 1,300 feet.

NAVIGATIONAL

CONSIDERATIONS

The islands fall well within the trade-wind belt and are far enough offshore to be unaffected by the mountains of Honduras. For much of the year the wind blows steadily out of the east, with minor variations to the south or north, at 15-25 knots. In the winter this pattern is sometimes broken by northers sweeping down from the Gulf of Mexico. In the summer calms are a little more prevalent, with a rare hurricane.

The deep water immediately offshore and between the islands, combined with the strong trade winds, creates an ever-present, often steep-sided swell which you encounter almost as soon as you poke your bow out of an anchorage. This can make working to windward wet and uncomfortable. Since the wind tends to ease at night, you should make your easting early in the morning. The northeast-to-southwest axis of the islands usually creates a partial lee close in along the north shore, making it easier to work to windward here than on the south shore. The confused seas in the open water between the islands are aggravating because of swells hooking around the ends of the islands. The lumpy cross-seas can really kill your boat speed, even when under power. When you make passage upwind from one island to another, be sure to time the crossing so that you have plenty of daylight in which to find an anchorage at the other end.

Many Bay Island anchorages are entered through narrow, coral-bound channels. The same rough conditions can make coming in and going out a little hair-raising. *Under no circumstances attempt any of the entries outlined in the following pages unless you have a good view of the bottom and full control of your boat.* If in doubt, stay out!

HISTORICAL BACKGROUND

The people of the Bay Islands are an unusual mixture. Though the islands were discovered by Columbus, early Spanish settlements didn't prosper. Later, the many natural harbors on the islands provided occasional refuge for pirates, privateers, and buccaneers who preyed on the Spanish Main and its treasure fleets. Still later, British settlers used the islands as a base from which to organize scattered logwood and mahogany-cutting operations along the mainland coast. The British brought with them a mixture of African slaves and Black Caribs.

The islands have been indisputably Honduran now for over a century, and with the Hondurans have come a Hispanic bureaucracy and the resettlement of mainland Hondurans on the islands. Nevertheless a large proportion of the population is white and English-speaking, tracing its ancestry (for the most part erroneously) back to an assortment of British pirates. These people, some of whom cannot and others of whom will not speak Spanish, dominate island politics and many do not even consider themselves to be a part of Honduras. They resent the government's mandate that made Spanish

Cayucos heading home at sunset.

the official language in the public schools. The Black Caribs and blacks seem to live in another world, in isolated spots along the coast, where life in the fishing villages has continued relatively unchanged for 100 years.

Most islanders live in small, picturesque settlements consisting of houses built on piles either at the water's edge or in the water on shallow reefs. There are few roads and transportation is almost exclusively by *cayuco*, large dugout canoes. Bay Islanders call these *dories* and power them by single-cylinder inboard diesels. A series of mangrove-lined canals make it possible for the cayucos to work long stretches of the coastlines without having to brave the open sea.

For 20 years there has been talk that Roatan and the Bay Islands are about to be "discovered." In 1978, Caribbean Sailing Yachts (CSY) opened a charter operation at Brick Bay, Roatan, which grew to a fleet of 36 boats. The influx of charterers spawned new marinas, restaurants, and other services. The predictions seemed set to come true, but then the pace faltered and CSY folded, as did the restaurants and marinas it spawned. The islands slid back into a quieter era.

I believe the time for the predictions' realization has come. Roatan now has the infrastructure to support a major tourist expansion. The airport at Coxen's Hole has been expanded to accommodate jets and now has direct flights to and from Miami, New Orleans, and Houston. The road out of Coxen's Hole is being paved. The island will be electrified in 1991. Telephones and cable TV are available in many places. The Fantasy Island Resort—a multi-million-dollar hotel complex, the first of an international caliber—opened its doors in 1989. If it is successful, other similar projects are bound to follow since many an equally beautiful spot on the islands is ripe for development.

This is not necessarily bad news for cruisers. The rugged nature of the islands keeps many of them accessible only by boat. Utila and Guanaja, in many ways more fascinating than Roatan, are likely to remain relatively isolated, and the Cayos Cochinos to the south, quite possibly the most beautiful group of islands in the whole Caribbean, will probably be unscathed. In all probability the tourists will be constrained to a few more or less self-contained resort areas. For a while, at least, cruisers will

be able to enjoy the unspoiled nature of the islands and have access to improved facilities. (In 1990, there was talk of at least one new marina.)

NORTH SHORE REEF ENTRIES FOR ROATAN AND GUANAJA

The reef is almost continuous along the north shores of Roatan and Guanaja, lying between one-half mile and one mile offshore. It is punctuated by a series of openings, most of which are narrow and deep with reef awash on both sides. When the prevailing trade winds are blowing, the swells close to the reef are quite moderate. Under these conditions you can safely approach the reef to identify the channels. However, *when a norther is blowing, both coastlines are very dangerous lee shores and no anchorage is safe to enter.* If you are already inside an anchorage and get caught by a norther, you will proabably have to wait it out since it would be unsafe to brave the swells in any of the reef entrances.

The channels are as deep as 100 feet and, in the right light, form a pencil line of deep-blue water through the shallower reef on either side. When you are approaching the reef, keep a sharp lookout, preferably in the ratlines or on the spreaders rather than the bow pulpit. None of these passages should be attempted by singlehanders except in the most settled conditions. Most channels are too narrow to turn around in—once you have started you are committed. It is therefore essential to keep an accurate, up-to-date record of your position, and to be certain of your position before heading in. One or two blind alleys in the reef resemble channels but peter out in a maze of shallow coral heads.

When you come around onto a southerly heading to enter a channel, you will feel the full force of the trade wind amidships. The wind, wave action, and possibly the current, will all be pushing westward. You should stay up toward the east wall of the channels to give yourself a little room to maneuver.

All channels can be entered under sail in normal trade-wind conditions, but this requires a high-cut headsail for good visibility forward and very strong nerves. We prefer to drop the sails and go in slowly under power, which gives us more control. Obviously this carries its own risk: If the motor were to die, we would most likely be into the coral before we could set enough sail to regain control of the boat.

CLEARANCE PROCEDURES

As with Mexico, not only must you clear in and out of Honduras, but you must also clear from port to port and island to island on your itinerary. The specific procedures are covered in the relevant sections.

Region 1: Utila

Utila is low-lying, swampy, and uninteresting. Aside from the town of Puerto Este, the only other area of interest to cruisers is the group of cays to the southwest of Utila. The cays are well worth a visit—in fact, with the exception of the Cayos Cochinos, the area southwest of Utila was our favorite spot in the Bay Islands.

Pumpkin Hill, in the island's extreme northeast, is visible for miles and forms a useful reference point when approaching from the north, east, or south. The light indicated on the charts was not operating in 1990. The water is deep and free of hazards on all sides of Utila except to the west and southwest. These areas are rife with reefs and small cays—any approach from these directions should be made in daylight and with extreme caution since the landmarks are all low-lying and visible only shortly before you enter the reef area.

PUERTO ESTE

Chart: DMA 28143. This is based on a very old British survey with little updating, but is nevertheless surprisingly accurate. The reef has grown in a couple of critical areas—enough to run us aground!

Note: A canal leads from the lagoons (to the west of Puerto Este) clear across Utila to Black Rock Basin on the north shore. However, this is very shallow—even the cayucos have to be dragged through the mud in places.

The bay at Puerto Este is protected by a headland to the east and a fringing reef across its mouth, some of it awash but much of it just submerged. In normal trade-wind conditions, the entire harbor provides excellent protection. Even with the winds in the southwest and heavy swells running outside the reef, reasonable protection can be found in the southeast corner of the harbor.

UTILA

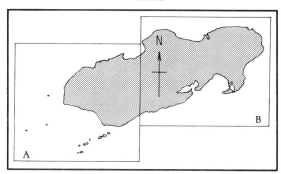

APPROACHES.

From the East. There are no hazards. Just stay one-quarter mile or more off the coastline, continuing westward for one-quarter mile past the lighthouse at the entrance to the harbor until you pick up the ranges given below.

From the West. Here, the coastline tends to draw you in! To stay clear of the shoals at the mouth of the harbor, keep outside of a line drawn to the light on the east side of the entry (approximately 077°T) until you pick up the ranges given below.

Traditionally entry has been made on a heading of 020°T for the Methodist chapel on the waterfront; however, the chapel is now obscured by a large new building. In any case this track comes rather close to a shoal on the west side, just inside the entrance. We found a better approach to be on a heading of 038°T for the large, conspicuous satellite dish on the waterfront, which belongs to a cable TV company. (Since cable TV is in the islands to stay, this should be a reasonably permanent feature.) Once well inside the entrance to the bay, come around to the north (007°T toward the Lighthouse View Restaurant) to avoid another shoal. The restaurant is also conspicuous—its name is painted on the roof.

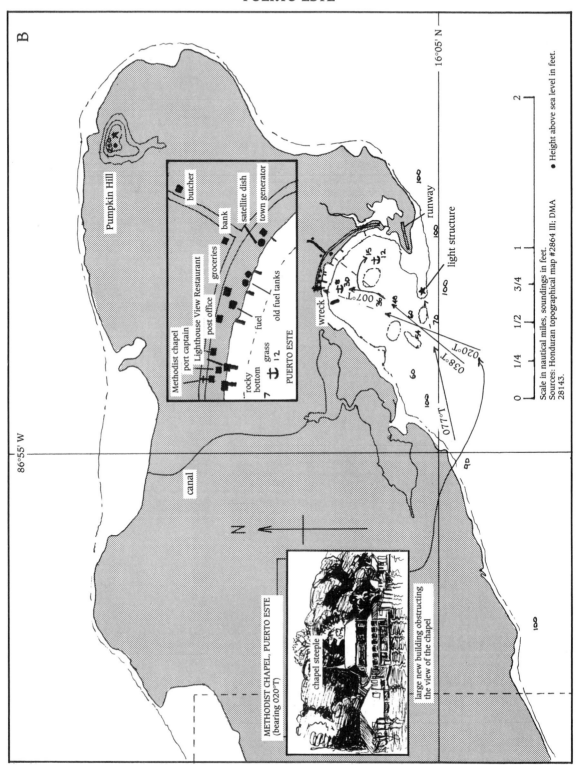

B

16°05' N

Pumpkin Hill

86°55' W

canal

N

Methodist chapel
port captain
Lighthouse View Restaurant
post office
groceries
bank
satellite dish
town generator
butcher

rocky
bottom
7
fuel
old fuel tanks
grass
12
PUERTO ESTE

wreck
007°T
038°T
020°T
077°T
runway
light structure
qb

METHODIST CHAPEL, PUERTO ESTE
(bearing 020°T)

chapel steeple

large new building obstructing
the view of the chapel

Scale in nautical miles, soundings in feet.
Sources: Honduran topographical map #2864 III; DMA
28143.

● Height above sea level in feet.

0   1/4   1/2   3/4   1   2

ANCHORAGE. Anchor a couple hundred yards southeast of the Lighthouse View Restaurant dock. Water depths in this area range from 7 to 30 feet. The holding is good in a grassy bottom. However, note that the bottom shoals to 7 feet over rock to the west of the dock. In a rare southwesterly this part of the bay will be rolly; you have better protection by coming around the waterfront toward the east and anchoring off the airport runway.

CLEARANCE PROCEDURES. Puerto Este is not an official port of entry, nevertheless the port captain will grant you permission to stay for a few days and will issue the necessary zarpe when you leave. There is no immigration office on Utila so you will still need to clear in or out properly at Coxen's Hole on Roatan before proceeding to any other destination.

Dinghy in to the Lighthouse View Restaurant. You can leave the dingy on the dock or on a patch of sand immediately behind the restaurant to the west side. Watch out for a couple of submerged piles close to the building when coming around. The port captain's office is immediately behind the restaurant. He will take your zarpe and hold it until you are ready to leave, at which time he will issue a new one. The charge is L20 (lempiras, 1990). Most of the people on Utila are white and English-speaking, although the officials come from the mainland and speak Spanish, the official language of Honduras.

PROVISIONS/FACILITIES. The people of Utila are exceptionally friendly, but the sand flies are not! We found them to be fierce all day long, not just at dusk. You need to wear long sleeves and pants, and carry bug repellant.

Puerto Este is a very clean and pretty little town, which took us by surprise since it looks rather dreary from the anchorage. It has a couple of small grocery stores, fresh milk (which we found throughout the Bay Islands but nowhere else in the Northwest Caribbean), a butcher, a bank, and a post office. You can buy diesel but have to haul it in jerry cans (see the town plan). A ferry leaves at 0600 hours on Monday mornings for the mainland, returning Tuesday evening. The crossing takes 2 1/2 hours. There are three flights daily from the airfield to La Ceiba.

UP AND DOWN

Chart: DMA 28143.

Just to the southwest of Utila are a couple of small, inhabited cays called Suck-Suck and Pigeon—known locally as Up and Down, which describes their relationship to the prevailing trade winds. Although Up and Down barely stick up above the water, they are covered with clapboard houses, some quite substantial, which are built on piles and spill off the islands into the surrounding sea. The two cays are joined by a rickety boardwalk. This relatively prosperous community comprises primarily white people who make their living fishing in large cayucos powered by single-cylinder inboard diesels. Immediately to the northeast of Suck-Suck lies Diamond Cay, and in its lee is a well-protected, reef-enclosed anchorage. To the southwest of Pigeon Cay are several small, almost uninhabited sand-and-coconut cays with lovely beaches and excellent snorkeling. To the northwest are three more reef-bound cays, again with excellent diving and snorkeling on the outside of the reef. Up and Down is a fine area in which to stay a few days—not to be missed by anyone coming to the Bay Islands.

APPROACH. Make your approach to the anchorage north of Diamond Cay from the east since you must check in at Puerto Este before proceeding to Up and Down. Follow the coastline to Diamond Cay, but when one-half mile off pay close attention to the entering directions that follow since there is a substantial patch of shallow coral in the middle of the approach channel.

Enter on a heading of 277°T on Sandy Cay, which brings you just to the west of the coral patch to the east of Diamond Cay. This heading carries you almost into the anchorage. Maintain a close watch for the coral patch, perhaps making a minor course adjustment; the coral can be passed to both north and south. You need to make a dogleg to come into the anchorage. You will see another substantial patch of almost-awash coral immediately to the north of Diamond Cay. Pass between this and Diamond Cay, coming north around the western end of the coral and then anchoring anywhere in

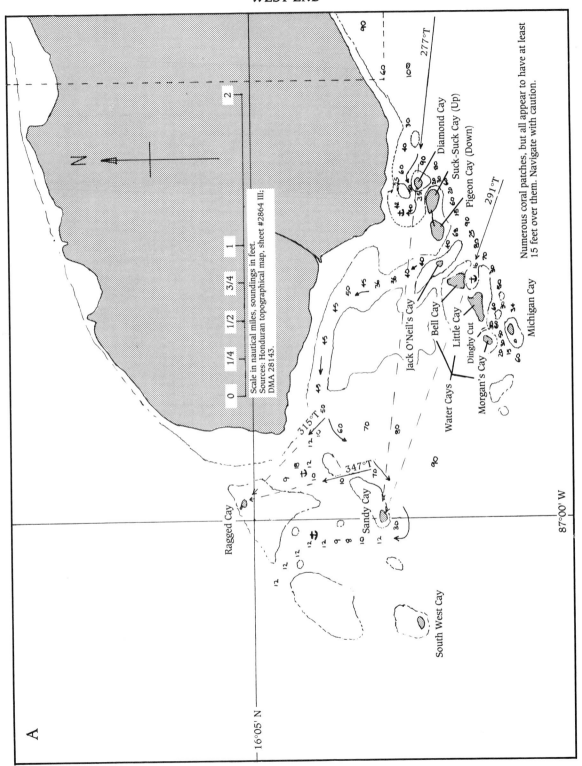

Scale in nautical miles, soundings in feet.
Sources: Honduran topographical map, sheet #2864 III;
DMA 28143.

Numerous coral patches, but all appear to have at least
15 feet over them. Navigate with caution.

Diamond Cay

Suck-Suck Cay (Up)

Pigeon Cay (Down)

277°T

291°T

Jack O'Neil's Cay

Bell Cay

Little Cay

Dinghy cut

Morgan's Cay

Michigan Cay

Water Cays

315°T

347°T

Ragged Cay

Sandy Cay

South West Cay

87°00' W

16°05' N

the area between this coral and a large shoal area to the west and northwest.

ANCHORAGE. The holding in this relatively deep (up to 40 feet) anchorage is good in sand. Pay out adequate scope and make sure the anchor is well set; the wind sometimes whistles through here. Since swinging room can be a little restricted, you may need a running moor. Some old wire cables foul the bottom so I recommend you buoy your anchors.

When you leave you can round the reef area in the anchorage on its eastern side. The channel narrows, but is easily seen in the right light. A narrow channel also exists between Diamond Cay and Suck-Suck on a heading of approximately 154°T, but this involves a slight dogleg at its outer end. Good light and calm seas are essential; I would not try coming *in* to the anchorage this way under any conditions.

PROVISIONS/FACILITIES. The town is fascinating, although with few supplies. A couple of small grocery stores have a small stock of canned goods and fresh produce, while diesel and ice are available at the fish plant. If you ask around, you can buy homemade cakes and jam at some of the houses.

THINGS TO DO. The Water Cays can be explored by dinghy from the Diamond Cay anchorage or by your big boat. Quite a few coral patches dot the surrounding waters, but in good light the intervening deep water permits you to work around them.

A particularly beautiful and picturesque anchorage can be found tucked into a small lagoon between the two easternmost Water Cays. Entry is made on a heading of 291°T on Sandy Cay, which will be visible midway between the two Water Cays. A minimum 16 feet of water will be found in the narrow cut between the reefs, and 36 feet in the lagoon, with good holding in a sandy bottom. You will be anchored off a lovely, shallow sandy beach (perfect for children). You can snorkel the coral right off the boat.

Sandy, West, and Ragged Cays are on a coral-bound, somewhat-exposed shelf to the northwest of

Beach scene in the Water Cays.

Diamond Cay. Sandy and West Cays are beautiful sand-and-coconut islets, while the surrounding reef offers some excellent snorkeling and diving. In normal trade-wind conditions, the area is reasonably well protected, enabling you to anchor to the north of Sandy Cay, but this should be a daytime stop only — retreat to Diamond Cay at night.

The sketch chart indicates the approach from Diamond Cay. Sandy Cay is rounded to the south and west, staying clear of the shallow coral. An alternative approach is to stand out to sea from Diamond Cay, coming all the way around the outside of Michigan Cay and then making up directly to Sandy Cay.

To the north of Sandy Cay the depths are mostly 10 to 12 feet, but with isolated coral heads. This is strictly eyeball navigation. The holding varies from reasonable in a grassy bottom, to poor in thin sand over rock. You must make sure there are no coral heads in your swinging circle, or set a running moor. The best snorkeling and diving are on the outside of the reef. A 12-foot-deep cut in the reef to the north exists approximately where I show it, but I would not advise traversing it in anything but a dinghy since it is none too clear.

Region 2: Roatan, Morat, and Barbareta

Roatan is a long, skinny sliver of an island, quite hilly for most of its length. The interior is green, lush, and almost uninhabited, the vast majority of the population choosing to live in picturesque clapboard houses set on piles and strung out along the coastline. Away from Coxen's Hole and French Harbor, almost all transportation is by cayuco through a series of coastal canals weaving in and out of the mangroves.

The south coast is punctuated by a number of fiord-like inlets cutting back into the encircling hills, each one guarded by a shallow reef with a narrow opening and offering superlative protection. The north shore is fronted by an almost continuous barrier reef, one-half to one mile offshore, that drops into the ocean depths. A series of narrow breaks in the reef give access to several wonderfully protected anchorages, while the drop-off on the outer reef face provides some of the best diving and snorkeling in the Western Hemisphere. Here and there between rocky headlands are beautiful beaches.

All of the reef entries require good light and eyeball navigation. Those on the north shore should not be attempted under any circumstances during a norther, or if the swells are running hard onto the reef. Fortunately, in normal trade-wind conditions, the northeast-to-southwest axis of the island creates a partial lee on the north shore, and the swells calm down considerably as you near the reef.

Coxen's Hole is the port of entry. If coming from anywhere other than Guanaja, you should go to

ROATAN, MORAT, AND BARBARETA

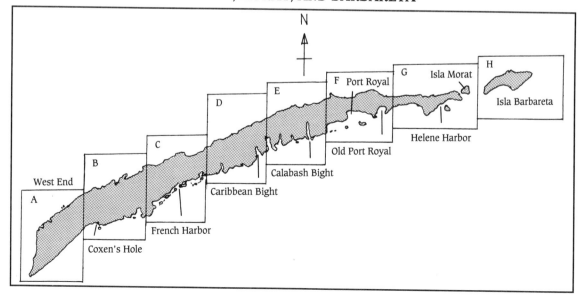

WEST END

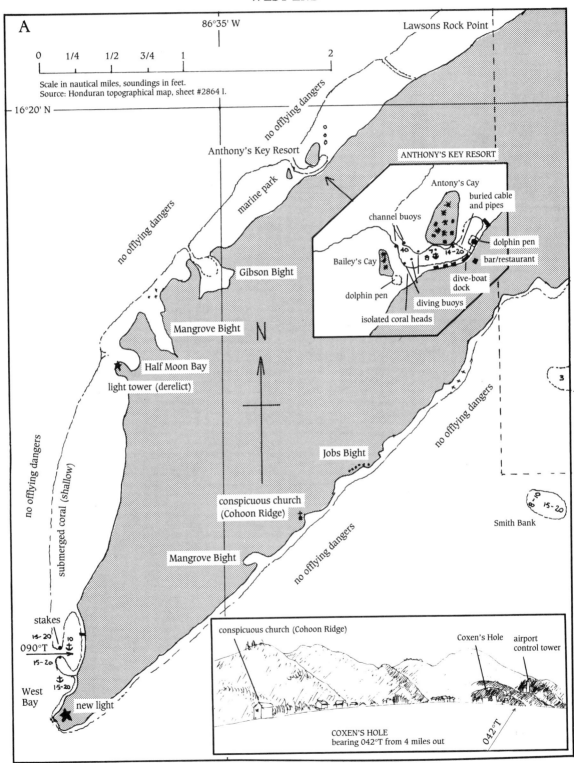

A

86°35' W

Lawsons Rock Point

Scale in nautical miles, soundings in feet.
Source: Honduran topographical map, sheet #2864 I.

0   1/4   1/2   3/4   1   2

16°20' N

no offlying dangers

Anthony's Key Resort

ANTHONY'S KEY RESORT

Antony's Cay

marine park

channel buoys

buried cable
and pipes

no offlying dangers

Bailey's Cay

40

8   7
14-20

dolphin pen

bar/restaurant

Gibson Bight

dolphin pen

dive-boat
dock

Mangrove Bight

diving buoys

isolated coral heads

N

Half Moon Bay

light tower (derelict)

no offlying dangers

3

Jobs Bight

no offlying dangers

Smith Bank

8-10   15-20

submerged coral (shallow)

conspicuous church
(Cohoon Ridge)

Mangrove Bight

no offlying dangers

stakes

15-20

090°T

15-20

West
Bay

15-20

new light

conspicuous church (Cohoon Ridge)

Coxen's Hole

airport
control tower

COXEN'S HOLE
bearing 042°T from 4 miles out

042°T

Coxen's Hole to clear in before doing any further cruising. If you have already cleared in at Guanaja, you are still expected to clear with the authorities in Coxen's Hole. However, normally no objections are made if you take a week or so making your way between the two islands, stopping at the numerous anchorages en route.

The most detailed chart of Roatan was DMA 28150, but this is to a scale of 1:300,000, which is of no use for inshore work. DMA 28154 and 28151, to a scale of 1:80,000, are a great improvement, but still lack any inshore details. The Honduran government has two topographical maps to a scale of 1:50,000, which between them cover all of Roatan. These have an accurate geographic outline of the island and the surrounding reefs, but with no charted depths. In the following pages, I have used the topographical maps to develop a series of detailed sketch charts that cover the entire island, but obviously the nautical information is limited to those places we were able to visit and those soundings we were able to take. I have used the names on the Honduran maps to label bays and cays.

COXEN'S HOLE

Chart: DMA 28154.

APPROACHES.

From the West. The coast drops off steeply and is free of hazards, with the exceptions of Smith Bank, to the south-southwest of Coxen's Hole, and an unnamed bank to the southwest. Smith Bank has 15 to 20 feet of water over most of it, but in places it shoals to 8 or 10 feet. The unnamed bank shoals to 2 or 3 feet. The best approach is inside both of these, seeking the calmer water as you come up into the lee of Big Cay. The new airport control tower is conspicuous from miles away.

From the East. Head around the southern end of Big Cay. The Cordelia Shoal, to the southeast, has no more than a few inches over it in places—and at one point a pile of conch shells left by local fishermen sticks up a foot or so. It is roughly crescent shaped. In calm conditions you can anchor in the arms of the crescent, in water 20 to 30 feet deep, to snorkel and dive the reef, but it is difficult to find a patch of bottom free of coral and the holding is none too good.

A passage with least depths of 30 feet leads between the light to the west of Big Cay and the unnamed bank. *Note that the light is set back on the reef, not on its end, and must be given a wide berth* (200 or so yards). In 1990 the light was not operational.

ANCHORGE. The water is deep (100 feet) almost to the west side of Big Cay, but then shoals from 30 feet into the shore. It is possible to anchor in 12 to 20 feet off the northwest shore of the cay, but swinging room is somewhat restricted at present due to a sizable freighter that was allowed to sink off Little Cay in 1990. The holding is good in a muddy bottom. A very protected anchorage is in the lagoon to the southeast of Coxen's Hole. It is entered either to the north or south of Little Cay, staying in mid-channel. The least depth to the south is 7 feet; to the north 8 feet. The northern channel is the wider of the two. Inside the lagoon the depth increases to 24 feet in the center, shoaling toward the edges. The holding is good in a muddy bottom. The recent extension of the airport runway into the lagoon increases the protection from the east without decreasing the pleasant breeze that comes in across the remaining reef area to the east.

CLEARANCE PROCEDURES. When checking in, be sure to fly your yellow flag and a Honduran courtesy flag. The Hondurans can be sticklers for flag etiquette—our flag was rejected because the stripes were not blue enough! Take your paperwork ashore to the town dock, which is immediately opposite Big Cay. The immigration office is on the dock, the customs immediately behind, and the port captain behind that. You should take your zarpe from the last port of call to the port captain, who will probably organize a boarding party. (This seems to be a racket since all the officials then charge L20 for the "inspection"—I suspect this charge is illegal.) You need a new zarpe—the form must be purchased from customs for L3 (this is the extent of their involvement in the procedures) and taken to the port captain. He charges L20 for filling it out (also, I believe, an illegal charge). The immigration officers have a history of charging whatever they can get away with for the visas in your passports—up to $10

(U.S.) each; the official charge is L5. In any event, it is best to pay in lempiras rather than dollars, since the rate of exchange on the dollar is lousy—generally about half the street rate. After we complained to the Minister of Tourism for Honduras about the extraction of *mordida* at Coxen's Hole, the total charges on our next visit fell to L3, but I don't suppose they remained L3 for long. (Just to keep things in perspective, it should be noted that even with the bribery, it is still cheaper to check into Honduras than the United States!)

When you are checking out, go first to the customs to buy a zarpe (L3) and take this to the port captain for him to fill out. If you are leaving Honduran waters, you take the zarpe to the immigration office and have your passports stamped, but if you are just sailing between the islands this is not necessary.

PROVISIONS/FACILITIES. Coxen's Hole is a grubby little town with not much to recommend it, but it does have quite reasonable grocery shopping at Warren's Supermarket (by the town dock). Better-quality fresh produce is available here than at most places in the Bay Islands—quite a backhanded compliment! In town are a post office, telephones, a bank, and a number of restaurants and bars. If you need to change money, try Warren's, or one of the restaurants, rather than the bank. Some places will even cash personal checks. Just the other side of Warren's Supermarket is a large new dock. Fuel is available at the head of the dock on the north side; this was the filthiest fuel we have ever taken on board. You can carry 6 to 7 feet alongside, but only by hugging the dock since the bottom shoals rapidly to the north. The fish plant on the dock has water and ice.

DIXON COVE BAY

Chart: DMA 28154.

Dixon Cove Bay is about one mile long, opening out to one mile or so wide at its mouth, with two small cays (Stamp Cay and Green Cay) over toward the western shore. You can enter the bay on either side of these cays, but cannot work around the in-side of the cays from one side of the bay to the other.

APPROACHES. The entry to the west of Stamp Cay is made on a heading of 017°T for the house in the center of the head of the bay. Going in the water has least depths of 12 feet; about two-thirds of the way to the inner shore, it shoals to 6 feet on all sides. There is a primitive wooden boat-building yard on the west bank.

The entry to the east of Stamp Cay is made in mid-channel, heading straight for the wreck at the top of the bay, with another wreck to port. There is a coral patch in the middle of the entrance, but it has 10 feet of water over it. The depth of the surrounding water varies from 20 feet to 140 feet. The water up the center of the bay is deep, shoaling slowly toward the far end. The western cove is shallow, but the eastern has deep water almost into the mangroves in most places, with the exception of its eastern shore where the bottom comes up quite suddenly. You need to proceed carefully here since the water is generally too cloudy to provide good visibility.

THINGS TO DO. Dixon Cove is exceptionally well protected with good holding but not much to see. The snorkeling around the outside is mediocre. The outer wreck was the subject of a salvage dispute with Lloyds of London. The owners won the right to retain the contents, but the salvagers got the ship. They stripped it clean and ran it up on the reef. The inner wreck sprang a leak and the load of cement on board set solid; it too was deliberately run in here and abandoned. A local conservation group is trying to get both wrecks hauled out to sea and scuttled.

BRICK BAY

(see map page 210)

Chart: DMA 28154.

Brick Bay is rather more open than other anchorages on the south shore, but is well protected by Jesse Arch Cay and a fringing reef with just one narrow entry. On the port side as you enter is a lovely private development along a couple of canals
(Continued on page 211)

COXEN'S HOLE TO DIXON COVE BAY, MUD HOLE, AND TURTLING BAY

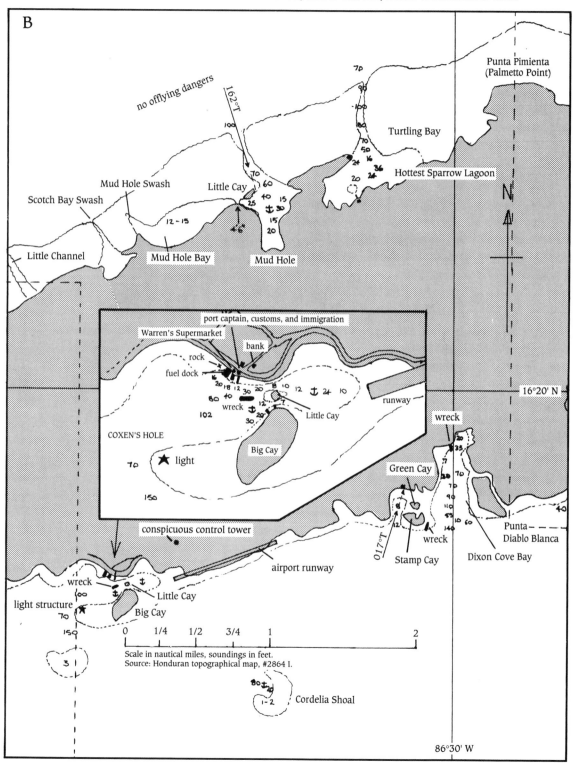

Punta Pimienta
(Palmetto Point)

no offlying dangers

162°T

Turtling Bay

Mud Hole Swash

Little Cay

Hottest Sparrow Lagoon

Scotch Bay Swash

12 - 15

Little Channel

Mud Hole Bay

Mud Hole

N

port captain, customs, and immigration

Warren's Supermarket

bank

rock

fuel dock

runway

16°20' N

wreck

COXEN'S HOLE

Little Cay

wreck

Big Cay

light

Green Cay

017°T

wreck

conspicuous control tower

Stamp Cay

Punta
Diablo Blanca

Dixon Cove Bay

airport runway

wreck

Little Cay

light structure

Big Cay

| 0 | 1/4 | 1/2 | 3/4 | 1 | | 2 |

Scale in nautical miles, soundings in feet.
Source: Honduran topographical map, #2864 I.

Cordelia Shoal

86°30' W

BRICK BAY TO FRENCH HARBOR AND PUNTA PIMIENTA TO BIG BIGHT

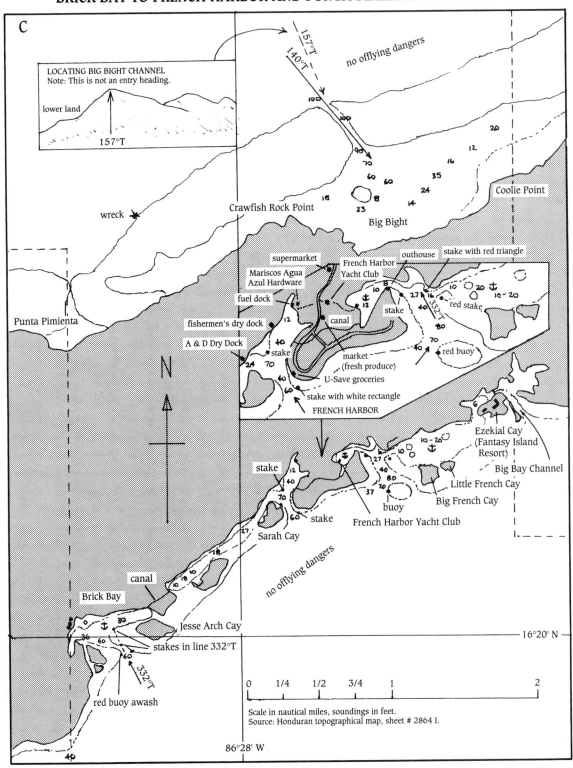

C

LOCATING BIG BIGHT CHANNEL
Note: This is not an entry heading.

lower land

157°T

157°T
140°T

no offlying dangers

Coolie Point

wreck

Crawfish Rock Point

Big Bight

supermarket

Mariscos Agua
Azul Hardware

fuel dock

Punta Pimienta

fishermen's dry dock

A & D Dry Dock

French Harbor
Yacht Club

outhouse

stake with red triangle

red stake

332°T

canal

stake

red buoy

N

market
(fresh produce)
U-Save groceries

stake

stake with white rectangle

FRENCH HARBOR

stake

Ezekial Cay
(Fantasy Island
Resort)

Big Bay Channel

Little French Cay

buoy

Big French Cay

French Harbor Yacht Club

Sarah Cay

stake

no offlying dangers

canal

Brick Bay

Jesse Arch Cay

stakes in line 332°T

16°20′ N

0   1/4   1/2   3/4   1   2

332°T

red buoy awash

Scale in nautical miles, soundings in feet.
Source: Honduran topographical map, sheet # 2864 I.

86°28′ W

(Continued from page 208)

cutting through a sandy, coconut-clad point. The old CSY facility, now a dive resort, is just to the north in the lagoon that leads off the west side of the bay. There is not much else to see at Brick Bay.

APPROACH/ANCHORAGE. At one time CSY had the various reefs and channels reasonably well staked out. However, several of these markers are gone now. The ones that remained in 1990 were a red buoy to be taken to starboard on entry, with an almost submerged red buoy to be taken to port. A little inside the reef entry were two range stakes.

Entry is made on a heading of 332°T, leaving the principal buoy about 100 feet to starboard while keeping the two range stakes in line. The channel is narrow and 60 feet deep. The two stakes are on a shoal; when you near the first one, come around onto a heading of 297°T toward a group of houses in the western extremity of the bay. Then curve around to the east to anchor over toward the northeastern shore. Alternatively, you could continue into the old CSY lagoon.

PROVISIONS/FACILITIES. The current owners of the CSY facility are Romeo's Resort Dive and Yacht Club. The CSY marine railway is still operational and able to haul boats of up to 40,000 pounds. The controlling depth is 6 feet. If you wish to haul out, you need to make arrangements with the resort and to bring all your own supplies (Romeo's Resort Dive and Yacht Club, Brick Bay, Roatan, Honduras, Central America. Tel: (011 504) 45-13-37 and 45-11-27.

A canal leads from the eastern end of Brick Bay into a channel that runs up to French Harbor. I am told that 6 feet can be carried through this canal, although we did not check it. There is certainly plenty of water in the channel on the other side.

FRENCH HARBOR

Chart: DMA 28154.

French Harbor is the second principal town on Roatan, and the center for a large, modern shrimp-boat fleet. Many of these million-dollar boats would be just as at home in Louisiana or Texas. The town itself is spotty, sometimes pretty, and sometimes pretty dreary! However, with the possible exception of Warren's Supermarket in Coxen's Hole, it is the best place in the Bay Islands to stock up on groceries and other supplies.

APPROACHES/ANCHORAGES. Entry is straightforward through a 60-foot-deep channel between Sarah Cay and the headland to the east. A white rectangle on a stake marks the tip of the reef to the east and is left to starboard. Once inside you can turn either to port or to starboard—a shoal dead ahead is marked by another stake.

A turn to port takes you into a channel that continues for 1 mile, as far as the canal running through to Brick Bay. There is no passage back out to sea through the fringing reef that runs from Jesse Arch Cay to Sarah Cay. In 1990 a resort was in the early stages of development on the cay at the southern end of this channel. Depths vary from 10 to 30 feet. The protection is excellent and the holding good—you could anchor anywhere along here and be well out of the way of French Harbor's in-and-out shrimp-boat traffic. However, a more pleasant anchorage will be found 1 mile northeast behind Big and Little French Cays, and a more protected anchorage off the French Harbor Yacht Club (the next two anchorages in this guide).

A turn to starboard takes you into French Harbor. This is a very busy base for the shrimp-boat fleet, and it is also a small commercial harbor. It is not a suitable place for pleasureboats. The only reason to come here is to fill your tanks at the fuel dock, which is tucked into the northeastern corner of the bay. This is a commercial fuel dock with high-pressure hoses capable of pumping thousands of gallons of fuel an hour—the shrimp boats take on as much as 20,000 gallons—but the hoses have adaptors suitable for the 1½-inch deck-fills normal on pleasureboats. Nevertheless, the fuel comes out fast so keep a close eye on your tank level or you will end up with a big mess!

PROVISIONS/FACILITIES. To service the shrimp-boat fleet, the town has a couple of supermarkets, a bank, a fuel dock, a large hardware store with a number of marine items (most much too large for pleasureboats), various professional services (listed under "French Harbor Yacht Club"), a couple of marine railways, and the expected crop of restaurants, bars, and brothels. The two dry-docks are almost the only places in the Northwest Caribbean where a boat can be hauled for major repairs (see page 23).

FRENCH HARBOR YACHT CLUB

(see map page 210)

Chart: DMA 28154.

The French Harbor Yacht Club is in an extremely protected lagoon just to the east of French Harbor. An insalubrious dinghy canal, which doubles as the principal local sewer, connects the two.

APPROACH/ANCHORAGE. Big French Cay is encompassed by a substantial reef, much of it awash. To its southwest is another large coral patch with a red buoy on its western end. The reef on the mainland also juts out to the northwest of this coral patch.

From the West. You simply make toward the red buoy, then come around between the coral patch and the mainland reef.

From the East. You can take a narrow channel between Big French Cay and the coral patch. However, in anything other than calm conditions and good light, you had better stand toward the west and round the buoy as above.

The reef around Big French Cay extends to the northwest. You must come up the west side of this reef, on a heading of approximately 332°T to enter. You pass a red stake on the reef to starboard, then a red stake with a triangle, which marks a small shoal extending out from the mainland. Almost immediately opposite this last stake is another stake to be left to port. Ahead is a small spit of land with shoals off its tip. At this point you must come around to the west, cutting close into the southern side of the entrance into the lagoon (there is a conspicuous outhouse on this point) since the water shoals immediately to the north. The depth here is 8 feet, but increases to 10 or 12 feet once you are in the lagoon. You can either moor to the yacht club dock or anchor off.

PROVISIONS/FACILITIES. The French Harbor Yacht Club has a well-constructed dock with 7 to 8 feet of water alongside, and fresh water and 110/220VAC power on the dock. There is a restaurant and bar in the hotel at the top of a small hill overlooking the bay. The yacht club monitors channel 16 on the VHF and will hold mail. This is quite the best place in the Bay Islands to leave a boat to go sightseeing or to fly home to visit family and friends. For those coming from the West Coast, it is the first secure spot since leaving Panama. There is a drawback: The dock is small, with just 6 to 8 berths. If you wish to lay your boat up, plan to book ahead. The address is: French Harbor Yacht Club, French Harbor, Roatan, Honduras, Central America. Tel: (011-504) 45-1478/1460. Fax: 45-1459.

The yacht club can contact professionals to help with various problems. In particular, Searle Bodden of TMR (Transcoastal Marine Refrigeration), who monitors channel 16; Dale Werdon of Dale's Electronics (channel 68); and Bobby Reiman of Casa Reiman, who does woodworking repairs (channel 66).

BIG AND LITTLE FRENCH CAYS

(see map page 210)

Chart: DMA 28154.

A continuous breaking reef runs from Big French Cay northeast to Ezekiel Cay. The area behind is well protected from the ocean swells while a strong breeze generally blows in across the reef. This is a more pleasant anchorage than the French Harbor Yacht Club lagoon, which tends to be hot and airless.

APPROACHES/ANCHORAGES. To enter the anchorage you come into the channel toward the French Harbor Yacht Club as above, but then hook around to the east through a relatively narrow passage off to starboard, fairly close to the shore. The red stake previously mentioned marks the south side of the entry channel and should be kept to starboard, while the stake with the red triangle should be kept well to port. The entry heading is approximately 032°T; the entry depth shoals to 10 feet. Once inside there are two obvious shoal patches to be avoided (you can go around them or between them) with another patch to the northeast. The depths vary from 10 to 20 feet. You can anchor anywhere. The holding is good.

PROVISIONS/FACILITIES. A multimillion-dollar resort (the Fantasy Island Resort) has been developed on Ezekiel Cay at the northeast end of this anchorage. The hotel has a fine bar and restaurant, lovely beaches, and all kinds of tourist-oriented sports—diving, windsailing, Jet-Skis, etc. A 6-foot draft can be carried through the channel and behind the resort, where the mangroves provide extreme protection. A bridge obstructs access to the rest of the lagoon back here. Just on the other side of the bridge, the resort has built a substantial dock for visiting yachts—it has plans for a marina with water and shorepower in all the slips. Access is via the Big Cay Channel. Take it slowly since there are one or two rocks, and the bottom shoals as you come around the back of the resort onto the dock—stay close to the dock, which has 6 to 7 feet of water alongside.

EVERTIME BIGHT

Chart: DMA 28154.

APPROACHES/ANCHORAGES. Entry is straight-forward—up the center of the bay and then curving around to the west. Once around the point, the protection is excellent and the holding is good. The bay is mostly mangrove-lined, uninhabited, and mundane. The head of the bay is all shoal water as shown on the sketch chart.

CARIBBEAN POINT BIGHT

Chart: DMA 28154.

Caribbean Point Bight is a very picturesque anchorage with a rocky cliff face to the west and green hills all around. The bay is uninhabited.

APPROACH/ANCHORAGE. Entry is on a heading

of 335°T. The channel is fairly narrow but easy to see due to its depth (70 to 90 feet). Inside an extensive shoal runs from the center of the bay to the northern shore. To the east of this shoal, the water is deep in most places, but there is a shelf in the area of the wreck. The bottom comes up quite suddenly to 20 feet or so, and then shoals slowly. When you anchor, get well on the shelf and make sure your hook is set. If it drags off the edge of the shelf, it won't get another bite before you are on the shoal in the middle of the bay. A dinghy canal runs east through the mangroves to Bodden Bight: This is one of the neater canals on Roatan and well worth exploring. The mangroves join overhead to form a tunnel for much of the way.

BODDEN BIGHT

Chart: DMA 28154.

APPROACH/ANCHORAGE. The entry is narrow, but straightforward. The southern half of the bay has good depths, but the northern half is riddled with shoals that come up quite suddenly and are hard to see since the water is murky. We ran aground twice poking around! The sketch chart gives a pretty good idea of the areas to avoid.

Bodden Point is particularly interesting. It has a line of colorful houses built on piles strung out along a steep, rocky shore. Behind are cliffs with hanging creepers and a cave of sorts—very different scenery from elsewhere. When approaching stay to the east until you are past the shoal that comes out from Bodden Point, then make over toward the houses on the western shore since there is another shoal on the eastern side of the bight. The bottom is rocky here so you may have some trouble setting an anchor, but make the effort. From time to time strong winds come whistling up the bight with little warning.

A substantial settlement clings to the shoreline behind Cat Island from Bodden Bight to Hog Pen Bight. This channel is only negotiable by dinghy.

FIRST BIGHT TO BODDEN BIGHT AND JOHNSON BIGHT TO POLYTILLY BIGHT

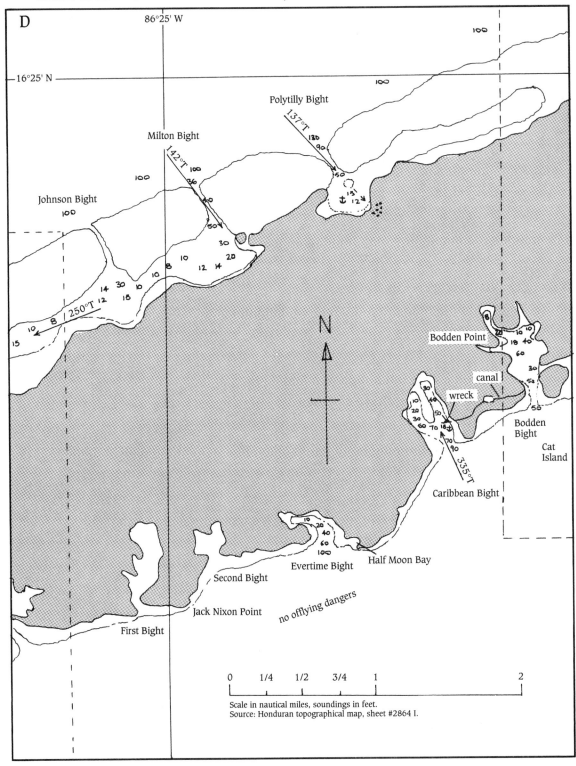

D

86°25' W

16°25' N

Polytilly Bight

137°T

Milton Bight

142°T

Johnson Bight

250°T

N

Bodden Point

canal
wreck

Bodden Bight

Cat Island

335°T

Caribbean Bight

Half Moon Bay

Evertime Bight

Second Bight

Jack Nixon Point

no offlying dangers

First Bight

0   1/4   1/2   3/4   1   2

Scale in nautical miles, soundings in feet.
Source: Honduran topographical map, sheet #2864 I.

HOG PEN BIGHT

Chart: 28154.

APPROACH. Enter on a heading of 345°T leaving a yellow buoy to starboard. This is another narrow channel but it is easily seen, with 50-foot depths going in, shoaling to 36 feet at the inner end of the passage. Once inside you find an extensive shoal in the middle of the bay. In 1990 it was marked with a white float toward its northern end. This shoal can be passed either to east or west, but the deeper water is to the east. Head over toward the substantial new blue-roofed building, which is set on piles out from the eastern shore, leaving this building to starboard and then curving around to the northwest to avoid a shoal extending out from the shore.

ANCHORAGES. You can anchor anywhere up here. An overhead power cable with a clearance of approximately 20 feet now closes off the northern half of the bay. Seven feet can be carried to the west

of the shoal in the middle of the bay. You also can anchor south of Long The Shore behind the reef, but keep well away from the docks, which are busy. Carter Point has a lovely beach.

OAK RIDGE HARBOR

Chart: DMA 28154.

APPROACH. This is another narrow but straightforward entry; head 350°T and leave the light structure to starboard and the remnants of a wreck on the reef to port. The reefs extend a little way out to sea on both sides of the entrance so keep off until lined up to come in, and don't cut any corners. Favor the east side of the channel coming in since parts of the wreck partially obstruct the west side. The light was working in 1990 (Fl 5 secs). The channel shoals to 12 feet about midway through and then deepens on the inside to 30 feet. An extensive shoal obstructs the center of the harbor. It is

Houses at Oak Ridge Harbor.

BODDEN BIGHT TO PORT ROYAL AND THE NORTH SHORE
FROM CANABRAVAL TO ALLIGATOR NOSE

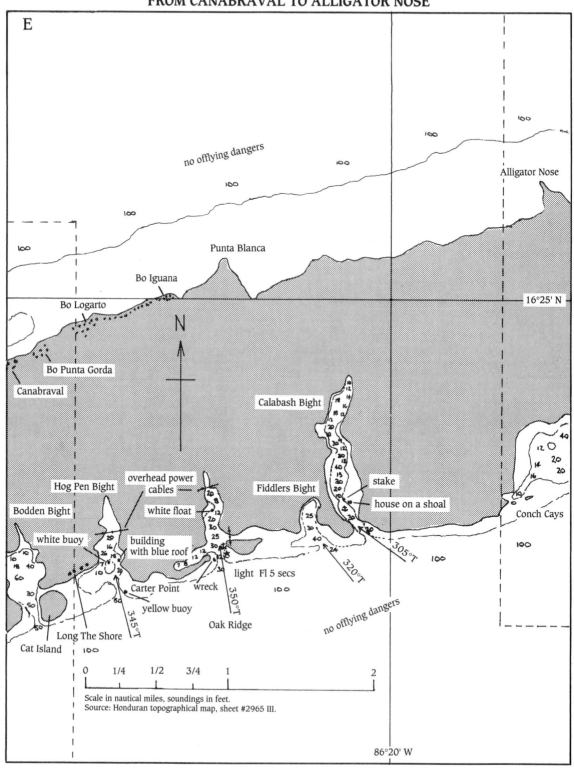

E

no offlying dangers

100

100

100

100

100

Alligator Nose

Punta Blanca

Bo Iguana

Bo Logarto

N

16°25' N

Bo Punta Gorda

Canabraval

Calabash Bight

Hog Pen Bight

overhead power
cables

Fiddlers Bight

stake

house on a shoal

Bodden Bight

white float

Conch Cays

white buoy

building
with blue roof

light Fl 5 secs

305°T

100

100

320°T

Carter Point

wreck

350°T

no offlying dangers

yellow buoy

100

Oak Ridge

Long The Shore

345°T

Cat Island

100

| 0 | 1/4 | 1/2 | 3/4 | 1 | | 2 |

Scale in nautical miles, soundings in feet.
Source: Honduran topographical map, sheet #2965 III.

marked by a white float on its southern end. The deeper water is over toward the eastern shore. Once you are up to the old dry dock, depths are pretty good all over.

ANCHORAGE. You can anchor at the head of the bay away from all the traffic (this is a busy harbor with a sizable shrimp-boat fleet), or tuck in behind the light at the harbor entrance where the water is deep almost into the docks running around to the canal. You need to come close to the dock to keep out of the channel and yet leave enough room for boats to get on and off the dock. A running moor would be a good idea in case the wind comes around in the night and sets you onto the dock. Here you will have a pleasant breeze, no bugs, and a good view of all the activity around the harbor.

CALABASH BIGHT

Chart: DMA 28154.

APPROACH/ANCHORAGE. One of the trickier entries, requiring good light. The narrow part of the channel is longer than most. Entry is made on a heading of 305°T up the center of the channel with 20 feet going in and 30 feet just inside. Here you can anchor south of the house that stands on a shoal in the middle of the bay. The bottom is rocky with poor holding—we dragged a considerable way before getting a good bite.

There are numerous shoals in Calabash Bight, which is not very picturesque. However, the upper part of the bay is considered to be the best local hurricane hole. We surveyed it in some detail; the results are shown on the sketch chart. Northwest of the house on the shoal is a stake that is left just 10 feet to starboard (the channel is only 30 feet wide at this point, with a depth of 10 feet). Once north of the stake, stay pretty much in the center of the bay. At its head you can run almost into the mangroves along the eastern shore. In a hurricane, however, you would be sharing this area with a lot of trawlers, which, if any broke loose, would tear up a yacht in seconds.

PORT ROYAL

Chart: DMA 28154.

Port Royal is a 2½-mile-long bay, protected to seaward by a string of cays and a reef, much of it awash, which has three navigable passes. Inside the bay are numerous anchorages. The bay is quite deep and free of hazards, although we did find one shoal patch over toward the western end and there may well be others in this area. The water is shoal between the Cow and Calf rocks, but there is an 8-foot-deep passage to the north as well as deep water to the south. During the heyday of the CSY charter fleet, a couple of marinas and a resort lodge opened in Port Royal Harbor, but all are now defunct.

APPROACH. Breaks in the reef occur both to the east and west of Lime Cay. To the west the entry is straightforward, entering on a heading of 355°T, leaving a yellow buoy to port. The water is at least 12 feet deep. The channel to the east of Lime Cay runs between reefs for one-third of a mile in the general direction of the Cow and Calf rocks. It is relatively wide, but good light is essential. Just short of the rocks, you can head into the bay both to port and starboard. The third channel is to the west of Fort Cay. This is a straightforward entry on a heading of 325°T up the center of the channel.

ANCHORAGES. You can anchor anywhere in the bay. Our two favorite spots are at the extreme western and eastern ends, tucked in behind the barrier reef. Both spots have picturesque beaches backed by coconuts and a cool breeze blowing over the reef. The western anchorage needs to be approached with caution since shoals extend northward from the Conch Cays and southward from the mainland.

OLD PORT ROYAL

Chart: DMA 28154.

APPROACH/ANCHORAGE. The entry is straightforward on a heading of 345°T in the center of the channel. The wreck of a shrimp boat sits high and

PORT ROYAL AND OLD PORT ROYAL

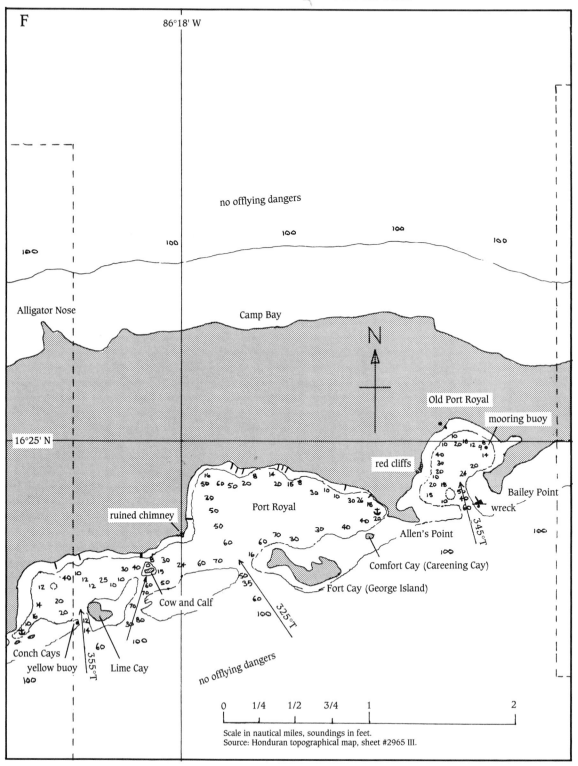

F

86°18' W

no offlying dangers

100

100

100

100

100

Alligator Nose

Camp Bay

N

Old Port Royal

mooring buoy

16°25' N

red cliffs

Bailey Point

ruined chimney

Port Royal

wreck

345°T

Allen's Point

Comfort Cay (Careening Cay)

100

100

Cow and Calf

Fort Cay (George Island)

325°T

Conch Cays
yellow buoy
100

355°T

Lime Cay

no offlying dangers

0   1/4   1/2   3/4   1   2

Scale in nautical miles, soundings in feet.
Source: Honduran topographical map, sheet #2965 III.

dry on the reef to starboard. On the inside of the entrance, to the northwest, is a coral patch awash. The center of the bay is deep, shoaling toward the shore. The eastern end of the bay is particularly shallow, with a maximum of 4 feet leading into a mangrove-lined canal that heads east. This is a large, secure bay with excellent holding and protection just about anywhere. With just one house and one scrubby beach, it is not very interesting.

HELENE HARBOR

Chart: DMA 28151.

APPROACH. An almost unbroken reef stretches the 2¹/₂ miles between Bailey Point and Rocky Point. There is a break toward its eastern end leading into McField Bay, but the entry is tricky with a number of coral heads and requires good light. There is, in any case, nothing much to see in here, except for a small beach at the eastern end.

Heading East. Keep one-quarter mile or so offshore after rounding Rocky Point since there are coral heads and rocks closer inshore. The water comes up quite suddenly from 80 feet to less than 20 feet in places.

Coming from the East. You must swing wide of Rose Island, holding over toward Bentley Bay until south of Big Rock, at which time you can make up for the rock. Bentley Bay has a pretty beach with coconuts. Big Rock is conspicuous, with a minimum of 12 feet of water fairly close to it. Interesting rock formations abound, with numerous palms on the hillsides providing a dramatic backdrop to the houses lining the shore.

ANCHORAGES. You can anchor anywhere in the bay to the southwest of Helene Harbor, or on the western edge of the shoal extending to the west of Rose Island, lying 200 to 300 yards off a lovely beach. A channel, leading into a small anchorage with 12-foot depths, rounds the northern end of the sandspit projecting to the northwest of Rose Island. This anchorage has limited swinging room and is surrounded by shoal water. One mile off to the east is a break in the fringing reef. I was told it is possible to carry 6 feet through the shoals between Rose Cay

and this break, but we could not see the channel—if heading east, you will need to go back out and around to the south of Rose Cay.

ISLA DE MORAT

Chart: DMA 28151.

APPROACH/ANCHORAGE. Morat is a small, attractive, verdant island with one failed restaurant on it. A reasonably protected anchorage can be found off the old restaurant dock, entering to the west of Hog Reef on a heading of 328°T. Hog Reef is awash in a number of places and therefore easy to spot. Note, however, that it has a number of coral heads immediately to the west of it. You should favor the western side of the channel to stay clear of these heads.

PASCUAL BIGHT,

ISLA DE BARBARETA

Chart: DMA 28151.

Barbareta is a lush, green island, rising to almost 500 feet and covered in tropical rain forest teeming with bird life. Along its rocky shores are several beautiful beaches. The western end is the site of several large homes, all of which appear to be closed up, and a failed tourist condominium project. Moves are afoot to try to purchase the whole island and turn it into a permanent wildlife refuge.

APPROACH/ANCHORAGE. A protected anchorage with good holding can be found off the beach at Pascual Bight. If you are coming from Morat, keep careful watch for a couple of shoals south of the west end of Barbareta. Coming from the east, you can either pick your way through the coral around the Pigeon Cays, or pass these to the south until the highest point of Barbareta is to the north, at which point you head north. A long shoal extends from a point to the northeast of Pelican Rock, in a southeasterly direction past Pelican Point. It is broken in

OLD PORT ROYAL TO MORAT

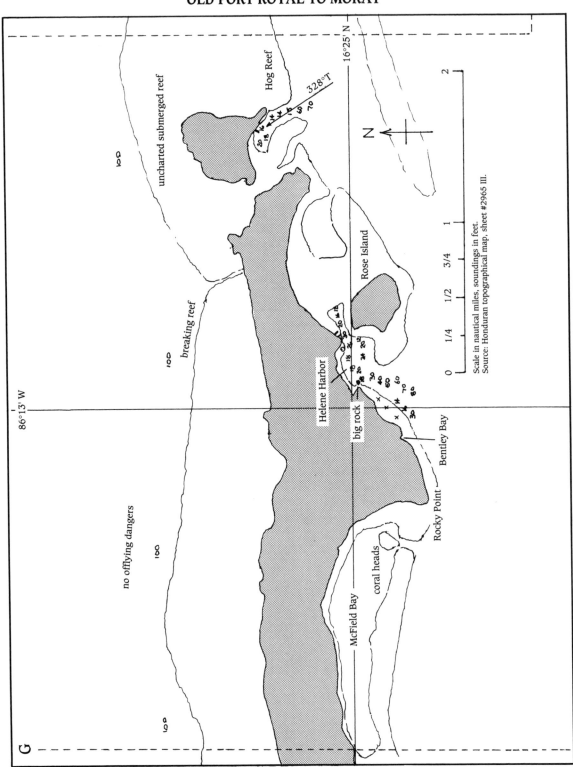

Hog Reef

uncharted submerged reef

328°T

16°25' N

N

Rose Island

breaking reef

Helene Harbor

big rock

Bentley Bay

Rocky Point

McField Bay

coral heads

no offlying dangers

86°13' W

Scale in nautical miles, soundings in feet.
Source: Honduran topographical map, sheet #2965 III.

0   1/4   1/2   3/4   1   2

Fishermen selling lobsters on Isla Barbareta.

APPROACH. A channel leads broadly northwestward between the two western cays up to Pascual Bight on Barbareta. The southern end of this channel is easy to follow since the water is deep (60–70 feet) and the surrounding reefs shallow. Up toward Barbareta the channel shoals to less than 30 feet; the shoals are less clear-cut, and the water colors are not so easy to read—it becomes a little more difficult to pick your way through the coral.

From Pascual Bight. Stand south past Pelican Point until the middle Pigeon Cay (the easternmost of the two conspicuous cays) bears approximately 113°T. At this point you should be lined up on the channel and can head straight for this middle cay. Alternatively, continue south in deep water until the Pigeon Cays are a little to north of east, then come at them in the deep water from the south.

From the East. Stay south of all three cays and then come up into the channel between the two western cays. Note that the channel entry is over toward the westernmost cay. Water depths going in are a minimum of 20 feet, rapidly deepening to 60 feet in the basin between the reefs.

ANCHORAGE. The reef comes up sharply on all sides of the 60-foot basin that lies to the northwest of the middle cay. Drop a hook on the shelf close to the reef, or anchor in the deep water with lots of scope. This area is somewhat exposed to swells rolling in from the east and may be uncomfortable. It should in any case be treated as a daytime stop only.

two places. The westernmost break is the wider of the two and affords an easy aproach to the beach with no water shallower than 26 feet in the cut.

PIGEON CAYS

Chart: DMA 28151.

The Pigeon Cays are three sandy spits, the two western islands each having a stand of palm trees, but the easternmost being swept almost bare. The cays hug the southern edge of an extensive area of shoals and reef extending more or less all the way northward to the southeastern shore of Barbareta. The two western cays are very picturesque and the surrounding water colors are glorious—the prettiest we saw in the Bay Islands.

NORTH SHORE OF

BARBARETA TO

POLYTILLY BIGHT, ROATAN

Chart: DMA 28151.

More than 16 miles lie between the eastern tip of Barbareta and Polytilly Bight, the easternmost reef entry on Roatan. Thirty-three miles separate the Pine Ridge Channel on Guanaja and Polytilly Bight. Whether sailing east or west, you must take these distances into account and allow adequate time to make a secure anchorage in good light.

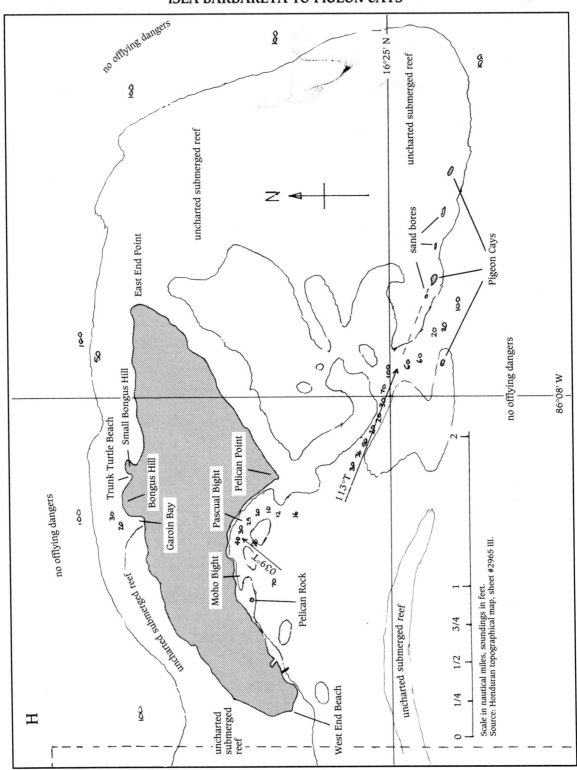

16°25' N

no offlying dangers

uncharted submerged reef

uncharted submerged reef

N

East End Point

sand bores

Pigeon Cays

100

50

Small Bongus Hill

Trunk Turtle Beach

Bongus Hill

Garoin Bay

Moho Bight

Pascual Bight

Pelican Point

no offlying dangers

86°08' W

100

no offlying dangers

uncharted submerged reef

30
20

40 30 25
30
45

039°T

Pelican Rock

113°T

20
30
40
50
60
70
80
90
100

20

20

100

60

16

12

10

uncharted submerged reef

West End Beach

100

H

2

Scale in nautical miles, soundings in feet.
Source: Honduran topographical map, sheet #2965 III.

0   1/4   1/2   3/4   1

The north shore of Barbareta is exceptionally beautiful with rocky headlands enclosing sandy beaches backed by steep hillsides clad in luxurious, green, tropical vegetation. Here and there a palm pokes its head above the surrounding canopy, and there is no sign of human habitation. The offshore reef does not form a continuous wall; instead there is a roughly half-mile-wide shelf with scattered coral nearing the surface. The coral is fairly close to the shore at the eastern end of the island but extends further offshore toward the western end.

APPROACHES/ANCHORAGES. Between the eastern end of the island and Bongus Hill, in settled conditions and with care, you can come in toward the coast. There is no reason to do this except that I am reasonably sure you can work into a gorgeous little bay (Garoin Bay) just to the west of Bongus Hill. Bongus Hill provides good protection from the trade winds, making it a snug little anchorage off a lovely beach. However, a shallow reef extends from the western half of the bay out to the northwest a considerable distance. If there is an entry, it is from the northeast coming in fairly close to the cliffs. (The day we tried it the swells were running just a little too hard, the water visibility was not as good as it might have been, and I chickened out when still in 20 feet of water but fairly close in.) To the west of Bongus Hill, you should stand one-half mile out to sea since the reef does come out a considerable distance. The northern shore of Morat is inaccessible. To the west of Morat the reef is almost continuously awash along the whole coast of Roatan. The outer edge of the reef drops off into the ocean with no offlying hazards. If the conditions permit, you can sail quite safely just a couple of hundred yards off the reef.

The eastern end of Roatan is low-lying for 2 or 3 miles. North of Port Royal the mangroves give way to hills, and on the north shore is a lovely long beach in Camp Bay. We were told there is an entry to Camp Bay and made for what looked like a sufficiently submerged section of reef (as opposed to an obvious channel). We had a school of a dozen spinner dolphins playing in the bow wave. As we closed the reef under power, it became clear that, if this was an entry, it was not an easy one and we would have to dodge a coral head or two. The dolphins began to get extremely excited, jumping out of the

water just ahead of us and then scattering in all directions. We couldn't make out whether they were trying to show us the way in or warn us off. We got into some shallow heads and had to back out; however, we decided to give it another shot. The dolphins, who had swum off a distance, came back and repeated the same agitated behavior—once again we had to back out. We decided to give up. The dolphins stayed with us long enough to see that we were headed away from the reef, then took off!

The western end of Camp Bay is bounded by a conspicuous headland known as "Alligator Nose" or "Alligator Head." Two miles further west is another prominent headland, Punta Blanca. Pollytilly Bight is 2 1/2 miles to the west of Punta Blanca. In between lie a series of isolated, poor settlements primarily of Black Caribs.

POLLYTILLY BIGHT

(see map page 214)

Chart: DMA 28154.

APPROACH/ANCHORAGE. The entry at Polytilly Bight is clear enough, even in overcast conditions, because of the depth of the water in the channel in contrast with the reef on either side. The channel is wide at its mouth but narrows to 100 feet or so (at which point it is 90 feet deep with sheer walls of coral to port and starboard!). You come in on a heading of 137°T for the center of the small village at the head of the bay. Once inside the bay, watch out for a small shoal, with just 6 feet over it, right on this heading. The bay is mangrove-lined with good protection and holding. The village is small and mundane. We saw more parrots here in the evening than anywhere else on Roatan.

MILTON BIGHT TO

BIG BIGHT

(see maps pages 214/210)

Chart: DMA 28154.

APPROACHES/ANCHORAGES. Enter Milton Bight on a heading of 142°T through a narrow channel between approximately 200 yards of jagged coral walls, but expect to do a little weaving in the channel. Ahead of you as you emerge from the channel is a lovely pastoral scene with green fields, dotted with palm trees, coming down to the water's edge. You can anchor anywhere in 10 to 18 feet of water with good holding.

Eight feet can be carried behind the reef between Milton Bight and Big Bight. Southwest of Johnson Bight the channel narrows and a shoal extends out from the shore. You have to stay over toward the reef, holding a heading of approximately 250°T on Crawfish Rock, which will be more or less in line with Punta Pimienta (Palmetto Point)—these are the two northernmost tips of land visible from here. Another shoal extends to the north of Coolie Point—once again you must keep over to the inside of the reef.

Big Bight has a relatively wide channel, which is approached on a heading of 157°T for the eastern-most of the two hills that rise up just to the west of a lower section of the island (see the sketch on page 210). Once into the channel itself, the entry course is closer to 140°T down the center of the channel. The depths in Big Bight Bay are extremely variable, 12 to 60 feet with the occasional shallow coral patch (see the sketch chart). The best protection is in the lee of Coolie Point. The bay is not particularly interesting, but as with all these north shore anchorages, a short dinghy ride to the reef gives access to spectacular snorkeling and diving.

TURTLING BAY
(HOTTEST SPARROW LAGOON)

(see map page 209)

Chart: DMA 28154.

APPROACH/ANCHORAGE. This is a very narrow channel at its entry (70 feet wide, but 90 to 100 feet deep), which requires a couple of small course changes and for which there are no obvious ranges. The point immediately to starboard on entering has a conspicuous white sand pile on its tip. A shoal sits

in the southeast corner of the bay; a picturesque house on piles stands immediately behind it. Apart from this you can anchor just about anywhere. There is nothing special to see.

MAN OF WAR CHANNEL
AND MUD HOLE

(see map page 209)

Chart: DMA 28154.

APPROACH. Entry is on an approximate heading of 162°T for the eastern tip of Little Cay with a couple of small course changes, finally hooking to the east at the inner end of the passage. Beware the coral wall jutting out into the channel halfway along the western side. Mud Hole is a mangrove-lined, well-protected bay that has a backdrop of verdant hills. The holding is good. A narrow channel appears to lead around the southern shore of Little Cay into Mud Hole Bay, but this channel shoals to 4 feet 6 inches immediately to the southwest of the cay.

ANTONY'S CAY AND
ANTHONY'S KEY RESORT

(see map page 206)

Chart: DMA 28154.

A road from Coxen's Hole leads down past Sandy Bay to Antony's Cay. With the road has come a steady trickle of development so that now the lovely beaches to either side of Antony's Cay are lined with resort homes. This cay and Bailey's Cay, its neighbor to the southwest, are home to Anthony's Key Resort, a long-established dive operation.

APPROACH. The entry at Antony's Cay is straightforward, heading in between the two cays that are conspicuous from both the east and the west. The channel narrows to 50 feet at one point. In 1990, there was a red buoy on the reef to starboard and a white buoy on the reef to port, but these markers tend to come loose in northers and may change (I knocked one of them loose with our dinghy during our stay). As you close the shore, hook around to the northeast toward the channel between Antony's Cay and the dive dock on the mainland. The water shoals to 8 feet and then deepens off the cay to 14 to 20 feet.

ANCHORAGE. It used to be possible to continue past the cay and anchor in a small basin just the other side. This can no longer be done since a substantial dolphin pen has been built out into what was the anchorage, leaving insufficient swinging room. You will have to anchor off to one side of the channel immediately to the south of Antony's Cay. The reef recedes a little at this point, forming a small bay with 7-foot depths. A half-deflated red mooring buoy is already in place; otherwise, you will need a running moor. This is a tight spot with no room for more than two or three boats, and there is frequent dive-boat traffic. Don't moor to the dock—periodically it is fully occupied with dive boats—and don't drop a hook between the dive dock and the dock on the cay since water and electricity lines run across here.

PROVISIONS/FACILITIES. The resort, which monitors channel 16 on the VHF, has a great bar and restaurant (book ahead) situated on the hill overlooking the cays and anchorage, as well as other facilities. Bailey's Cay is being developed as the nucleus of a marine park and wildlife sanctuary that extends from Gibson Bight (to the west) to Lawson's Rock Point. All fishing and lobstering are banned in this area.

THINGS TO DO. A second dolphin pen has been built between the cay and the mainland. It is possible to feed these dolphins by hand—I understand that there is only one other place in the world (in Australia) where this can be done.

GIBSON POINT TO WEST BAY

(see map page 206)

Chart: DMA 28154.

APPROACH/ANCHORAGE. Between Gibson Point and West Bay the reef is partially submerged in many places, but nevertheless too shallow to sail across. Toward the southern end of West Bay, you have 15 to 20 feet of water over much of the reef, with a shallower reef closer inshore. A little farther south the shallow reef hooks into the coast, enabling you to close West Bay Beach, anchoring in sandy patches among the coral 200 or so yards off the beach. This can be a rolly anchorage, and the holding is none too good.

A little to the north of the point where the shallow reef closes the shore, a narrow passage cuts through the reef into a small sheltered basin in which you can carry 6 feet close to the beach. Two substantial steel stakes mark either side of the channel. Entry is made on a heading of 090°T. You will find 8 feet in the channel with 10 feet inside, shoaling toward the beach. The beach is the private property of Anthony's Key Resort.

Region 3: Guanaja

Guanaja is a relatively high island (1,300 feet) visible from many miles away. As with Roatan the interior is sparsely inhabited, the people preferring to live in small communities clinging to the shoreline. The only sizable community—Guanaja Settlement—is crammed onto two low-lying cays (Shin Cay and Hog Cay) with the houses spilling off on all sides into the surrounding water. Little cayuco-size canals cut through to the heart of the settlement.

Guanaja Settlement, which has a considerable shrimp fleet, is a busy and relatively prosperous place. This is a port of entry for Honduras and a very convenient place for cruisers coming from or going to the West Coast and Panama Canal to clear in or out. If you are coming from Roatan or the Cayos Cochinos, you will still need to leave your zarpe with the port captain, collecting a new one when you leave.

GUANAJA SETTLEMENT

Charts: BA 1718; DMA 28123. These two are the same, based on very old British surveys with little updating, but are nevertheless surprisingly accurate.

APPROACHES.

From the West. You are likely to be faced with a wet and lumpy beat from Roatan through confused, steep-sided waves. Coming from the Cayos Cochinos, you might want to work to windward, into the lee of Cabo de Honduras at Trujillo on the mainland, which would then put you on a close

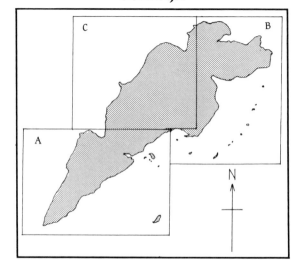

A banana boat at Guanaja Settlement. This cayuco regularly makes the open-water crossing from the Honduran mainland.

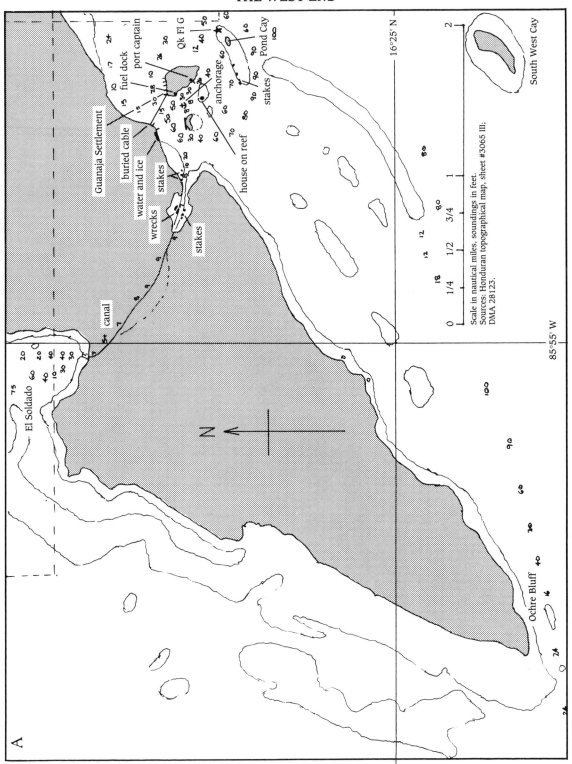

A

THE WEST END

El Soldado

75

20
40
60
40
10
30
20

canal

7

Guanaja Settlement
buried cable
water and ice
wrecks
fuel dock
port captain
stakes
stakes

24
17
10
15
15
Qk Fl G

30
78
30
50
15
40
30
60
22

30
24

12 40 50
60
50
60
90
90
90

80

80

70
60
70

Pond Cay
anchorage
stakes

house on reef

90

86

12
18

12

80

80

100

90

60

40

24

Ochre Bluff

South West Cay

2

Scale in nautical miles, soundings in feet.
Sources: Honduran topographical map, sheet #3065 III;
DMA 28123.

0   1/4   1/2   3/4   1   2

16°25' N

85°55' W

N

reach to Guanaja. A reef extends one-half mile to the west of Ochre Bluff, the cliffs at the southern tip of the island. This reef parallels the northwestern coastline, lying up to a mile offshore. Another series of reefs lies off the southern shore of Guanaja, broadly paralleling the coastline. There are numerous relatively shoal patches up to one-half mile off the southwestern tip of the island. Keep out of this area since conditions are frequently fairly rough, making it hard to see the bottom. In good light, once past the tip of Guanaja, the final approach can be made close to the southern shore, inside the various reefs (providing a fair measure of protection). Otherwise come to the west or east of South West Cay, making for Pond Cay.

From the East. Either come inside the reef through the break at North East Cay (see page 230), or stay outside the line of cays extending to the southwest, making for Pond Cay as above.

Pond Cay sits on a half-mile-long reef with a deep-water channel around both ends. On the northern end of the reef is a light (Qk Fl Green). Entry is easy through both channels. Inside you have plenty of deep water, although there is a series of shoals to the west and southwest of the settlement.

ANCHORAGE. The anchorage is between the settlement and the crescent-shaped cay to the west. You can enter it either by hugging the southwest tip of the settlement, where the water is at least 26 feet deep, or by coming around to the west and north of the crescent-shaped cay, where water depths are 40 to 60 feet or more with no water shallower than 30 feet. The water is fairly deep between the settlement and the crescent-shaped cay. However, it shoals to 8 to 10 feet over toward the cay, and a little to the south is another small 8-foot patch. Try to anchor on the eastern edges of these shoals in 20 or so feet of water, dropping back into 8 to 10 feet. This limits the amount of scope, and therefore the swinging room, you need. The holding is variable. At times our plow bit straight away; on other occasions it took up to three attempts to set it.

CLEARANCE PROCEDURES. The port captain's office is set back from a little dock toward the south end of the settlement's western side. If you are clearing in or out of Honduras, he will direct you to the immigration office to take care of your visas.

PROVISIONS/FACILITIES. The town has a supermarket about as well stocked as any in the Bay Islands, a post office, and a number of restaurants, hotels, and so on. The fish plant on the mainland immediately north of the anchorage will give you limited quantities of fresh water and ice at no charge. Larger amounts have to be purchased. Fuel is available from a dock at the northern end of the west side of the settlement but usually must be hauled in cans since the dock is normally occupied.

Guanaja Settlement has a minor problem with thieves. Keep your outboard locked to your dinghy during the day, and take it off at night. Chain the dinghy to your boat at night if you don't take it on board.

THE CANAL TO EL SOLDADO. A canal cuts across Guanaja to El Soldado and the Pine Ridge Channel. This has recently (1987 or '88) been dredged, supposedly to 9 feet, but by 1990 it was already silting up, particularly at its northern end where the banks are sandy and easily undermined by boat wash. At low water the controlling depth is now only a little more than 5 feet. It is likely to decrease steadily over the years. This is a pity since most of the canal has 7 to 9 feet in it; if it were not for this one section, you could take your big boat through here to the various lovely anchorages inside the reef on the northwestern shore. When entering from the southern end, stay close to the stakes on the north side of the lagoon entrance, then ease across to stay close to the stakes on the south side opposite the two wrecks. From here, head straight for the mouth of the canal. Coming from the north, when you emerge from the canal into the lagoon, hold a course of 117°T. This brings you south of the wrecks but north of the stakes. Hold over toward the stakes, then ease over to the north shore of the entrance to the lagoon.

EL BIGHT

Charts: BA 1718; DMA 28123.

El Bight is an extremely protected anchorage with good holding and pleasant beaches on the coast just to the north of the anchorage. A bar has

THE OFFLYING CAYS

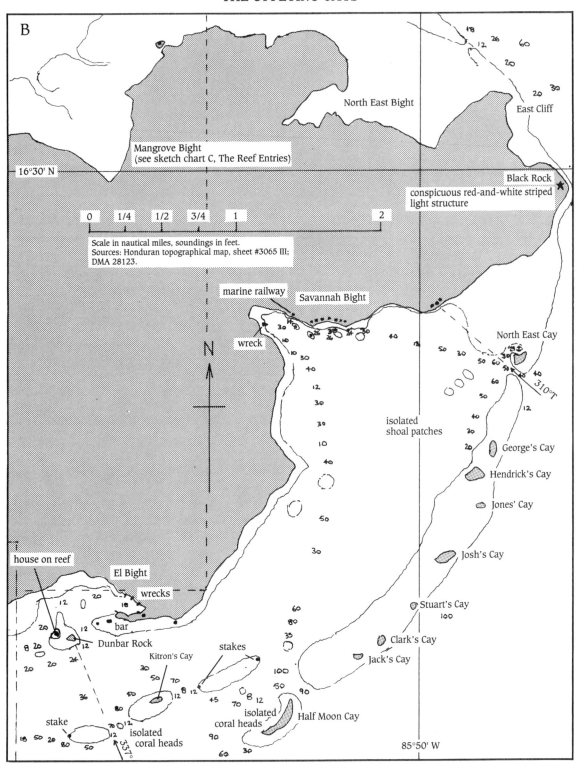

B

North East Bight

East Cliff

Mangrove Bight
(see sketch chart C, The Reef Entries)

16°30' N

Black Rock

conspicuous red-and-white striped
light structure

| 0 | 1/4 | 1/2 | 3/4 | 1 | 2 |

Scale in nautical miles, soundings in feet.
Sources: Honduran topographical map, sheet #3065 III;
DMA 28123.

marine railway

Savannah Bight

wreck

North East Cay

310°T

isolated
shoal patches

George's Cay

Hendrick's Cay

Jones' Cay

Josh's Cay

house on reef

El Bight

wrecks

Stuart's Cay

bar

Dunbar Rock

Clark's Cay

stakes

Kitron's Cay

Jack's Cay

stake

isolated
coral heads

Half Moon Cay

337°

isolated
coral heads

85°50' W

been built on piles on the reef extending from Peak Rock. In the mangroves is a collection of wrecks.

APPROACH. Dunbar Rock is conspicuous. Shoals extend to the west and north, with a house built on a section breaking the surface to the northwest. There are other scattered shoals in the vicinity of the rock as shown on the sketch chart, but the approach is reasonably straightforward either to the north or the east of the rock.

THE CAYS TO

SAVANNAH BIGHT

(see map page 229)

Charts: BA 1718; DMA 28123.

APPROACHES/ANCHORAGES. A line of cays set on a reef runs broadly northeast from Pond Cay up to North East Cay. Between these cays and the mainland, the sailing is great in protected water, with the trade wind blowing in over the reef—the experience is similar to sailing behind the reef in Belize but on a much smaller scale. Most depths are 40 to 60 feet, but there are one or two shoal areas as I have indicated and perhaps a few more we didn't spot. As a result you should keep a good watch. You can find protection more or less anywhere behind the reef if you can find a shallower spot in which to drop your hook. Carefully check the set of your anchor since the wind can whistle in over the reef. The cays are mostly private.
    Channels will be found:

1. Between Kitron's Cay and the reef to the southwest. Note that there is a coral shoal in the center, and the navigable area free of heads is quite narrow—good light is essential, especially since the reef is not awash and is therefore harder to see. Come in on 337°T for Dunbar Rock.
2. North of Kitron's Cay, where the least depth is an 8-foot shoal in center channel, which has 12 feet of water on either side.
3. To the north and south of Half Moon Cay where the water is deep and free of hazards.
4. Between Half Moon Cay and the reef to its

northwest, staying over toward the reef where the water is deep. Closer to Half Moon Cay an extensive shoal has isolated heads, which may have less than 6 feet over them.
5. Between the reef to the northwest of Half Moon Cay and the continuous reef with the rest of the cays on it—this channel is deep and free of hazards, save for one coral patch with 6 feet of water over it located a little to the north of the channel (see the sketch).
6. Immediately south of North East Cay (see below).

SAVANNAH BIGHT

Charts: BA 1718; DMA 28123.

    Savannah Bight is a picturesque settlement of brightly painted clapboard houses on piles at the water's edge, with a beautiful backdrop of green hills and pastureland dotted with palm trees.

APPROACH. Two shoals immediately south of the settlement now have buildings on them—a bar on one and a private house on the other—so they are easy to spot. You have 14 feet between the western shoal and the shore, and 26 feet between the eastern one and the shore. Southeast of the settlement are more shoals as shown on the sketch chart.

PROVISIONS/FACILITIES. The town has little in the way of supplies, but there is an operational marine railway that is quite clearly large enough to haul just about any pleasureboat.

NORTH EAST CAY

(see map page 229)

Charts: BA 1718; DMA 28123.

    A channel leads through the reef immediately south of North East Cay. The reef extends northward from the cay to the mainland, barring all passage in this direction. However, there is a small basin on the north-northwest side of the cay, which makes a lovely, protected anchorage off a sandy, coconut-lined beach. The breeze blows in over the reef and the surrounding coral offers interesting snorkeling—definitely one of the prettier anchorages on Guanaja.

APPROACH/ANCHORAGE. To enter this basin stay approximately 100 yards off the northwest tip of the cay so that you avoid a shoal area jutting out at this point. But don't stray much further off since it is all shallow reef to the north. The water here is 20 to 30 feet deep. Anchor off the beach.

If you are entering through the North East Cay channel, come in on a heading of 310°T for the houses on the point to the east of Savannah Bight. This is straightforward, with least depths of 40 feet. A note on the old British chart reads, "Very dangerous as the heavy swell breaks in three and four fathoms"; we found this channel no more difficult than many others. Exiting through the North East Cay channel is also straightforward. You encounter the prevailing swells the minute you are through the reef.

THE NORTHERN COAST

OF GUANAJA

Charts: BA 1718; DMA 28123.

This is a very picturesque coastline with high rolling green hills behind rocky headlands that enclose beautiful palm-lined beaches. There is hardly a sign of habitation. Black Rock Point has a conspicuous new red-and-white striped light structure approximately 100 feet up a cliff. If it is anything like other Honduran lights, it is unreliable.

The reef forms an almost continuous arc between East Cliff and Mangrove Bight, with one small break into North East Bight. This large, shallow (the chart shows 6 to 15 feet) bay is wide open to the trade winds. We made no attempt to enter since the reef is a dangerous lee shore with substantial swells driving up onto, and over, it. You need exceptionally calm conditions before trying this passage, and you do not want to get caught inside in case the wind kicks back up.

If you remain one-quarter mile outside the reef, you will clear all shoal areas on the northern shore (which is not shown on the sketch chart). A channel now exists through Black Rock Point so that its tip forms an independent, rocky cay with a house on it.

MANGROVE BIGHT

Charts: BA 1718; DMA 28123.

With its backdrop of cliffs, hills, green fields, and palms, we found Mangrove Bight to be the most picturesque settlement in the Bay Islands.

APPROACH. The entry is tricky, requiring good light and calm conditions. Approaching from the east, if you maintain a heading of 222°T on Michael Rock, the conspicuous headland to the southwest, you have deep water (80 to 100 feet) and are clear of all dangers until the western reef at Mangrove Bight looms up ahead. When the head of the bight bears 142°T, start coming in. The breaking section of the western reef will still be some way off. Maintain this distance, staying in 100 feet of water. Although the reef shoals gradually to 30 feet on this side, you will find one or two heads dotted around with less than 6 feet of water over them if you come any closer to the reef. As you come in, curve around to the east onto a heading of 112°T for the headland formed by the hill (Athens Hill) on the east shore of the bight. The water to this point is all deep (80 to 100 feet). On the last stretch you must come back toward the settlement in 20 to 25 feet of water, dodging shoals in front of the settlement and also in the center of the bight.

ANCHORAGE. You can anchor northeast of the settlement in 20 to 25 feet with good holding and protection. Alternatively, you could head further into the bight, but note that the shoal in the center continues to the east shore—there is no passage around this east side.

THE REEF ENTRIES

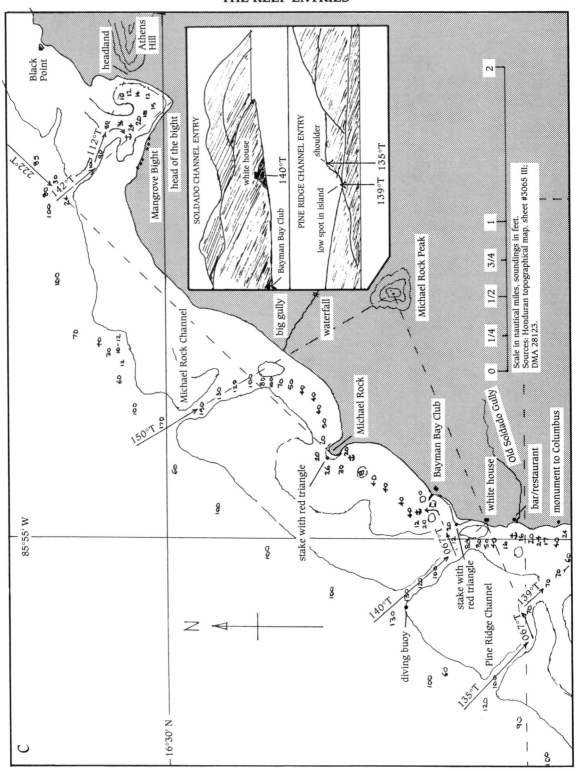

Black Point

headland

Athens Hill

222°T

142°T

112°T

Mangrove Bight

head of the bight

SOLDADO CHANNEL ENTRY

white house

140°T

Bayman Bay Club

PINE RIDGE CHANNEL ENTRY

shoulder

139°T 135°T

low spot in island

big gully

waterfall

Michael Rock Peak

Michael Rock Channel

150°T

Michael Rock

stake with red triangle

Bayman Bay Club

white house

Old Soldado Gully

bar/restaurant

monument to Columbus

2

1

3/4

1/2

1/4

0

Scale in nautical miles, soundings in feet.
Sources: Honduran topographical map, sheet #3065 III;
DMA 28123.

067°T

140°T

diving buoy

Pine Ridge Channel

stake with red triangle

135°T

067°T

139°T

N

85°55′ W

16°30′ N

C

MICHAEL ROCK CHANNEL

Charts: BA 1718; DMA 28123.

The reef to the northeast of the Michael Rock Channel is less uniform than much of the reef along this coast. There are several coral patches with no more than 12 feet over them up to one-quarter mile beyond the main line of the reef—you might want to stand off a little at this point.

APPROACH. Michael Rock Channel is found by approaching the reef on a heading of 150°T for Michael Rock Peak, the tallest hill on the island. Once the channel is located, you simply eyeball your way in. The water is exceptionally deep—170 feet at the outer end, reducing to 100 feet at the inner end—making the channel easy to see. A substantial coral patch is in the center of the channel at the inner end but the water between it and the reef to the northwest is still upwards of 100 feet deep and the channel easy to follow around. A stream cuts down through the mountains at this point—if you care to anchor and hike up its watercourse you will find a dramatic waterfall about a mile inland.

To the southwest of Michael Rock Channel the water steadily shoals to 40 feet, and then to 20 feet when rounding Michael Rock. The channel at this point is relatively narrow with the main reef immediately to the northeast, and a small coral shoal extending to the northwest of Michael Rock, marked with a stake on its outer end. You should round Michael Rock just off this stake.

In the lee of Michael Rock you will find one of the prettiest anchorages in the Bay Islands, off a small sandy beach in the low spot between Michael Rock and the mainland. The holding, however, is poor in a grassy bottom, and the wind tends to funnel around Michael Rock from different directions.

A quarter mile south of Michael Rock you will find a coral patch with no more than 8 feet over it, more or less in the center of the channel. Still further south there are several shallow coral patches, awash in places, in the vicinity of the Bayman Bay Club (see below).

THE SOLDADO AND
PINE RIDGE CHANNELS

Charts: BA 1718; DMA 28123.

APPROACHES/ANCHORAGES. The Soldado Channel is entered on a heading of 140°T for a white house about one-half mile southwest of the Bayman Bay Club. This is another deep and straightforward entry. In 1990, a diving buoy was on the reef on the south side of the entrance. The inner end of the channel runs up on a coral patch with channels to north and south.

Heading North. Make for the Bayman Bay Club dock when it bears 067°T. Keep a good watch since this track crosses a narrow neck between reefs with least depths of 12 feet. You are soon over it. Maintain the 067°T heading for the Bayman Bay Club dock—you pass a coral patch to your north, and then see another directly ahead about 150 yards off the dock. Swing to the north between the two and anchor northwest of the dock in 40 feet with a sandy bottom and plenty of swinging room.

South from the Soldado Channel. There is plenty of water, except for one coral patch shown on the sketch chart. The prettiest spot is unquestionably off the small beach where the Old Soldado Gully runs into the sea. A beach bar and restaurant has just (1990) been opened here. A little more than one-quarter mile to the south is a memorial to Christopher Columbus, who made a landfall here in 1502. However, the memorial is a miserable affair and not worth visiting.

Pine Ridge Channel has a pronounced dogleg midway through. The initial entry is made on a heading of 135°T for the shoulder of land immediately to the south of the lowest part of the island (see the sketch). When the highest visible peak on the island (Michael Rock Peak) bears 067°T, head for it. When the lowest point of the island bears 139°T, come back around for it. Once inside, if heading north, watch for the coral patch southwest of the Soldado Gully—you should stay over toward the beach.

PROVISIONS/FACILITIES. The Bayman Bay Club is a divers' resort that is set back on the hillside; it has a lovely beach in the bay below and excellent diving and snorkeling all around—even in 3 feet of water at the head of the dock! The water is 12 feet deep on the end of the club's dock, but watch out for the coral patches to the west, southwest, and north-west (which have already been mentioned). The club welcomes visiting sailors to the bar and restaurant, but make reservations ahead of time for meals (channel 9 on the VHF).

Region 4: The Cayos Cochinos

No cruise of the Northwest Caribbean should omit the Cayos Cochinos. It is an area of outstanding natural beauty and interest. Cochino Grande and Pequeno are relatively high islands covered in dense tropical vegetation with rugged headlands enclosing gorgeous sandy beaches; the surrounding cays are low-lying, coconut-clad, sandy islets as pretty as any to be found in Belize—or elsewhere. The reefs offer spectacular snorkeling and diving.

A small village clings to the east shore of Cochino Grande, while another fishing community lives in palm-thatched huts on Lower Monitor. A few fishermen have established a primitive camp with their families on South West Cay. Two or three of the other cays are privately owned by expatriate Americans who have built substantial homes. Apart from this, the islands are almost uninhabited. *There are no facilities for cruisers.*

In normal trade-wind conditions, plenty of protected anchorages can be found in the lee of the islands and reefs, but in a norther, particularly the early stages when the wind tends to be in the west, or even the southwest, shelter is hard to find—you will probably have to shift your anchorage more than once as the wind shifts.

Chart DMA 28150, with a scale of 1:300,000, was the most detailed chart available. It does not show most of the small cays in the Cayos Cochinos group and is completely useless for navigating around the area. The new DMA 28154, to a scale of 1:80,000, is a great improvement, though still not adequate for detailed navigation. My sketch charts are derived from a Honduran government topographical map with a scale of 1:50,000. The geographic outlines on this map are accurate. It also shows most of the coral in the area but fails to distinguish between shallow and deep coral. We have modified and supplemented this map with numerous soundings and other observations.

Inaccurately charted extensive reef areas extend more than 8 miles to the southwest of Cochino Grande, with shoal depths of as little as 3 feet in places. The southwesternmost reef, in particular, may be as much as 1 mile south of its charted posi-

The fishing village on Lower Monitor.

CAYOS COCHINOS

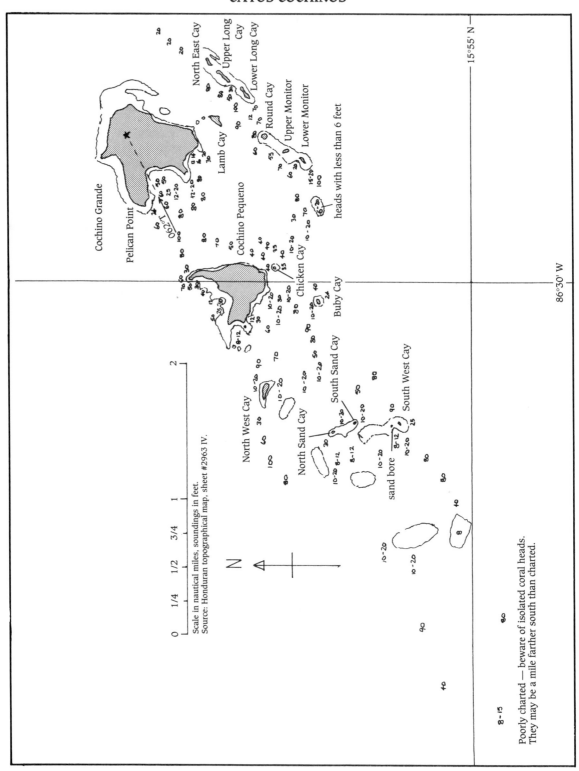

North East Cay

Upper Long Cay

Lower Long Cay

Round Cay

Upper Monitor

Lower Monitor

Lamb Cay

Cochino Grande

Pelican Point

Cochino Pequeno

Chicken Cay

Buby Cay

heads with less than 6 feet

North West Cay

North Sand Cay

South Sand Cay

South West Cay

sand bore

Scale in nautical miles, soundings in feet.
Source: Honduran topographical map, sheet #2963 IV.

0   1/4   1/2   3/4   1   2

N

15°55′ N

86°30′ W

Poorly charted — beware of isolated coral heads.
They may be a mile farther south than charted.

tion. If approaching the Cayos Cochinos from the southwest, or leaving to the southwest, give this region a wide berth.

COCHINO GRANDE

Chart: DMA 28154.

The principal anchorage for the Cayos Cochinos is on the west side of Cochino Grande. This island rises to a height of 471 feet and is visible from many miles away. Close to its summit is a new (1985) red-and-white striped light structure, charted as Fl (3) 32 secs but probably Fl White, and in any case unreliable.

APPROACHES.
From the North. Come around the western tip of Cochino Grande (Pelican Point) keeping one-quarter mile or so offshore.

From the West. You want to keep well to the north of the string of cays and reefs running to the southwest. These are poorly and inaccurately charted. You can come east in the deep water just to the north of Bonkes Nose Point (the northernmost tip of Cochino Pequeno).

From the South and East. You can come around the southern tip of Lower Monitor into the lee of the cays and reef, or come through the pass between Round Cay and Lower Long Cay. You will find shoal patches on both approaches. The reef extends for one-quarter mile southwest of Lower Monitor, but has 15 to 20 feet of water over it until within a 100 yards or so of the beach. To the west is another patch of coral, mostly with 10 to 20 feet of water, but this one does have one or two shallow coral heads—you need to stay away. The approach is in the deep water between these two reef areas. There is a patch of coral in the center of the channel between Lower Long Cay and Round Cay, with least depths of 12 feet. Nevertheless pass it on either side.

You need to clear the southwestern side of

Jan Jones' Clinic

Jan Jones is a registered school nurse from Texas who first went to the Cayos Cochinos in 1970 to scuba dive. Her clinic, which is now just around Pelican Point to the northwest of the anchorage on Cochino Grande, started by accident in 1975 when a man who had pneumonia came to her for help. She was able to treat him with medicine she had brought for emergencies. By 1988, Jan had 2,000 patients on her records, some coming from as far as 100 miles away, all of them by boat and leaky cayuco—most without motors!

The clinic is open for seven to nine weeks in the summer during the school holidays. Patients begin arriving at 4:30 a.m. Some have never seen a doctor before and most have never seen a dentist. Apart from the needed medical care, Jan tries to give each and every one a toothbrush and tube of toothpaste. When she leaves at the end of August, the patients are given one year's supply of medicine to see them through until Jan's return.

The clinic does not charge for any services and Jan is not paid by anyone. Many of her medicines are donated because they are date-expired. If you would like to help, here are some of the things she could use:

- Cash (of course!).
- Just about anything you might throw away when cleaning out your medicine cabinet—partly used and date-expired medicines; bandages; bandaids; and so on.
- Clean medicine bottles (no glass; no childproof caps) and plastic spoons.
- Toothbrushes and toothpaste.
- Bars of soap.
- Eyeglasses (but not for astigmatism).
- Contraceptives (pills and foams).
- Vitamins (especially children's).

Physicians and dentists might consider spending a little time at the clinic. The diving and snorkeling, including right off the clinic's dock, are spectacular—you could do a little in between working hours.

In addition, Jan specifically needs medicines for asthma (especially medihalers), arthritis, high blood-pressure, and elixirs for children (cough syrups, antihistamines, etc.).

Contact Jan Jones, c/o the Honduran Fund, First Baptist Church, P.O. Box 656, Fort Stockton, TX 79735, USA; or, 3507 Tanglewood, San Angelo, TX 76904. Tel: (915) 944-8015.

COCHINO GRANDE AND COCHINO PEQUENO

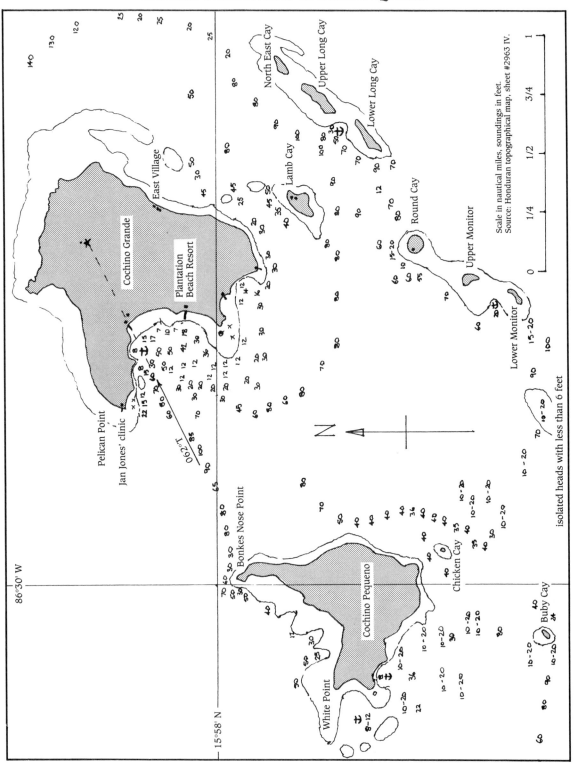

Scale in nautical miles, soundings in feet.
Source: Honduran topographical map, sheet #2963 IV.

isolated heads with less than 6 feet

Cochino Grande by one-quarter mile or so. The Honduran map shows an extensive area of coral reef off the western coast of Cochino Grande. However, the majority of this coral has 12 to 20 feet over it and is no hazard—you can cross it safely. A heading of 062°T on the light stays clear of all coral and keeps you in a 60-foot-deep channel, which starts to shoal only when you are well into the bay.

ANCHORAGE. The north part of the bay has a gradually shoaling shelf that drops off quite suddenly to 30 feet and keeps on going down to 50 feet or more. You can carry 6 feet almost onto the beach or the rocks to the north, but not to the east where the bottom shoals farther out. You should come up toward the small sandy bay in the north and drop your hook in about 8 feet. The bottom is hard sand with eel grass in which it can prove very difficult to set an anchor, but once set it will hold well. On a couple of occasions we had to snorkel down and physically jam the flukes in the bottom. The wind whistles down off the hillsides, boxing every point of the compass with no two boats swinging in the same direction. If the anchorage is at all crowded (unlikely!), you need a running moor to limit your swinging room.

THINGS TO DO/PROVISIONS. The snorkeling is excellent on the reef all around Pelican Point, particularly just to the northwest off Jan Jones' clinic.

The Plantation Beach Resort is a divers' resort on the hillside to the southeast overlooking the anchorage. The managers are very friendly and welcome visiting sailors at their bar. Meals are available with prior reservations—the hotel monitors channel 12 on the VHF, answering to "Trinity," and can give you an up-to-date weather forecast.

EASTERN SHORE OF
COCHINO GRANDE

There is plenty of water between the southern coast of Cochino Grande and Lamb Cay, with just a couple of coral patches as shown on the sketch chart. In spite of the cays and reefs to the northeast, the prevailing swells tend to run up on the east coast of Cochino Grande, but further north they are partially broken by an arm of submerged reef extending southward a little over one-quarter mile off the coast. This is not usually a comfortable spot in which to anchor, but it is *one of the best places to seek shelter during the early stages of a norther*. A small settlement—East Village—lines the shore at this point.

NORTH EAST CAY TO
LOWER MONITOR

Chart: DMA 28154.

These cays are strung out in a northeast to southwest axis along a reef that is broken between Lower Long Cay and Round Cay.

APPROACHES/ANCHORAGES. The reef awash extends one-quarter mile to the north of North East Cay. It then continues to the northeast for another mile or so, with depths from 20 to 25 feet and perhaps some shallower coral heads. We came running onto this shoal area from the north on a wild reach in substantial breaking swells; we were expecting to be in deep water and got the fright of our lives when we suddenly saw coral heads looming up in the wave troughs! Unless the sea is calm, stay away from this area, especially since it is not the best approach to the anchorage on Cochino Grande.

North East Cay is principally coral rubble with a small beach at its southern end, but Upper Long Cay and Lower Long Cay have lovely sandy beaches. In normal conditions there is no comfortable anchorage (since the swells hook around North East Cay and run to the south), save for a small bight tucked in to the southwest of Upper Long Cay. The reef all along these cays drops off suddenly into 80 to 100 feet of water, but in this bight is a small shelf with 20 to 30 feet over a grass-and-sand bottom, with reef all around.

The channel between Lower Long Cay and Round Cay is 70 to 90 feet deep with a 12-foot shoal patch in the center. This patch is not a hazard to navigation.

Round Cay is an attractive, private island with

an extensive coral shoal, particularly to the northwest. This coral has 15 to 20 feet over much of it, shoaling to 10 feet on the western side of the island. Upper Monitor is largely composed of coral rubble and coconuts, but has a beautiful beach on its southwest shore. It is surrounded by shallow coral. Lower Monitor is a jewel, a little sliver of a sandy islet covered in coconut trees among which are scattered the palm-thatched palapas of a small fishing community. In normal conditions, you find excellent anchorage in a gently shoaling sandy bight cutting in to the reef off the northwestern end of the island. The bottom shoals steadily from 20 feet to 7 feet fairly close inshore. The holding is good. The reef awash between Upper Monitor and Lower Monitor breaks all swells.

Ashore in the village of Chachahuate you will find a small bar, a very limited supply of groceries, and exceptionally friendly people in a wonderfully ro-

mantic setting. This is one place that should not be missed.

COCHINO PEQUENO

Chart: DMA 28154.

Another relatively high island with some gorgeous beaches and scenery, Cochino Pequeno is virtually uninhabited with just a couple of houses on the south shore next to Jim McDonald's small grass airstrip. It has some beautiful anchorages.

APPROACHES/ANCHORAGES. The east coast of Cochino Pequeno is free of hazards with deep water fairly close inshore. The northern point, Bonkes Nose Point, can also be rounded 100 to 200 yards off. The entire western shore is another matter: Ex-

The school bus bringing children home to Lower Monitor from Cochino Grande.

tensive reef areas jut out in fingers for up to one-quarter mile. I have tried to show them as accurately as possible on the sketch chart. You have to be extremely careful in this area. Usually these reef fingers have 10 to 20 feet of water over them, but dotted around are heads and coral patches with less than 6 feet. Two 25- to 30-foot-deep sandy bights extend into the reef, providing protected anchorages for snorkeling the coral. With care you can pick your way in toward the beaches in a couple of places, but only during the daytime in good light and calm conditions.

White Point is a low-lying, coconut-covered, sandy point. The reef comes out a considerable way in a broad arc to the north and west, much of it awash, then as it trends to the south, it breaks up into substantial coral patches that are just submerged. Inside this arc the water is mostly 8 to 12 feet deep with a reasonably clear approach to the sandy beach. The best entry is from the southeast toward the rock off the tip of the southwest point of the island. Approximately 200 yards off the rock, curve northward in sand between coral patches, then hook around to the east toward the beach. Here you have plenty of sand and grass to anchor in. Good light is essential. There is another anchorage in the westernmost cove on the south shore, immediately to the east of the rock mentioned above. Entry is straightforward from the south, anchoring in 8 to 12 feet, good holding in a grass-and-sand bottom. The bay has a delightful mix of sand, coconut palms, rocks, low cliffs, verdant hillsides, and birdsong. Further to the east, the south shore of the island has a bit more coral close inshore, with some extension to the southeast as shown. Yet another lovely, but not so protected, anchorage is found off the beach and coconut groves just to the east of the homes and grass airstrip.

CAYS AND REEFS TO

THE SOUTHWEST OF

COCHINO PEQUENO

(see map page 236)

Chart: DMA 28154.

Note: In this area we found some discrepancies with the topographical map and our charts, particularly with the reef areas well to the southwest. I have done my best to present an accurate picture in the sketch chart, but with few reliable fixed objects on which to take sights with a hand-bearing compass—and poor crossing angles with the bearings we took—the margin of error is greater here than with any of the other sketch charts in this guide. Good light and great caution are needed.

APPROACHES/ANCHORAGES. North West Cay, known locally as Culebra, is coral rubble with coconuts, but the south coast does have a pretty beach. A reasonable anchorage can be found in scattered sand patches about 150 yards off the south shore. The coral extends a couple of hundred yards to the east, north, and west of the island.

North Sand or Timon Cay has about 10 straggly palms and a rather exposed anchorage immediately to the west. South Sand Cay is just a heap of sand and coral rubble with some ground cover. It is almost certainly farther north than charted, although the extensive reef area to the west has at least 8 feet of water over much of it. You should keep out—there is no reason to go here.

South West or Bulano Cay is another pretty sand-and-coconut island with a small fishing community that lives in palm-thatched huts. The reef extends 200 to 300 yards to the southwest where it is awash. A predominantly sandy bight leads up into the coral just to the west of the cay with good holding in grass and sand in 8 to 12 feet of water. You have to watch out for a certain amount of scattered coral in this area. The reef and a sandspit to the northwest of the cay provide excellent protection in normal trade-wind conditions.

A series of reef areas (Providence Shoal on BA charts) extend another 5 or 6 miles to the southwest. Although there is plenty of deep water between them, and 8 feet of water or more over much of the coral, areas with shoal depths down to 3 feet do exist. To make matters worse the most southwesterly reef may be charted as much as one mile to the north of its actual position. My advice is to give this entire area a wide berth when approaching or leaving the Cayos Cochinos.

Region 5: Mainland Honduras

A narrow lowland plain is backed by high mountains rising in places to 9,000 feet. None of the peaks are particularly conspicuous so they are of little use in fixing your position. As mentioned previously, there is an extreme lack of shelter for small boats along almost the entire mainland coast. With the exception of Laguna El Diamante, even where protection does exist in the lee of headlands, the anchorages are all wide open to the northwest.

The mountains influence the prevailing trade winds to a considerable degree. At night the wind along the coast is often calm, or moderately strong out of the west. During the morning the trades reassert themselves, building to a peak of intensity, commonly 20 to 25 knots from the east, in mid-to late afternoon. You will almost always find an underlying swell from the east, which increases in size and steepness during the day, forming whitecaps by late afternoon, then diminishing during the night.

The continental shelf off the coast is poorly charted, with some question as to the location and depth of several dangerous shoals, particularly those to the southwest of the Cayos Cochinos (see page 241). The Salmedina Shoal, to the northwest of La Ceiba, is another that should be given a wide berth. A third is shown on the charts northeast of Puerto Cortes, 1 mile off the coast near Cardona Hill. Aside from these and in appropriate weather conditions, you should be able to safely sail along the coast so long as you keep out 1 mile or so and keep an eye on your depthsounder. Between ourselves and associate editor Peter Hancock, we have sailed the full length of the coast from Trujillo to Cabo Tres Puntas without any nasty surprises.

The pilot charts for Central American waters show an eastward-setting countercurrent sweeping along the coast and up to the north of Utila. We found no discernible current in this region when we were there, but Peter found a 1- to 1½-knot *westward-setting current* when he was passaging between Guanaja and Trujillo.

The principal reason for sailing the mainland coast is to use its partial lee at least as far as Laguna El Diamante, so that you can make easting to the Bay Islands (see page 57). In certain circumstances a tack down into Trujillo Bay may also prove to be good tactics. In general this is not a coastline to be trifled with. Particularly in the winter months when it becomes a dangerous lee shore during northers, you should stay away.

TRUJILLO

Chart: DMA 28154.

Trujillo is on the south shore of the bay named after it. It is the site of one of the oldest Spanish settlements in Central America, defended by a castle that is in a good state of preservation. The town's atmosphere is relaxed and friendly, but this is not a port of entry and lacks both facilities and a secure anchorage. You will have to make for Puerto Castilla on the northern side of the bay where you can find a reasonable anchorage, the port captain, and fuel and water.

APPROACHES. When making for Trujillo Bay, it is prudent to allow for a westward- or northwestward-setting current of up to 1½ knots.

From the North. The prominent water tower at Puerto Castilla is visible from 8 to 10 miles away. Closer in, the light structure on Punta Caxinas can be picked out among the dense vegetation on the low-lying Cabo de Honduras. There are no offlying dangers to the north of the cape, which can be approached to within one-quarter mile, but discolored shoal water extends one-quarter to one-half mile to the west and southwest of Punta Caxinas.

From the East. On this approach a dangerous shoal breaks the surface 1 to 1½ miles north of Punta Betulia.

TRUJILLO

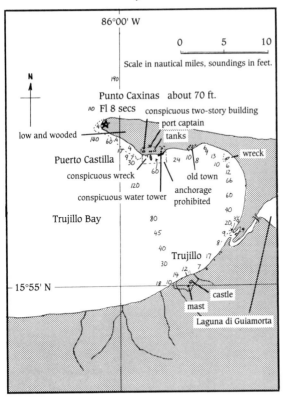

86°00' W

0   5   10

Scale in nautical miles, soundings in feet.

N

190

Punto Caxinas about 70 ft.

110 Fl 8 secs conspicuous two-story building

port captain

low and wooded 140 60.4 tanks

17·4 9·7 24 10 8 13 wreck
Puerto Castilla 30 60 10 6
conspicuous wreck old town 12 66
120 anchorage 60
conspicuous water tower prohibited 40

Trujillo Bay 80 20 1 3½
45 9·₂
40 8· Trujillo 17
30 14 12 7
18 19 castle
mast
Laguna di Guiamorta

15°55' N

The 5-mile-wide bay is easy to enter. Once inside, follow the peninsula eastward from Punta Caxinas, keeping one-half mile or more offshore, until abeam of a large building (a derelict hospital). Inshore a conspicuous wreck and the modern quayside buildings of the recently built (1983) Puerto Castilla can be clearly seen.

ANCHORAGE. Anchorage is prohibited in this area (the army threatened to use Peter's boat for target practice!) so you need to continue an additional 1¹/₂ miles to the old town of Puerto Castilla, closing to within one-quarter mile of the coast. Here you can anchor among the fishing boats in 8 to 10 feet of water over a sand-and-weed bottom with good holding. In strong east winds you can find better protection farther to the east in 8 feet, one-half mile off another conspicuous wreck that will be bearing 077°T.

CLEARANCE PROCEDURES. You have to dinghy ashore and walk the 1¹/₂ miles to the new port terminal. The port captain's office is in a modern building outside the terminal complex. He will take your old zarpe and issue a new one.

PROVISIONS/FACILITIES. Diesel and water are obtainable at the quayside, but lying alongside in company with large merchant vessels is not recommended.

If you wish to visit Trujillo, do so in the morning before the wind rises. Anchor in 8 feet over sand off the mouth of a small river about three-quarters of a mile west of the small pier. Ashore are a number of bars and restaurants in a quiet but colorful town, all watched over by the cannon in the castle.

The Laguna de Guiamoreta has inside depths of 8 to 9 feet but just 3¹/₂ feet of water over the narrow sandbar across its entrance.

LA CEIBA AND TELA

Charts: BA 513; DMA 28154.

APPROACHES. La Cieba is an open roadstead. The small headland to the east provides no protection at all from the easterly swells. A substantial dock comes straight out into the bay, but it is a lattice-work structure rather than a solid quay. Even in its lee, there is a good deal of wave action and surge. *This is no place for a small yacht.*

The coastline between La Ceiba and Puerto Cortes is low-lying and relatively featureless with the exceptions of Punta Izopo and Punta Sal, both of which can be seen from miles away either to the east or west (Punta Sal from 20 miles). The two headlands appear initially as islands with the lower-lying land filling in as you approach more closely. I imagine they make good radar targets, but in both cases the higher ground is inland one-half mile or more, and there are nasty offlying rocks—give both a wide berth.

Tela is tucked into the large bay between Punta Sal and Punta Izopo. The anchorage is another open roadstead. The two capes do nothing to break the prevailing swells that sweep around and head straight for the shore. This is potentially an extremely dangerous lee shore; I can think of no reason why a small yacht would want to sail in here.

LAGUNA EL DIAMANTE

(TINTO)

Charts: BA 513; DMA 28150.

Some confusion exists regarding this anchorage, so let me clear it up. The actual Laguna Tinto lies some distance up a tributary of the Rio Ulua (see the sketch chart). The Rio Ulua is supposedly navigable, but we could not find adequate maps when we were there and there are no charts, so we did not attempt it.

In the lee of Punta Sal lie three bays, increasing in size from north to south. The northernmost offers no protection. The middle bay, Puerto Escondido, provides good protection in normal trade-wind conditions but would be uncomfortably rolly in a norther. The southernmost bay, Laguna El Diamante, offers excellent protection in anything short of a hurricane. In fact, it would make a reasonable hurricane hole. Both Puerto Escondido and Laguna El Diamante are often confused with Laguna Tinto by crusing sailors (El Diamante is misnamed "Laguna Tinto" on BA 513). A little to the west of Laguna El Diamante lies the Rio Tinto, also reported to be navigable, from which a canal (Canal Martinez) heads inland.

APPROACHES/ANCHORAGES.

From the East. You need to round Punta Sal staying one-half mile to the north to give the dangerous rocks off its tip a good clearance. The west side of Punta Sal is deep (40 or so feet of water) and free of obstructions. You can come into its lee. You will see a conspicuous flat-topped hill to the southwest in an otherwise low-lying area—a heading of 217°T on this hill brings you to both anchorages.

From the West. Punta Sal will be clearly visible as soon as you round Punta Ulua.

If you are coming from Puerto Cortes, beware a shoal patch 1 1/2 miles to the northwest of Cardona Hill (the only hill in this area). If you head northeast from Puerto Cortes until Punta Sal can be seen just to the north of Punta Ulua, you will remain clear of all dangers. The entrances to Puerto Escondido and Laguna El Diamante are visible from many miles out. From 3 to 4 miles out, they appear roughly as

shown in the sketch, the northernmost break being Puerto Escondido and the southern one Laguna El Diamante. You can head directly for either.

Puerto Escondido is bounded by cliffs on both sides with conspicuous offlying rocks, and beyond those, rocks awash. An approximately 200-yard-wide channel runs more or less midway between the rocks with no water shallower than 36 feet. Enter the bay on a heading of 162°T straight up the middle of the channel. This is a straightforward entry. Once inside the bay, curve around and anchor in the northeast corner for the most protection in 8 to 10 feet of water, about 200 yards off the beach. The holding is good in sand. A lovely coconut-lined beach rings almost the entire bay; parrots squawk in the trees and howler monkeys roar—this is a very pleasant anchorage.

Laguna El Diamante has a fairly wide entrance bounded by low rocky cliffs, but there is a large rock in the center of the entrance. The lay of the land and the rock is such that, coming from the north, you can see only the break between the rock and the north shore with a clear channel apparently opening up on a heading of 162°T. *Do not attempt to enter through this channel.* The bottom shoals steadily to 10 feet and then suddenly hits solid rock with just 3 to 4 feet over it! The entry channel is to the south of the big rock, entering in mid-channel on a heading of 107°T for the south side of the prominent stand of trees on the point on the far side of the lagoon. Once inside you must hook around for the highest point of land to the northeast (Punta Sal hill), staying 200 to 300 yards off the shore. The bottom shoals steadily in the entry channel to 9 feet, then to 8 feet just inside. To the south of the entrance the lagoon is shoal. An extensive shoal also lies immediately to the north of the entrance, but 7 or 8 feet can be carried up the lagoon all the way into the northernmost arm as shown on the sketch chart (see page 246). You can anchor anywhere. The holding is good and the protection excellent, but the scenery is uninteresting (mangroves) and there is nothing to do except to listen to the parrots and monkeys. Puerto Escondido to the north is a far more attractive anchorage.

To leave, run up the center of the channel, heading for Punta Ulua (291°T).

PUNTA SAL TO PUNTA ULUA

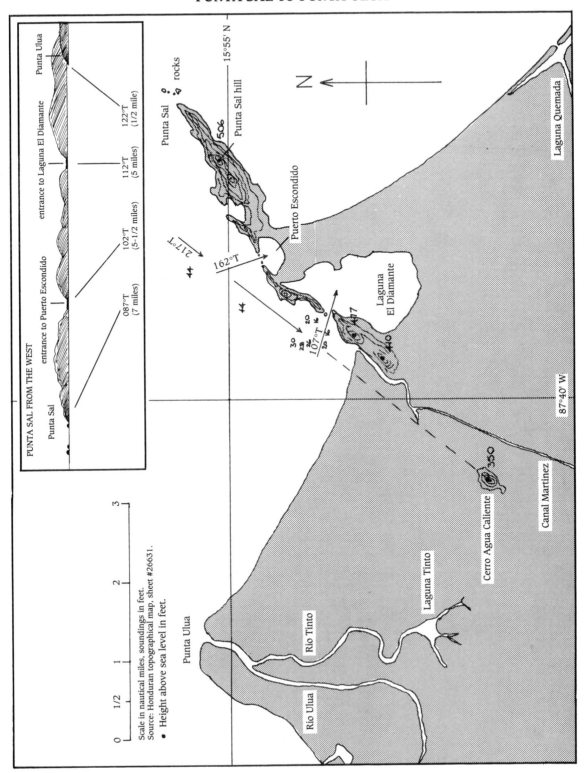

Scale in nautical miles, soundings in feet.
Source: Honduran topographical map, sheet #26631.
● Height above sea level in feet.

PUNTA SAL FROM THE WEST

| Punta Sal | entrance to Puerto Escondido | entrance to Laguna El Diamante | Punta Ulua |

087°T (7 miles)　　102°T (5-1/2 miles)　　112°T (5 miles)　　122°T (1/2 mile)

15°55′ N

Punta Sal

rocks

506　Punta Sal hill

Puerto Escondido

217°T

162°T

Laguna El Diamante

107°T

30　29　20　17

350

Cerro Agua Caliente

Laguna Tinto

Canal Martinez

87°40′ W

Laguna Quemada

Rio Tinto

Rio Ulua

Punta Ulua

0　1/2　1　2　3

PUERTO ESCONDIDO AND LAGUNA EL DIAMANTE

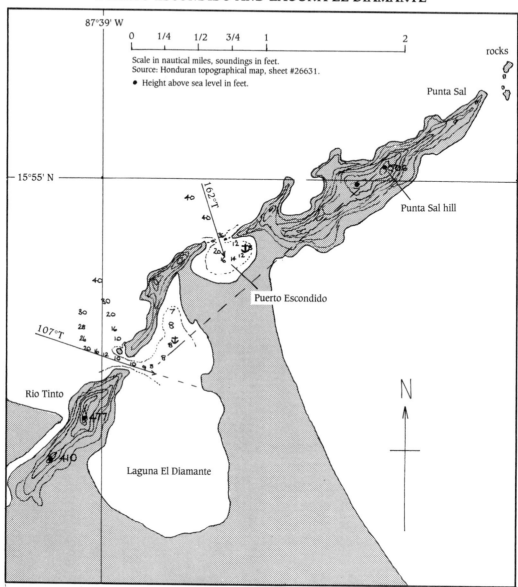

87°39' W

0   1/4   1/2   3/4   1   2

Scale in nautical miles, soundings in feet.
Source: Honduran topographical map, sheet #26631.

● Height above sea level in feet.

rocks

Punta Sal

15°55' N

162°T

Punta Sal hill

Puerto Escondido

107°T

Rio Tinto

N

Laguna El Diamante

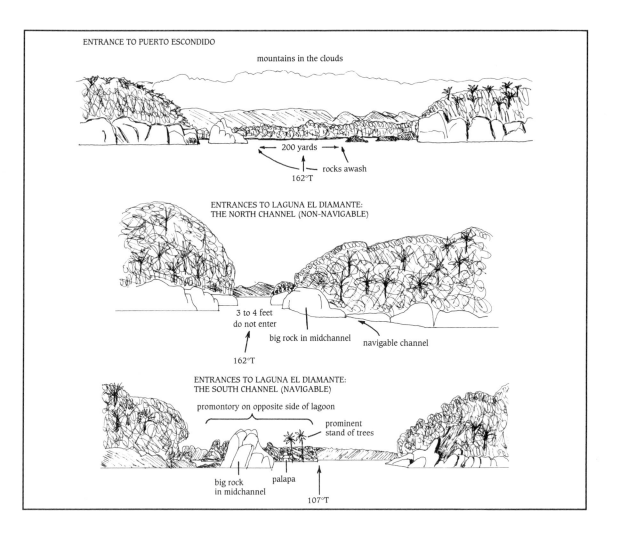

ENTRANCE TO PUERTO ESCONDIDO

mountains in the clouds

←— 200 yards —→

rocks awash

162°T

ENTRANCES TO LAGUNA EL DIAMANTE:
THE NORTH CHANNEL (NON-NAVIGABLE)

3 to 4 feet
do not enter

big rock in midchannel

navigable channel

162°T

ENTRANCES TO LAGUNA EL DIAMANTE:
THE SOUTH CHANNEL (NAVIGABLE)

promontory on opposite side of lagoon

prominent
stand of trees

big rock
in midchannel

palapa

107°T

PUERTO CORTES

Charts: BA 513; DMA 28150.

Puerto Cortes is a drab town. Checking in and out here involves more walking than in the Bay Islands, but it was much cheaper since there was no mordida. The anchorage is reasonably protected in normal trade-wind conditions, but uncomfortable most nights when a west wind develops. It would be no good in a norther.

APPROACHES. From the east, the only offlying danger is the shoal patch 1½ miles northwest of Cardona Hill (7 to 8 miles to the east of Puerto Cortes). The water is deep close in around Punta Caballos, and channel buoys (red to starboard, green to port) mark the ship channel.

From the west, the approach is a straight shot from Cabo Tres Puntas into the bay at Puerto Cortes. At night the lights of Puerto Cortes are visible from Cabo Tres Puntas. (Conversely the lights of Puerto Barrios are visible all the way from Puerto Cortes, though obviously there is no direct passage since you must round Cabo Tres Puntas.) None of the Honduran navigation lights were working in 1990.

ANCHORAGE. Head toward the conspicuous water tower, decorated with the "Pepsi" logo, in the southeast corner of the bay. Just to the north of this tower is a navy base. More or less in front of the tower, you should see a couple of bars on the beach. Anchor in 10 to 12 feet of water off the bars; it is

PUERTO CORTES, HONDURAS

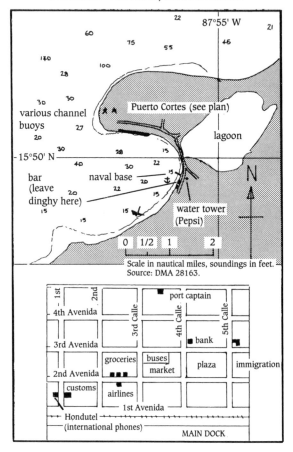

good holding in sand and mud. The people in the bar nearest the navy base are very friendly and will watch your dinghy for you. You can catch a bus or taxi to town from outside the bar.

CLEARANCE PROCEDURES. If you are checking in, first go to the port captain, then immigration for entry visas (L5 per passport), and then customs (see the town plan). The immigration office is up a narrow stairway in the side of the building. The sign over the door is: *Delegacion Seccional; FSPY Transito; Pto. Cortes.*

To check out, go first to customs to buy a zarpe (L3), then to immigration for exit stamps (L5 per passport), and finally to the port captain for a zarpe.

PROVISIONS/FACILITIES. Puerto Cortes is a sizable town with quite reasonable grocery shopping, banks, a post office, telephones, and so on. Diesel is available from gas stations only. There is nothing special to interest tourists. We could see no reason to go here except en route to somewhere else or to check in and out of Honduras. The navy will sometimes haul civilian boats on their marine railway, but it is expensive.

Appendix A: Supplemental Reading

OFFICIAL PUBLICATIONS

Atlas of Pilot Charts for Central American Waters, DMA pub. 106, provides essential wind, temperature, current, and seastate information for the region, broken out into the 12 months of the year. An indispensable aid in cruise planning.

Sailing Directions. These are volumes that list additional information of interest to navigators. Both the British Admiralty and the Defense Mapping Agency publish a series covering the whole world. Although they are of limited value to small-boat sailors, the relevant volumes are: *Sailing Directions for the Caribbean Sea* (DMA pub. 144) and *East Coasts of Central America and Gulf of Mexico* (BA Sailing Direction (pilot) #69A).

Light Lists. Both governments publish light lists for the region but, since half the lights are out and many of the others have altered characteristics, these lists are of limited use.

Tide Lists. Throughout the region tides are small—no more than 18 inches in range—and erratic, being influenced by winds and other factors to a considerable extent. The only point at which tide information is likely to be critical is when crossing the bar at the mouth of the Rio Dulce, Livingston, Guatemala (see page 173). Tide tables, therefore, are of little use.

Topographical Maps. During the past 20 years, all the countries of this region have produced updated topographical maps to a scale of 1:50,000 and 1:250,000. These are based on aerial surveys and, while they contain little information of use to the navigator and still contain some quite surprising errors, they nevertheless have more accurate geographic outlines of land masses than most of the corresponding charts. I have made extensive use of these maps in drawing the sketch charts for this guide.

"UNOFFICIAL" PUBLICATIONS

A Cruising Guide to the Caribbean, by William T. Stone and Anne M. Hayes (formerly Hart and Stone), published by G.P. Putnam's Sons, New York. This book covers an enormous area. Coverage of this region in particular is a little thin on details, but it has nevertheless a lot of useful information.

Commodores Bulletin, by the Seven Seas Cruising Association (SSCA). The SSCA is an organization of cruising sailors with more than 3,000 members and associate members. Its monthly magazine contains information from members in far-flung places all over the world—a veritable treasure-trove, but it requires quite a bit of digging through past issues of the bulletin to find all the available information on a specific cruising area. The address is: SSCA, 521 South Andrews Avenue, Suite 10, Ft. Lauderdale, FL 33031; (305) 463-2431.

Belize Cruising Guide, by Bill Sorem, published by Belize Marine Enterprises, Ltd., Box 997, Belize City, Belize, C.A. A limited guide to some of the cays in Belize. Available at the Angelus Press in Belize City.

Cruising Guide to the Bay Islands, by Julius M. Wilensky, published by Westcott Cove Publishing, P.O. Box 130, Stanford, CT 06904. A detailed guide to the Bay Islands prepared for the Caribbean Sailing Yachts (CSY) charter fleet in 1978. Much of the shoreside information is now out-of-date, but most of the navigational data still stands. This guide is out of print.

The South American Handbook, by Trade and

Travel publications, Bath, England, and distributed in the U.S.A. by Rand McNally. An unbelievably detailed compendium of useful shoreside information—places to go, hotels, restaurants, buses, etc. Very useful for planning trips inland.

Guide to the Yucatán, by Chicki Mallan, published by Moon Publications, P.O. Box 1696, Chico, CA 95927. A very good shoreside guide to the Yucatán.

Belize Handbook, also by Chicki Mallan and Moon Publications. This is the only shoreside guide to Belize. It is also very good and truly captures the flavor of Belize. It will be an essential companion for those traveling inland.

Few places in the Northwest Caribbean stock charts and nautical books. You had better get all you need before you leave. The Cozumel Yacht Club (Club Nautico) has local charts; and the Angelus Press in Belize City has a few charts of Belize and Bill Sorem's *Belize Cruising Guide*. In Guatemala City, the Instituto Geografico Militar carries a couple of charts of Guatemalan waters at very low prices, but it takes hours to obtain them—the military is paranoid about charts and maps falling into the hands of the guerillas, so their sale is strictly controlled.

Appendix B: Light Lists for Mexico,

Belize, Guatemala, and Honduras

Note: Many of the lights, particularly in Mexico and Honduras, are unreliable or have changed characteristics. Where we were able to observe characteristics, these are shown on the relevant sketch charts—you will notice some discrepancies with this list.

Key:
Fl	Flashing, with shorter periods of light than dark
Fl (...)	Group flashing, with the number in brackets indicating the number of flashes in the group
F	Fixed
Iso	Isophase, having equal periods of light and dark
Aero	Aircraft beacon
Q	Quick flashing, generally red (QR) or green (QGr), sometimes orange (QY)
Oc	Occulting, with longer periods of light than dark
Lt	Light

The information is tabulated as follows:

Column 1. The international number of the light.
Column 2. The location and name of the light.
Column 3. The approximate latitude and longitude in degrees and minutes; e.g., 21 36/87 04 = 21°36'N; 87°04'W.
Column 4. Characteristic, giving the flash pattern and the time it takes to complete each cycle (sequence).
Column 5. The elevation (height above sea level) of the light in *meters* (m).
Column 6. The range of the light in nautical miles (M).
Column 7. A description of the light structure and its height, in *meters*.

Light #	Location and Name	Latitude/ Longitude	Characteristic	Height Above Sea Level in Meters	Range in Miles	Description of the Light and its Height in Meters
			MEXICO'S YUCATÁN COAST			
4428	Cabo Catoche	21 36 87 04	Fl(4)W 20s	15	25	White concrete tower and dwelling, 14
4430	Isla Contoy. Near N Point	21 33 86 49	Fl W 7s	32	21	White concrete tower and dwelling, 31
4430-5	El Dormitorio	21 22.5 86 46.7	Fl W 6s	3	5	Black triangular concrete tower, red bands, 2
4431	El Cabezo	21 19.3 86 46.7	Fl(2)W 10s	3	5	Black triangular concrete tower, red bands, 2
	ISLA MUJERES					
4432	- SE point	21 12.2 86 42.8	Fl(4)W 16s	23	14	White 8-sided concrete tower, 12
4433	- Piedra La Carbonera	21 14.9 86 45.0	Fl R 3s	6	6	White square concrete tower, 5
4433-1	- Punta Norte	21 15.4 86 45.0	Fl(2)W 10s	19	20	Red masonry tower, white stripes, 18
4433-8	- Roca Yunke Canal Las Pailas, S side	21 15.1 86 45.3	Fl G 5s	5	6	Triangle masonry tower, 4

4435	Bajo de la Bandera (Roca Beckett)	21 09.0 86 44.0	Fl(2)W 10s	4	11	Red truncated pyramidal tower, black bands
4436	El Meco	21 12.7 86 48.4	Fl W 6s	8	11	White square tower, 5
4436-5	Punta Cancún	21 08.9 86 44.8	Fl(3)W 12s	15	11	White round concrete tower, 12
4437	Punta Nizuc	21 02.1 86 46.7	Fl(4)W 16s	10	11	Silver metal framework tower, 9
4438	PUERTO MORELOS	20 50.8 86 55.5	Fl W 6s	17	18	White round concrete tower, 15
4438-5	- Mole	20 50.4 86 52.7	Iso R 2s	5	11	Dolphin
4440	Punta Brava	20 48.4 86 56.3	Fl(4)W 16s	11	11	Silver metal framework tower, 9
4440-5	Punta Maroma	20 43.7 86 57.7	Fl(2)W 10s	11	11	Silver metal framework tower, 9
4441	Playa del Carmen	20 37.0 87 04.5	Fl(3)W 12s	12	11	Silver metal framework tower, 10
4441-5	Caleta de Chachalet	20 34 87 14	Fl(2)W 10s	11	11	Silver metal framework tower, 8
4441-7	Caleta de Xel-Ha	20 29.5 87 14.0	Fl W 6s	12	11	Silver metal framework tower, 8
	ISLA DE COZUMEL					
4442	- Punta Molas. N Point	20 35.3 86 43.5	Fl(3)W 8s	22	20	Red round masonry tower and dwelling, 20
4443	- San Miguel de Cozumel	20 30.2 86 57.0	Fl(2)W 5s	17	15	White round concrete tower and dwelling, 15
4444	- Government Pier. Head	20 30.7 86 57.1	Iso R 2s	6	6	Hut, 5
4445	-	20 30.6 86 56.6	Aero A1Fl WG 10s	25	14	Framework tower, 22
4445-4	- Caleta S	20 28 86 59	Fl R 5s	9	7	Silver metal framework tower, 7
4445-6	- Caleta N	20 28 86 59	Fl G 5s	9	7	Silver metal framework tower, 7
4446	- Punta Celarain	20 16.3 86 59.3	Fl W 5s	26	20	White truncated conical masonry tower and dwelling, 25
4447	- Banco Playa. Entrance, N side	20 31.6 86 57.2	Fl G 5s	9	6	Green structure, 5
4447-2	- Banco Playa. Entrance, S side	20 31.6 86 57.2	Fl R 5s	9	6	Red structure, 5
4447-4	- Ldg Lts. Front	20 32 86 57	Fl W 3s	5	5	Lantern on structure
4447-41	- Rear	20 32 86 57	Iso W 2s	11	5	Red metal mast, 6
4448	Tulum	20 13.0 87 25.0	Fl W 6s	24	15	White square concrete tower, 11

4450	Bahia de La Ascension. Punta Allen	19 47.5 87 28.0	Fl(4)W 16s	22	16	White round concrete tower, 20
4450-5	Punta Vigia Chico	19 48 87 30	Fl(4)W 16s	12	11	White round concrete tower, 10
4450-7	Cayo Culebras	19 40.6 87 27.0	Fl(3)W 12s	14	11	White round concrete tower, 12
4450-9	Punta Nohku	19 38 87 27	Fl(2)W 10s	12	11	White round concrete tower, 10
4451	Punta Pajaros	19 34.4 87 24.6	Fl W 6s	11	11	Silver metal framework tower, 9
4452	Bahia del Espiritu Santo. Punta Herrero	19 19.2 87 27.6	Fl(2)W 10s	23	15	White metal framework tower, 22
4453	Isla Chal	19 20 87 27	Fl(3)W 12s	12	11	White round concrete tower, 10
4454	El Uvero	19 04 87 34	Fl(3)W 12s	10	11	Aluminum tower, 10
4455	El Majahual	18 43 87 41	Fl(4)W 16s	10	11	White metal tower, 9
	ARRECIFE DEL CHINCHORRO					
4456	- Cayo Norte	18 45 87 19	Fl W 6s	16	11	White round concrete tower, 10
4456-5	- Cayo Centro	18 36 87 20	Fl(2)W 10s	15	11	Metal framework tower, 13
4456-7	- Cayo Lobos	18 24 87 24	Fl(3)W 12s	15	11	Metal framework tower, 13
4457	Punta Gavilán	18 24.9 87 46.3	Fl W 6s	11	11	White round concrete tower, 10
	XCALAK					
4462	-	18 16 87 50	Fl(3)W 12s	13	17	Round concrete tower, 12
4462-4	-	18 16 87 50	Fl W 3s	8	5	Aluminum tower, 7
	BELIZE					
	LIGHTHOUSE REEF					
5934	- Sandbore Cay	17 28.1 87 29.2	Fl W 10s	25	17	Red metal framework tower, 25
5936	- Half Moon Cay. E end	17 12.3 87 31.6	Fl(4)W 15s	24	14 .	White metal framework tower, 24
	GLOVER'S REEF					
5937	- N end	16 53.7 87 41.8	Fl W 5s	—	9	White metal framework tower, 11
5937-5	South West Cays	16 42.7 87 50.9	Fl(2)W 5s	—	9	White metal framework tower, 11

TURNEFFE ISLANDS

5940	- Mauger Cay	17 36.5 87 46.2	Fl(2)W 10s	19	13	White metal framework tower, 19
5942	- Cay Bokel	17 09.8 87 54.4	Fl(3)W 15s	10	8	White metal framework tower, 10

BELIZE CITY HARBOR

5943	- ENGLISH CAY CHANNEL. English Cay. Ldg. Lts about 300° - Front	17 19.5 88 02.8	Q W	7	9	Concrete pillar, 7
5943-1	- Rear. 300 m from front	17 19.6 88 02.9	Fl W 2.5s	19	11	White tower, 19
5943-2	- Goff's Cay. Sandbore	17 20.4 88 02.0	Fl R 5s	5	3	Red concrete pile, 5
5944	Water Cay Spit	17 21.4 88 04.4	Q R	5	5	Red concrete pile, 5
5945	- North-East Spit	17 23.0 88 05.3	Q G	5	—	Green concrete pile, 5
5946	- White Grounds Spit	17 22.8 88 06.8	Fl W 2.5s	5	5	Red concrete pile, 5
5947	- Spanish Cay Spit	17 22.7 88 08.2	Q G	5	5	Green concrete pile, 5
5948	- One Man Cay Channel. Halfway	17 22.2 88 09.5	Q R	5	5	Red concrete pile, 5
5948-4	- SW side	17 22.0 88 09.7	Q G	5	5	Green concrete pile, 5
5950	- Robinson Point	17 22.0 88 11.7	Q W	12	8	White framework tower, 12
5950-2	- Three Triangles	17 21.5 88 12.3	Fl G 5s	5	5	Black concrete pile, 5
5950-4	- Frank Knoll	17 23.8 88 11.7	Q W	5	5	Concrete pile, 5
5950-6	- Sugar Berth. B	17 23.5 88 10.6	Fl R 2.5s	5	5	Black concrete pile, 5
5950-7	- Sugar Berth. A	17 25.5 88 08.9	Fl G 2.5s	5	5	Black concrete pile, 5
5951	- Westward Patch	17 25.5 88 11.3	Q R	5	5	Red concrete pile, 5
5952	- Middle Ground	17 28.0 88 10.5	Fl R 2.5s	5	5	Red concrete pile, 5
5954	- Baron Bliss Light	17 29.6 88 10.7	Fl R 5s	16	8	White concrete pillar, red band on base, 16
5955	-	17 32.5 88 18.5	Aero QW	—	30	Radio mast
5957	Manatee River	17 13.8 88 18.2	F W	10	2	—
5958	Colson Point	17 04.3 88 14.4	Fl W 10s	12	9	White metal framework tower

5962	Commerce Bight Pier	16 55.8 88 14.2	Lt	—	—	—
5964	Sittee Point	16 48.3 88 14.9	Fl W 5s	9	8	White metal framework tower
5967	Placencia Lagoon	16 32.0 88 25.2	Aero FR	96	35	Mast
5968	Bugle Cay	16 29.2 88 19.4	Fl(2)W 10s	19	10	White framework tower, 19
5970	Monkey River	16 21.8 88 29.1	F W	16	8	White mast, 16
5972	East Snake Cay	16 12.5 88 30.5	Fl W 3s	20	13	Metal framework tower, 20
5974	Hunting Cay	16 06.6 88 15.8	F1 W 10s	17	13	White metal framework tower, 17
5976	Punta Gorda	16 06.3 88 47.9	F W	17	9	White mast, 17

GUATEMALA

5982	Ox Tongue Shoal. W end	15 53.9 88 41.1	Fl W 3s	4	12	White and orange framework structure
5984	Heredia Shoal	15 51.1 88 40.3	Fl R 6s	6	—	White and orange framework structure

BAHIA DE SANTO TOMAS DE CASTILLA

5985	- Puerto Barrios	15 43.8 88 35.8	Fl W 8s	—	25	
5986	- Bajo Villedo	15 45.3 88 36.9	Fl W 2s	5	—	Aluminum framework tower
5988	- Muelle de Puerto Barrios Head	15 44.1 88 36.6	Oc W 4s	—	5	—
5989	-PUERTO SANTO TOMAS DE CASTILLA. Ldg Lts 189° 30'. Front	15 41.6 88 37.2	Q Y	11	—	Red on metal framework tower
5989-1	- Rear. 347 m from front	15 41.4 88 37.2	Oc Y 4s	24	—	Red on metal framework tower
5989-3	- Wreck	15 42.9 88 37.8	Fl W 3s			
5989-4	-	15 42.2 88 36.7	Fl W 3s			
5990	- Lights in line 237°. Front	15 41.7 88 37.4	FR			
5990-1	- Rear. 290 m from front	15 41.6 88 37.5	FR			
5992	Cabo Tres Puntas . 1.5 M east of extremity	15 57.8 88 35.0	Fl W 10s	40	17	White framework tower

HONDURAS

PUERTO CORTES

5994	- Punta Caballos	15 50.5 87 57.8	Fl W 5s	58	20	Tower

5994-2	- No 1	15 51.2 87 57.8	Q(3)G	—	—	Single pile beacon pivoted at base
5994-4	- No 2	15 51.0 87 58.2	Q(3)R	—	—	Single pile beacon pivoted at base
5995-2	- No 3	15 50.6 87 57.9	Q(3)G	—	—	Single pile beacon pivoted at base
5995-4	- No 4	15 50.5 87 58.3	Q(3)R	—	—	Single pile beacon pivoted at base
5996	- Pier. On shoal off head	15 50.5 87 57.4	Fl R 2s	—	—	Red on pile
5997	Punta Sal	15 55.5 87 36.1	Fl(4)W 30s	84	15	White framework tower, 15
5998	Tela. Pier. Head	15 47.2 87 27.6	Fl W 10s	14	6	Red metal tower, 18
5999	Punta Obispo	15 50.9 87 22.5	Fl W 5s	40	20	White framework tower, 15
	ISLA UTILA					
6002	- Utila Peak	16 07 86 53	Fl W 10s	99	20	Red metal framework tower, 11
6003	- Puerto Este E side	16 05 86 55	F W	—	4	Small wooden building
	PUERTO LA CEIBA					
6005	- Pier. Head	15 47.5 86 47.8	Fl W 5s	5	—	Wooden tower
	ISLA ROATAN					
6008	- W end	16 18.0 86 35.3	Fl W 20s	—	10	Red framework tower
6008-2	- Punta Oeste	16 16.1 86 36.1	Fl W 5s	23	19	—
6008-4	- Coxen's Hole. Coxen off southwest end	16 17.9 86 35.2	F W	8	—	—
6009	- French Harbor	16 23.5 86 23.0	Q W	—	15	Mast, 9
6009-2	- Oakridge Harbor	16 23 86 21	Fl W 5s	7	4	Concrete column
	CAYOS COCHINOS					
6009-6	- Cochino Grande	15 58.5 86 28.5	Fl W 7s	157	40	
6009-7	PUNTA CAXINAS	16 01.4 86 00.6	Fl W 7s	23	19	
6010	ISLA GUANAJA. Pond Cay-Off E end	16 26.3 85 54.5	Q G	—	2	Grey concrete column, 9
6010-5	- Black Rock Point	16 29.9 85 49.0	Fl W 10s	61	25	

Cruising Index

U

Upper Long Cay, 239
Upper Monitor, 240
Utila, 199-204

W

Water Cay, 126
Wee Wee Cay, 128
West Bay, 225

X

Xcalak, 87-92

General Index

A

Anchoring, 17-21
Asthma/bronchitis, 32

B

Barracuda, 34
Bay Islands, circumnavigation of, 58
Bearings, in this guide, viii
Boatyard facilities, 23-24

C

Carribean, crossing the, 55
Charts, 38-40
Ciguatera poison, 35
Cooking aboard, 32
Coral
    anchoring on, 20
    fire coral, 35
    navigating around, 41-42
    ratlines or mast steps and, 15
Credit cards, 7-8
Current patterns, and route planning, 50

D

Dental care, 32
Diarrhea, 32-33
Docking, 25-26
Dress code, 10
Drugs and piracy, 6

E

Energy systems, 13-14
Eyeglasses, 32

F

Firearms, 6-7
Fishing licenses, 9
Flags, 9-10
Fuel, 14-15
    sources of, 22-23
    for stoves, 15

G

Groceries, sources of, 22
Guanaja, landfall strategies, 58

Gulf of Mexico, route planning for, 51-53

H

Hardware, 23
Health
    asthma/bronchitis, 32
    bites, 34-35
    cleanliness of food/water, 31-32
    cooking aboard, 32
    cuts/scratches, 34
    dental care, 32
    diarrhea, 32-33
    eyeglasses, 32
    fungal infections, 33
    hepatitis A and B, 34
    innoculations, 29-30
    lice, 33
    malaria, 30-31
    medical kit checklist, 35-36
    personal hygiene, 31
    prickly heat, 33
    protection from sun, 31
    seasickness, 28-29
    shoes, 32
    worms, 33
Hepatitis A and B, 34
History, 2-5
Holidays, 10
Hurricanes, 45-46, 48